Rock, Paper, Scissors: Positions in Play

Hammad Nasar

الجناح الوطني لدولة
الإمارات العربية المتحدة
بينالي البندقية

National Pavilion
United Arab Emirates
La Biennale di Venezia

In its capacity as Commissioner of the National Pavilion of the United Arab Emirates (UAE), and with the support of the UAE Ministry of Culture and Knowledge Development, the Salama bint Hamdan Al Nahyan Foundation is proud to present "Rock, Paper, Scissors: Positions in Play."

Curated by Hammad Nasar, the UAE's fifth contribution to la Biennale di Venezia's International Art Exhibition explores the concept of play as an unbroken thread connecting generations of seemingly diverse UAE-based artists over the last four decades. The exhibition features the works of five headline artists and includes a combination of existing works, the remaking of "lost" works, and new commissions.

The added inclusion of creative interventions from some of the most inventive artists, writers, and publishers in the UAE today infuses the exhibition with greater playfulness, currency, and resonance. Living up to its title, "Rock, Paper, Scissors" unashamedly plays with the form by allowing echoes of the exhibition to spill out into this program, into the streets of Venice, and back to the UAE.

The fresh perspective that fuels "Rock, Paper, Scissors" is consistent with the ambition of the Salama bint Hamdan Al Nahyan Foundation to showcase untold aspects of the artistic and cultural landscape of the UAE to international audiences in engaging ways. However, the beauty of the Venice Biennale is that conversations here flow in multiple directions. In keeping with that tradition, this exhibition does not just tell the world something new about UAE art. Its deep dive into play has also revealed to the UAE arts community a distinctive aspect of our own artistic DNA that has never before been so clearly identified, simply articulated, and sharply brought into focus.

"Rock, Paper, Scissors" would not have been possible without the commitment and creativity of its curator, Hammad Nasar. An accomplished curator and writer based in the UK with longstanding ties to the UAE, and most recently the Head of Research and Programmes at the Hong Kong-based Art Asia Archive, the Lahore-born Nasar brought a unique combination of familiarity, objectivity, curiosity, and expertise to the curatorship of this original exhibition.

We wish to congratulate him on the outcome and officially welcome you to the National Pavilion of the UAE for "Rock, Paper, Scissors: Positions in Play."

Salama bint Hamdan Al Nahyan
Foundation
Commissioner

The exhibition 'Rock, Paper, Scissors: Positions in Play' enables us to celebrate and shine a light upon what the United Arab Emirates brings to its people, its region, and the world. The United Arab Emirates is an open, safe, pluralistic country where people from all over the world live together peacefully in prosperous harmony. Furthermore, around 20 million tourists visit the country annually, most of them to enjoy the marvelous offerings of this enchanting, welcoming place.

The game 'Rock, Paper, Scissors' is universal. It has been played for thousands of years all over the world since spreading from ancient China. It is played by people of all ages and backgrounds. Compelling in its simplicity and decisive in its outcomes, this game has provided a wonderful metaphor for curator Hammad Nasar to assemble a richly talented and diverse group of UAE artists to showcase their innovation and creativity. These artists provide an insight into the country they each call home. The United Arab Emirates is proud of them and values its role in nurturing their talent.

In the streets of Venice, children will be playing 'Rock, Paper, Scissors' amongst themselves, or with their parents or grandparents, while inside the National Pavilion of the United Arab Emirates a collection of wonderful artistic achievement will be on display that is inspired by that simple game. This exhibition provides further evidence of our country's commitment to culture, the arts, and all creative endeavors. It is indicative of the richness, vitality, and diversity of our culture and Arts.

The world is a much richer place thanks to the hard work, talent, and creative endeavors of artists and to the organizers of events such as Venice Biennale, who provide artists with an outlet for their work to be displayed. I express my sincere thanks and appreciation to the Salama bint Hamdan Al Nahayan Foundation, the commissioner of this National Pavilion of the UAE, for its continued support of this important cultural and artistic initiative. Her Highness Sheikha Salama is a strong supporter of culture and the arts, including sculpture, poetry, architecture, music, jewelry, painting, printing, pottery, stories, plays, films, and photography. She inspires us all with her commitment to enhancing the UAE's dedication to the universal values of dialog and collaboration, as well as to our own culture and identity. The Ministry of Culture and Knowledge Development is honored to be supporting this wonderful event.

Our greatest desire in the UAE is to enrich the lives of our people and to provide them with everything that would enable them to enjoy happy lives. And, of course, the arts contribute fundamentally to human happiness. Under the leadership of the President, His Highness Sheikh Khalifa bin Zayed Al Nahayan, and with the strong support and guidance of His Highness, the Vice President, Prime Minister and Ruler of Dubai, Sheikh Mohammed bin Rashid Al Maktoum, and the Crown Prince of Abu Dhabi, the Deputy Supreme Commander of the Armed Forces, His Highness Sheikh Mohammed bin Zayed Al Nahayan, we, in the United Arab Emirates, have a profound commitment to promoting the arts and preserving the heritage and cultural values of our country. The cultural achievements of our country are due in no small measure to their leadership, their vision, and their efforts.

Nahayan Mabarak Al Nahayan
Minister of Culture and Knowledge Development, United Arab Emirates

Contents

Rock, Paper, Scissors: Notes on Play

Hammad Nasar

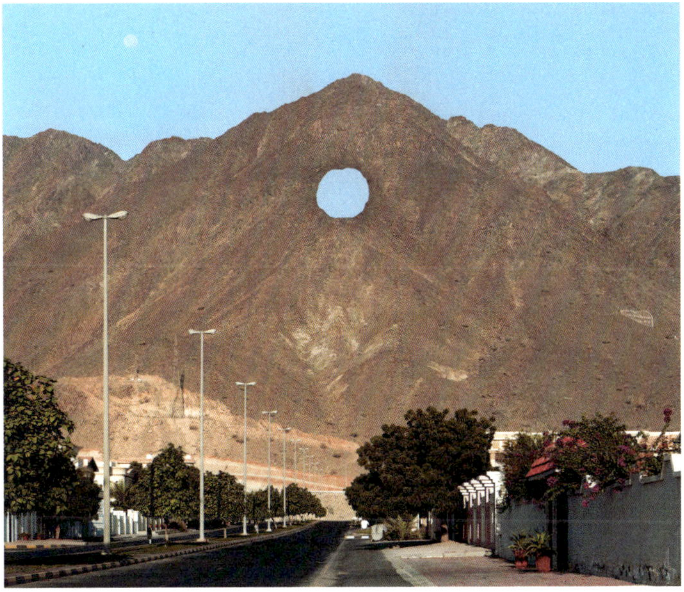

Mohammed Ahmed Ibrahim, *Sunset*, 1993–2013, flex print, 500 × 600 cm
Courtesy of Abu Dhabi Tourism & Culture Authority

Why Play?

Ten years ago, while looking through the catalog for the exhibition "Window: 16 UAE Artists" (2006), I came across a proposal by the artist Mohammed Ahmed Ibrahim to cut a hole in the mountain facing his home in Khor Fakkan so that he could follow the setting sun behind it.[1] Entitled *Sunset* (1993–2013), this digital rendering of a violent yet poetic intervention in the landscape struck me as an audacious act of imagination.

Turning the pages of "Window", I noted numerous examples of diverse artistic strategies with which artists were engaging the everyday: an archive of photographs of people's hands (Ebtisam Abdulaziz); arrangements of banal objects collated, woven, and glued together (Hassan Sharif); documentation of an artist's attempt to stick his tongue into a keyhole and the handle of a pair of scissors (Mohammed Kazem); and an eccentric collection of twigs, knotted rope fragments, and chipped stones that recorded a mother's visits to an absent son's house (Abdullah Al Saadi). Many of these works addressed issues of social import but were realized through an eclectic array of gestures or acts that shared

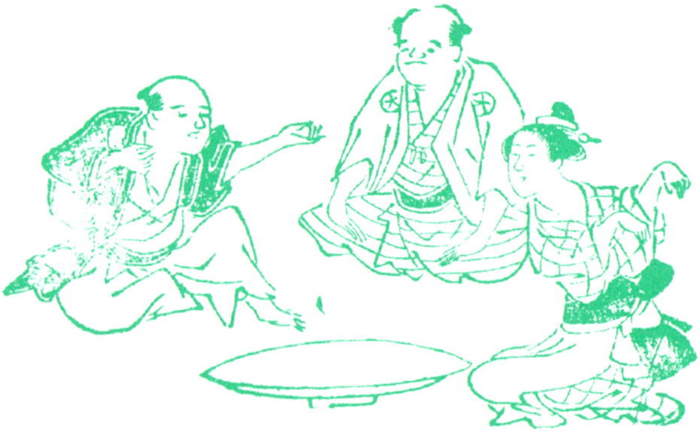

Rock, Paper, Scissors

The playground game of Rock, Paper, Scissors originated in China, was popularized by the Japanese, and can be seen on playgrounds everywhere.[2] To play, two players make hand signals corresponding to three positions: a fist (rock); a flat hand, face down (paper); and a partial-fist with the index finger and middle finger forming a V(scissors). If both play the same shape, it's a tie; otherwise there is always a winner determined by a simple one line rule—rock breaks scissors; scissors cuts paper; paper covers rock. The game's three component shapes have no inherent bias and no internal hierarchy, and all three shapes have an equal chance of wining.

Playing regularly against the same opponent can, however, lead to strategy recognition and predictability. New players, new strategies and new energies are essential to keep the game interesting.

The game has also been used in business settings—most notably in 2005 to settle whether Christie's or Sotheby's were awarded a $20million art consignment by the Japanese electronics company, Maspro Denkoh Corporation.[3] The corporation required the rival auction houses to play a game of Rock, Paper, Scissors to determine the winner.

Kanae Ishibashi, the president of Christie's in Japan, prepared for Christie's winning bid by taking advice from the 11-year old twins of her colleague.

Scissors won.

Drawing of an early Japanese Rock, Paper, Scissors (or sansukumi-ken) game. Published in the Genyoku sui bento in 1774

a *playful* intent—characterized by whimsy, imagination, performance, experimentation, arbitrary rules, and chance.

On being invited to curate the fifth official presentation of the UAE's National Pavilion at the Venice Biennale of contemporary art, it was this attitude of *playfulness* in art practice in the UAE that I was drawn to, in proposing an exhibition that would explore the analogy between "playing" and artistic strategies that used "play." Where does this artistic impulse to play come from? On which sites do different forms of play take place? How are they nurtured? Who can play?

What does play do?

The Fruitful Ambiguity of Play

"Play" is a productively ambiguous term, whose definitions, functions, limits, and characteristics suffer from the twin problems of being simultaneously too broad and too narrow.[4] Numerous fields have wrestled with attempts to tame play.[5] In 1794, Friedrich Schiller proposed an idea of play as "surplus energy" that children "accrued" and subsequently "transformed" into art. Herbert Spencer introduced play as a principle in evolution in his 1864 book, *The Principles of Biology*. Johan Huizinga advanced a conception of *Homo Ludens* ("Man the Player") in 1938 to address the limitations of *Homo Sapiens* ("Wise Man") and *Homo Faber* ("Man the Maker"), and positioned play as a "free activity" separated from ordinary life. Roger Caillois refined and expanded Huizinga's definition twenty years later, framing play as "free, separate, uncertain, and unproductive, yet regulated and make-believe"; and within the past decade, David J. Getsy has offered an alternative trajectory in 20th century art through play and "nonserious activity."

In *The Ambiguity of Play* (1997), a work of broad-ranging scholarship, Brian Sutton-Smith distilled the literature on play theory from a range of disciplines—anthropology, education, ethology, folklore, history, philosophy, sociology, and even pop culture—into categories based on what "ends" play serves (e.g. acquisition of skills) or the "values" play supports in the individual or the wider culture (e.g. excellence). He identified play's avatars as progress, fate, power, identity, imaginary, self, and frivolity. He saw play everywhere, and noted that it is ambiguous and fluid, applicable to adults as much as children, and independent from ideas of work and recreation. Out of this primordial soup of undulating discourses, he channeled evolutionary biology to make his own argument of play as a mode of "adaptive variability"—promoting the possibility for species and individuals to achieve their potential and survive.

The import of this final point was made clear to me watching my own six-year-old adjusting to moving between continents last summer. His first demand upon arrival was to unpack his toys and his first action to rush outside to play with the neighbor's children—gestures that carried echoes of his elder brother's four years before when we moved the other way.

We know that play is where children first encounter difference; where they learn to interact with others as social beings; and where, in so doing, they learn both the rules—of games (and behavior)—and how to bend them. They learn to push boundaries, to say and do things "playfully" that could not be said or done otherwise. But above all the significance of play in a child's development, it seems to me from my own simple parental observations, is that play is a crucial part of making a place "home." And then learning to navigate its rules: seemingly arbitrary, often changing, and always open to chance.

Playing in the UAE National Pavilion

The artists in "Rock, Paper, Scissors" enact a habitation of home through playful gestures and acts, in which bodies mark time and transform space.

LANTIAN XIE measures time in cigarettes, chai, and daily conversations with friends. SARA AL HADDAD counts stitches and records them in diurnal drawings. VIKRAM DIVECHA converts time into value, hourly wage rates an oft-used medium. HIND MEZAINA tracks time's impact on the construction (and representation) of identity in popular media. DR. MOHAMED YOUSIF is concerned with cyclical time: tides, seasons, generations.

RAMIN HAERIZADEH, ROKNI HAERIZADEH, and HESAM RAHMANIAN have a shape-shifting practice that cannot be contained within physical space. For NUJOOM ALGHANEM, space is a construction of the imagination that one could disappear in. DEEPAK UNNIKRISHNAN spins stories about *veed*, an expanded notion of the space of home in Malayalam, which "encompasses a family's soul, where ancestors are cremated, where the soil remembers your footprint."[6] Mezaina frames space, and Xie seeks to extend it—both make work about hotels. WTD MAGAZINE maps marginal spaces that become pirate playgrounds. In these practices there is an exploration of which spaces can be called public, and which can be shared.

The artists in this exhibition demonstrate a commitment to *affect*—art's capacity to carry an emotive charge—and to the belief that this charge "does not reside in a person or thing but is produced through the circulation of things;"[7] but they have a promiscuous understanding of what these "things" could be.

Artworks by the Haerizadehs and Rahmanian privilege the performing body through videos and photographs, which circulate primarily through exhibitions, but also through social media. Divecha smuggles in unlikely fragments of the real—dynamited chunks of rock, paving bricks, hedge trimmings, boxed toys—gently tweaking the art world's orderly circuits. Xie follows the trajectories of music as a carrier of histories, meanings, and imaginaries. Yousif renders, in sculptural assemblage, music's capacity to move the body in space. Alghanem's films choreograph movement. *WTD Magazine*'s photographs record the playful body. Mezaina's work tracks how particular bodies are permitted to move in specific ways. Unnikrishnan's texts release bodies from the tyranny of the real: his protagonists become suitcases and passports and consume airplanes.

The body is not always directly visible, but remains a palpable presence that can be felt as an absence, residue, or metaphor.

This group of artists work through paradox, analogy, appropriation, repetition, symmetry, rhyme, rhythm, and, occasionally, even reason. They make artistic gestures that are whimsical, imaginative, follow arbitrary rules, and are open to chance. In so doing these artists engage in the business of living a life; of making a home.

The various positions espoused in these works add to the genealogies of "play" in artistic practice in the UAE.[8] By working across generations, the Pavilion attempts to make visible some of the "hinges" on which the young art history of the UAE rests. This contrasts with a common stereotype about contemporary art, which I have previously called the "unhinged contemporary": art practices or discourses that are not understood as being in critical conversation with the work of prior generations of artists.[9]

This group of artists also represents the diverse and complex demographics of the UAE, where most of its population does not hold Emirati citizenship. Home is thus only superficially the passports we carry. As a place of belonging, home is much more the food we share, the songs we sing, the stories we tell, and the games we play. The potential of play to transform a place into home presents a counterpoint to the mercantile forms of cosmopolitanism that rely on the UAE's, and in particular, on Dubai's, role as an entrepôt.

The "undisciplined" diversity of practices, approaches, and positions sketched out above demands a curatorial response that can allow this multiplicity to be in productive tension with time and space.[10] For "Rock, Paper, Scissors," this has meant reimagining the possibilities of the conventional structure of a representational exhibition at the Venice Biennale and its accompanying catalog and program. The UAE's National Pavilion can be thought of as a platform where the three components will play with each other in the form of:

An EXHIBITION whose components include a dialogue between multiple art practices spanning three decades, whose physical manifestation in the Sale d'Armi of the Arsenale spills out into a larger space and duration: the city of Venice—with things that happen, and *could* happen, in different times in different places; the accompanying publication; and, the realm of the imagination.

A PUBLICATION that not only introduces the art and the artists exhibiting in Venice, but also serves as an additional *site* of the exhibition itself, presenting three new commissioned artistic projects within its pages. Given the project's ambitions to explore the multifarious notions of play as a *life* practice, the publication also ventures beyond regimented definitions of art—seeping into cricket, music, folklore, heritage, and social clubs.

A collaborative PROGRAM with a number of cultural institutions in the UAE and elsewhere, which catalyzes multiple conversations between the artists, contributors, ideas, and practices contained in the exhibition and publication, and the diverse publics who may wish to engage with them in ways that are left deliberately undefined. The program extends these conversations beyond the sites of the exhibition and publication, and in particular, brings them back to the UAE. This component will host a new artist commission as the Pavilion's contribution to the collaborative program.

Exhibition as Moderated Conversation

Exhibitions can be sites for thinking in public—with artists, and through art. They are discursive spaces as much as aesthetic ones, where different practices and forms can come together in a "moderated conversation."[11] As with all modes of dialogue, different points of view, that are given the space and opportunity to develop into positions, enrich the conversation. It is in this spirit that I have invited Sara Al Haddad, Nujoom Alghanem, Vikram Divecha, Lantian Xie, and Dr. Mohamed Yousif to contribute to the exhibition at the Venice Biennale.

Nujoom Alghanem and Dr. Mohamed Yousif were contemporaries of Hassan Sharif, and while their practices are in dialogue with his conceptually grounded oeuvre, they are deeply informed by their affiliations to poetry and theater, both of which have longer genealogies within the cultural history of the UAE than the visual arts. Both are pioneers in testing different trajectories of play in the UAE, but given the paucity of artistic infrastructure in 1980s UAE, their works were not collected and preserved by institutions, and their artistic contributions are not well circulated, documented, or known. This exhibition includes works originally produced between 1980 and 1995 mostly remade or expanded.

Sara Al Haddad, Vikram Divecha, and Lantian Xie have all come of age professionally in Dubai's last decade, during which a growing constellation of opportunities—scholarships, commissions, institutional exhibitions, and commercial representation—presents a different nature of challenge for artists: how to retain space for criticality while continuing to play. While they were aware of the practices of Hassan Sharif and his students, their relationship with the earlier generation of artists in the UAE is not one of direct "influence" as much as of resonance and shared sensibilities or concerns.

Al Haddad, Divecha, and Xie have produced new commissions and extended previous projects for the Pavilion. They engage with the

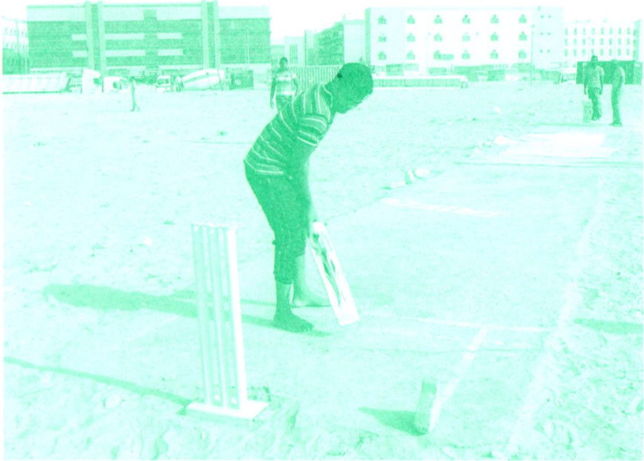

It's just not cricket

The phrase "it's just not cricket" is an admonishment for all that is unjust, underhand and morally dubious. "Sticky wicket" (tricky situation); "googly" (unpleasant surprise); and, "played a good innings" (led a good life or had a good career), are other common examples of cricket's gifts to the English language, and its capacity to serve as an expanded metaphor for life. Cricket does not just have rules and laws; its players are expected to uphold the "spirit of the game." It is a sport that fosters ambitions to be not only played, but *lived*.

The game originated in medieval England, but in its contemporary formulation it has its spiritual heart in the South Asian subcontinent, its financial engine in India, and its administrative home in the UAE.

Cricket's journey from imperial export to its postcolonial comeuppance is not linear. Alongside empire, cricket has had to cross lines of race and class; and continues to navigate new lines of power, privilege and access that often echo a previous century. Cricket's capacity to navigate this treacherous terrain has made it a fecund field for cultural production—often narrating stories of resistance to racial injustice of empire and the malodorous residue it left behind.[12]

Contemporary art is a more recent entrant into cricket's cultural possibilities, its most prominent example being Rayyane Tabet's *Home on Neutral Ground* (2011); an exploration of the singular story of the Sharjah Cricket Club.

Elevated sandpit co-opted as cricket ground, Al Quoz

physical site (Al Haddad, Divecha), and extend beyond it into the city (Xie); address the systems of value that accrue to the institution of the Venice Biennale (Divecha); and tap into the realm of the imagination (all three). Chance plays a role in how, and what, the viewers can experience.

Works by these five artists, with interventions within the exhibition space by Unnikrishnan and *WTD Magazine*, embody play as a mode of navigating the complex and ever-changing mix of social norms, geographical specificities, economic structures, and demographic peculiarities that shape the UAE.

Publication as Site

In addition to a consideration of the artists and artworks in the Venice exhibition (pp. 185–263), this publication contains newly commissioned texts, interviews, and translations that anchor the exhibition in wider cultural practices and sites in the UAE, and offers possibilities for its speculative expansion.

The search for wider cultural context takes the UAE's art history as its point of departure. MURTAZA VALI'S essay (pp. 28–41) offers insightful readings of works by Hassan Sharif and Abdullah Al Saadi through the lens of play. He articulates their use of "the ludic as a strategy," helping us recognize the commonality in approaches and impulses between Sharif, Al Saadi, and the artists in the Pavilion.

Extracts from an extended interview (pp. 148–167) with NUJOOM ALGHANEM and the poet KHALID ALBUDOOR, punctuated by archival research and new translations (in particular, *A Letter to Ahmed Rashid Thani*, pp. 168–172), point to the intellectual and cultural ferment in the formative years of the UAE that informed the collaborative, experimental, and sub-versive spirit of the Aqwas collective. In conjunction with Vali's text, the interview makes visible some of the "hinges" on which contemporary practices rest.

UZMA Z. RIZVI mines how discourses of the past are used in the present to propose the notion of "fluid subjectivity" (pp. 42–48), where "repeated gestures" of everyday life lead to a belonging that is "unstable, uncertain, and yet resolutely in place," and crafted through "aesthetic and cultural resonance." DR. AISHA BILKHAIR explores this idea of resonance through the musical genre of *Laywa* and the "folk [performance] art" of *al nuban*, which originated in African ritual (pp. 84–93). Rizvi and Bilkhair offer vistas into an idea of home as a project of the imagination—a cultural settling.

Through an evocative tour of the multiple sites and histories of cricket in the UAE (pp. 72–83), and in particular the historic Sharjah Cricket Club, OSMAN SAMIUDDIN asks if home can be "the team you represent"? REEM FADDA and MAISA AL QASSIMI bookend a selection of images from artist LAMYA GARGASH considering the import of social clubs as addressed in their exhibition "Emirati Expressions IV: Conventions of Arts" (2015–16). The texts and images collectively invoke sports and social clubs as sites where Benedict Anderson's "imagined communities" could be nurtured within the newly emerged nation of the UAE (pp. 94–107).[13]

Three new artistic commissions expand the "positions" presented in the Venice exhibition and are a contemporary "response" to the "call" of *Silsilat Al Ramad* (pp. 173–183), a self-published art journal produced by Alghanem, Albudoor, Hassan Sharif and Yousif Khalil, which is included in the exhibition as an early UAE example of the role played by publications (in particular artist-made publications) as carriers of artistic practice, not just of discourse.

RAMIN and ROKNI HAERIZADEH are brothers who work with their friend HESAM RAHMANIAN in a collaborative practice that defies classification and makes no distinction between life and art. They are best known for installations that overflow with references (to Persian miniatures and *ta'ziyeh* passion plays), meanings, and forms. They create theatrical assemblages peppered with bric-a-brac, artworks, films, and especially commissioned objects used as props for their performances, which offer oblique points of entry to history, philosophy, and contemporary life. Their performances mix rites, myths, cross-dressing, and digital culture, and are often staged in their Dubai living room, which subsequently decamps to institutions around the world, in the form of an exhibition.

In their commission for the UAE's Pavilion, they have fashioned a playground in book form, *Untitled* (pp. 118–147). Through the millennial DIY tools of WhatsApp, scanning, and printing, they have created a set of collaged images that recall the Surrealist game of *cadaver exquis* (exquisite corpse) in its openness to chance.[14] The ideas and sites they engage with include Walter Benjamin's notions of aura and reproduction, Hito Steyerl's framing of the "poor image," their Dubai garden, and images taken from news broadcasts on TV.[15] In combining these elements, they seek to examine what kind of "aura" could be conveyed through social media. Their collages also reveal their hidden collaborators, the South Asian carpenters and masons who fabricate their props but with whom the artists often share no common language and thus have to *perform* their instructions. The props that result from these directions never precisely meet, but always exceed, the artists' expectations.

DEEPAK UNNIKRISHNAN writes fiction that plays with forms, language, and structures of meaning. His writing is laugh-out-loud funny, gut-wrenchingly painful, myth-like in its epic span, and haiku-like in its compressed charge. His debut novel, *Temporary People* (2017), is a complicated love letter in multiple vignettes, to his family, to himself, but above all to those (like him) who have grown up to call the UAE home.

Unnikrishnan's contributions to the Pavilion—six new mini fables (pp. 49–71)—propel his ambition for activating his readership into a shared experience to a broader and more diverse audience. One of his texts is realized as a scratch card. Yet others are hidden in French folds—reading them is a violent, willful act. He has given an existing text, "Gulf Return," wings: it now exists as a paper plane that lives within the space of the publication and the Pavilion itself.

WTD MAGAZINE is the Dubai-based editorial practice behind the eponymous architecture and design magazine. Named after the thin-headed nail that anchors a tent to the ground, it aims to address "the forgotten, the current, and prospective spaces that represent us." *WTD Magazine* does so with a wide-ranging curiosity that can encompass, in a single issue, the Al Ain Hilton as a nation-building tool, a photo-feature on seven UAE churches, and the story of the so-called "Pirate Coast" where the *Qawasim*—tribal leaders of what is now Ras Al Khaimah and Sharjah—resisted British imperial control of trade routes through naval attacks.[16]

For the UAE Pavilion, *WTD Magazine* has expanded its ongoing inquiry into the informal sites of play in Dubai (pp. 109–117), mapping an alternative topography of play in marginal spaces—on roads, in malls, in the desert, sidewalks, under trees, on beaches, in parks. Recalling geographic surveys based on rainfall or crops, *WTD Magazine*'s *Gamescapes* record the capacity of play to mark territory through a photographic cartography.

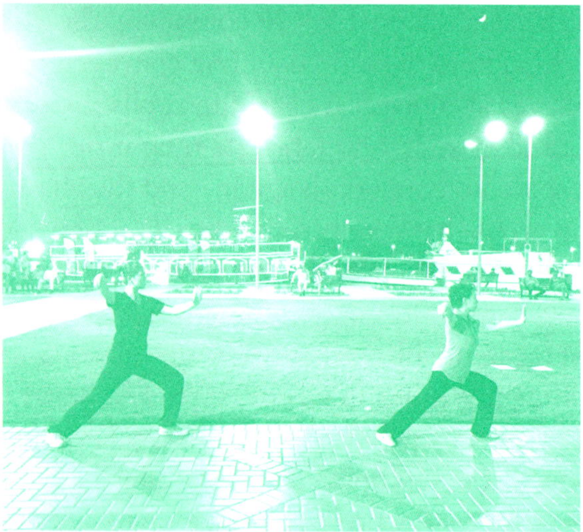

Pushing Hands

T'ai chi chuan (T'ai chi) aims to enhance the flow of chi (life-force or energy) through the body's "meridians"—a principle it shares with acupuncture, and other branches of Chinese medicine. T'ai chi is both a form of moving meditation and a martial art for self-defense.

The use of t'ai chi as a martial art privileges the idea of "listening" and "yielding" to an attack rather than opposing it with force, and is taught through a two-person exercise known as "pushing hands." Demanding a highly trained sense of balance, it requires practitioners to flow with the attacker's force without losing their own balance. Students progress from basic patterns of movements that are fixed at one point; to combining these with moving steps, and finally ending up with "freestyle" that can, on first glance, look like children fighting.

The objective is for practitioners to train their reflexes so that they meet incoming aggression not with strength or resistance, but with softness; moving *with* the force, alert to its intent, and either redirecting it or allowing it to exhaust itself.

These exchanges between practitioners are known as "questions" and "answers"; echoing the Socratic method of argumentative dialog; the longstanding rhyming game in Urdu poetry called *bait baazi*; and the improvisational, and almost conversational, play of "freestyle" rap.

Tai Chi along Dubai Creek, Tian Fei and friends

The program is conceived as a potluck (a one-dish party)—an open-ended invitation to institutions (in the UAE and elsewhere) to be in dialogue with the Pavilion's explorations of play and home, developing strands of activities that reflect their own interests and priorities but enrich the cumulative and collective conversation. The intent is to catalyze independent thinking—not direct a singular curatorial voice—through different formats in multiple venues.

The initial group of confirmed institutional partners includes The Art Gallery at New York University Abu Dhabi and Warehouse 421 in Abu Dhabi, Alserkal Programming and Tashkeel in Dubai, and Maraya Art Centre and Sharjah Art Foundation in Sharjah. The first program—a film series by Nujoom Alghanem—was held at The Art Gallery at NYU Abu Dhabi in April.

The Pavilion's contribution to the program takes the form of an artist commission by HIND MEZAINA, who is engaged in an ongoing "visual archaeology" of Dubai, which she realizes as photographs, video works, and installations. Alongside her art practice she maintains an expansive blog called *The Culturist*. She is interested in the city's accelerated pace of change, its representation in the media, and its relationship with its inhabitants in the form of memory. Her past projects have included a display of her pirated cassette tape collection, a look at the changing cultural norms in relation to folk dance, and the UAE's representation in the 1979 edition of the now defunct World Disco Dancing Championship.

For the Pavilion, Mezaina is developing a program series that will engage with multiple sites of play in the UAE for different strands of publics during the course of the exhibition in Venice.

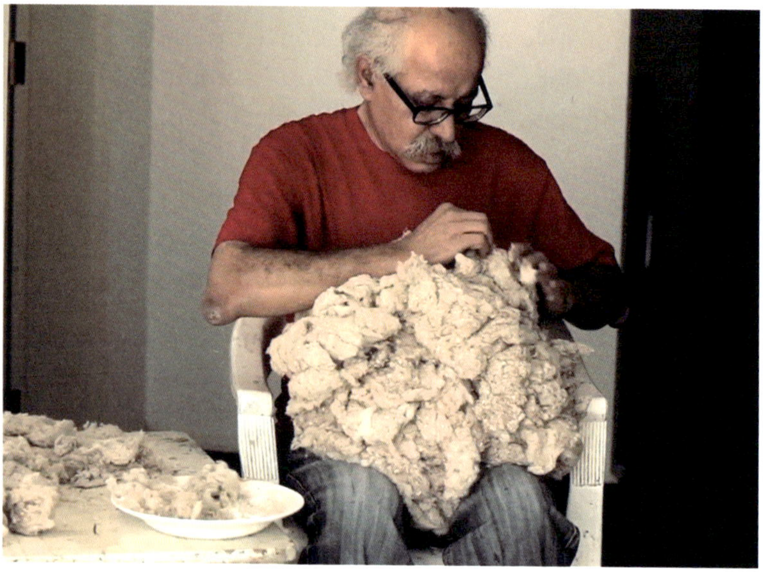

Hassan Sharif, *Cotton*, 2013
Cotton and HD video, silent, color, single channel,
20 × 67 × 46 cm, 08:26 min
Courtesy of the Estate of Hassan Sharif and
Gallery Isabelle van den Eynde, Dubai

Be you, however you are and more ...
Be the sea ...
Be Khor Fakkan ...
Be the entire world ...
Be the citizen, the wretched and the human ...

– Ahmed Rashid Thani, *A Letter to Ahmed Rashid Thani* (p. 168–172)

Let's end with another mountain—a more modest one than the one in Khor Fakkan that inspired Mohammed Ahmed Ibrahim's fantasies of cutting a hole through it.

In 2013, Hassan Sharif made a new work, *Cotton*, that combined a mound of cotton with a simply shot video documenting the mechanics of its making: handfuls of raw cotton from one pile on a table are dipped into a bowl of binding agent and piled into another rough pile on the artist's lap, until the pile on the table is exhausted. The task complete, the artist slowly looks up to meet the viewer's gaze. What do we see? Satisfaction? Challenge? Mischief? A man occupying space and time according to rules of his own choosing; making objects that the world had begun to value more highly— after a series of high profile exhibitions, including one at the Venice Biennale—than the hundreds he had produced over the prior three decades?[17]

Cotton presents an artist "pushing hands", keeping his balance. With its underlying whimsy, challenge, and rhythm, it seems to *rhyme* with many of the works in the Pavilion exhibition and publication, evidencing a shared interest in time and space, and in their unhurried occupation.

For the scientifically minded, any discussion of time and space elides neatly from banal considerations of everyday life to existential questions about Life, meaning, and our place in the universe all the way back to the Big Bang—the "initial singularity" when matter was infinitely hot and dense, and space itself was formed through its infinite expansion and cooling.

The Big Bang is one hypothesis that emerges from Albert Einstein's general theory of relativity rooted in "classical" physics. But classical physics is an awkward fit with quantum mechanics, the study of the subatomic realm. Quantum mechanics does not subscribe to the bedrock of classical physics: the independent particle with a "position" and singular characteristics such as "velocity," or even a fixed notion of space.[18]

Rather, quantum mechanics uses as its building blocks structures called "wave functions"—regarded as the most complete way of representing reality—which allow us to observe physical systems. And while wave functions can reveal the state of physical systems and make predictions about how systems may behave under given conditions, they are unable to predict outcomes with certainty. Chance and unpredictability raise their conjoined heads, opening up the possibility that the universe may have behaved differently in the extreme conditions of its creation.

In Ahmed Rashid Thani's imploration to "Be the sea;" in quantum mechanics' "wave functions;" and, in the notion of "pushing hands," we can detect an underlying commonality. An "attitude" that can be characterized by the willful and playful refusal to meet force with force; to predict the future; or attempt to control the circumstances and rules through which one negotiates the present. In navigating the "physical systems" that govern our lives, the best course of action may be to ride these waves—to play.

The practices of artists in "Rock, Paper, Scissors" resonate with this idea. Each on their own, but also as part of a "system," a community, a shared space, a home.

1 *Window: 16 UAE Artists* (Total Arts, Dubai, 2006) accompanied the exhibition at Total Arts at Courtyard, Dubai, curated by Mohammed Kazem, with Ebtisam Abdulaziz as assistant curator.

2 See Michael E. Moore and Jennifer Sward, *Introduction to the Game Industry*, Pearson Prentice Hall, Upper Saddle River, New Jersey, 2006, p. 535. But the earliest references to a finger-flashing game are traced to a tomb-wall painting in Egypt, circa. 2000 BCE. See Katharine Schwab, "A Cultural History of Rock-Paper-Scissors," in *The Atlantic*, December 23, 2015, available online: www.theatlantic.com/entertainment/archive/2015/12/how-rock-paper-scissors-went-viral/418455/

3 Carol Vogel, "Rock, Paper, Payoff: Child's Play Wins Auction House an Art Sale," *The New York Times*, April 29, 2005,available online: www.nytimes.com/2005/04/29/arts/design/rock-paper-payoff-childs-play-wins-auction-house-an-art-sale.html?_r=0

4 On the ambiguous nature of play, see Brian Sutton-Smith, *The Ambiguity of Play*, Harvard University Press, Cambridge, Massachusetts, 1997.

5 Key texts that have framed ideas of "play" include: Friedrich Schiller, On the Aesthetic Education of Man, Dover Publications, Mineola, New York, 2012 (originally published in 1794); Herbert Spencer, The Principles of Biology, Williams and Norgate, Oxford, 1864; digitized by Google from the library of Oxford University; Johan Huizinga, *Homo Ludens: A Study of the Play-Element in Culture*, Angelico Press, Kettering, Ohio, 2016 (originally published in 1938); Roger Caillois, *Man, Play, and Games*, University of Illinois Press, Chicago, 2001 (originally published in 1958); David J. Getsy (ed.), *From Diversion to Subversion: Games, Play, and Twentieth-Century Art*, Pennsylvania State University Press, University Park, Pennsylvania, 2011.

6 Deepak Unnikrishnan, "Veed," in *Temporary People*, Restless Books, New York, 2017.

7 Nan Enstad, "Smoking Hot," in Ronald Radano and Tejumola Olaniyan (eds.), *Audible Empire: Music, Global Politics, Critique*, Duke University Press, Durham, North Carolina, 2016, p. 47.

8 The previous four editions of the UAE National Pavilion included the work of Ebtisam Abdulaziz (2009); Abdullah Al Saadi (2011, 2015); Mohammed Kazem (2013, 2015); and Hassan Sharif (2009, 2015). The Abu Dhabi Authority for Culture & Heritage (ADACH) Pavilion (2009) in Venice included work by Abdulaziz, Al Saadi, Mohammed Ahmed Ibrahim, Kazem, and Sharif. There have also been numerous initiatives in the UAE to showcase many of this same group of artists (often referred to as "The Five") who were directly influenced by Sharif, most notably "But We Cannot See Them: Tracing a UAE Art Community 1988–2008," curated by Maya Allison with Bana Kattan at The Art Gallery at NYU Abu Dhabi (2017). The work of Hassan Sharif and Abdullah Al Saadi is also featured in the central pavilion of the 57th Venice Biennale.

9 See Hammad Nasar, "Reimagining the Museum," in *Think*, no. 8, January 2014, pp. 51–56

10 Hammad Nasar, "Interview with Irit Rogoff," in Iftikhar Dadi and Hammad Nasar (eds.), *Lines of Control: Partition as a Productive Space*, Herbert F. Johnson Museum at Cornell University, Ithaca, New York, and Green Cardamom, London, 2012, pp. 101–110.

11 Julia Cerqueira Leite, "Interview with Hammad Nasar" in *Naked Punch*, no. 10, Spring 2008, pp. 101–110.

12 See C. L. R. James's magisterial semi-autobiographical account of the Caribbean, *Beyond a Boundary* (1963); Joseph O'Neill's novel, *Netherland* (2008), exploring post 9/11 New York; the Bollywood blockbuster *Lagaan* (2001); and the British documentary *Fire in Babylon* (2010).

13 Benedict Anderson, *Imagined Communities*, Verso, London, 1983.

14 See Claudia Mesch, "Serious Play: Games and Early Twentieth-Century Modernism," in David J. Getsy (ed.), *From Diversion to Subversion: Games, Play, and Twentieth-Century Art*, Pennsylvania State University Press, University Park, 2011, pp. 64-65

15 See Walter Benjamin, *The Work of Art in the Age of Mechanical Reproduction*, Penguin, London, 2008 (originally published in 1936); and Hito Steyerl, "In Defense of the Poor Image," *e-flux Journal*, no. 10, November 2009, available online: www.e-flux.com/journal/10/61362/in-defense-of-the-poor-image/

16 See "ANNEX," *WTD Magazine*, no. 6, Winter 2015

17 Hassan Sharif's presentation in the ADACH Pavilion (2009), curated by Catherine David, was followed by a major retrospective of his work, 'Hassan Sharif: Experiments & Objects', 1979–2011, curated by David and Mohammed Kazem, and accompanied by a monograph edited by David, *Hassan Sharif: Works, 1973–2010*, Hatje Cantz, Ostfildern, Germany, 2011.

18 For an introduction to the general themes, see Sean Carroll, "The Big Bounce," in *FT Weekend Magazine*, March 18–19, 2017, pp. 20–23. For a fuller consideration, see Sean Carroll's *The Big Picture: On the Origins of Life, Meaning and the Universe Itself*, Oneworld, London, 2016.

Objects at/of Play

Murtaza Vali

For Hassan

In the early 1980s, during summers spent back home while he was attending art school in London, Hassan Sharif executed a series of simple actions in the harsh desert landscape outside Dubai. Documented in a few black-and-white photographs (below), these early performances involved simple activities—walking, jumping, throwing stones, digging, and then standing in a hole in the sand—that resemble elementary forms of child's play, the kinds of basic movements through which we, especially as children, map out and acquaint ourselves with the spatial and material conditions of our surroundings. These actions seemed to embody a desire—possibly borne of time spent away—to situate himself, literally, back in his homeland. They enacted emplacement through a retrieval of basic child's play. More complex task-based actions would follow, carried out in the confines of his modest home and studio back in the city. Composed of sets of simple instructions, these resembled the sorts of made-up games one might concoct to relieve the unrelenting boredom of the sultry days of summer in early 1980s Dubai. Sharif continued to produce such provocative "Experiments" and "Performances,"

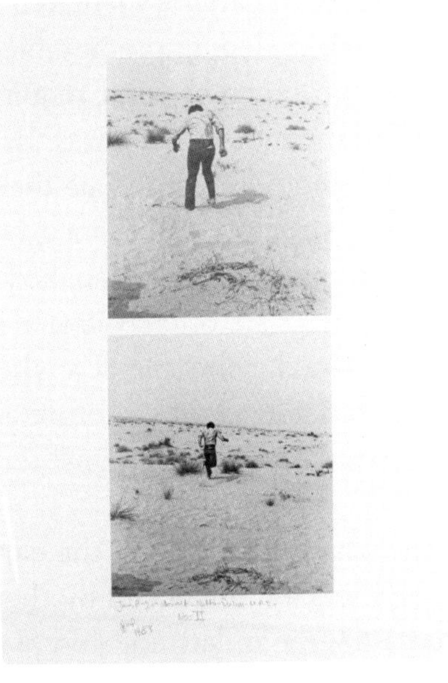

Hassan Sharif, *Jumping No. 2*, 1983
Collage, photographs and pencil on mounting board, 73.7 × 56 cm
Courtesy of the Estate of Hassan Sharif
and Gallery Isabelle van den Eynde, Dubai

as he called them, during his studies at the Byam Shaw School of Art, and brought this commitment to radical and experimental art practice back with him to the UAE upon completing his degree in 1984. Through a close analysis of the work of Sharif, and of his younger compatriot Abdullah Al Saadi, I will attempt to trace some of the genealogies of play at play in the short history of contemporary art production in the UAE.

Though play is a fundamental human experience, it was only first theorized in the 20th century by Dutch anthropologist Johan Huizinga, who, in *Homo Ludens: A Study of the Play Element in Culture* (1938), provides a succinct definition of play as "an activity which proceeds within certain limits of time and space, in a visible order, according to rules freely accepted, and outside the sphere of necessity or material utility."[1] The French surrealist Roger Caillois built on Huizinga's landmark study, and critical of his fellow surrealists' growing predilection for esoteric rituals, sought to secularize play by distinguishing the ludic from the sacred. In *Man, Play and Games*, Caillois developed an elaborate structural typology of play which could then be used to analyze and classify the games of a culture. Caillois divided various kinds of play and games into four distinct but not exclusive categories: *agôn* (competition), *alea* (chance), *mimicry* (simulation), and *ilinx* (vertigo), with games in each category situated on an evolutionary spectrum between *paidia* (open-ended, unpredictable, and spontaneous activities) and *ludus* (activities governed by rules, requiring strategy and calculation).[2] What emerges from these theorizations is the notion that play constitutes an exceptional and unproductive terrain that is characterized, somewhat paradoxically, by both structure and chance, both constraint and freedom—a definition that could just as easily be applied to art itself. In play, the deterministic structures of rules are often balanced by the indeterminacy of chance, through the cast of a die, the spin of a wheel, or the uncertainty of an acting body. This coincidence of structure and chance, though it appears in a myriad of distinct guises, is a consistent trope across much of Sharif's oeuvre.

Take Sharif's "Semi-System" works, which he began in the early 1980s and would revisit two decades later. Heavily influenced by the British Systems Group, Sharif introduced a degree of latitude and play into their strict use of mathematics, systems, and structures. He subverted the totality of the system by reintroducing the potential for chance and

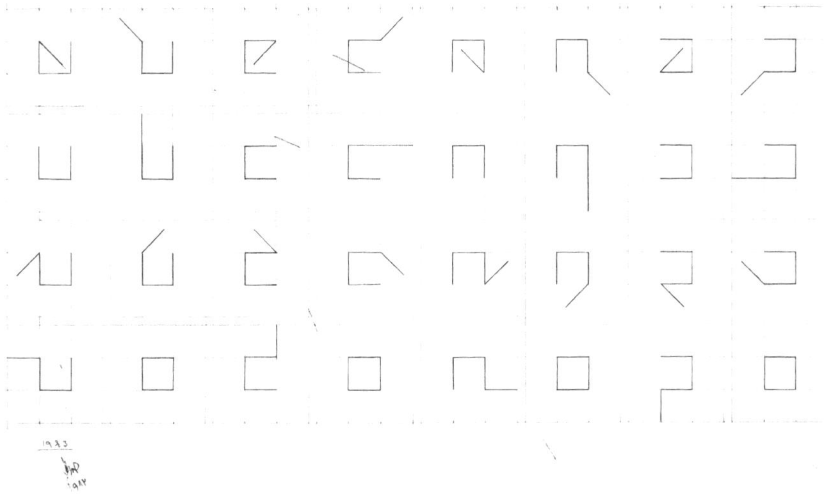

Hassan Sharif, *Movement of Square's Side*, 1983
Ink on paper, 62.9 × 47 cm. Courtesy of the Estate of Hassan Sharif and Gallery Isabelle van den Eynde, Dubai

human agency through his own hand, allowing varying qualities of mark, line, and form to emerge out of a predetermined structure. And while a grid is often featured, its orthogonal order is thrown into disarray through the playful introduction of diagonal lines, as in *Movement of a Square's Side* (1983, above), which presents thirty-two hand-drawn permutations of an open square, with its errant edge pivoting at various angles and in different directions. While Sharif's "Semi-System" works appear to abide by sets of rules, these rules do not necessarily create order or close down multiplicity, but rather enable play.

Sharif's sense of play was not limited to formal exercises. *In Drum (Barrel)* (1985), which was included in his first solo exhibition at the Emirates Fine Arts Society in Sharjah after his return from London, and *Wooden Column* (1985), drawn-out calculations and notes function as a playful ruse, a diversion of sorts, through which a wry critique of authority is smuggled in.[3] In the former, the calculations work out the dimensions of a simple cylindrical object, a life-size replica, handmade out of cardboard, paper, and paint, of the sorts of repurposed oil drums used by police to prevent drivers from off-roading to circumvent traffic. In the latter, a wooden structure, boasting a simple, elegant geometry, is housed in a white vitrine with a glass front. Mimicking the types of obstructions commonly used to reserve parking spaces, it too is an instrument of control itself marshaled into being a witty Duchampian readymade.

•••

Influenced by Marcel Duchamp and Fluxus International, Sharif turned his attention to the ordinary and commonplace, to investigating the artistic potential of banal objects and everyday actions. These strands of inquiry came together most powerfully in the "Objects" he began making in 1984 and continued to construct until his death in 2016. Sharif's process is humble and straightforward. It involves the seemingly obsessive repetition of mundane manual tasks—cutting, folding, rolling, twisting, knotting, tying, plaiting, weaving, binding, gluing, wrapping. Monotonously reiterated, the process resembles that of a machine on an assembly line, mirroring an industrial system of production. These actions produce numerous small discrete units, which are then simply piled, bundled, or strung together and hung to create a larger form. Paulina Kolczynska has suggested that a possible source for the forms and materials Sharif began to use is the displays of goods and foodstuffs commonly found in Dubai's traditional souqs, encountered with fresh eyes after his time abroad.[4]

The earliest known "Object" is the now lost *Nylon Rope* (1982), a piece of rope dangling off a hook on the wall, with knots of varying sizes and shapes tied at irregular intervals down its length.[5] Eventually, such knots would hold other objects, or parts of objects, in place, creating

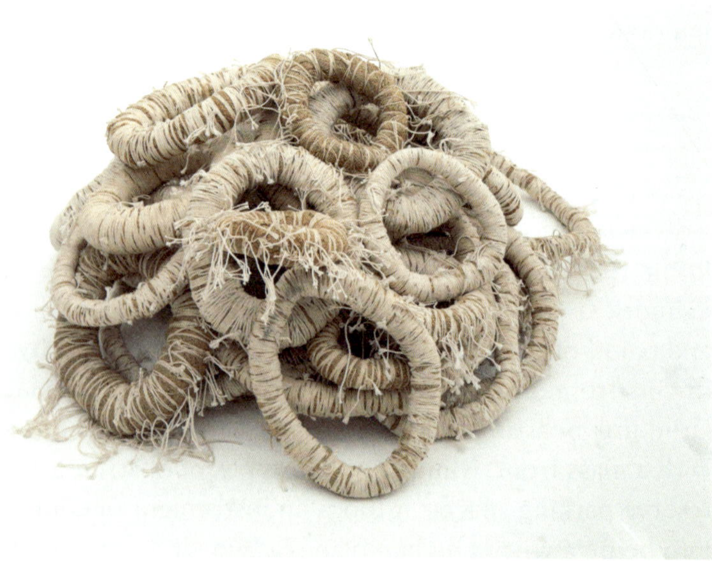

Hassan Sharif, *Jute, Cloth and Rope*, 1985
Coir, cotton, rope and jute, 110 × 110 × 50 cm
Collection of Sharjah Art Foundation

a string or matrix of smaller units. Sharif's "Objects" are made out of modest materials, listed, like the nylon rope, in their matter-of-fact titles. The earliest ones exclusively featured organic materials like coir, jute, cloth, rope, paper, and papier-mâché, as in *Jute, Cloth, and Rope* (1985, facing), in which these very materials form a heap of stringy circles of varying sizes and thickness. In 1986 Sharif began using staplers and hole punches, stapling strips of scrap paper together to form bundles and collecting punched-out discs of paper in little plastic bags, which were then displayed in piles. Playfully and somewhat absurdly repurposing these basic office tools as mark-making devices, Sharif critiqued the ineffectualness of bureaucratic structures and the tedium of corporate labor. Increasingly wary of growing wasteful consumption, Sharif also began to use waste material, tying discarded cardboard packaging material together into simple bundles.[6] And Sharif's more recent "Objects" specifically draw from the unbranded underbelly of global trade—the cheap, mass-produced commodities that fill the old souqs and small neighborhood groceries known as *baqalas* but are notably absent from the countless hypermodern air-conditioned malls dotting the UAE. In *Slippers and Wires* (2009, p. 35), garishly colored rubber slippers have been cut, folded, strung together, and piled high, while *Suspended Objects* (2011) consists of hanging bundles of strings overloaded with bits of other consumer effluvia which, somewhat unexpectedly, resemble date palm branches heavy with ripening fruit.

Though the physical qualities of an object might limit how Sharif can manipulate it, the simplicity of his methodology makes it very versatile, allowing it to be adapted to a variety of objects and materials, as Sharif ably demonstrated through his more than three decades of experimentation. And the raw materials are rarely transformed through the sculptural process—their original form and function remain identifiable. Though the "Objects" are recognizable as works by Sharif to those in the know, they are simultaneously unexceptional and anonymous—capable of simply and seamlessly blending into the existing urban landscape.[7]

There is a conscious and perverse purposelessness to the way Sharif works. He foregrounds process; the act is more important than the final result. Channeling Duchamp, he rejects the authority of authorship by repeatedly performing a type of unspecialized task, a process that could extend endlessly and that does not produce use or surplus value. Made through obsessive, repetitive labor, the completion of these objects is somewhat arbitrary and dependent on exhaustion, raw material, time, space, energy, desire, and interest. Sharif repeatedly downplayed the significance of his process and dismissed the value and status of the final product, dubbing it "useless, an exercise in construction"—a phrase that emphasizes the insignificant, routine, and repetitive quality of the process, and links it to the notion of art as a set of instructions to be followed.[8] For Sharif, the act of making art is neither heroic nor transcendent but a simple extension of daily life. It is an immanent practice that rejects artistic virtuosity by firmly embedding the aesthetic in the everyday.

In the title of an important essay from the mid-2000s, Sharif characterized his practice as a type of "weaving."[9] An ancient technique for creating surfaces, forms, and structures, weaving is central to various indigenous craft practices. Traditionally, the leaves of date palms were dried, dyed, and plaited to make mats, trays, and baskets. Similarly, the stronger wooden midribs of the palm fronds were used for making crates and boxes, as roofing, and to construct *garagir*, the dome-shaped fishing traps typical of the region, which are now commonly made out of wire. Bedouin women in rural communities continue to practice a traditional form of fabric weaving called *al sadu* to produce soft furnishings and decorative accessories for camels and horses. By linking his art practice to such indigenous craft practices, Sharif claimed solidarity with the bodies, primarily female, that traditionally perform these and countless other unacknowledged domestic tasks, acts distinguished through their endless nonproductive repetition. Sharif's final tapestry-like wall pieces have made this link to weaving explicit.[10] A longstanding critic of conservative constructions of heritage that fetishize elements of pre-oil existence, decontextualizing and re-presenting this lived past as hollow icons and displays, Sharif, instead, revitalizes an ancient handicraft technique as a viable medium of contemporary art. Though enacted through his male body, his practice reveals and revels in a strong feminist aesthetic and ethic of labor and care.

In that same essay, Sharif also positions his practice as a conscious critical response to the alienating effect of consumer capitalism spreading across the globe and transforming society and culture in the UAE. His response is to turn himself into a type of pointless nonproductive machine

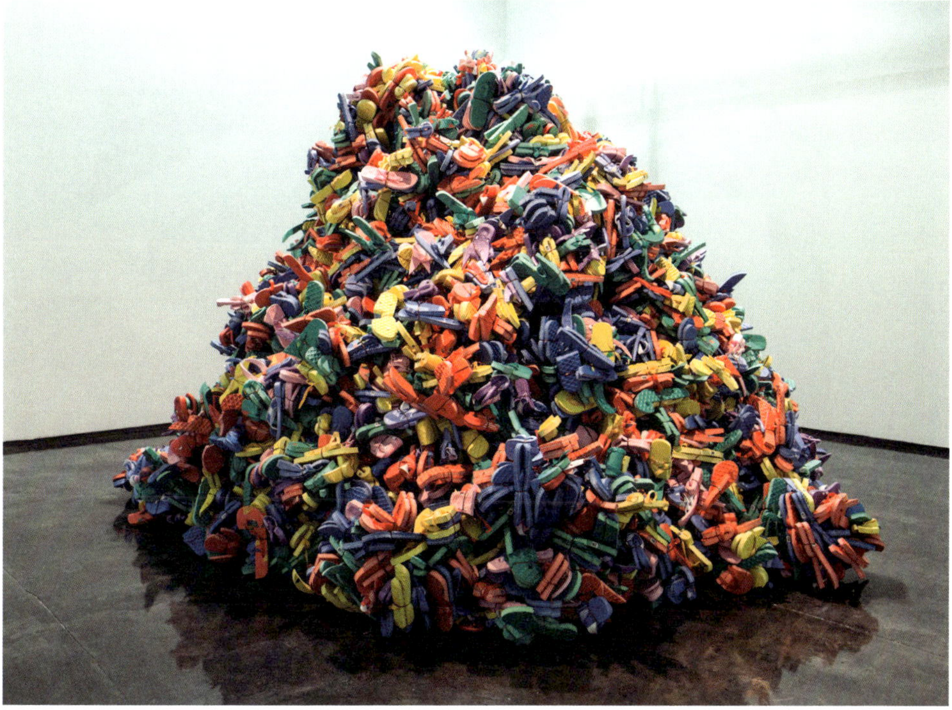

Hassan Sharif, *Slippers and Wire*, 2009
Slippers and copper wire; dimensions variable
(as shown: 300 × 400 × 500 cm)
Courtesy of the Estate of Hassan Sharif and Gallery Isabelle van den Eynde, Dubai

engaged in "redundant repetition," perversely reenacting through a human body the conditions of mass production.[11] Dubai has enjoyed great success as an exemplary entrepôt—a tax-free trading post optimized to facilitate the streamlined movement and trade of commodities. Sharif stalls these never-ending cycles of consumption by extracting goods from incessant circulation and reducing them to a raw material for sculpture. Objects are folded and bound, immobilized, enmeshed in nets and weighed down, sometimes embedded in a muddy substrate of papier-mâché and glue. Everyday utilitarian objects are rendered useless; they are, instead, transformed into material anchors—objects that insist on and enable attachment.

Though superficially Sharif's sculptural practice appears to have remained methodologically and morphologically consistent, there have

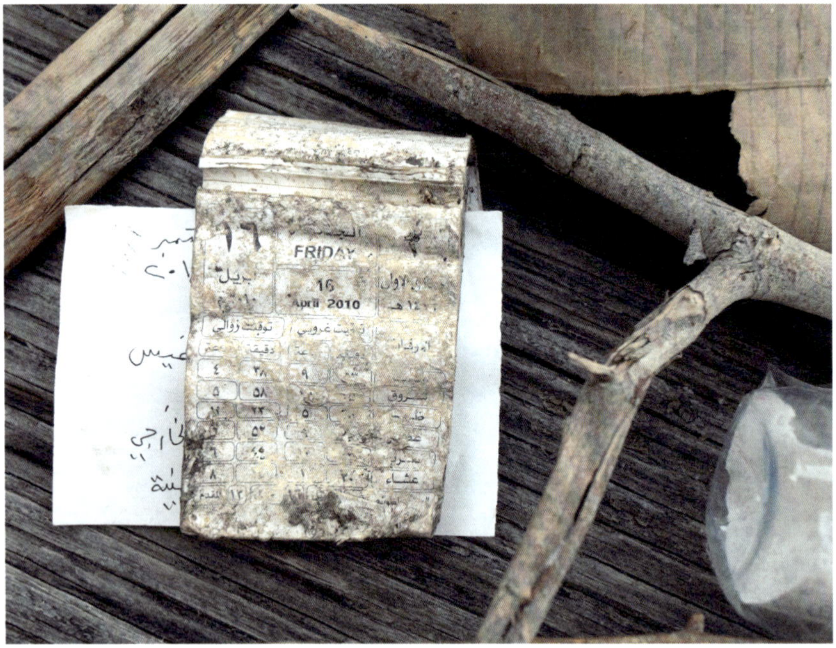

Abdullah Al Saadi, *My Mother's Letters*, 1998–2013
Installation, mixed media; dimensions variable

been important shifts, as Kolczynska's careful chronological survey identifies. Like an open-ended game, the simplicity of Sharif's process affords it infinite potential, allowing the "Objects" to be interpreted in many different ways: as revitalizations of traditional handicraft practices; as valorizations of domestic and other types of unacknowledged labor; as gestures of care against injury, aggression, and violence, if binding is read as a form of bandaging; as metaphors for societal repression and building frustration, if binding is read as a gesture of restraint and control; and as critiques of the alienating effects of consumer capitalism. Sharif, however, once also compared his sculptural process to the never-ending testimony of a guilty person on trial, who must keep talking to delay the verdict.[12] Repeated to the point of ritual, Sharif's simple manual actions enact an endless deferral, forestalling judgment, evaluation, opinion, criticism, and eventually, even death.[13] Most forms of play involve comp-etition with an adversary; in Sharif's case, play is an ongoing struggle against boredom, convention, and closure. And the final lesson is to figure out a way to always stay in the game.

•••

If Sharif's practice repeatedly introduces an element of chance into a defined system, Abdullah Al Saadi's does the reverse, constructing elaborate, if somewhat idiosyncratic, structures of representation around the seemingly incidental and accidental, around the observed and excavated. As in Sharif's work, found objects also play a central role. Al Saadi does, however, focus somewhat exclusively on objects discarded by others, on trash, debris, and detritus, often gravitating to the abject. These objects—which have included animal bones, insects, and soda cans—are often collected on everyday wanderings or longer meticulously planned multiday journeys conducted on bicycle or on foot, accompanied by his donkey and dog, through the mountainous landscape/terrain of the northern UAE. Carved out of the temporal and spatial routine of daily life, these journeys are also a type of mimetic play, evoking the Bedouins' nomadic past and the itineraries of fabled explorers like Ibn Battuta.

While Sharif's practice is materially transformative to a degree, Al Saadi minimally manipulates the objects he collects. Casting himself as an amateur entomologist, natural historian, or archaeologist, he carefully collects, cleans, categorizes, classifies, catalogues, and displays them, as if they were merely evidence of his expedition, field samples for further study, or artifacts of an archaeology of the present. Objects are catalogued and analyzed; data and information is studiously and obsessively recorded. Al Saadi stresses, correctly, that he is an amateur; derived from the Latin root amare or "to love," the term refers to a person driven by sheer passion rather than the promise of professional recognition or financial compensation. His status as an amateur allows him the latitude to play, testing the limits and conventions of these scientific disciplines.

It is hardly surprising, then, that one of his most important recent works arises out of an intimate relationship. *My Mother's Letters, 1998–2013* (2013, facing) consists of a collection of objects—litter, scraps, twigs, and tree branches found close to his home—left at his doorstep in his absence as messages by his illiterate mother. It's a material and tactile, if enigmatic, form of communication. Forced to decipher these messages, Al Saadi began to systematically study and categorize these objects, collecting his sketches, notes, observations, and findings in a handmade book filled with richly but cryptically annotated diagrams, attempting to translate a set of material signs into linguistic ones, to translate unspoken intimacies into collective utterances. Despite the appearance of scientific rigor, Al Saadi's data and analysis does not promise or provide answers; legibility is suggested but never guaranteed. With the objects displayed in a manner somewhere between that of relics and artifacts, the project playfully presents an encounter between two distinct and irreconcilable epistemologies.

Linguistic play is a key component of Al Saadi's practice, and he frequently creates new systems and spaces for communication. A key characteristic of play, as Huizinga notes, is that it unfolds in an exceptional space and time that lies outside of the ordinary routines of daily life. Seven novel alphabets (six based on Arabic and one based on English), developed by the artist over more than two decades, are showcased in his handmade book *Alphabets* (1990–2013). Al Saadi's artistic practice draws significantly from the flora, fauna, and landscape of the mountains near Khor Fakkan where he lives, and his novel alphabets incorporate minutiae from his daily life in these rural surroundings. Two are based on the lines, curves, and shapes suggested by male and female bodies. Others take their cues from the anatomy of his donkey companion, Camar Cande, the bodies of local birds, or the pollinating patterns of bees. By translating careful observations of his natural environment into an idiosyncratic linguistic system, Al Saadi reminds us of the pictographic origins of many alphabets, and that languages are rarely abstract systems but are profoundly influenced by the social, cultural, and physical contexts out of which they emerge.

Al Saadi's use of the human anatomy as the basis of some of his invented alphabets is significant. His linguistic play may represent a conscious strategy through which to circumvent and subvert conservative societal proscriptions on representations of the human figure. His made-up letters cleverly sublimate the forms and contours of bodies into the syntax of language. They reintroduce the abject body, otherwise repressed, back into plain view as code. As code they escape censorship and avoid surveillance, allowing knowledge and representations of the body to continue to circulate freely.

This coded return of the repressed abject body is best exemplified in Al Saadi's *Naked Sweet Potato* (2000–2010, above), a multifaceted project that celebrates the humble sweet potato—a root vegetable indigenous to the rural area where he lives and works. Fascinated by their

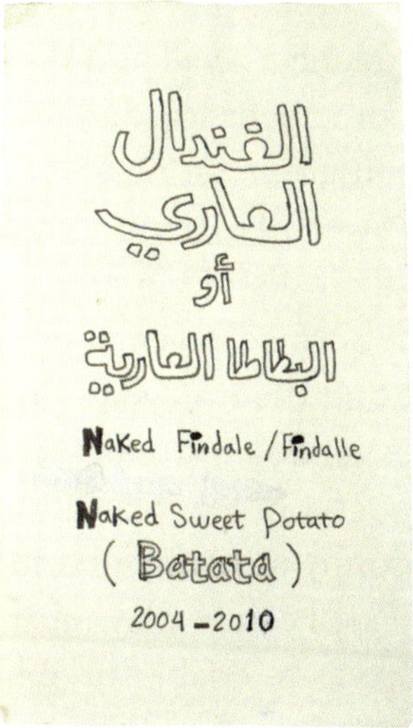

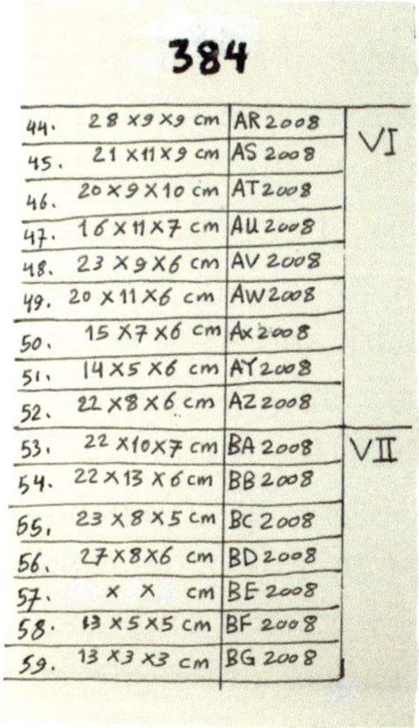

Abdullah Al Saadi, *Naked Sweet Potato*, 2000–2010
Book page, pen on paper, 11 × 19 cm

biomorphic forms, Al Saadi began cataloging and analyzing the varying bulbous shapes he encountered in daily life, developing elaborate formal taxonomies of these bodily forms. Over the years, Al Saadi has repeated these suggestive forms, which are simultaneously sexual and scatological, in different media—small ink drawings; large, colorful oil paintings; engravings on rocks; delicate clay replicas; larger found metal sculptures; handmade bronze jewelry, and precious, but deliciously perverse, versions cast out of solid gold. These forms have also served as the basis of another novel alphabet, one that celebrates the breathtaking diversity of the artist's surroundings and is literally rooted in his native land.[14] For Al Saadi, ludic and diaristic methodologies cultivate and maintain intimacy with the rural landscape that is his core subject. Play enables him to comprehend and represent his natural environment without reducing its richness, contingency, and complexity, without forcing it to conform to rational demands of culture, without alienating himself from it.

•••

Elaborating the relationship between play and subversion, David J. Getsy has noted that "Play's capacity for diversion from the everyday—both in the sense of a light distraction from the mundane as well as a skewed push away from it—also enables its potential for subversion and critique. Accordingly, the liminality of play and its potential for acting and being otherwise, if even temporarily, has made it a powerful metaphor for artistic creation and for the aesthetic encounter."[15] In their distinct practices, both Sharif and Al Saadi appear, at least on the surface, to embed the ludic back into the materiality of the ordinary and the everyday through their use of the found object, seemingly domesticating a strategy that gains its criticality from alterity and exceptionality. In a public culture where standards of decorum invalidate open confrontation and criticism, especially when it originates from outside, the position of play must remain elusive and inside, carefully calibrated so as to enable an oblique perspective that results in just the right parallax effect. Neither Sharif nor Al Saadi openly rejects established structures, but rather they use the ludic as a strategy to make such structures expand from within, creating some space for contingency, multiplicity, and ambiguity. Under the sign of play, the critical becomes not an outright rejection or negation but a much-needed space of negotiation, where the pressing issues of the day, artistic and otherwise, may be discussed and debated.

1 Johan Huizinga, *Homo Ludens: A Study of the Play Element in Culture*, The Beacon Press, Boston, 1955, p. 132.

2 Roger Caillois, *Man, Play and Games*, University of Illinois Press, Urbana and Chicago, 2001.

3 Paulina Kolczynska, "Hassan Sharif: A Rare Bloom in the Desert," in Catherine David (ed.), *Hassan Sharif: Works 1973–2011*, Hatje Cantz, Ostfildern, Germany, 2011, pp. 54–55.

4 Ibid, p. 56.

5 Ibid, p. 56. An image of the work appears on p. 202 of the book.

6 Ibid, pp. 56–67. In her detailed survey Kolczynska carefully traces the subtle shifts in materials, and resulting meanings, Sharif's "Objects."

7 This quality is illustrated best by Sharif's contribution to Sharjah Biennial 7 in 2005. "Objects" made of glued cardboard placed in the square outside the Sharjah Art Museum were mistaken for garbage and hauled away by street cleaners just before the opening.

8 Sam Bardaouil and Till Fellrath, "Hassan Sharif," in *Summer Autumn Winter... and Spring: Conversations with Artists from the Arab World*, Skira, Milan, 2014, p. 99.

9 Hassan Sharif, "Weaving," in Ismail Al Refai and Patricia Millns (eds.), *Window 2006: 16 UAE Artists*, Total Arts at Courtyard, Dubai, 2006, p. 208. In this bilingual catalogue to a group exhibition curated by Mohammed Kazem at Total Arts at Courtyard, Dubai (April 18–May 15, 2006), the text appears under the Arabic title of "*al nasij*" which technically translates to "the weave" in English. The same Arabic text was first published in 2005 in the catalogue for the Sharjah Biennial 7, where it appeared under different titles in both Arabic and English. The Arabic is "*al tamuj*," which translates to "the roll," and the English is "rolling," and featured a different English translation. See Hassan Sharif, "Rolling," in Kamal Boullata (ed.), *Sharjah Biennial 7: Belonging*, Sharjah Biennial, 2005, p. 390.

10 Such works featured prominently in some of Sharif's recent solo exhibitions including "Approaching Entropy" at Gallery Isabelle van den Eynde, Dubai (November 18, 2013–January 2, 2014) and "Hassan Sharif" at Alexander Gray Associates, New York (April 7–May 14, 2016).

11 Ibid.

12 Hassan Sharif, interview with the author, January 5, 2014.

13 Ibid. Though Sharif never acknowledged this during my interview, this analogy bears an uncanny structural similarity to Scheherazade's predicament in *One Thousand and One Nights*, where storytelling becomes a way to forestall certain death.

14 A selection of works from this project were exhibited in "Second Time Around: The Pavilion for the UAE at the 54th Venice Biennale curated by Vasif Kortun. See Vasif Kortun, *Second Time Around: The Pavilion for the UAE at the 54th International Art Exhibition – la Biennale di Venezia*, Abu Dhabi, National Pavilion of the United Arab Emirates at the Venice Biennale, 2011. The gold versions were commissioned for "Emirati Expressions: Realised" curated by Reem Fadda, see Reem Fadda (ed.), *Emirati Expressions: Realised*, Abu Dhabi Tourism & Culture Authority, 2013.

15 David J. Getsy, "Introduction," in David J. Getsy (ed.), *From Diversion to Subversion: Games, Play, and Twentieth-Century Art*, Pennsylvania State University, University Park, 2011, p. 12

Sea/Sand/Wind/Internet: On States of Fluidity and the Aesthetics of Critical Heritage in the UAE

Uzma Z. Rizvi

I don't want to be an artist with deep roots in any one thing and then merely branches out to other disciplines. I'm not a tree; I'm a small bush, or only sand, or only the sea. Sand and the sea are small. Their roots are not too deep. And the winds can blow through and carry them off, like a Bedouin. This is what I am.[1]

– Hassan Sharif

In his own uniquely whimsical, yet politically clear manner, Hassan Sharif (1951–2016) embodied the various contradictory possible histories of the UAE by claiming to be both the sea and sand. Hailing from a federation whose heritage is located in both milieus, Sharif's ability to locate sea/sand in the body of the artist gives critical meaning to aesthetic forms ripe with the possibility to destabilize articulations of the nation through artistic expression. He is utterly complete in his statement: while the winds may blow through, those natural processes do not detract from his existence, but rather are intrinsic to it. Although this essay is not about Hassan Sharif per se, it is about the paradoxical condition of being and belonging in the UAE he so uniquely inhabited; it is about the necessity of a fluid subject position in a place where unauthorized positions are categorically impossible and yet exist; and finally, it is about how critical heritage discourse in the UAE has an aesthetic that can be traced to a fluidity of self that is often and necessarily found within complicit systems of cosmopolitan otherness.

Critical heritage discourses are, by their very nature, political acts in which power relations are exposed, insisting on uncomfortable negotiations of what constitutes heritage narratives, particularly within the constructs of the nation.[2] Within a new federation such as the UAE, one that was not quite colonial, thus not quite postcolonial, and yet oddly neocolonial, discourses related to ways of being and belonging through practice do not follow known global political frameworks, such as liberal democracies, within which to critique heritage. Complicating further the usual narratives of belonging and heritage is the question of citizenship (or lack thereof), which creates its own complicit systems simultaneously forcing a positionality for those with and without such privilege, generating subsets of hierarchies based on race/class/gender within each.[3] The manner in which critical heritage discourse is framed in this piece has little to do with questions of citizenship, and this is significant, as it revolves entirely around the claims to place, history, and a negotiated sense of belonging through aesthetics.[4]

Fluidity as Subject Position

In order to claim a place in history, concepts of the modern state require heritage to settle. Modernity and its relationship with history-making is dominated by histories of settlements. In the UAE, narratives of mobility are presented as authorized heritage discourse for a federation that requires a claim of stability and settled-ness in order to be part of global narratives of world order.[5] This paradoxical requirement can be found along all scales of experience in the UAE. In this gentrification of belonging, the subjectivity of those individuals who have always been from "spaces of motion" are also made static. Any aesthetic that represents static notions of others and selves does so as a screen shot—a moment in time that is made into a representation that stands in for much mobility, movement, and trends. These representations of fluid belonging then need not be monumental, but rather, as they become the grounds upon which the experience of the representation leaves a trace, they depict the everyday. The claim to heritage then becomes an acknowledgment of the banal, of the everyday, of the quotidian.[6] And it is the location of the practice of the everyday that gives fluidity as a subject position its complexity in form and nature.

Fluid subjectivity lays claim to being and belonging through the context, the wind, and the place. The simultaneity of subject location is precisely where the complexity is most apparent. Fluid positioning means that even though there is mobility and flow, the claim to belonging will be in the repeated gestures of living life. It is for this reason that critical heritage discourses in the UAE require locatedness, even if precarious, for the crafting of meaning. If you are not breathing the air, blowing in the wind, mixing in the waters, unstable, uncertain, and yet resolutely in place, you are not of here.[7] Fluidity as a conceptual framework allows for a simultaneity of positions, standpoints, forms of belonging, identities, and landscapes.[8] It escapes definition, which is in itself its definition. It takes the form of the vessel, the citizenship, the occupational visa provided to it, but it also spills over, making surfaces slippery and slimy, helping aerate the vessel's contents, and it is not one form, but waves of multiples.

Thresholds of Form

Form is often thought of in absolute terms. In focusing in on the threshold, the form itself has the capacity to engender spaces of marginal subject positionality and considers the impact such a position makes on subsequent aesthetic forms and critical heritage discourse. This threshold can be thought of as the melding of practices, the specific vagaries of the Internet, transdisciplinary approaches to understanding contemporary heritage practice, or metaphorically as the coast, gulf, and straits.[9] Locating practice and thought at thresholds shifts conversations from being on the margins to occupying the multiple spaces in-between. It is not just about the sand, it is not just about the sea; it is not just about the public or the private: the threshold breaks down binaries and forces multiple spaces of contention open. Thresholds of form allow for a flexible subject position to exist organically, representing multiples as possibilities, and providing the form as a potential universal.[10] And thus the condition of being of here and elsewhere becomes a valid criteria of belonging, and as such, other claims of authenticity can be anchored within states of fluidity.

These thresholds are not only of geographic concern, but also of temporal significance, as they embody linkages from the past to ways of being in the future. Encountering a form from another time within the contemporary landscape breeds a false sense of intimacy with a period that is not known, yet informs one's person. And with that intimacy comes a desire to maintain the residue of time, sometimes as a way to perpetuate a sense of self, but often to create it, as one might create memories. An easy example of such creations of memories is easily witnessed in the discourses surrounding the historic preservation of architectural structures and facades. A quick glance at newspapers such as The National illustrates the contemporary nature of these concerns, positioning the process of memory restoration as something intrinsically connected to the protection of buildings.[11] What is or should be protected is a topic that many have weighed in on with a diversity of opinions shared in the papers,[12] but at the core of this is often a question: whose memories are we preserving? Each geography has its own concerns and histories, and in some cases can be a site for critical interventions.[13] However, as we see in many other examples worldwide, this question of creating memory as history quickly becomes the realm of the state. In fact, it is of national importance to have a memory, to have a heritage, to have a history, in order to claim a space in a global world order.[14] Having a sense of heritage provides the nation with memory, aiding and abetting the gentrification of belonging. And that belonging necessarily entangles futurity with knowing and appreciating the past—the past that has been settled and made static in order for the future to soar in those same winds.[15]

A Note on Locating Critical Aesthetics as Critical Heritage Discourse

On May 1, 2016, the Arabic newspaper *Al Bayan* reported on the winning design, inspired by a falcon (saqr) in flight, for the UAE Pavilion of the next World Expo to be held in Dubai in 2020.[16] A bulk of the article focused on authorizing the criteria, emphasizing Expo 2020's theme, "Connecting Minds, Creating the Future," which through the image of the falcon was able to illustrate a balanced, and yet authentic, expression of heritage and

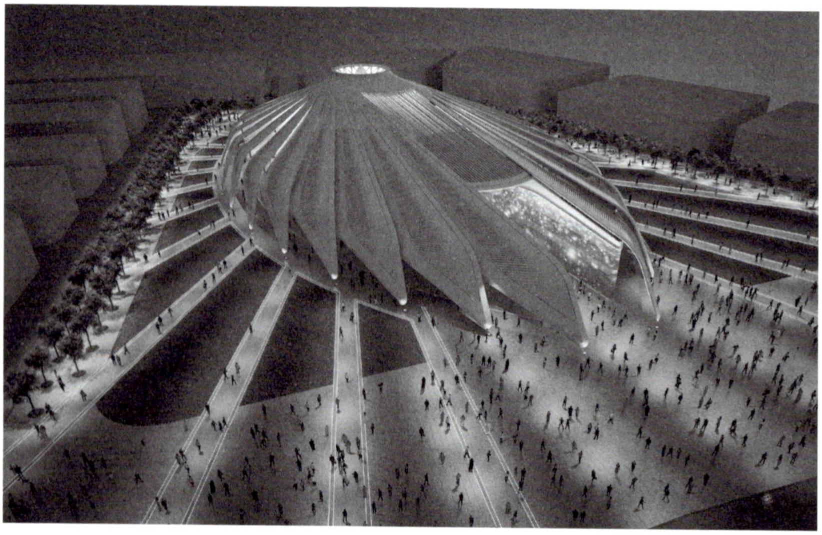

UAE Pavilion at Expo 2020
Image courtesy of the National Media Council, UAE and Calatrava International LLC

the future.[17] If we consider the image of the falcon as the aesthetic choice of authorized heritage discourse, it exemplifies the fluid subject position of the federation, utilizing mobility and flight as a way to forge connections between tribes on the ground. And yet, in that moment, the federation is also settling/grounding the falcon, literally making it concrete in order to house the pavilion. In response, the aesthetics related to critical heritage discourses employ visual tropes that negotiate the meaning, belonging, and heritage of those authorized aesthetics—and rather than settling in the service of the nation, they complicate it by maintaining the fluidity of subject positions. The irony of all critique lies in the institution's ability to disarm dissent through co-option, eventually making disagreement representative of itself. Importantly, it is also precisely in those spaces that we encounter the aesthetics of critical heritage discourse.

1 Interview with Hassan Sharif in Sam Bardaouil and Till Fellrath, "Hassan Sharif," in *Summer Autumn Winter... and Spring: Conversations with Artists from the Arab World*, Skira, Milan, 2005, p. 301. Many thanks to Murtaza Vali for this quote, and for being a constant sounding board throughout the process of writing this piece.

2 For contemporary topics related to Critical Heritage, see the Association for Critical Heritage Studies (ACHS) www.criticalheritagestudies.org.

3 See also *Neha Vora, Impossible Citizens: Dubai's Indian Diaspora,* Duke University Press, Durham, North Carolina, 2013, for an ethnographic account of ways of belonging within the Indian business community in Dubai, and Naomi Hosoda's article, "Kababayan Solidarity? Filipino Communities and Class Relations in United Arab Emirates Cities," *Journal of Arabian Studies*, no. 1, 2013, pp. 18–35.

4 I have written about this elsewhere as crafting a sense of belonging through aesthetic and cultural resonance—see Uzma Z. Rizvi, "Crafting Resonance: Empathy and Belonging in Ancient Rajasthan," *Journal of Social Archaeology*, no. 2, 2015, pp. 254–273.

5 In a very simple sense, "Authorized Heritage Discourse" (AHD) is an academic phrase within Heritage Studies, which generally refers to state-sanctioned, hegemonic forms of heritage discourse, and as such, often in service of the state.

6 These ideas have been developed in response to Murtaza Vali's 2015 show "Accented" at Maraya Art Center, Sharjah.

For context see Murtaza Vali, "Searching for the Voice of Difference," *Al Nafas Magazine*, 2015. www.u-in-u.com/nafas/articles/2015/accented/, last accessed January 19, 2017.

7 The concept of Dubai as a hotpot has been developed by Rahel Aima (in conversation with Lantian Xie) in "Gulf Return," *Binary States*, exhibition catalog, Kochi-Muziris Biennale, Kerala, 2016, pp. 18–24.

8 The idea of a fluid subject position and a different way of understanding history was first developed by me in "Once Upon a Time: On Pirates, Poetry, and the Portuguese," *ArteEast Quarterly*, Spring 2015. www.arteeast.org/quarterly/once-upon-a-time-on-pirates-poetry-and-the-portuguese/, last accessed January 19, 2017.

9 On the uses of the 'gulf' as a metaphor and its relation to belonging, see MurtazaVali, "Gulf Studies," *ArteEast Quarterly*, Fall 2012. And also Raja'a Khalid, "An Arm of an Ocean or Sea: Editorial Note," in *ArteEast Quarterly*, Spring 2015. www.arteeast.org/?post_type=issues&issues_season=spring&issues_year=2015, last accessed January 19, 2017.

10 These ideas are in conversation with ideas developed in the work of Ahmad Makia, "Treading Gulf Waters," Ibraaz, 2016 (www.ibraaz.org/essays/142), and Rachael Goss and Robert Garfield McInerney, "Becoming Threshold Researchers in the Community," in *Journal of Humanistic Psychology*, no. 3, 2016, pp. 286–308.

11 Ramola Talwar Badam, "Old Structures Are Part of UAE's Memory Construction," *The National*, January 15, 2017. www.thenational.ae/uae/heritage/old-structures-are-part-of-uaes-memory-conservationists-say, last accessed January 19, 2017.

12 Brett Debritz, "In the City of the Future, What's Worth Protecting?" *The National*, November 2, 2015. www.thenational.ae/opinion/comment/in-the-city-of-the-future-whats-worth-protecting, last accessed Jan 19, 2017; Nick Leech, "Brisk Cycle of Construction and Demolition in Abu Dhabi a Threat to Capital's History," *The National*, February 13, 2014. www.thenational.ae/arts-culture/brisk-cycle-of-construction-and-demolition-in-abu-dhabi-a-threat-to-capitals-history, last accessed January 19, 2017.

13 Ramola Talwar Badam, "Calls to Preserve UAE's Modern Architectural Heritage," *The National*, January 15, 2017. www.thenational.ae/uae/heritage/calls-to-preserve-uaes-modern-architectural-heritage, last accessed January 19, 2017.

14 WAM/Emirates News Agency, "New Law to Protect and Preserve Abu Dhabi's Heritage a Step in Right Direction: Paper," *WAM*, October 15, 2016. www.wam.ae/en/news/emirates/1395301220351.html, last accessed January 19, 2017. See also Lynn Meskell and Christoph Brumann, "UNESCO and New World Orders," in Lynn Meskell (ed.), *Global Heritage: A Reader*, Wiley-Blackwell, Oxford, 2015, pp. 22–42.

15 Nick Leech, "Abu Dhabi's Heritage as Guide to Future," The National, April 9, 2014. www.thenational.ae/uae/heritage/abu-dhabis-heritage-as-guide-to-future#full, last accessed January 19, 2017.

16 مستوحى من الصقر واعتمده المجلس الوطني للإعلام:تصميم جناح الدولة في إكسبو 2020 مزدان بقيم الإمارات www.albayan.ae/economy/local-market/2016-05-01-1.2629919, last accessed January 19, 2017. For the announcement in English, see "Falcon Design Wins Dubai Expo 2020 Pavilion Prize," *The National*, March 30, 2016. www.thenational.ae/uae/falcon-design-wins-dubai-expo-2020-pavilion-prize, last accessed January 19, 2017. Also important to note is that the falcon wings are the central design of the Zayed National Museum, Abu Dhabi, as well. www.e-architect.co.uk/dubai/zayed-national-museum, last accessed January 27, 2017. Thanks to Elizabeth Derderian for discussions of art and heritage and for her comments and feedback on this piece.

17 See Sarina Wakefield, "Falconry as Heritage in the United Arab Emirates," *World Archaeology*, no. 2, 2012, pp. 280–290.

Eulogy 1

[redacted] died last week, he no longer [redacted] and English.

If Amma was still around, I could've roped her in to decipher the Malayalam. But [redacted], no dice.

There must have been two hundred people on Acchan's list, half of whom I didn't know. From his immediate and extended family, only my sister and, Shiva Well-y-Acchan, made the cut. So did Detective Columbo. [redacted] And if Columbo succumbed, then I'd certainly be able to snare the other guest of honor, Acchan's old boss, local, who'd grown fond of him and gifted Acchan his Cartier. At the very least, tell him I've sort of died, Acchan's note said, so that he knows I'm gone.

And I? Who, or what was I to my father? It's relevant, this question. If Acchan could be resurrected from ashes and bone, he'd appear [redacted] assume you've got access to a full-length mirror. Quick, wheel Acchan there. Make small talk.

Ask him about Suitcase Face, the friend who'd swallowed a plane in order to turn himself into [redacted] in a Mallu kiln, fierce, dark, and apprehensive, like Mallu crows. He'll notice all that. At some point—believe you me—he'll offer a sentence best saved for story night. Something like: I've always looked like this boy, more than his father ever will/did. But [redacted] man, he'd add, people confused us all the time. As Acchan told it, Suitcase Face was his brother from another mother. He didn't put it quite like that, but I [redacted] on account of inclement weather. Whenever the power of his meds ebbed, Acchan would return to the possibility that his friend had died in a crash. But the aviation authorities in either country weren't helpful, he said. Suitcase Face's flight had caused a scandal, Acchan said. He hadn't given notice to his employer. He'd just missed slamming into a parked airliner. The question of looking for a black box didn't come [redacted] of the Gulf, escaping whatever he became.

Eulogy 1

When my father died last week, he no longer remembered his name, but he'd wanted a [redacted] and English.

If Amma was still around, I could've roped her in to decipher the Malayalam. But [redacted], no dice.

There must have been two hundred people on Acchan's list, half of whom I didn't know. From his immediate and extended family, only my sister and, Shiva Well-y-Acchan, made the cut. So did Detective Columbo. [redacted] And if Columbo succumbed, then I'd certainly be able to snare the other guest of honor, Acchan's old boss, local, who'd grown fond of him and gifted Acchan his Cartier. At the very least, tell him I've sort of died, Acchan's note said, so that he knows I'm gone.

And I? Who, or what was I to my father? It's relevant, this question. If Acchan could be resurrected from ashes and bone, he'd appear [redacted] assume you've got access to a full-length mirror. Quick, wheel Acchan there. Make small talk.

Ask him about Suitcase Face, the friend who'd swallowed a plane in order to turn himself into [redacted] in a Mallu kiln, fierce, dark, and apprehensive, like Mallu crows. He'll notice all that. At some point—believe you me—he'll offer a sentence best saved for story night. Something like: I've always looked like this boy, more than his father ever will/did. But [redacted] man, he'd add, people confused us all the time. As Acchan told it, Suitcase Face was his brother from another mother. He didn't put it quite like that, but I [redacted] on account of inclement weather. Whenever the power of his meds ebbed, Acchan would return to the possibility that his friend had died in a crash. But the aviation authorities in either country weren't helpful, he said. Suitcase Face's flight had caused a scandal, Acchan said. He hadn't given notice to his employer. He'd just missed slamming into a parked airliner. The question of looking for a black box didn't come [redacted] of the Gulf, escaping whatever he became. [redacted]

Eulo

Eulogy 2

I walked into Acchan's room one day to find him in conversation with an empty chair. I caught snippets of the conversation. He'd been lucky, he was saying. When he showed up in bell-bottoms, platforms, and curls, the water was good, ACs too.

When Acchan saw me, he paused. You who? A friend of your son's, I said. OK wait, he replied, a bit busy.

And I waited, and watched him speak to the chair for another hour, deep in thought. When the good Zayed passed, he continued, I felt my heart sink into my tummy, where it waited to be freed. In Kerala, we've got these   in power. For them politics is a hustle. Now, Zayed, man, Zayed was different.

Mostly, I remember the quiet, as my father nodded, at the invisible figure in front of him, sitting in the chair he stared intently at. His nurse had requested me to ask him to stop stealing the salt from the tables. He takes the shaker, she said. Puts out his hands, then dumps the salt into his pockets. Then, she continued, he's back here, dumping the salt on the chair. Or, she animated, he collects a week's ration of salt, pours it over his reading chair. Then takes the chair out into the sun to watch everything dry. Sure, I said. That's all you got, the nurse said, sure?

Listen, I said, you're probably sick of work, as much as I'm sick of dragging myself up here once a month, but if you knew what he was trying to do, you'd shut up and let him do it. You ought to thank him, I said, he doesn't soil himself, doesn't make passes at you. And then I turned the screw, explaining why the salt mattered so much to my old man.

My father knew one story he could recite from memory. Someone told it to him when he first got to Abu Dhabi. It was about a five hundred year old boy made of salt, this kid who lived in the sea. Who'd stop by land some time after midnight, along with his uncles and aunts, because he was an orphan. They'd show up at high tide, most people asleep. And my father, so he claimed, bumped into this child, on a walk one night. And they talked, he said. Mainly about parents, because they'd both lost their fathers early. And they'd ask about each other's lives. Mostly, Acchan would listen, as the little fellow chatted about the characters he's encountered over the years. There was the British sailor and murderer who'd abducted him in 1564. Thankfully his ship had sunk near Oman, allowing the boy to escape. In 1963 there was the American oilman who missed Chicago winters. Then there was Pritiva, the Sri Lankan nanny who befriended him in 1987. That was a decade before bumping into the tennis player Andre Agassi riding a jet ski. Or Abu-Laila, who'd park his Land Cruiser, and then linger by the water as he thought of his only daughter. When Abu-Laila passed in 1996, his spirit sought permission to stand guard by the sea, protecting the living. Which is where the boy made of salt met the man, where they became friends, looking after each other, as old friends do. And where they discovered that the boy knew Abu-Laila's great-great-great-grandfather, Sultan. But Acchan's biggest claim was that the boy made of salt was the one who'd taught him Arabic. In the beginning, he'd say, all I knew was La and Na'am. But I got better. Over time, Acchan said, he'd taught the boy some phrases in Malayalam. Before leaving, Acchan beamed, the little fellow would say poitu varaam. And he'd say it, Acchan swore, with the same inflections expected of Mallu children when they visited family they'd rarely seen/known. But what Acchan truly cherished was the walk home. The boy was a hugger, Acchan smiled. So when he'd return to his room, the one he shared with his cousin and two other people I've never met, Acchan would be covered in salt.

I'd never explain, Acchan said, I'd say Hello and then pass out, smelling like the waters that lapped the Khaleej.

gy 2

Eulogy 3

In 1976 Acchan found a jinn chained to a pole by the corniche. His captors had put him up for sale. His buyer was a Malayalee from Kottaikal who ran a traveling circus.

The jinn's captors had found him napping in the desert. Now if Acchan's reciting this tale, especially if he's had a peg two, he'll tell you he's not one to [redacted]. So your job would be to say, Of course, continue.

You need water jugs to capture desert jinns. They're allergic. And often cocky, the only explanation to why the jinn was snoozing in the sands, waiting to be caught. They'd tied him up like cattle because with the sea nearby, there's little the jinn could do. The Mallu was late, because (Acchan's words, not mine) Mallus usually are. And as the jinn lay waiting, his minders off to lunch, he spotted my father.

Now Acchan had never seen a jinn before, so when the fellow said, Look, whatever you want, name it, Acchan laughed. Look, man, two wishes, whatever you want. And Acchan said, OK, I'm in the mood for kappa and meen curry, served with cut-un chai. But, he continued, I'd like the meal to be prepared by meen from the sea before you. Fine, he was told. Within seconds, a school of meen jumped out of the water, and began to spar, in what Acchan described, was a battle that didn't make much sense. The meen were armed with teeth, tail, and scales. And they quite literally tore into each other. When the spectacle ended, the spot littered with fins, bones and eyeballs, the surviving meen built a makeshift stove, found some turmeric, chili powder, and curry leaves. Tamarind too. And kappa, of course, and cooked their friends/foes, in order to feed my father, who was now cursing himself for not having asked for something a little useful. Right, said the jinn, as my father tucked into lunch, you've got one more wish, yours for the asking, once you've set me free.

My father asked for an air conditioner. He wanted an AC that wouldn't break, or only break after his death. Now, Acchan used to say, I don't know the state of jinns today, what they do, where they get their news…etc. But back then, the age of telegrams and

Eulo

letters, this jinn didn't know what an AC was. So, according to my father, he spent a good twenty minutes trying to explain the science behind cooling. Now the jinn had stumbled upon a refrigerator somewhere. He'd been introduced to a Kelvinator, he said, but an AC didn't make sense to him. Explain it, he kept saying. And finally my father said, Look, I need cold air. I want you to give me something that produces cold air on demand. As he said this, the jinn noticed his abductors approaching. The Mallu buyer was with them too. W'allah, Unni! You've got to let me go, the jinn said. Not without an AC, my father said. I promise you'll have it, he said—untie me! So my father did, and the jinn escaped. But he kept his promise, just not how my father anticipated him to, that's all.

Remember there were four men, the gang of three and the Malayalee buyer. As soon as the jinn escaped, the quartet stopped walking. My father found that a bit odd. He was irritated about the AC, but he also wanted to see what was up. So he walked towards the men and introduced himself, to be met with silence. Fine then, he said, before turning around, homewards. The jinn stopped him. You should take your ACs with you, the jinn said. And that's when Acchan inspected the men who'd ignored him seconds ago. Acchan put his ear next to their hearts, which were beating. But their eyes were dead. And when the jinn instructed my father to open their mouths, out came cold air.

When the nurse called to ask why my father kept insisting the AC was broken, when it wasn't, and why he seemed to be burning up when he wasn't feverish, I asked her to calm down, and to do me a favor. It's going to seem odd, I said, but I'll need you to find four middle-aged men to stand in front of him with their mouths wide open. When his body temperature sorts itself out, or after he calms down, sedate him.

gy 3

Eulo

Eulogy 4

My last conversation with my father had him sobbing in my arms. At the time, he didn't know who I was. I was just a stranger who'd walked into his space.

Acchan had pissed Abu, his caretaker. I'd like to speak to Suitcase Face first, he'd said. I'd like you to call him, please. Medicine first, Abu insisted. Acchan told him to . He was polite about it. Please , he'd said. And Abu, not prepared to back down, asked Acchan whether he'd heard the news. News? They found your friend Suitcase Face, Abu said. The wreckage was found at sea, along with parts of the plane your friend's friend had transformed into. Acchan asked him to cut the crap. But Abu insisted on telling him how Suitcase Face's face, almost unidentifiable, had split open, to reveal letters, perfume, cassette tapes, dates, a VCP, gold, IDs. And muskets and jinns and henna and petrol. And poems and voices and kohl and silver and pearls. And sand and pickles and palm leaves and ghosts and joy. And hope and loss. And photographs, and seawater. And fish. And friends.

gy 4

Whaat

Whaat is Plan

In elementary school, we'd make bets on how we'd leave the Khaleej. My friend Bipin was going to catch a ride back to the homeland, on the back of a gold-finned Hamour. His mate Jacob, who wouldn't be my mate Jacob, was going to teleport. His cousin Nina was going to pray, while her neighbor Khadeeja was going to don bespoke plastic wings her mother had made for her birthday.

In secondary school, we'd make bets on how we'd leave the Khaleej. My friend Bipin was going to apply to colleges in the States. His mate Jacob, who never became my mate Jacob, wasn't going anywhere because he'd convinced himself that if he'd been born in the Khaleej, he'd also breed, then die in the Khaleej. His cousin Nina's future walked a predictable line, as her parents hoped to put her on the nuptial market after medical school, while her neighbor Khadeeja upgraded from plastic wings to actual wings after her parents admitted over karak that they came from a family of superheroes, like actual superheroes.

In college, our professors, blanketed by academia, didn't warn us about the world. At university in Dubai, my commencement speaker spoke of how we would impact, perhaps run, the world. And then the world fell on top of us, like a wave that had traveled thousands of miles to find us. My friend Bipin dropped out of his program in Computer Science, returned to the Khaleej on a tourist visa and moved to another emirate where he works as a medical ex-cue-tive. He's got the proverbial wife, kids, bank loan and credit card(s). Last I heard, he's hoping to move to Australia, but doesn't know what to do with his NRI parents, who'd like to come to Australia too if it wasn't so far away, so stay, they say. Bipin's mate Jacob, grateful he's not my mate Jacob, got deported after getting caught accepting kickbacks. In Kochi, he went into the cafeteria business, the real estate business, and the kickbacks business. Last report, his empire was flourishing, because Kochi's the [redacted], where everything's at, friend. His cousin Nina's life panned out like every NRI parents' [redacted] . Mother of two, wife of an attorney who made partner, tax write-offs, Platinum Card member of Etihad, card-carrying member of the NRA, green card, wedding announcement in *The New York Times*, board member, house in the States, summer retreat in the Balkans, flat in the homeland. Her neighbor Khadeeja didn't fare as well. The superhero gig didn't' work out so great. Language barrier.

Her superhero costume didn't win points with the pubic either. Last woman she saved berated her for not speaking Arabic, and asked her to find a tailor. When an Emirati chopper pulled her over in mid-flight to enquire about paperwork, she took a voluntary sabbatical, and decided on an MBA. She's now a consultant at ADCB, where I ran into her and joined her for lunch, when she [redacted] about alopecia, having no home, paying a bundle in rent. But she wouldn't buy in the Khaleej, she said, unless someone gave her some dough. That would be a game-changer, she said, money, because some of the properties are beautiful.

In elementary school, I didn't give much thought to leaving. I was too busy being a child. In grade school, I dreaded leaving, because that's all my parents talked about—leaving. As an adolescent, after being programed for years to pack one suitcase in a pinch, I stopped thinking about it, or romanticizing being the perpetual outsider, or talking about my parents, the dementia-ridden father and fat mother, who'd grown into nervy senior citizens during their stint in the Khaleej. So I turned practical, I turned towards money, which is what I'd always wanted. I didn't want a homeland. I didn't have one. I didn't want the house, or the jewelry, or the wife with the degrees, job, lipstick, heels, polished accent and the German sedan. What I wanted, ever since my father flushed his savings down the toilet, ever since the shurtha[1] and the collectors came for him, was money. To not only have it, but lend it too, which is what I really do for a living. From wanting to be someone important, with an important sounding title, I ended up a loan shark, lending to blue and white collar, men, woman, foreigner, citizen, the young and old. I became a young man who could put his conscience on standby, to squeeze anyone who defaulted on payment so thoroughly that I wouldn't kill them, but I'd do enough for them to worry about their collateral, whether it was their passport, shame, house or business. And they'd get the money to pay me interest, buying time until the first of the following month, when I'd hit them up again for more dough. Which is probably what I'll do to Khadeeja, who seems like a nice person, but she put down her wings as collateral, acquiesced to have me glue and then knot them in chainmail.

In elementary or grade school or college, irrespective of my leanings, my hopes and dreams, loyalties towards my friends, or my thoughts about my place in the Khaleej, all I was on paper was an Indian boy, the oldest of Mr. and Mrs. Unni's children, the son of NRIs. And I'd never promised to be nice. Ever.

is Plan

Bullet Points About Pady Sopnams (Nightmares)

Alathoor Bhagavané, pady sopnam Kaanarudna
Pady Sopnam Kandalo, vaalonde adichu onurtanay
Editum valatum garudayanama thalakilum Kaakilum garudayanama[2]
- Amma

I have pady sopnams. I am little. I am sitting with my father by the corniche. He doesn't recognize me.
I had a pady sopnam. I took my father, dementia sufferer, to the corniche. We're talking. Then without warning, he disappears into the sea, pulled in by the ghosts of pearl divers.
I have a pady sopnam. My father's lonely; Amma's death haunts him. We're at the corniche. He hasn't been sleeping. He tells me burglars whisper in his ear. They tell him they're going to take his ACs. Then they're going to rip out his soul.
I have pady sopnams. I am sitting with my father by the corniche. I'm telling him he used to live here once, that we used to live here once. And my father nods his head and asks why we used to live here once.
I have pady sopnams about my father turning into a ghost still obsessing about that house he couldn't build.
I had a pady sopnam. I went to Abu Dhabi to grieve for my parents. I didn't recognize it. I didn't understand it. Anymore.
I have pady sopnams, especially one that returns periodically, like chronic pain. I think this one at daytime, when I'm most alert. It's that by writing about my family, I've fetishized my parents, their experience(s), pravasiness, guest-worker-ness, expatness, normalness. I worry I've fetishized everything, my parents' place in the world, their home(s), two nations, people attached/detached to documents, and their memories, as though as I've taken ownership over their private moments, and turned them all mythical, into creatures and stories people of the Khaleej and anywhere else will return to generations from now, in order to wonder why my rotund Amma and OCD Acchan feel so exposed in my work, when what was needed as they aged was for a son to protect them, from the world of fiction and non-fiction. I worry I've hurt them. I worry I've let them down.
I have pady sopnams!

Gulf Return

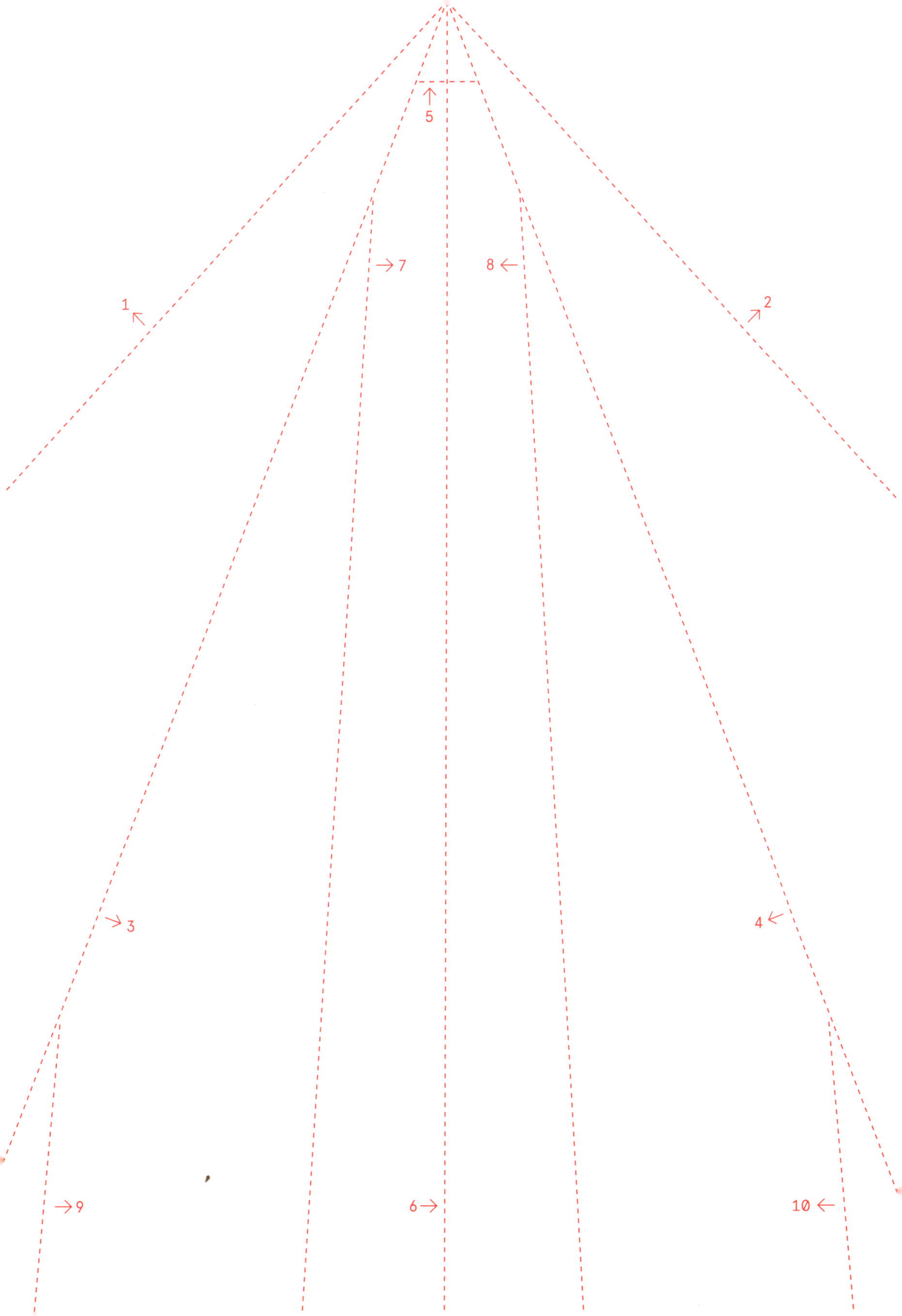
1
2
5
7
8
3
4
9
6
10

Somewhere nearby, a laborer from the Khaleej swallowed his passport and turned into a passport. His roommate swallowed a suitcase and turned into a little suitcase. When the third roommate, privy and vital to the master plan, ran away the next morning with the suitcase and the new passport, he made it past the guard on night duty, made it on the morning bus to the airport, past the bored ticket agent at Check-In, past Security, past pat-down and a rummage through his suitcase, past using the bathroom once, twice, thrice, to ▲ to ▼, to sit, past Duty-Free, where he stared at chocolates and booze and magazines and currencies, past families eating fast food in tracksuits or designer wear, past men and women sleeping on the floor, past his past, past his present, past the gold in the souks, the cranes in the sky, petrol in the air, dreams in his head, past God and the devil, the smell of mess halls, past humidity and hot air, past it all, until he found an empty chair in the Departures lounge, where he sat and held his future in his palms. It was then the little suitcase sprouted legs and ears, and the passport developed palms and long fingers as well as a nose and a mustache, and soon after boarding call, at the very moment the stewardess checked his documents, the third laborer was asked to wait. The stewardess needed time to figure out what protocol she should follow or what precedent the man and his possessions had set. The man preferred not to wait and ran as fast as he could through the door to boarding, past passengers who had already gone through and formed a line inside the tube with the little windows, waiting like blood in a syringe, now followed at an animal's pace by the little suitcase on legs, ridden like a horse by the passport with the long fingers, a sight that both fascinated and terrified and caused personnel, propelled by some odd sense of duty, to stand in the way of the trio and block their path, to protect the plane and its pilots and cabin crew from what they couldn't define. It didn't matter what they did, it wouldn't have mattered what they did, because the man leading the charge, in an act of despair, opened his mouth wide to ask them all to get away, get away, wide wide wider, until he swallowed the first person in his path, then the next, and the next, refusing to stop running, as the little suitcase did the same, opening and closing itself, running into people, sucking people in like a sinkhole, aided by the passport jockey, who assisted by stuffing those who fought desperately to escape. It happened so quickly, the running, the swallowing, the madness, the stuffing, that when the trio reached the aircraft doors, they seemed first surprised rather than jubilant, then relieved as pilots and the cabin crew stared from the other end of the tube, where everyone, including the remaining passengers, had now run to and watched them like cats watching dogs.

The little suitcase, the little passport, and the man caught their breath, inhaling and exhaling as though nails filled the air, while in the distance, like the sound of a million horses, well-meaning men with guns and gas rushed the gate where the stewardess had screamed then fainted. The trio realized it was now or never, abdi ya nabi, do or die, so they rushed into the empty plane, locked its door, with the little suitcase and the little passport finding seats in First Class and putting on their seat belts, while the man ran to the back of the plane and began swallowing everything in sight, starting with the two lavatories, the trolleys with the veg and non-veg options, the apple juice and the Bloody Marys, the seats and the magazines, the tray tables and the blinking lights, the blankets and the overhead bins, the socks and the TV monitors, the cabin air with its lingering halitosis and the candies, swallowing everything in sight, moving expertly from Economy to Business to First, swallowing even the little suitcase and the little passport, swallowing the carpets, the emergency exits, the airplane controls and smudged windows and the odor of pilots, slipping down the aircraft's nose and continuing to swallow as he moved from the aircraft's beak toward its base, swallowing wings, wheels, luggage, fuel, skin, presence, until the man was unrecognizable anymore, and had turned into an enormous jumbo, observed from the cordoned-off terminal by dumb-struck passengers and the men armed with guns and gas whose leader wondered on his walkie-talkie what sort of protocol ought to be followed here, but he needn't have bothered. The plane had begun taxiing down the runaway, past other waiting aircrafts, ignoring pleas from the Control Tower to desist, to wait a minute, to let's talk this through, to whadabout the hostages, but the plane didn't care, it went on its merry way, picking up speed, lifting its beak, tucking in its mighty wheels, returning its cargo.

1 *Police*

2 *O Lord Hanuman, please keep nightmares at bay. If I see them, nudge me awake with your tail. Praise the Lord Garuda who is everywhere, watch me from my head (north) to toe (south), from left and right.*

Marking Ground

Osman Samiuddin

So,
here you are
too foreign for home
too foreign for here.
never enough for both.[1]

– Ijeoma Umebinyuo, 'Diaspora Blues'

Three layers to this home, and at the bottom, the earth. This is not the pristine sand of the desert, the sand of imagination, which arranges itself artfully in waves, posing for photographs. This is real sand—scruffy, unkempt, and blemished. Tire tracks are dug into it; it is strewn with stray pebbles, stones, and the usual detritus of human civilization. This sand hurts. It's not like the desert sand, where you can bathe, surf, or ski.

Upon it, to no great choreography, are operating white specks of life. Some are round. Others are old. Almost none are what we might recognize as athletes. All are from the subcontinent. The action is slow—let's call it "considered physical activity;" "sport" is perhaps a stretch. It's slow enough to reveal the day of the week: this is, indisputably, a Friday.

The light around which these forces meander is at the center—the 22-yard strip of cement on which the game is really played—of this oval, otherwise known as the Abu Dhabi Cricket Club Ground #1.

High above them, the third layer—the Gulf sky. The Gulf sky is famously a beast of the evening, when it tarts itself up as a ploy to seduce the sun inside after another long, relentless day. Then it comes at you in a blaze of purples and oranges and shades of red so that you have to ignore the architecture—the marvels of man—and are instead transfixed by this, the ageless, unchanging marvels of beyond.

In contrast, the daytime Gulf sky, the third layer in *this* scene, goes underappreciated, especially in winter. Today its blue looks faded and with thinnish, indeterminate clouds, specifically like some well-worn stonewash denim. It stretches itself out, though not quite in the lordly manner the blue sky of Johannesburg does. That one knows it covers

1 In Ijeoma Umebinyuo, *Questions for Ada*, Create Space, Seattle, 2015

the entire world underneath it. Protruding into this sky, framing this #1 ground on one side are the red and white skeletal towers upon which overhead power cables are draped. To another side is the ground's parent, the Sheikh Zayed Cricket Stadium, its distinctive half-a-flying-saucer-at-a-tilt shade curving into the sky. The stadium is now over a decade old, a veteran of international matches and yet still looks like something out of a future that hasn't arrived.

Two sand-colored shamianas are the dressing room and pavilion for this ground, where a team from one bank is playing a team from another. It is part of an annual local league, organized by the Abu Dhabi Cricket Club, its matches played on this and other similar grounds that satellite around the main ground.

Soon comes a man on a bicycle. Indians will recognize it as the Atlas and Pakistanis as the Sohrab; it is the subcontinent's ubiquitous choice of cycling transport. The man is selling *karak chai* from a thermos and hot samosas from a plastic bag.

•••

Another home. Here, the earth is green and politely undulating. The grass is parched in patches but nowhere is it so deep or lush that you mistake this for a scene from some small English village, even if that is the intention. These are the east lawns of the Emirates Palace Hotel, the facade of which, on this stroll, is behind you. It is a hotel of famously unimaginable luxury, with, among other delights, ATMs that dispense gold bars. Ahead of you is a crowd of desert flora, mostly *ghaf* and palm trees. And then, with no hint to its emergence, the ground, "the most beautiful countrified cricket ground you've ever seen," according to Henry Blofeld, the most countrified English cricket commentator of all time.

The orientation of the ground is such that if the batsman has his back to the Hotel facade, the arc from his on drive to his pull opens up to the Persian Gulf, shimmering today, as always, in turquoise. On the off side, from his square cut to an off drive is the famous Corniche skyline, also shimmering, as always, in metal. This ground has four turf—not cement—pitches and an outfield of grass. It is nurtured and cared for by trained groundsmen. Still, the action is recreational, operating in slow motion even as everything around it moves as normal. Above them is the same sky, though the clouds today have acquired a backbone and are presenting themselves with greater belief.

The Abu Dhabi Gentlemen's Cricket Club is hosting a club side from Dubai. The vast majority of the players of this match are the other kind of expat in the UAE—from the First World (England, or Australia) perched now in a land where categories such as the First, Second, or Third World feel singularly unimportant as here this is the usual demographic; here, the other, older cricket, from within the greens of England; cricket as the idyllic watercolor scene, of picnics with cucumber sandwiches and tea; cricket as an indulgence and not an escape. Talking about cricket here means constructing multiple sentences using the word "tradition."

The ground has hosted club and school games for over a decade now, propelled in its early years by an English director of the Hotel's beach club, Andy Elliott. For a while after he left, from 2011, it fell into disuse—the oddest kind of white elephant for a luxury hotel in the UAE. The barrenness didn't last long. It just couldn't.

•••

And finally, another home. This one you can find in a number of places: the empty car park of a mall; the long, deserted road hemmed in by undeveloped land on either side; a park; in the spaces around labor camps; in the vacant crevices of an island of gleaming high-rise apartments, for each one of which there are two more under construction. Here, too, there is always a game, and though it is by name the same, it is in its doing nothing like the others. These are the *galli* games of India and Pakistan.

There is no identifiable kit. Most men wear *shalwar kameez*, or other clothes that give away the fact of their occupation. They are not midlevel executives. They are not corporate types. A lot of them play in slippers, or variants such as flip-flops. There is no marked ground as such. Just space. It doesn't seem to matter. In some areas you'll find several games on simultaneously in one lot.

The equipment is bare—one, maybe two bats, a tennis ball wrapped in layers of red or white electrical tape. This is to give it some heft, to help it mimic the real cricket ball with which they cannot play. The stumps are made out of flat stones piled one upon another, or an empty wooden crate. No one worries about the surface they are playing on.

One team may have six players, the other eight; both may have five; there may not be teams at all, just a few guys and a day to fill. Rules are created on the day. Fielding is an optional discipline. The action here is usually more urgent and the game played with a greater sense of abandon. There is no pretense to play as proficiently or efficiently as possible, to treat it as some clever strategic pursuit; only to play the game as maximally as possible: to hit the ball hardest and farthest, to bowl it fastest, to run at it most daringly. It is endearing, even if its order is impossible to make out.

The skies always seem greyer here, somehow less important. Games go on until the sun drops and here it does with less ceremony and fuss—the end of a free day. Others end the moment a person of authority rolls along to remind them the space is not for play. There is no reward other than the play itself.

•••

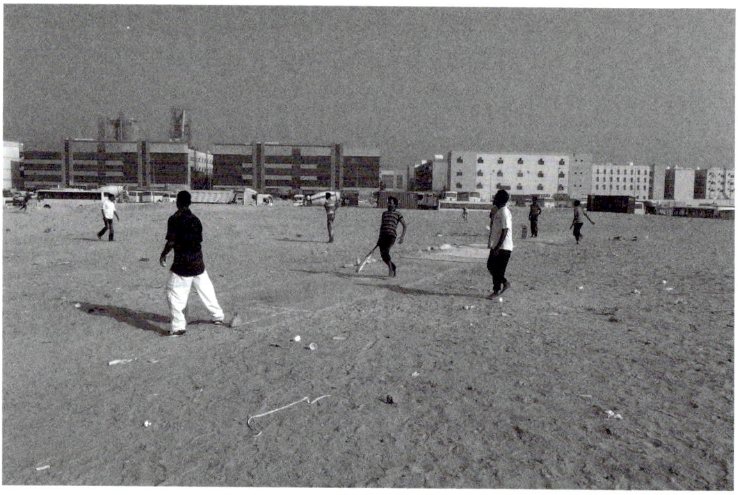

Elevated sandpit co-opted as cricket ground, Al Quoz

The plot of sandy land that confronted Asif Iqbal, a former captain of the Pakistani cricket team, one day in October 1980 was vast and ordinary, bereft of any distinguishing features. It was, in fact, a crater; the soil from it was being used at other sites for construction. It was around 200,000 square meters, and sat next to the Sharjah Sports Club. Iqbal had been brought there by Abdul Rahman Bukhatir, an ascendant and influential businessman. "Bring me two cricket teams," Bukhatir told Iqbal, "and I will have a stadium up and running by the following March."

At that point, Bukhatir was the game in this country. The son of a judge, Bukhatir had followed a reverse of the established migration pattern between the Gulf and the subcontinent. That is, he was an Emirati who went to Karachi to study at a Parsi school, and ended up bringing a bit of Pakistan back with him.

Until his return, what cricket there had been in the UAE was sporadic and without real texture. In the early 1960s, servicemen from the Royal Air Force played occasional games on the runways of Sharjah Airport, which was a British Army base. When oil lured expats from India and Pakistan in the 1970s, a clutch of businessmen found that weekends were best spent playing cricket wherever they could find land even enough to play on. One of them brought back from Kolkata a matting wicket—a mat made most often from coir (or jute), which was the surface on which the central theater of cricket between batsman and bowler was played out. They carried it around in a Land Rover, rolling it out on whatever suitable land they found and starting a game. Cricket lived by its most basic equation: if there was land, and the will, then there was a game. Otherwise there wasn't.

The return of Bukhatir, and the emergence of other Emiratis such as Abdul Rahman Falaknaz and Mohammad Redha Abbas (who had also learned the game during his schooling in the subcontinent), turned these irregular vignettes into a proper scene. Near the Al Khan roundabout in Sharjah, the first cement pitch was laid out on a ground. Bukhatir established the Sharjah Cricket Club, and expats soon followed, organizing themselves into their own clubs either by nationality or by employment. In 1975, by which time Bukhatir had already set up the Sharjah Cricket Council, a Bukhatir League began (now proudly in its 41st season). Bukhatir patronized several clubs and, in some instances, hired cricketers from the subcontinent in his companies to play for them.

The League provided a vibrant season, conducted mostly on four sandy grounds with cement wickets behind where Safeer Mall now stands on the Dubai-Sharjah motorway.

Two events propelled Bukhatir toward that meeting with Iqbal in 1980. In February 1976, he invited a strong team from Pakistan to play games against a local XI; the invitees included, among other stars, the starriest: Imran Khan. Fans from Dubai and Abu Dhabi arrived to watch, as did Dr. Sheikh Sultan bin Mohammed, the Ruler of Sharjah. Two years later Bukhatir took a side from the UAE to Pakistan, where they played against local teams. It was on this trip that he established greater contacts with Pakistani players and officials, and a plan began to take shape in his mind.

While in Karachi, Hanif Mohammad, one of Pakistan's earliest champions, a great but dour batsman capable of batting for days on end and of boring people away from the game, had become the object of Bukhatir's fandom. It was for Hanif Mohammad that Bukhatir wanted to organize a tribute and it was for him that Mohammad's path crossed with Iqbal's. Bukhatir's plan was to organize a game between two sides from India and Pakistan, the proceeds of which would go to Mohammad. Iqbal was the man to recruit the players.

Within five months Bukhatir had refilled the crater, leveled the land, grown grass for an outfield, and placed an Astroturf mat over a cement strip, which would be the wicket. Two scaffolding structures were put up, for spectators. The pavilion and dressing rooms were rudimentary, temporary structures, and for lunch the players had to go to the dining hall of the Sharjah Football Club next door.

Iqbal got the players, a task made easier by the fact that US $200,000 was on offer as prize money. Though not called India and Pakistan, as this wasn't an official international match, the teams would effectively be of India and Pakistan; they were named, instead, after their captains: a Gavaskar XI and a Miandad XI). By April 3, 1981, everything was in place. Tickets were sold in Indian and Pakistani restaurants, the cheapest at 25 dirham. Posters advertising the game went up around Sharjah and Dubai. The organizers were initially worried that people might not turn up. They didn't need to, as fans turned up in droves from all over the Gulf—there were eight thousand attendees, according to reports, and another eight thousand who couldn't get in.

A few years later, the pitch, now a proper stadium, hosted its first official international match, and by the end of the decade, Sharjah had become a fixture on the international cricket calendar, primarily but not exclusively as a bypass to the political clogging that prevented Pakistan and India from playing each other on home territory. Fridays in October and November, the day of rest, were now the scene: a setting Gulf sun, orange and golden sky, and under it, a frenzy in white on this piece of earth, Pakistan and India, India and Pakistan, a home in place of a home.

•••

I have a party trick. It isn't really a trick and it doesn't even need a party, but it is a great way to break into conversation. I pull it out when people ask me where I come from. Born in Tripoli, Libya. Grew up in Jeddah, Saudi Arabia. Studied and worked in Sheffield, Manchester, London, and Brighton. Became a journalist in Karachi. Got married in Delhi and now live and work in Abu Dhabi. And, by international law and to some degree in spirit, I'm Pakistani.

On paper as I read this, and even in my head as I tell people, it sounds fascinating. The cultures, the experiences, the people, the travels—oh, to live such a life, huh? In truth, I feel mostly rootless, unable to orient myself through any geographical allegiance. At university I remember being envious of friends around me who were all so well located within themselves: defined, formed, and identified by the lives they had led until then—lives spent mostly in one place. They shared tales of great, lasting friendships from their youth, tales I did not have: great, lasting friendships weren't easy to come by in Libya or Saudi Arabia, countries so transient in nature for their expatriates.

I've never been sure what home is. Is home where we are born? Is home where we grow up? Is home simply where we have spent most of our life? Is home where we become who we are, where we grow into the values and mores that make us adults fit for society? Is home where our family is? Is home where our friends are? Is home that country in which we work? Is home that country in which we take refuge? Is home that country which we escape? Is home that country in which we find love? Is home that country in which we can hate? Some days my life feels like the lesser-aired lie of the small village this world is. If anywhere can be home and anyone can be a friend, then really, nowhere is home and nobody a friend.

If nothing else, cricket has been the one buoy that I held on to as I grew up. As a student in England, I briefly let go but never let it disappear from sight. There I was too busy being a sponge, soaking in all manner of influences if not ever attaining a defined shape. Nothing gave me a greater sense of belonging, however, than covering cricket in Pakistan. Like many others, only to perhaps a more acute degree, Karachi exists as a city of bubbles—geographic, socioeconomic, and spiritual. You can go for days without stepping out of your own and experiencing other parts of the city or meeting people who are not like you—in this case, me, with a background of relative economic comfort, predominantly English-speaking, even Westernized (a kind of person known in Karachi, colloquially and with no little condescension, as a "burger"). Too foreign for home, too foreign for anywhere else.

Through cricket I pricked these bubbles, breaking out of one and slipping into another. I strived to not be a "burger," but a "bun kebab," a local, spicier variant of this imported cuisine. Over time, a sport once of the elites, a foreign sport, has become the country's most democratic pursuit, egalitarian in its construct like little else. Through its cricketers and cricket culture, I discovered the city of Karachi.

It was partially cricket fatigue, or at least a desire to broaden my scope beyond it, that brought me to Abu Dhabi. Fat chance. It ended up so that cricket was one of the ways I oriented myself to another new country. It was a crutch. The first road sign I noticed when leaving the airport the morning I landed, not ten kilometers out, was for the Sheikh Zayed Stadium. My very first assignment, on my second day here, was to go find some color in a club game being played at the very same stadium. Eventually I came to understand that its location couldn't help but be symbolic: away from the main city, but unmistakably part of it.

The first game of cricket I played in the UAE was at the impeccable picketed grounds of the International Cricket Council's (ICC) Global Academy in Dubai. They sit right next to the offices of the ICC; that is, the headquarters of the body that runs the world game. Here in Dubai, where it moved in 2005 from Lord's in London, the "Home of Cricket" was given free land to build offices on and a fifty-year tax exemption. Neither geographically nor professionally did I really get that far away

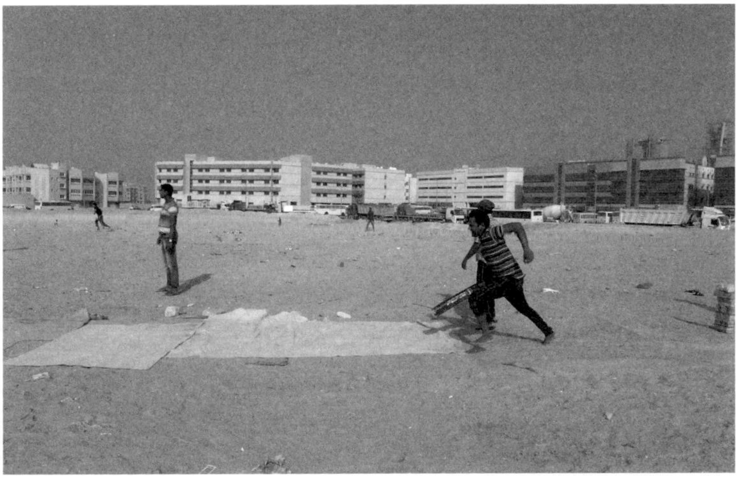

Elevated sandpit co-opted as cricket ground, Al Quoz

from Karachi, as I ended up covering Pakistan's international matches played in Abu Dhabi and Dubai that first winter.

Indeed, as for so many Pakistanis, the UAE has now become a home for Pakistani cricket—international teams no longer visiting Pakistan after a terror attack on the visiting Sri Lanka side in March 2009. It is here that the Pakistan Super League (PSL) takes place, a Twenty20 event with Pakistan's biggest stars and some of the world's best players. It is here that a number of Pakistan's former cricketers come to play league cricket. It is to here that the Indian Premier League (IPL)—the biggest, most lucrative, most globalized, and most glamorous cricket event—moved in 2014 for two weeks when security requirements for general elections in India meant they couldn't play there. The UAE felt like the most natural place for it to go, and it was, by most unscientific counts, probably among the best-attended sports events in UAE history. It is here that the game's administrators from around the world converge every few months to shape the game. It is here that they decide to hold a number of global tournaments for age-group sides and the second-tier world teams. It is, in other words and in many other ways, *there*, its specific location as yet undetermined and perhaps unimportant, within the fabric of this country.

The UAE has a national team—and has had one since 1989—historically composed mostly of expats from Pakistan, India, and Sri Lanka. It has just passed through one of its most successful phases and, rather charmingly, did so as almost an amateur side. Though it is on the verge of becoming genuinely professional, many of its cricketers wrestle with full-time employment commitments and the demands of being international sportsmen. Their greatest batsman, the recently retired Khurram Khan, originally from Pakistan, worked as a purser for Emirates Airlines throughout his international career, often turning up to play right after arriving back from work on a long-haul flight.

Is home, then, the team you represent, and the games you play? Perhaps. And perhaps it is so that this game that is too foreign for home, too foreign for here, is, all told, more than enough for both.

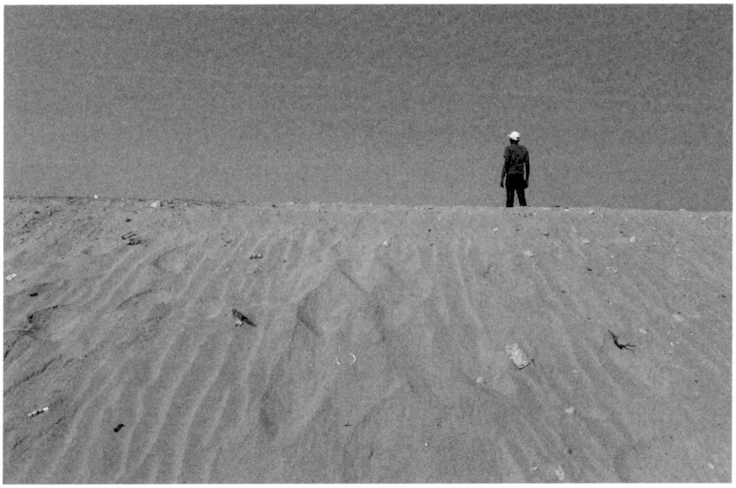

Elevated sandpit co-opted as cricket ground, Al Quoz

Music Shaping Identity

Dr. Aisha Bilkhair

Ever since its inception, music has contributed to shaping and influencing the experience and development of mankind. The spiritual interaction between human beings and sound can be detected in many aspects of life. Music can induce memories, celebrate sentiments, imitate nature, set the rhythm of work, as well as stimulate creativity, love, sleep, nostalgia, patriotism, and euphoria.

Tribal drumming's impact on music, in particular, turned out to be a crucial factor in the exportation of African culture and percussive instruments through the world. Traditionally drums were used by African populations as instruments to warn of danger, assemble gatherings, cure the unhealthy, call for war, and mark the moment of passage from boyhood to manhood. Some drums facilitated communication in codes as they were exclusively used for specific rituals and celebrations to ensure the secrecy of their practices. Furthermore, the interaction of drumbeats and heartbeats could result in a rhythmical pattern that affected the body and influenced the way brains operate.[1]

Members of the African Diaspora, regardless of their suffering, were able to adjust to life in their new countries by carrying with them their traditional music. On the Trucial Coast, this traditional music became

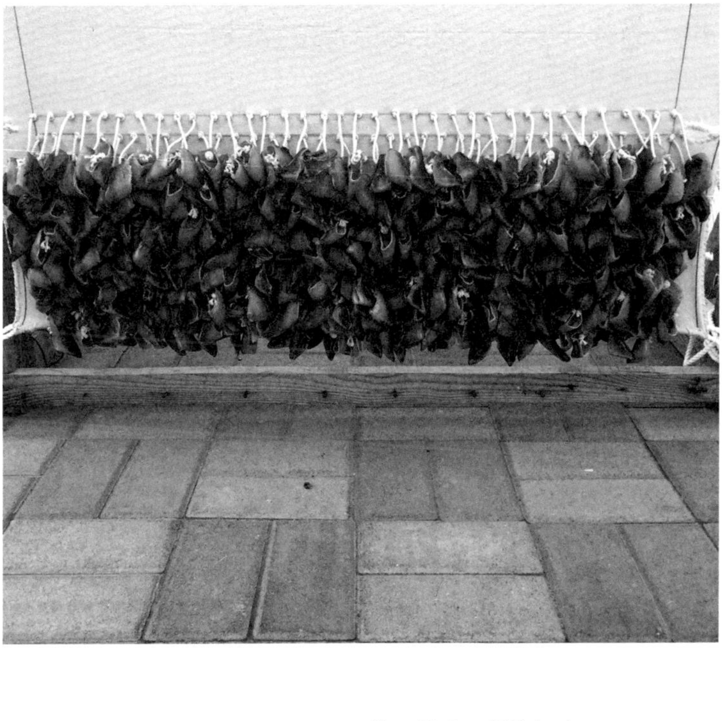

Al-manyur, a musical instrument made of a sail's cloth as a skirt to which goat hooves are attached. Manyur is also the name of the player who ties this skirt around his waist and shakes the lower part of his body to create the desired clacking sounds.

an integral part of the day-to-day activities of migrant workers, whether seamen chanting on pearl diving vessels or domestic help pounding grain.

Laywa, one of the musical genres originating from the Eastern coast of Africa, was brought to the Trucial Coast by immigrants who worked as seamen, pearl divers, and shipbuilders in the Arabian Gulf. The traditional dance that accompanied it is still routinely practiced.[2] It is performed in a circle, with a group of dancers taking two steps forward counter-clockwise while maintaining the shape of a drop of water. The undulation of the circle invokes images of the sea tide as it entices participants and audience members to join in as the circle opens and closes.[3]

Traditional performing arts in the Trucial Gulf involve pre-determined actions and each participant has a specific role and designation. Men who participate in the traditional tribal arts are referred to as *yarzf*, *Yazfin*, and *eyool*."[4] Laywa performances are more spontaneous and participants are referred to as "players" due to the improvisational nature of the dance, which is not viewed as serious when compared to "traditional" performing arts.

In the performance of *laywa* there is a simple yet complex relationship between the traditional use of the instruments and the conditions of the field of play. *Laywa* rules require all "players" to initially remove their shoes in order to participate. It also gives them ample space and freedom, so that they can evoke enjoyable and entertaining memories.

Laywa was passed down from generation to generation in the Trucial Gulf. The majority of *laywa* group members mechanically memorized the lyrics. Their expressions do not reflect their feelings about the words or their meanings. This foreign art had no linguistic or intellectual connection to the Trucial Coast and those who "played" it used it to establish their identity by modifying the lyrics from Swahili to Arabic. This modification left a permanent mark on *laywa*'s performance and further detached it from Africa. In essence there was an integration of two different cultures producing a distinctive local performance art. Arabization of *laywa*'s lyrics occurred in the 1970s, which served to safeguard *lawya*'s popularity and longevity, paving the way for its acceptance within a larger public.

Many Gulf and local Emirati composers[5] contributed to the perpetuation of *laywa* by incorporating its rhythms into their music. Consequently, this action further blended and transformed the art of the *laywa* performance by normalizing its existence within Emirati society. *Laywa* group members are convinced that the comprehensible Arabic *laywa* lyrics are a literal translation of the original Swahili despite the fact that they, themselves, do not speak or fully comprehend Swahili. This belief is based on the fact that the music and lyrics sounded the same as they were passed down from generation to generation and no one challenged its accuracy. The Arabization of the lyrics made *laywa* understandable and welcoming to others to join irrespective of its African cultural origin.

There is also the *al nuban* performance art, which migrated originally from Nubia (northern Sudan and southern Egypt). Even though it is called *al nuban*, it is also known in other regions under different names. In Egypt and Sudan, for example, it is performed with a lyre or harp-like instrument called *semsemia*; the same instrument is known in Uganda as *adungu*, while in some Arabian Gulf countries it is referred to as *tanboura*.

Al nuban is commonly considered one of the most effective spiritual healing methods used in Africa. It became rooted in the northern region of the continent and in parts of the Middle East more than a century ago. As a performance art, *al nuban* has its own rituals, symbols, and practices that were known to humans long before the advent of Islam and Christianity. However, the African performing arts were definitely influenced by both of these faiths and vice-versa.

This influence can be traced when visiting a Nubian house, which is highly dignified. Visitors are required to be clean and sober and to speak with the utmost respect to other participants when they enter these houses. Additionally, all musical instruments are stored in a private place and handled with care. The instruments resemble a divine holy book in how they function. Some Nubian songs have Islamic connotations because they mention Allah and the Prophet (peace be upon him). Paying respect to Allah at the beginning of the performance has become an established practice and fulfills social expectations.

During the pre-oil era,[6] in the absence of modern medical services, *al nuban* performance played a major role in healing mysterious physical and mental diseases that were difficult to cure. When spirit possession was suspected to be the cause of one's illness, the patient would initially be taken to a religious person to purify the body and soul from satanic contemplation by reciting verses from the Holy Quran. If the symptoms

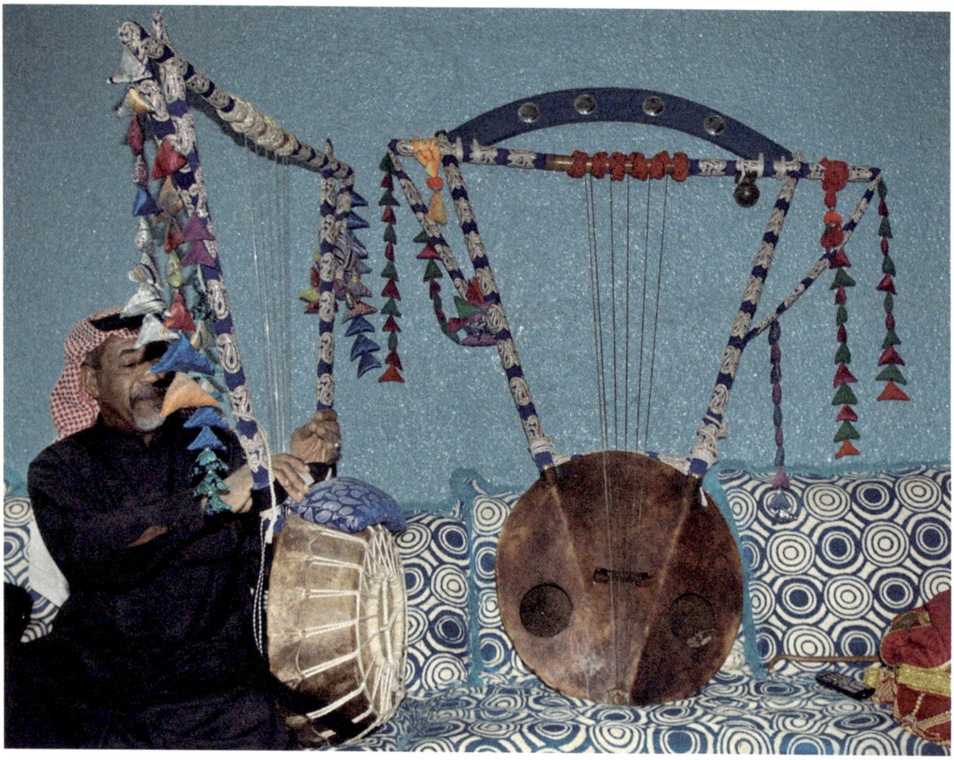

Taher Ismail tuning a tambura called "Naza'a" in preparation to play it.
Leaning against the wall is a tambura called "Jamila."

persisted, the patient would be subjected to common traditional beliefs and rituals. One of these rituals was called *al zar*. If this ritual failed to work, the patient would seek the *al nuban* ritual as a final resort. Although both the *al zar* and *al nuban* are used for spiritual healing rituals, the presence of *al tanboura* increases the potency of *al nuban* as a cure for spirit possession and other unknown symptoms.

According to the myths of prehistory as described in the *Encyclopedia Britannica* the *al tanboura* (a lyre-like instrument) has a magical impact on those healing practitioners. The head of the group communicates with the possessing spirits by presenting offerings that convince the spirit to exit the body. The popularity of such performance arts were endangered and declined after the introduction of Western medicine. The small group who continued to practice this art form added an entertainment element to its function which helped resurrect and sustain the practice of *al nuban* through present day.

Presently, *al nuban* is performed at weddings and heritage festivals where it is presented as a foreign folk art. It has maintained its Africanity through various features, two of which are mixed gender performances and language. The *al nuban* group is made up of male and female musicians, dancers, and performers. Some of the *al nuban* lyrics are sung in *rotana*[7] (a colloquial term used in the Gulf for an unfathomable language). Most songs are sung loudly and are incomprehensible to Arabic speakers since they are a mixture of African dialects imported by performing Africans who brought them from their motherland. Some of the comprehensible words refer to geographical locations and historical figures.

Al nuban Arabized songs tell of the courage of the first generation of Africans. They explain their living conditions and address issues of love and romance. Many of the songs speak of misery and nostalgia. The *al nuban* performances allowed participants the time and space to express themselves and heal their wounds by dancing and singing. As in *laywa*, participation in the *al nuban* dance is called "play," resulting in two conflicting elements: "play," whereby participants dance to traditionally choreographed music, and providing a professional performance in both recreational and therapeutic events.

The relocation and existence of African performance arts to the Trucial Coast region became a cultural mainstay for the participants, and a new identity evolved from these artistic forms. Over time, and since the era of maritime voyaging, the present Gulf (UAE) performing arts earned financial support from the government.

Missing from the public view are *laywa* and *al nuban* performance's secret rules, defined and unspoken customs that govern both rituals. The most important component is secrecy. The complexity of the participants' social upbringing and the implicit agreement by the participants enabled the African origin performing arts to keep their secrets in a cloistered yet refined way. During the performance, the public views secret elements as simple and naïve, trivializing the signs, symbolism, and their intuition by not inquiring about their meaning. This lack of curiosity kept the real meaning mysterious.

Folk games are settled in an individual's memory, contributing to his or her personality and perception of the world. Play involves fun, art, ethics, and morals. Some games depend on concentration, planning, physical fitness, and/or imagination. Games refine personal traits and boost self-confidence while stimulating discovery and interaction within a group and community.

Playing is a vital component in every child's life. It makes up half of their rearing and education. In the pre-union[8] days, Emirati families encouraged their children to play with their peers, as play was considered both pleasurable and rare. The reality of life, which could suddenly require all family members to work, made opportunities to play quite limited. Games engage children and teach them patience, endurance, compliance with social laws, values, principles, customs and norms.

There are three kinds of folk games. Some are associated with thinking and intellectual capacity; others are associated with physical and mental capabilities; and the third kind is for children's amusement. These games can be played individually or collectively. In Emirati society, play starts at birth as children are often showered with prayers, chants, and lullabies.

From the songs that are sung throughout the day, babies are able to associate a specific vocabulary with daytime or nighttime. This recognition develops their self-sufficiency and capability to play on their own as well as entertain themselves. In the next stage, children learn by observing and participating in games with their peers. When a child shares a toy with another child, this cooperation benefits the development of the children and of society in general.

The similarities between some adult activities and some games played by children in the UAE are no coincidence. Certain childhood games were carefully and thoughtfully designed by adults to meet specific objectives and purposes. This is particularly evident when girls are encouraged to play *al maryahana*, which is the gentle pushing of a swing while chanting traditional and improvised songs—an evident preparation for a future where they would need to use these activities while engaging in housework, such as shaking a bottle made of sheepskin to prepare buttermilk. Memories of play and chants return to fully grown women

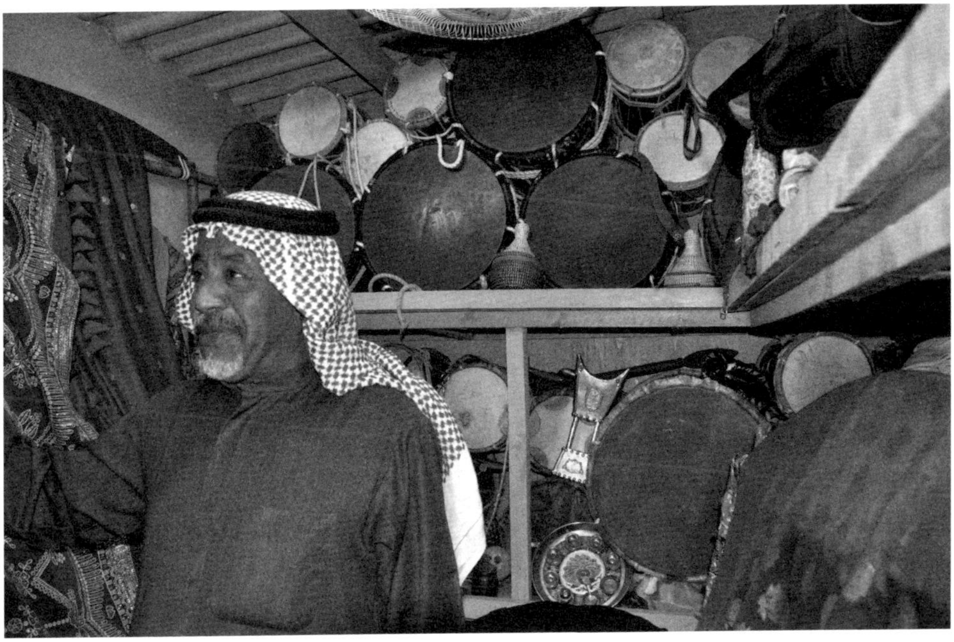

The musical instruments and relevant artifacts used in all aspects of *al nuban* performances are safely stored in a room that can only be accessed by a restricted number of members

and mothers when swinging the cradle and singing songs from their childhood to put their own offspring to sleep.

Interestingly, lullabies, childhood songs, and swing songs are inseparable components of a woman's intangible memory throughout the different stages of her growth and maturity. The girl becomes familiar with certain shapes, such as the triangle. For example, both a cradle and a tent share the same shape from the inside as well as from the outside. This is what the child sees from the inside, and when she comes out of the cradle to the larger tent. This is where she spends active time with her parents when she is not sleeping.

There are games that were designed to perpetuate the mother's role in protecting children. One such traditional game played by girls is called "I am the Wolf." In this game players are divided into two groups. The first group has one person who is the wolf. This child should be agile and flexible as she must strike the herd in order to catch the young ones. The second group consists of the mother and her young children. The tallest player assumes the role of the mother so that she can protect the children from the wolf who attempts to snatch them.

The play starts with the wolf threatening the young ones by saying "I am the wolf—I will devour you." The mother challenges him by saying "And I am your mother—I will protect you." The wolf then says, for example, "I want the red one," referring to one of the young children wearing a red dress; and the mother replies, "You will not get her." Then the wolf says, "I want the yellow one," referring to another child wearing a yellow dress. The mother replies, "You will not get her," and so on. The aim of the game is to unite the children together so the wolf will not be able to divide and separate them. The group is coherent and moves in harmony, thus the wolf cannot get any one of them. This is a vital exercise, because it teaches children how to shift their focus from play to problem-solving and how to best protect themselves from attack and abduction.

Conclusion

Music is a human legacy, and playing is a cultural activity. As elements of music and play combine, they merge identities and cultures in the same way sugar dissolves in water. Our memories are created in actions we undertake and remember. Society's traits are formed in this cumulative memory, and their core values and concepts are managed when playing and performing. These activities serve to revive skills and talents that unite people and prepare them to accept one another, and live and co-exist in good and bad times, even when divided by geography and history.

1 Hui-Min Wang and Sheng-Chiefh Huang, "Musical Rhythms Affect Heart Rate Variability: Algorithm and Models," *Advances in Electrical Engineering*, 2014. See www.hindawi.com/journals/aee/2014/851796/, last accessed March 21, 2017.

2 Rifcat Duaib, *Aghani al-acras fi dawlat al-imarat al- carabiyah al-muttahiddah*, Wizarat al-Iclam wa-al-Thaqafah, Abu-Dhabi, 1982, pp. 132–133.

3 Wahid Ahmed al-Khan, "The Leewah in Bahrain as an Art Form: A Textual Analysis of the Leewah Dance-Songs," *Al-Ma'thurat al-Shacbiyyah*, no. 21, January 1991, p. 8.

4 "*Zafin*" means literally "dance," which is associated with *Alsoot* music that was popular in the pre-union era. "Eyool" refers to men who participate in the traditional tribal music called *yolah* as they enter the circle of action to exhibit their masculinity and mastery of handling a cane and/or a rifle.

5 Some of these composers include Awadh Dwkhi and Faisal al Saad from Kuwait, Bilal Al Shami from Iraq, Khaled Abu Heshi from Bahrain, and Ibrahim Juma from the UAE.

6 An economic term referring to the impact of oil since its first discovery in the UAE in the 1950s and its exportation in the 1960s.

7 Ioan Myrddin Lewis, Ahmed Al-Safi, and Sayyid Hurreiz (eds.), *Women's Medicine: Zar-Bori Cult in Africa and Beyond*, Edinburgh University Press, 1991, p. 83.

8 The period predating the 1971 union of the seven Emirates.

Emirati Expressions IV

Reem Fadda
Maisa Al Qassimi

The exhibition "Emirati Expressions IV: Conventions of Arts," curated by Maisa Al Qassimi and me with the assistance of Munira Al-Sayegh, sought to raise questions about the functionality and usability of art. Can art be useful? What does art look like when it has a function? A vibrant and varied practice calls for the merging of use value and art in the UAE. Elements of design are incorporated, immersive experiences are developed, and engaged social art has become the norm.

The inspiration to delve into this line of questioning came from examining the makeup of the cultural scene in the UAE, which is primarily constituted from the social clubs and community associations around the Gulf. These interactive spaces dedicated to community engagement are the nuclei of modern cultural institutions within the UAE and particularly in Abu Dhabi. Dynamic and communal in their outlook, they serve a long list of functions: athletic, social, environmental, heritage, and so on. The clubs in Abu Dhabi also reflects the diversity of the communities that have resided in the city for decades, such as the Sudanese Social and Cultural Centre, the Jordanian Social Club, the India Social Cultural Centre, among others. There are also the popular sport clubs such as the Equestrian Club, Al Wihdah Club, Yacht Club, and many others that draw on a large audience. Visiting these institutions allowed us, the curators, an insight into a rich, diverse, and dynamic history of arts and culture within the city.

It was very important for us to address the issue of the lack or lag that many Arab or Third World countries face with when contending with the assumed absence of museums or cultural institutions. This thesis was a way for us to tackle this lack or lag and investigate what a cultural institution is, and what its remits and audiences are. Could we do without demarcations of high and lowbrow culture and instead open up a plethora of possibilities as to what constitutes culture and its institutions in these various societies? How do we question art's evolution from a nonstructured perspective, when nation-building projects came later, yet were not far behind? Having been born in Kuwait, I grew up in an extremely culturally active environment where the Palestinian community was allowed to prosper culturally, independently, and politically. I remember my first encounter with art was visiting one of the cultural centers in Kuwait, which was showing the monumental mural works of the preeminent Palestinian artist Ismail Shammout. As a child, I remember helping my mother as an usher at the many cultural events organized by the Palestinian Women's Organization in Kuwait. These were the experiences with music, theater, and art that shaped my cultural awareness, and they took place not in the Louvre or any museum but in the clubs and the community centers of the Gulf.

We felt strongly that there was a need to track and then take ownership of this trajectory of grounds-up cultural institutional growth. Additionally, it was important to revive these centers in our memory and not relegate them to the category of nostalgic or abandoned sites, especially since the urban growth of cities in the UAE is accelerating at an unprecedented pace. We also felt that a partnership with these institutions through the work of artists and the Tourism and Cultural Authority of Abu Dhabi was therefore necessary to achieve the above.

Throughout our research, we met with welcoming and hospitable representatives of these various centers and were invited to look into many of their archives. We came across many images of important dignitaries, both local and international, such as Indira Gandhi visiting the Indian Club of Abu Dhabi (which was actually founded preceding the union of the Emirates), or the current Minister of Culture Sheikh Nahyan bin Mubarak Al Nahyan, who was a devoted attendee of all cultural events in the city decades ago. We discovered through the archives of the Jordanian Club, which boasts a large hall, that it had hosted many events such as weddings, engagements, meetings, and even wakes for all communities. In the absence of museums and galleries, these clubs become the substitute in providing cultural and artistic activities with a sense of openness, community, and necessity.

Putting these clubs at the forefront of this exhibition, we decided to invite a group of fifteen Emirati artists and designers on this journey of discovery of the city and this vital scene. Many artists—such as Lamya Gargash, Alia Lootah, Ghaya Bin Mesmar, Khalid Mezaina, and Khalid Shafar—chose to create specially commissioned works inspired by the various historic social clubs. Other artists, including Ammar Al Attar, Afra Al Dhaheri, Zeinab Al Hashemi, Farah Al Qasimi, Salem Al Qassimi, Maryam Al Suwaidi, Sumayyah Al Suwaidi, Hind Bin Demaithan, Rami Farook, and Nasir Nasrallah, made works that spoke more straightforwardly about elements of community engagement, design, and function. Some of the artworks produced included wearable textiles, photography, furniture design, interactive installations, paintings, illustrations, large-scale sculptures, and performances. The exhibition ended with a section dedicated to showcasing the archives of an assortment of these communal clubs, including the Emirates Writers Union, Armed Forces Officers' Club, Jordanian Social Club, and India Social Cultural Centre, to name but a few. Photographs, memorabilia, guest books, albums, and models were all put on display in cabinets showcasing an important history of place and people—one that permeates a real sense of community and culture.

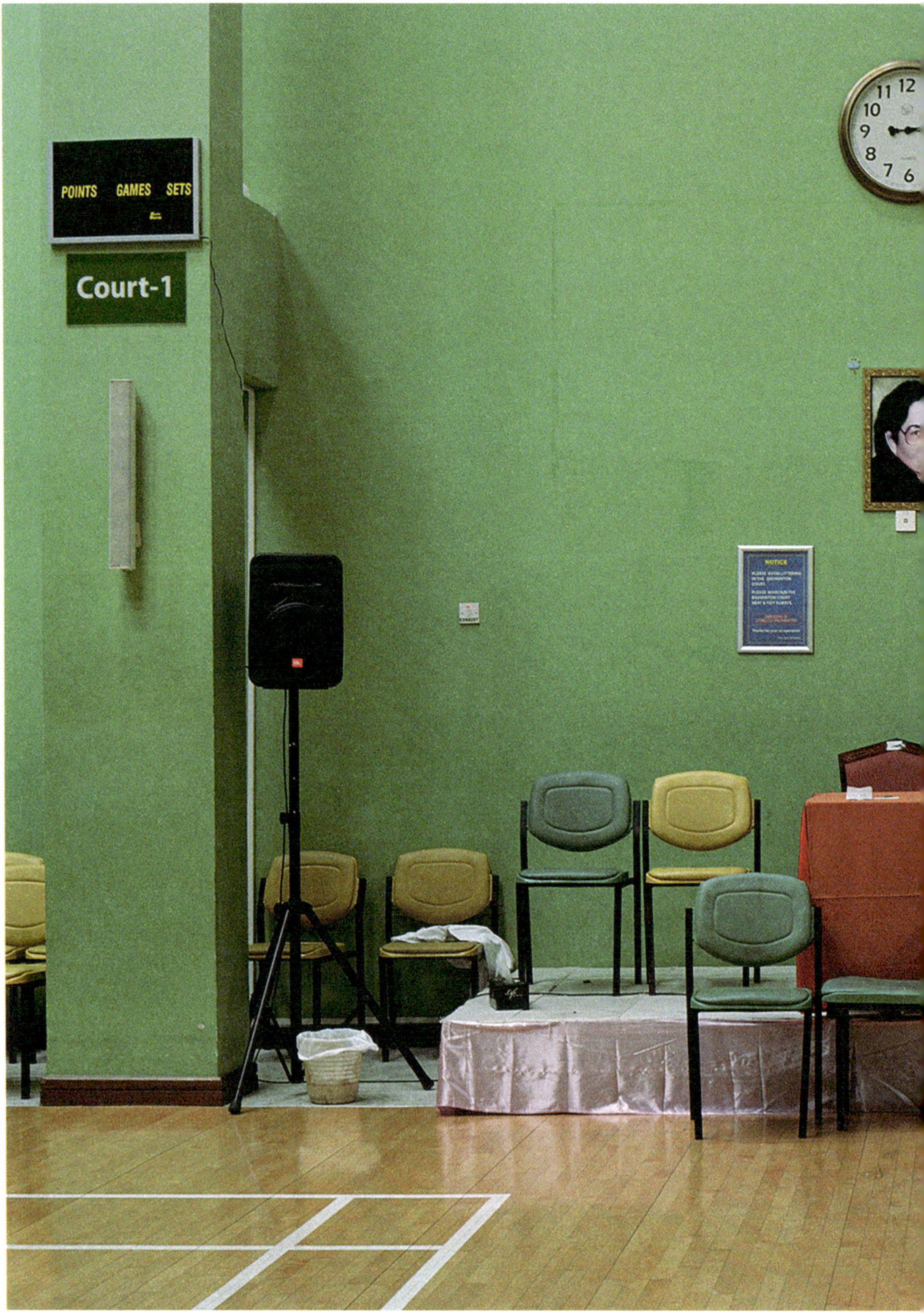
POINTS GAMES SETS
Court-1
NOTICE

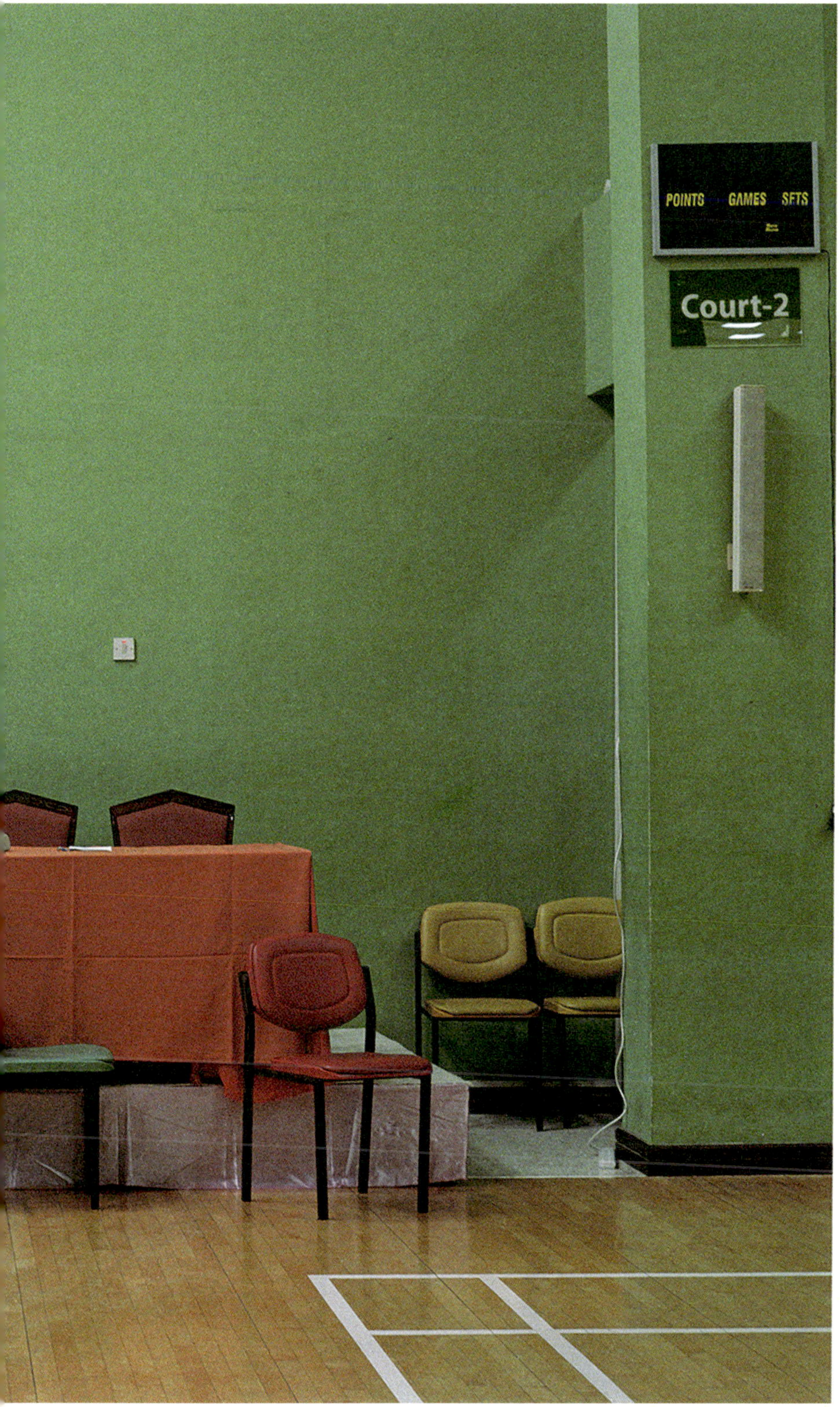

Lamya Gargash, *Court, The Indian Club*, Abu Dhabi, 2015
Chromogenic print, 70 × 52 cm

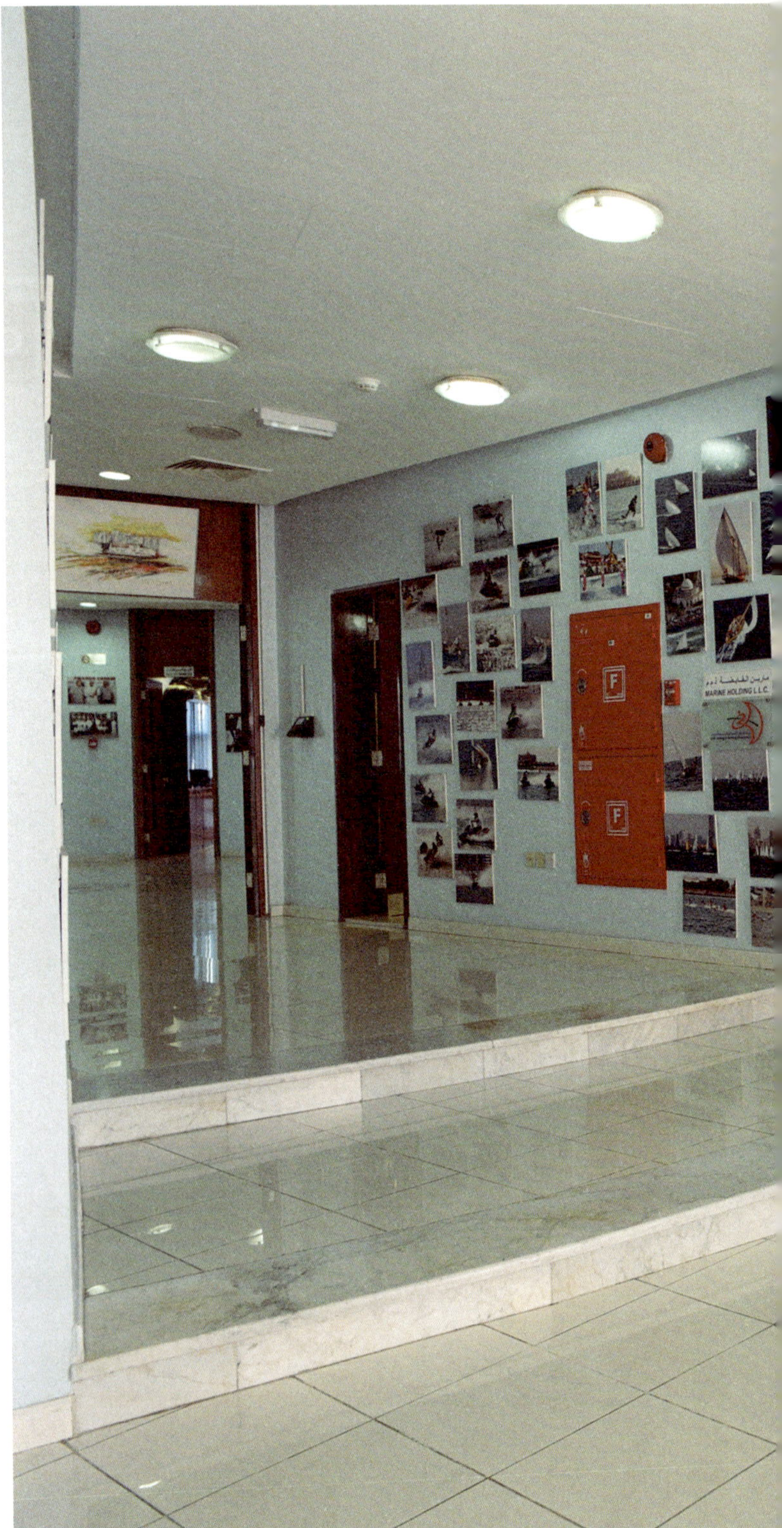

Lamya Gargash, *The Entrance, The Marine & Yacht Club*, Abu Dhabi, 2015
Chromogenic print, 70 × 52 cm

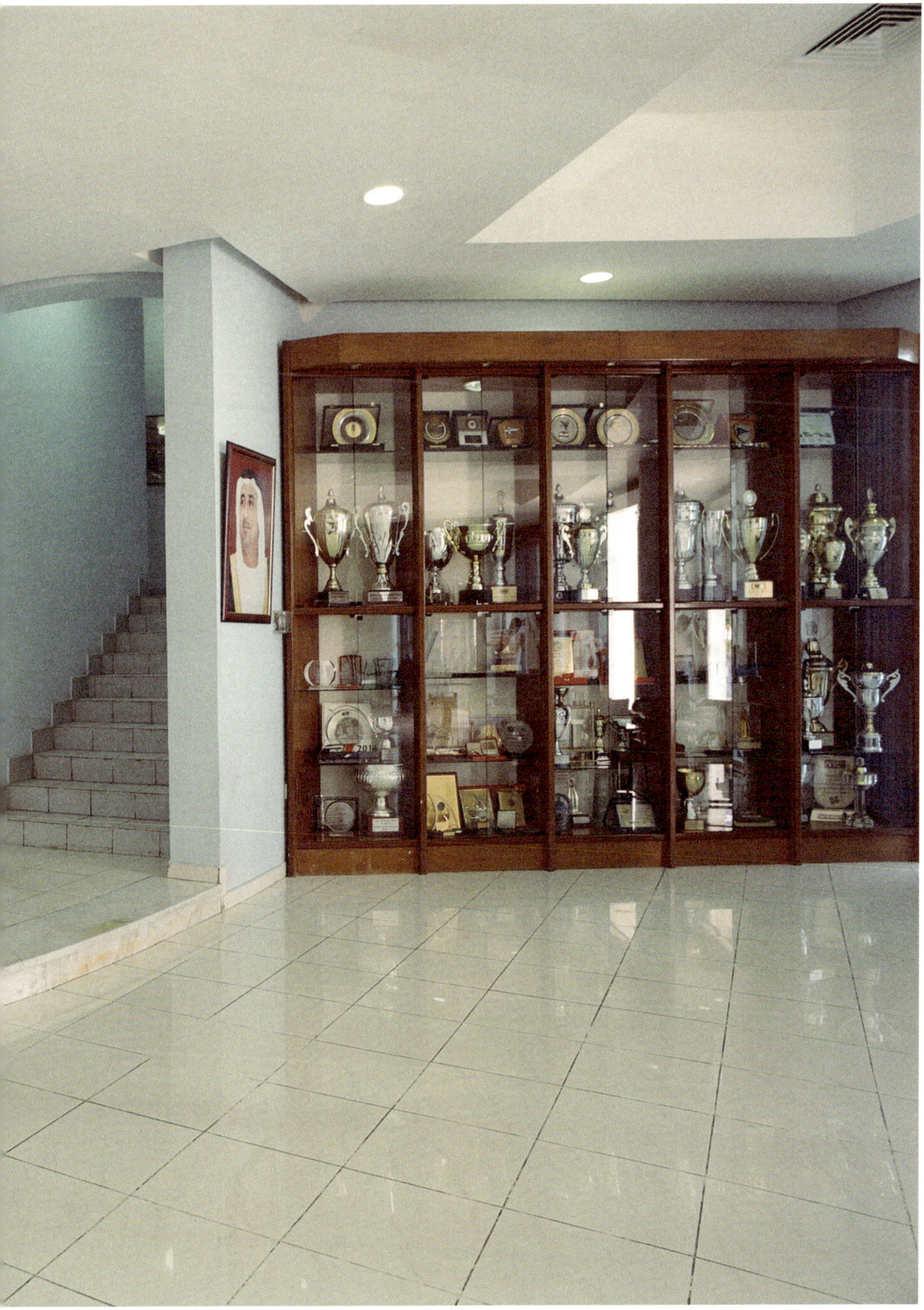

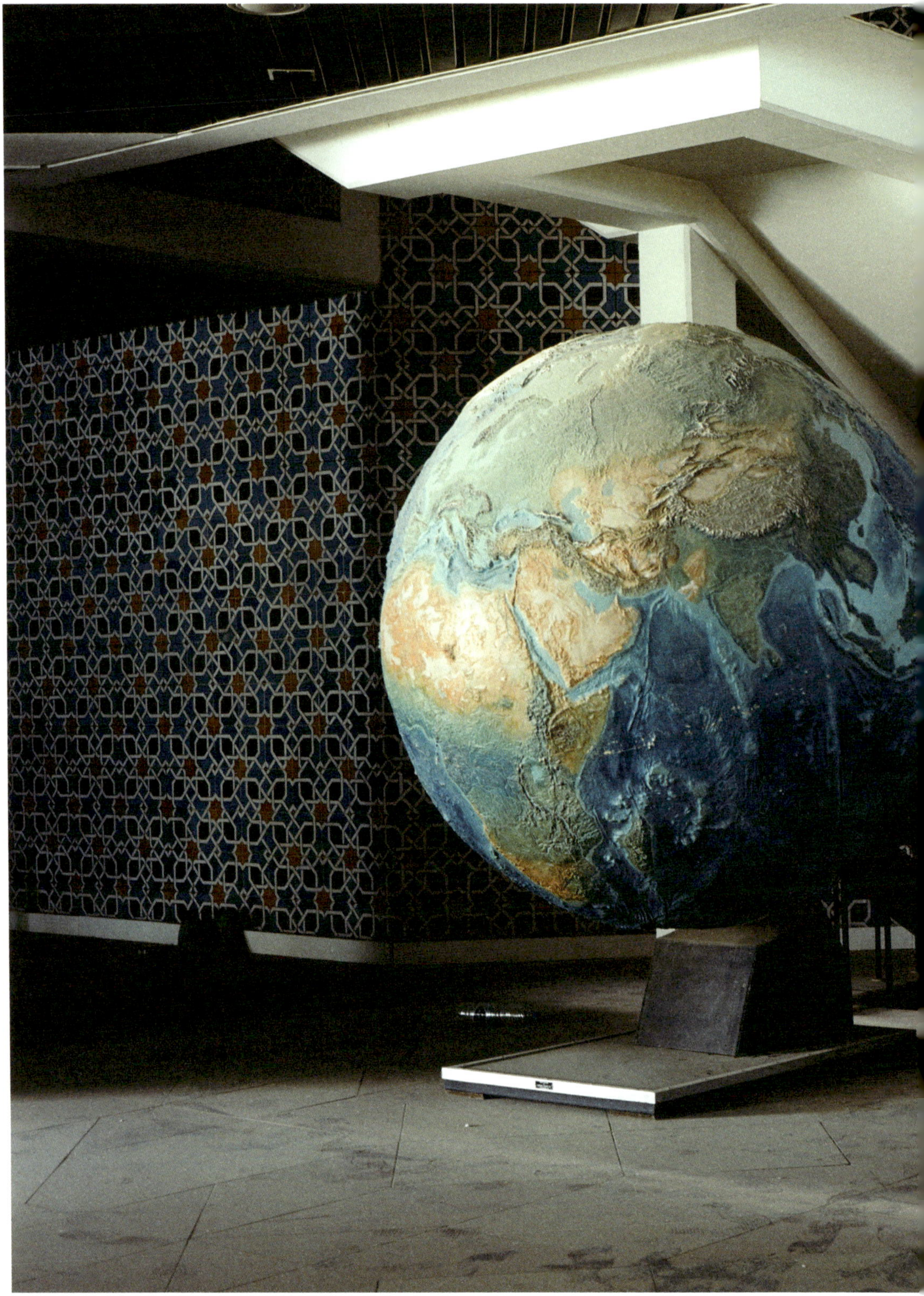

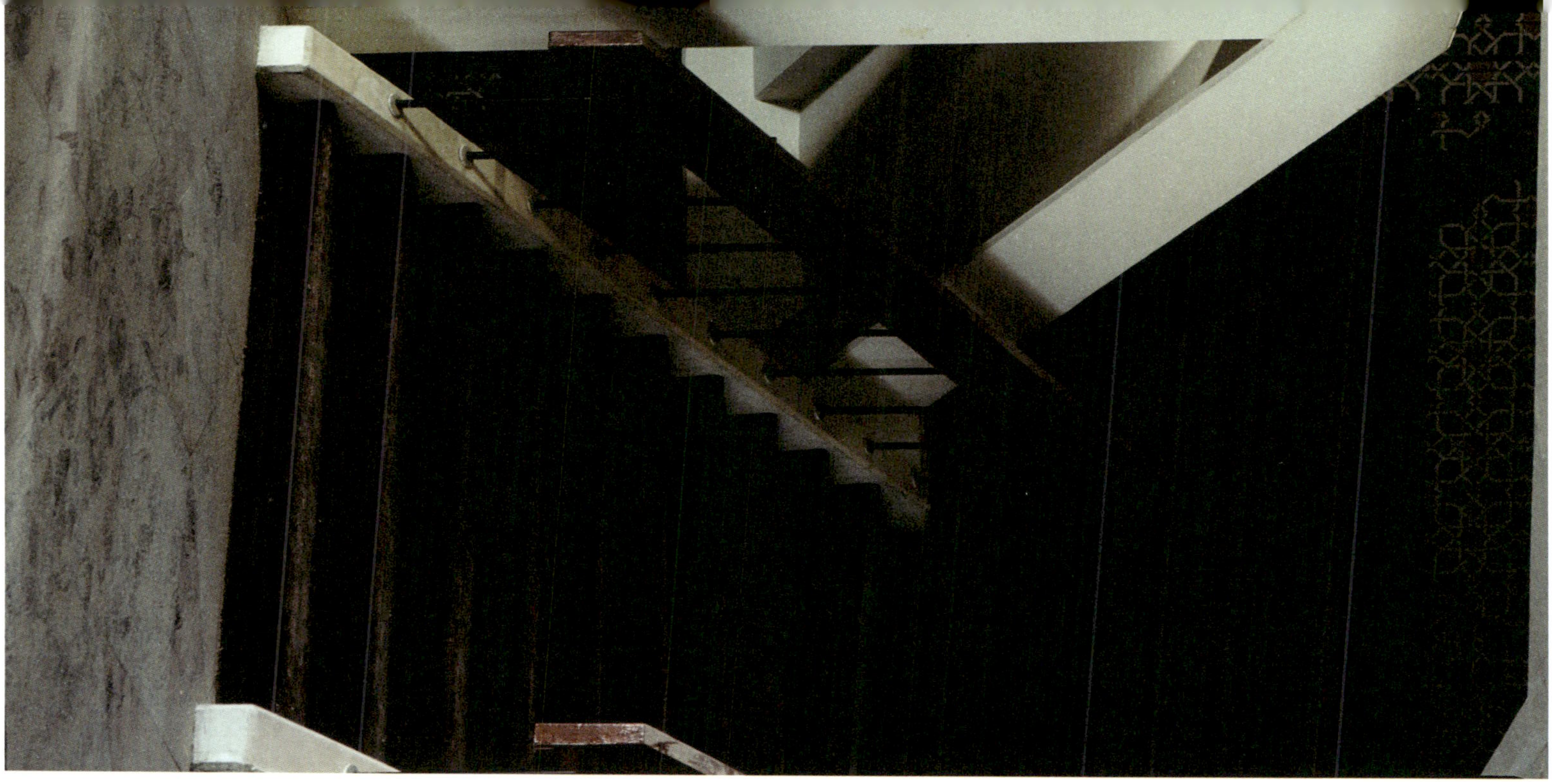

Lamya Gargash, *The Globe, The Cultural Foundation*, Abu Dhabi
Chromogenic print, 70 × 52 cm

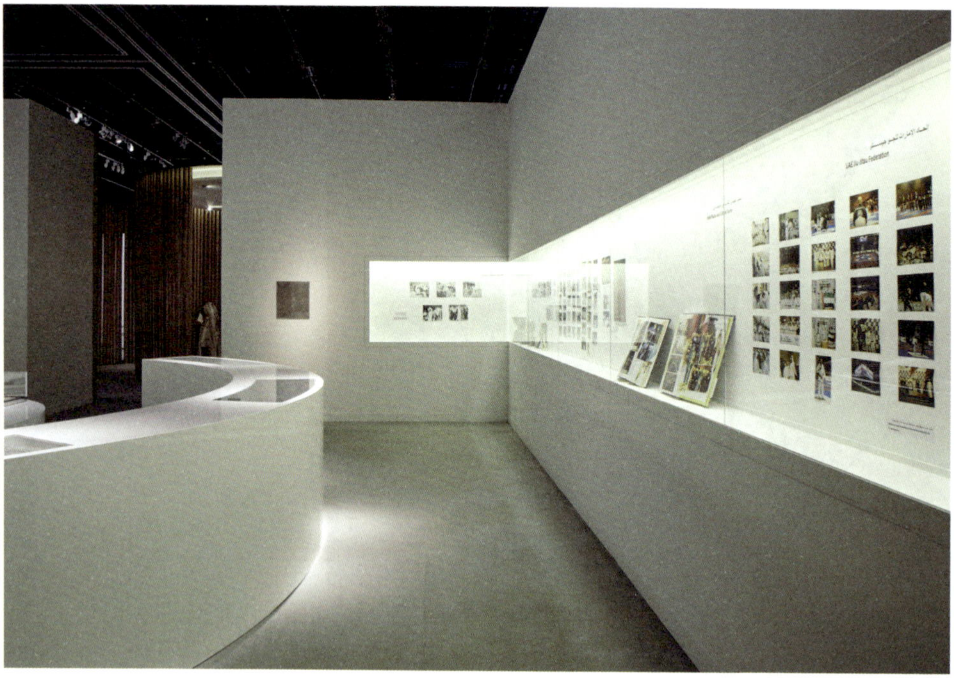

"Emirati Expressions IV: Conventions of Arts", 2005.
Installation view: Archival Room, Manarat Al Saadiyat
Courtesy of Abu Dhabi Tourism & Culture Authority

Whenever I think about my first "playgrounds" in the UAE, cultural and social clubs come to mind. These sites fed into the cultural and social ecology of the country, offering a range of activities in such diverse areas as sports, theater, and the arts, and bringing together both particular communities and society in general. In curating the exhibition "Emirati Expressions IV: Conventions of Arts" (2015) at Manarat Al Saadiyat and throughout the city of Abu Dhabi, Reem Fadda and I decided to use these clubs as an underlying/overarching framework. To that end, we commissioned the selected artists to produce works that responded to specific historic clubs in Abu Dhabi and dedicated a room in the exhibition to the display of archival photographs, publications, and memorabilia, which documented and offered insight into the history of these clubs.

Lamya Gargash (b. 1983, Dubai) made a series that documented various clubs and cultural centers through traditional film photography. Gargash captured the empty interiors and exteriors of the clubs, focusing on traces of human existence. The India Social and Cultural Center (ISC), for example, *Indian Club Court* (2015, p. 98–99) has its origins in the Unity Club, which was established in 1967, prior to the union of the UAE. ISC was founded by a group of Indians based in Abu Dhabi, who shared a vision to create a hub for social and cultural activities for the Indian community that would allow them to stay connected to their cultural roots. In the early days of its history, a number of leading political figures—among them His Highness Sheikh Zayed Bin Sultan Al Nahyan, founding father of the UAE, and Prime Minister Indira Gandhi—visited the ISC. Since its founding, the ISC has expanded its activities to include educational and literary programs, and today the Center, which has over 2,500 members, continues to serve as a sanctuary for the Indian diaspora.

Gargash also chose to document the Abu Dhabi Cultural Foundation. Founded in 1981 in the oldest building (dating from the late 1700s) in the heart of the city of Abu Dhabi, this cultural center hosts a variety of events such as plays, music concerts, and art exhibitions, and it also serves as the National Library in the capital. Gargash documented this space in *The Globe. The Cultural Foundation* (2015, see p. 102–103), and when on view in the exhibition, her photographs attracted attention from diverse generations of visitors. We were fascinated by the sight of crowds gathering as soon as they recognized the globe that was housed in the Cultural Foundation for decades and openly sharing stories and memories of their childhood with other spectators.

While conducting research for his commission, Khalid Shafar (b. 1980, Dubai) visited a number of clubs and was immediately drawn to an abandoned *dhow* (traditional sailing vessel) docked in the backyard of the Abu Dhabi Sailing and Yacht Club. He learned that Kuwait had gifted this boat to His Highness Sheikh Zayed bin Sultan Al Nahyan in the early 1970s, and it was subsequently used as a viewing deck for invited delegations to watch sailing competitions (see p. 100–101). Inspired by his ruminations on the many events during the life of Sheikh Zayed that must have unfolded in and on the historic dhow, Shafar created *The Cabin* (2015, see below), an interactive installation that invited visitors to step barefoot into a tubular structure. Once inside, they would encounter a carpet with a raised, wavelike pattern mimicking the physical sensation of sand and a ceiling composed of blue Plexiglas tiles and over 400 *egals*, the black ropes traditionally used in men's headdresses in the region. Watery blue reflections were cast onto the floor outside the structure, extending their reach and beckoning people to enter *The Cabin*. As with Gargash's

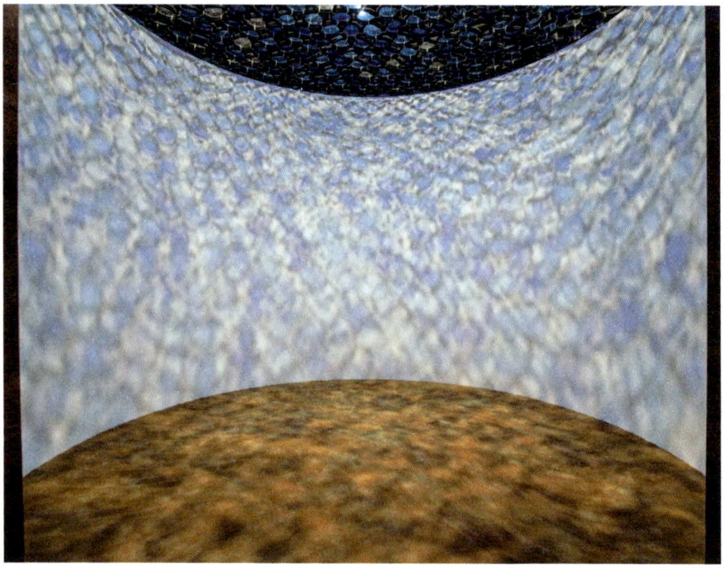

Khalid Shafar, *The Cabin*, 2015. Installation view © Khalid Shafar. Courtesy of Abu Dhabi Tourism & Culture Authority, from "Emirati Expressions IV: Conventions of Arts"

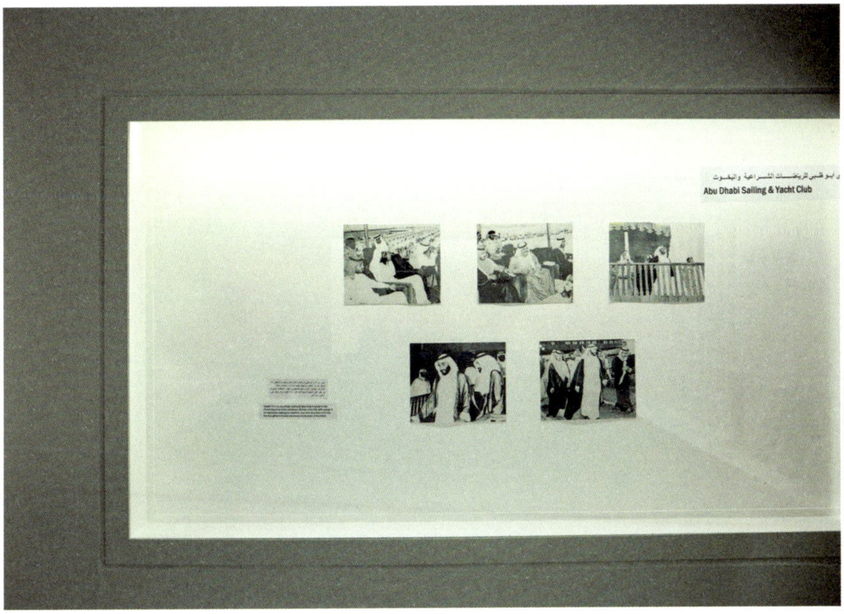

Installation view: Archival Room
Photo Courtesy of Abu Dhabi Tourism & Culture Authority,
from "Emirati Expressions IV: Conventions of Arts"

photographs, Shafar's installation sparked conversations about Abu Dhabi's past among visitors.

The experience of researching the history of the cultural and social clubs of Abu Dhabi—hospitable institutions that have encouraged many to learn, engage, come together, and participate in multicultural celebrations—coupled with the opportunity to see them through the eyes of both the commissioned artists and the visitors to "Emirati Expressions IV: Conventions of Arts" reinforces their important and enduring role as universal playgrounds that have nurtured communities and societies and set the foundations for cultural growth in the UAE.

Gamescapes

WTD Magazine

This is not a photographic survey.

Gamescapes is an unfinished template attempting to record various subcultures that convene to play. The compiled vignettes highlight the elements that mark the territory and narrate an ongoing distinctive condition of appropriating the public realm.

Locations:
Karama
Creek
Jumeirah
Al Quoz
Nad Al Sheba
Al Satwa

Reference	Notes
25.2489° N, 55.3061° E	The cat that saw the grass disappear in Karama. Within the tightly knit residential block, rumored to be the most populous in Dubai, the neighborhood's pockets house daily playoffs that include: badminton, football, and cricket among loitering kulfi-eating-hipsters.
25.1580° N, 55.1916° E	A new square by the Creek. Not along the newly extended body of water, but its natural parameter, a fountain transforms into a skateboarder's park. Defined as a traditional square, the blue tiled zone provides the ideal performance space. Whereas the periphery and imagined horizon allow for meditative sports to emerge.
25.2016° N, 55.2453° E	Punctual pastimes in Jumeirah. An area that is constantly reinventing itself through its inhabitants, currently characterized as a low rise residential neighborhood and chaotic commercial strip. The distinct mall typology that emerged in the early 1990s shelters a group of backgammon enthusiasts under the skylight right before the sun starts to set while resident surfers flock the beach at sunrise.
25.1514° N, 55.2508° E	Social movements (and escapism) in Al Quoz. A cocktail of services, amenities, residences, and art galleries, Al Quoz is one of the best examples of urban gentrification in Dubai. All daily needs (personal and professional) are housed within the dense industrial blocks, allowing for markets and cricket matches to be concealed within its walls.
25.1561° N, 55.3752° E	How should Nad Al Sheba be? A low-density residential neighborhood frequented once a year by avid horse racers, models, and the royal entourage. It houses the best conglomeration of resident designers and peculiar trees. Its empty parking lots become the ideal cricket grounds.
25.2194° N, 55.2729° E	Forming an eclectic in Al Satwa. The pedestrian-friendly, kitsch-commercial and charming residential neighborhood houses the best fabric stores, resident tailors, karak, and one-hour IT services. Ravi might be the main attraction but Satwa is layered with public interventions. Specifically the Public Arts and Rowing Association.

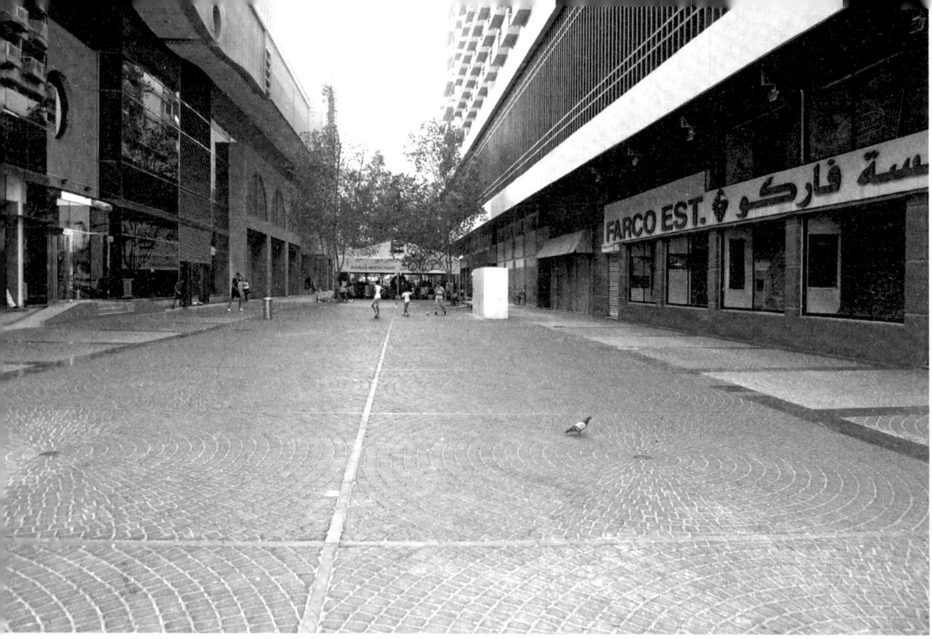

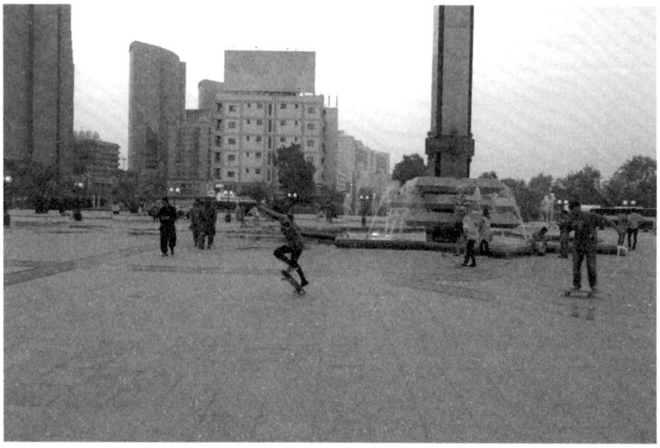

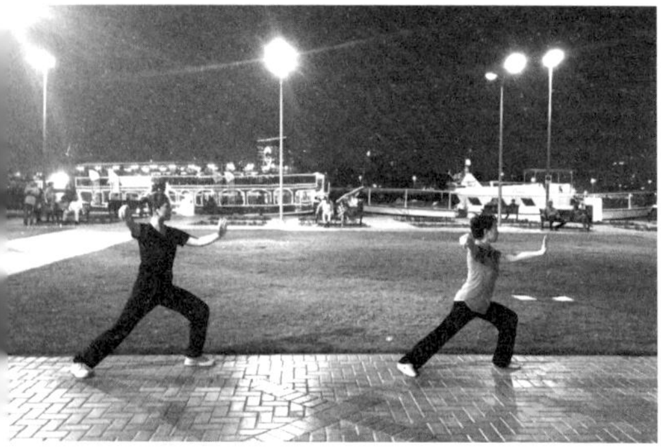

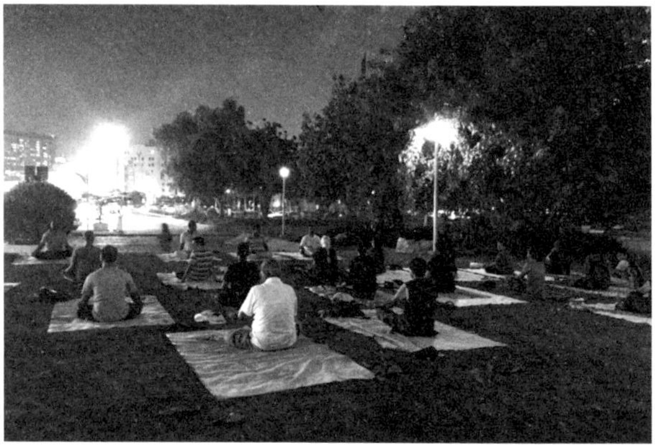

25.1580° N, 55.1916° E

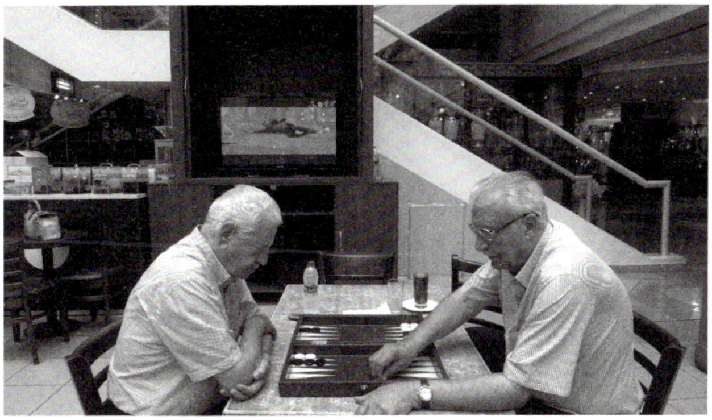

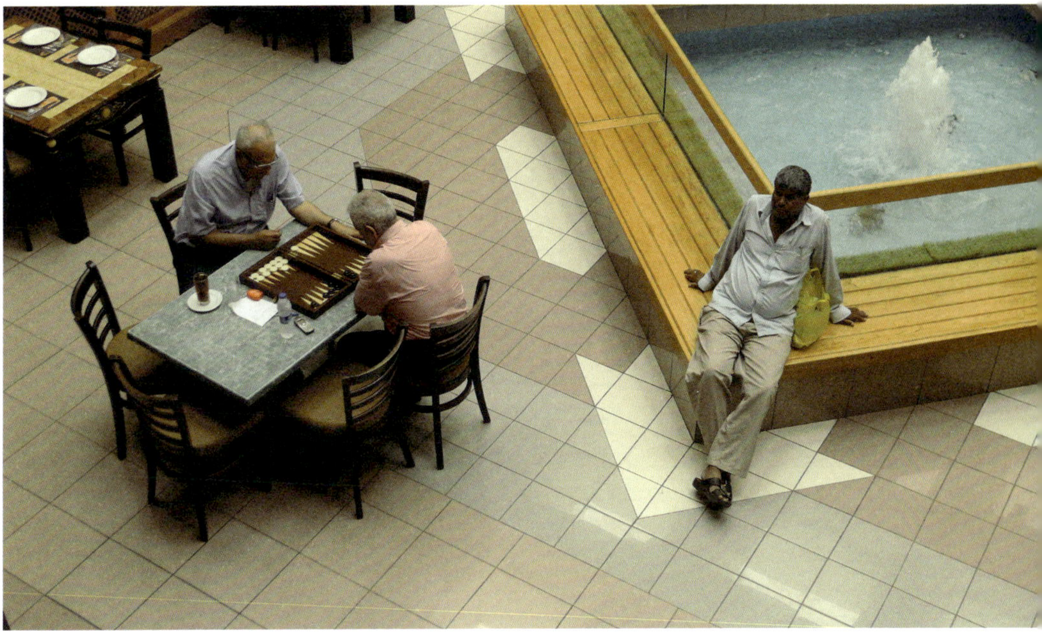

25.2016° N, 55.2453° E

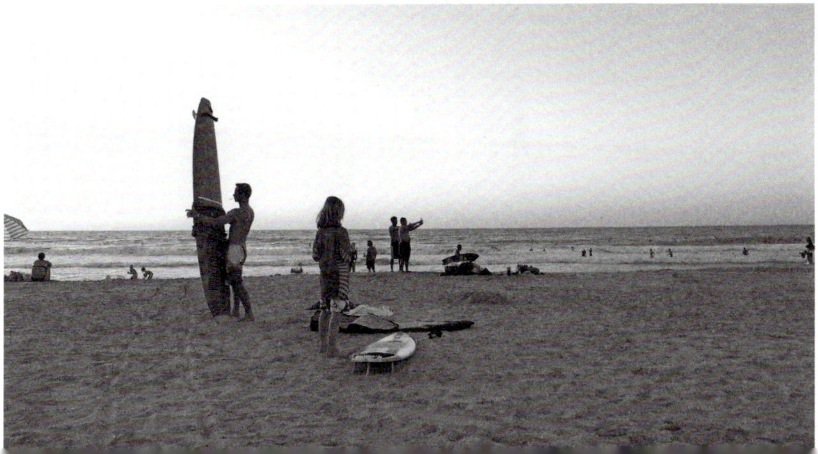

25.1514° N, 55.2508° E

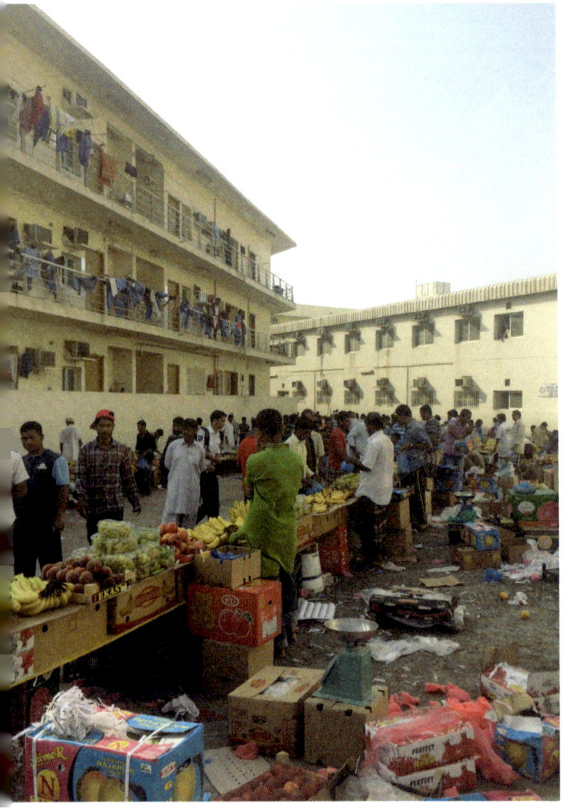

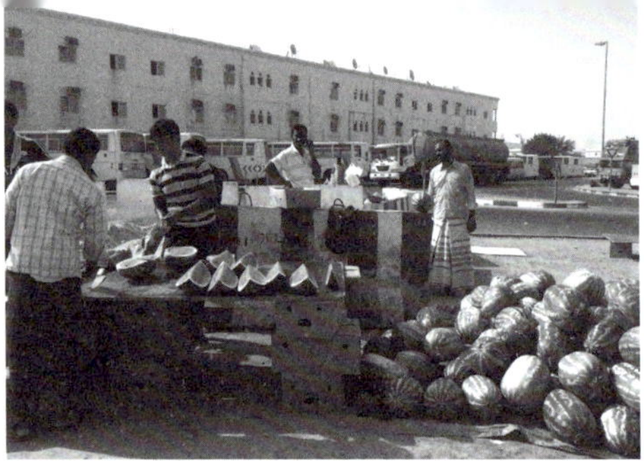

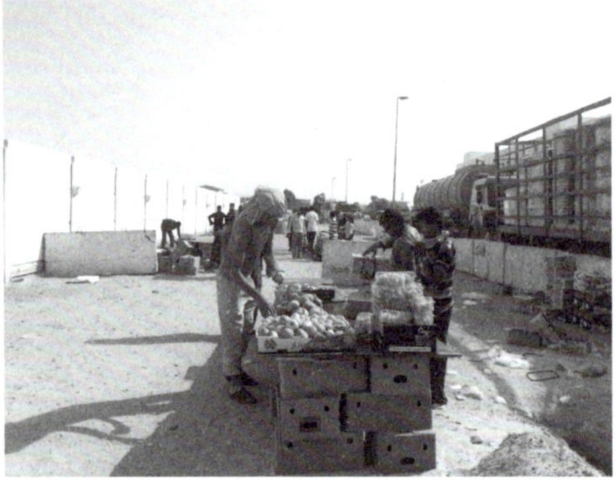

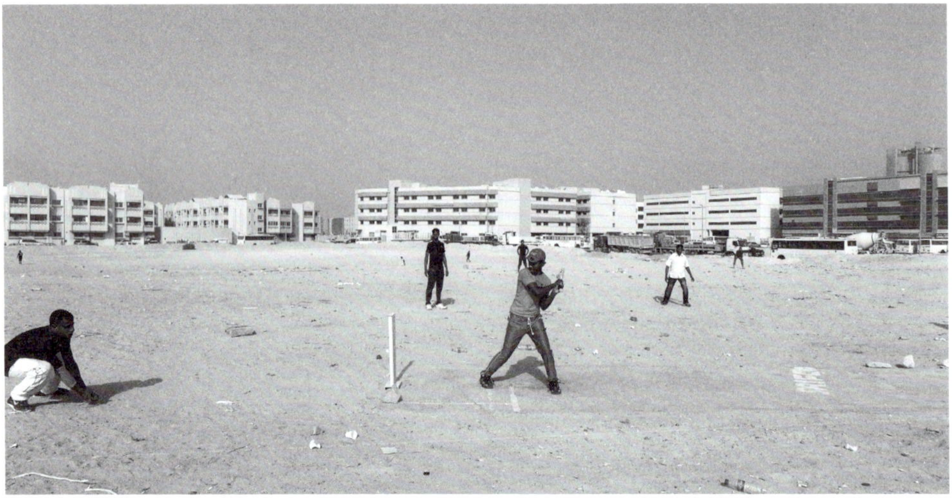

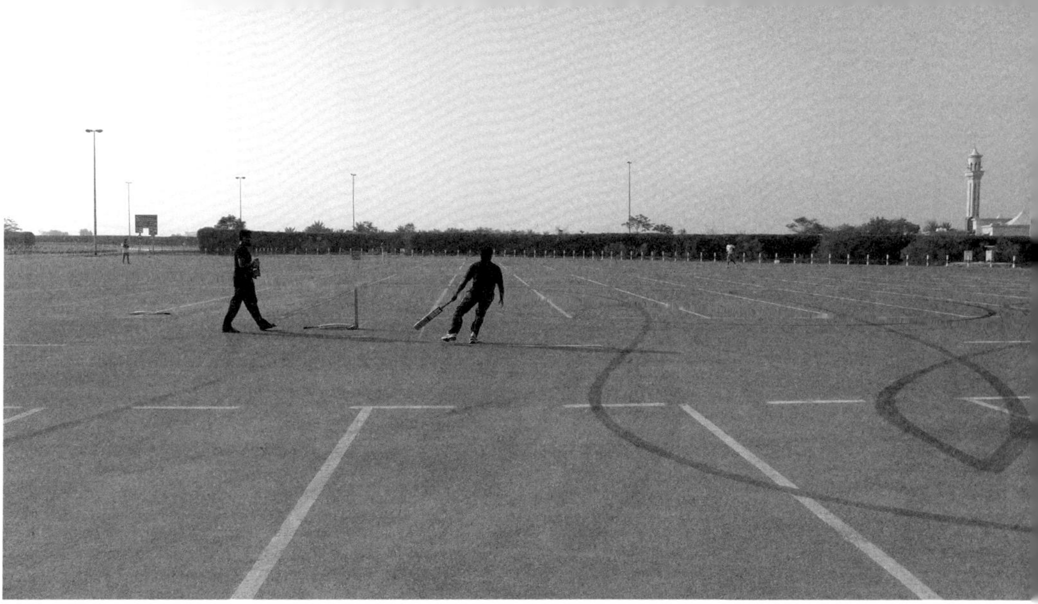

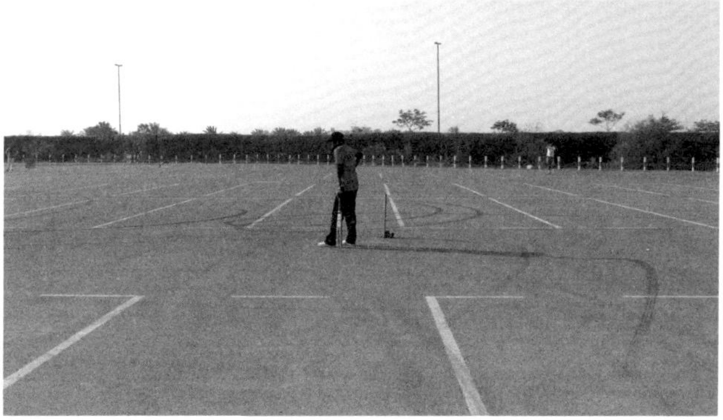

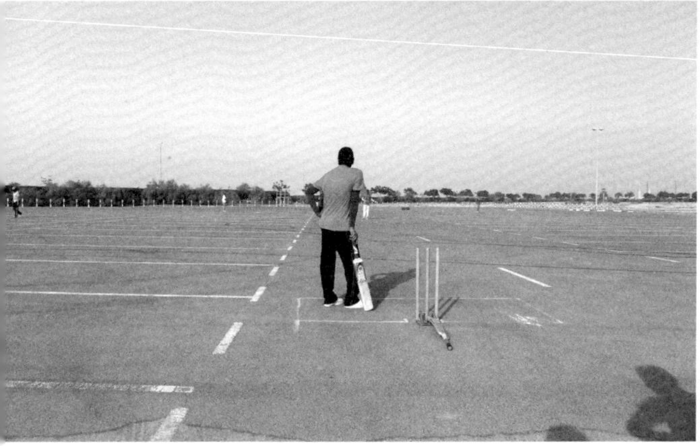

25.1561° N, 55.3752° E

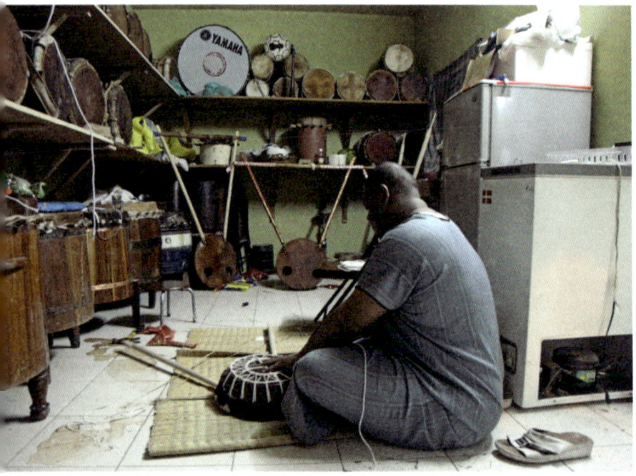

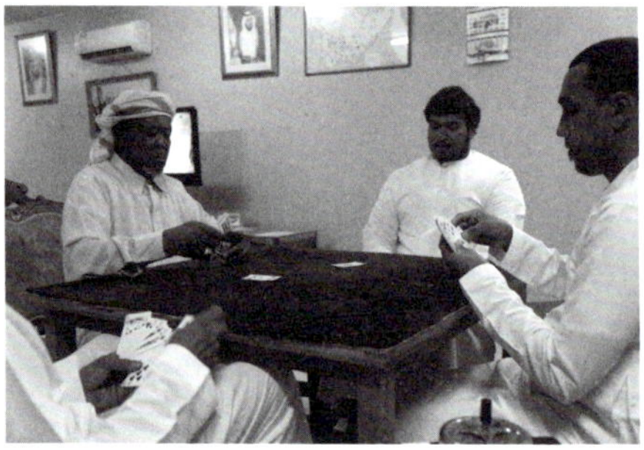

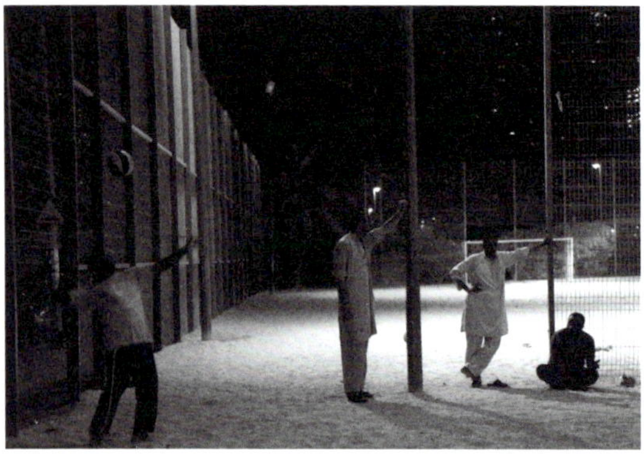

25.2194° N, 55.2729° E

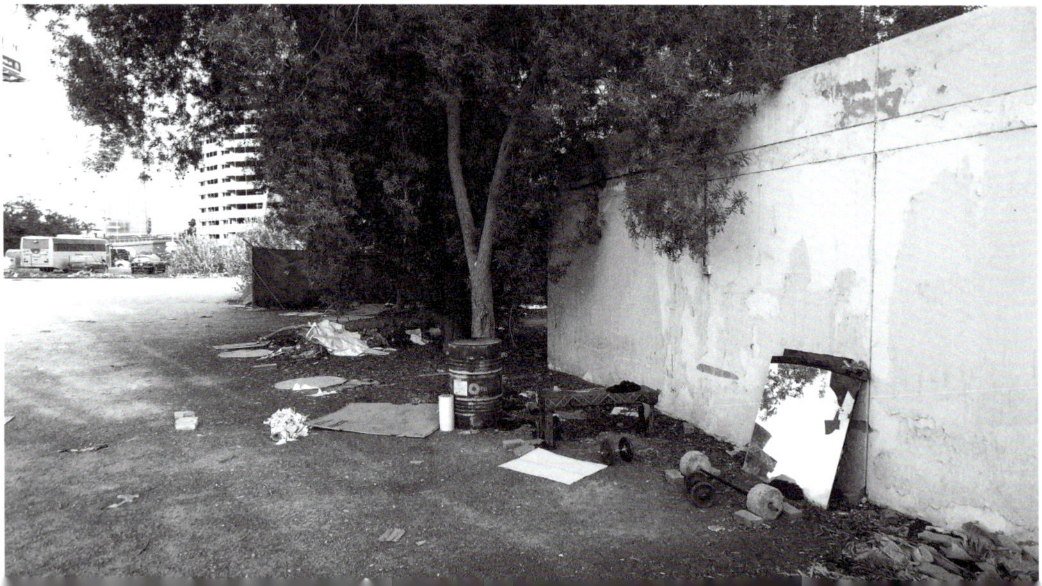

25.2489° N, 55.3061° E

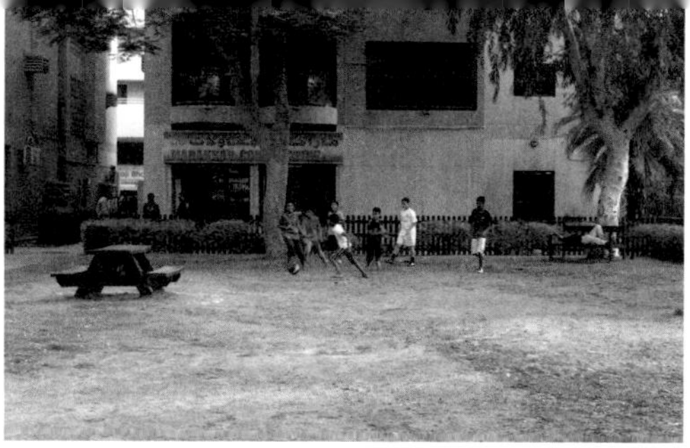

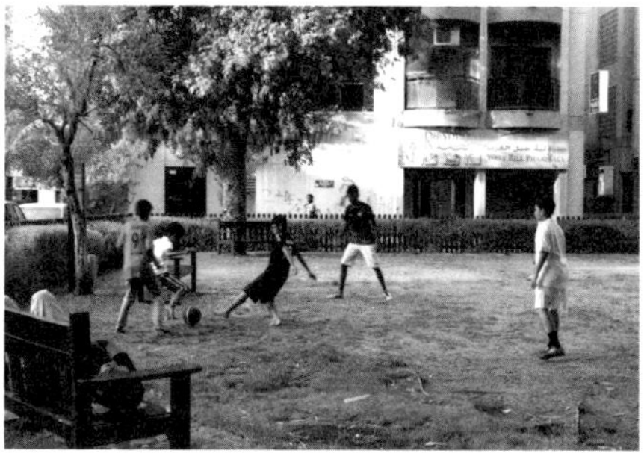

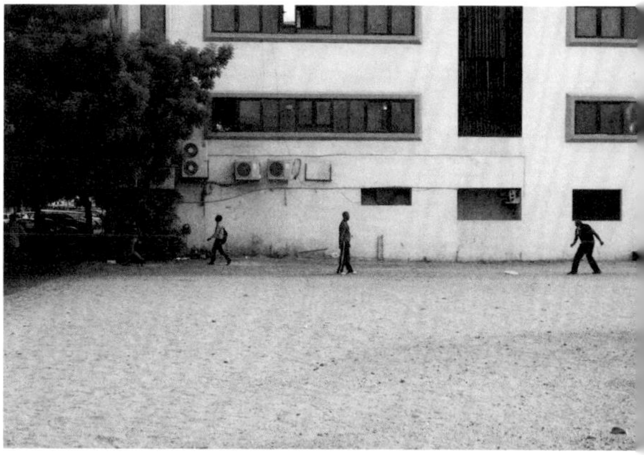

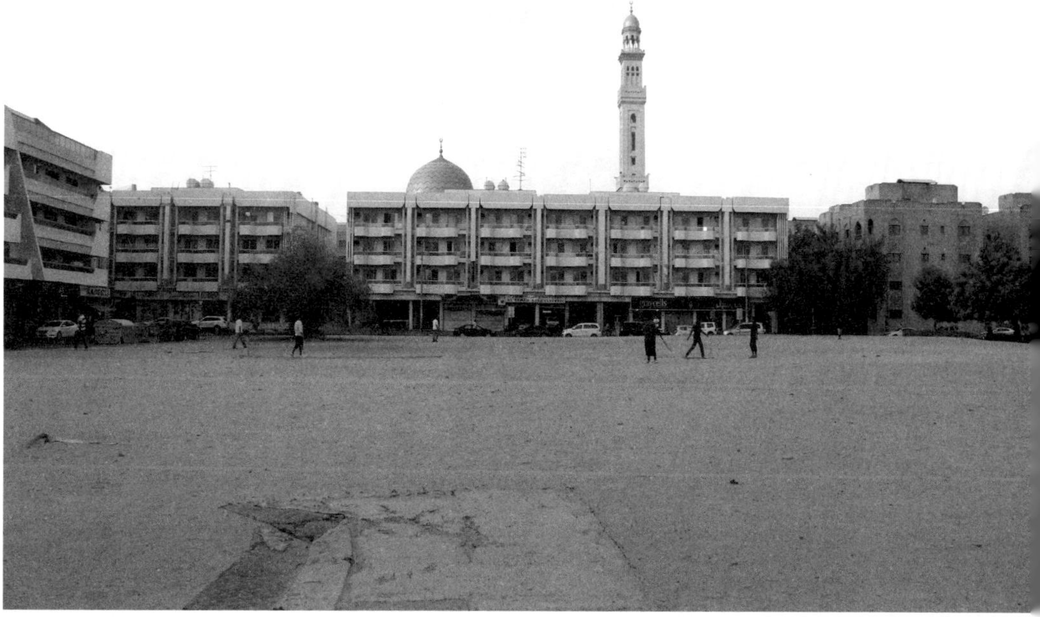

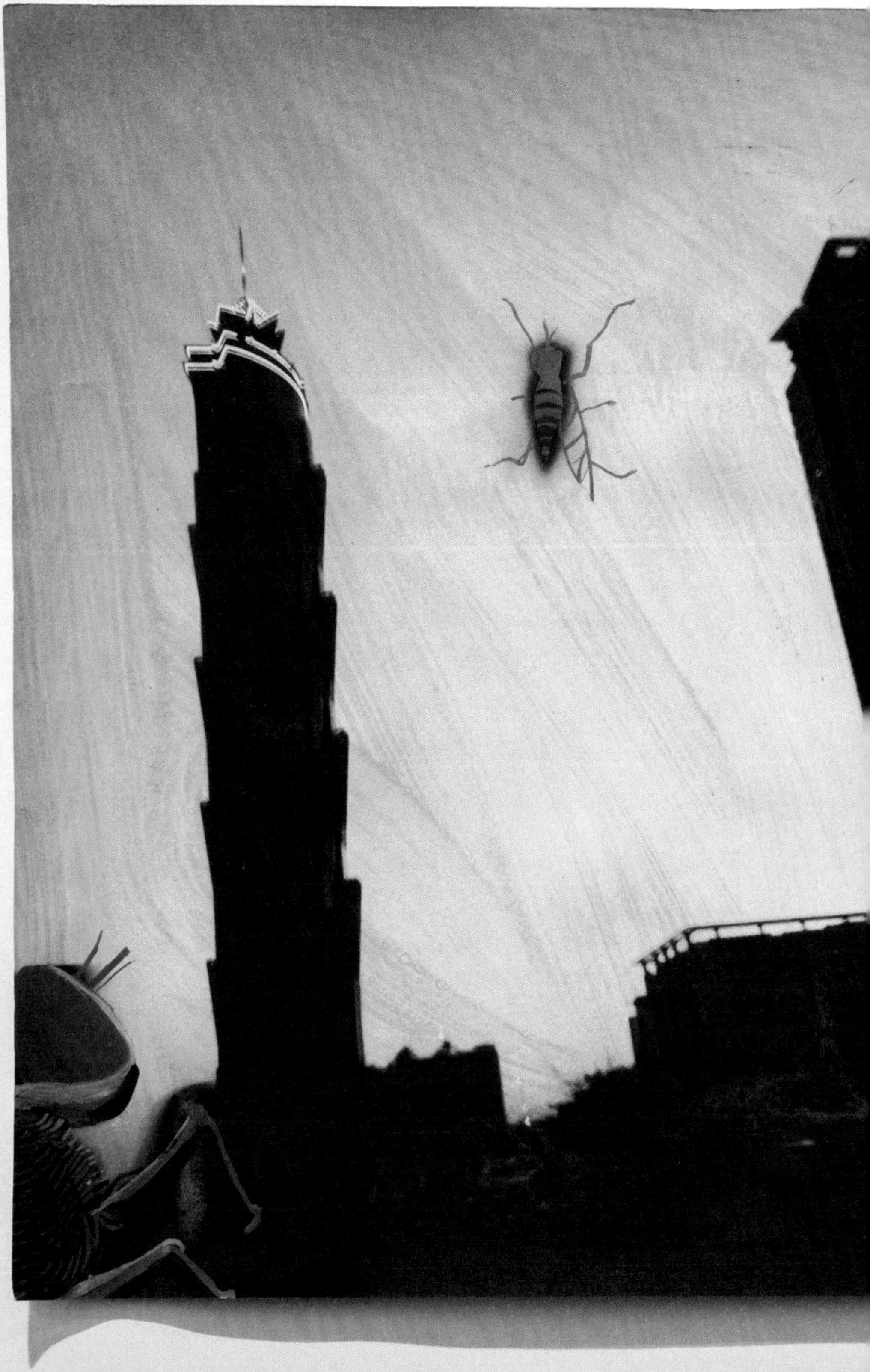

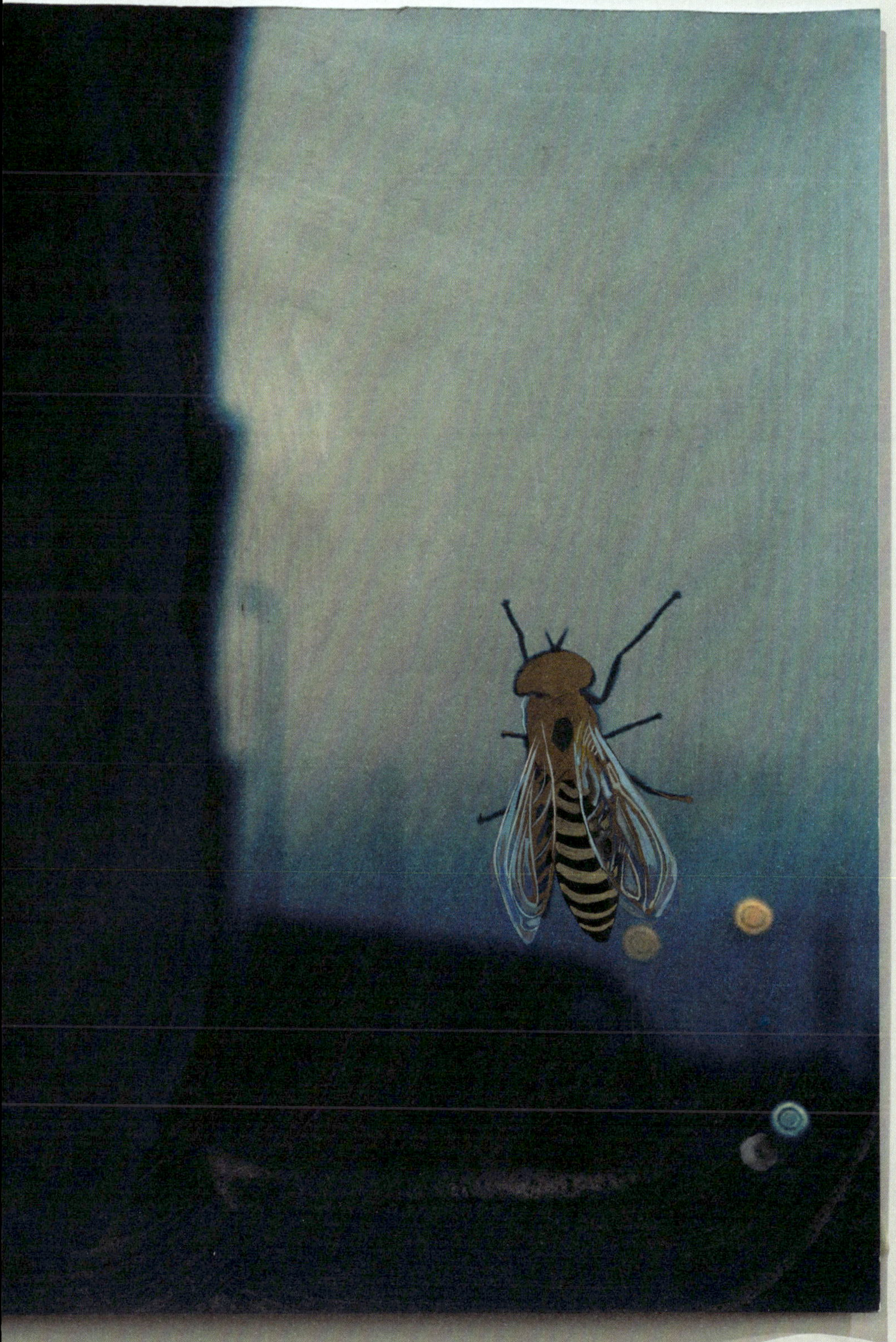

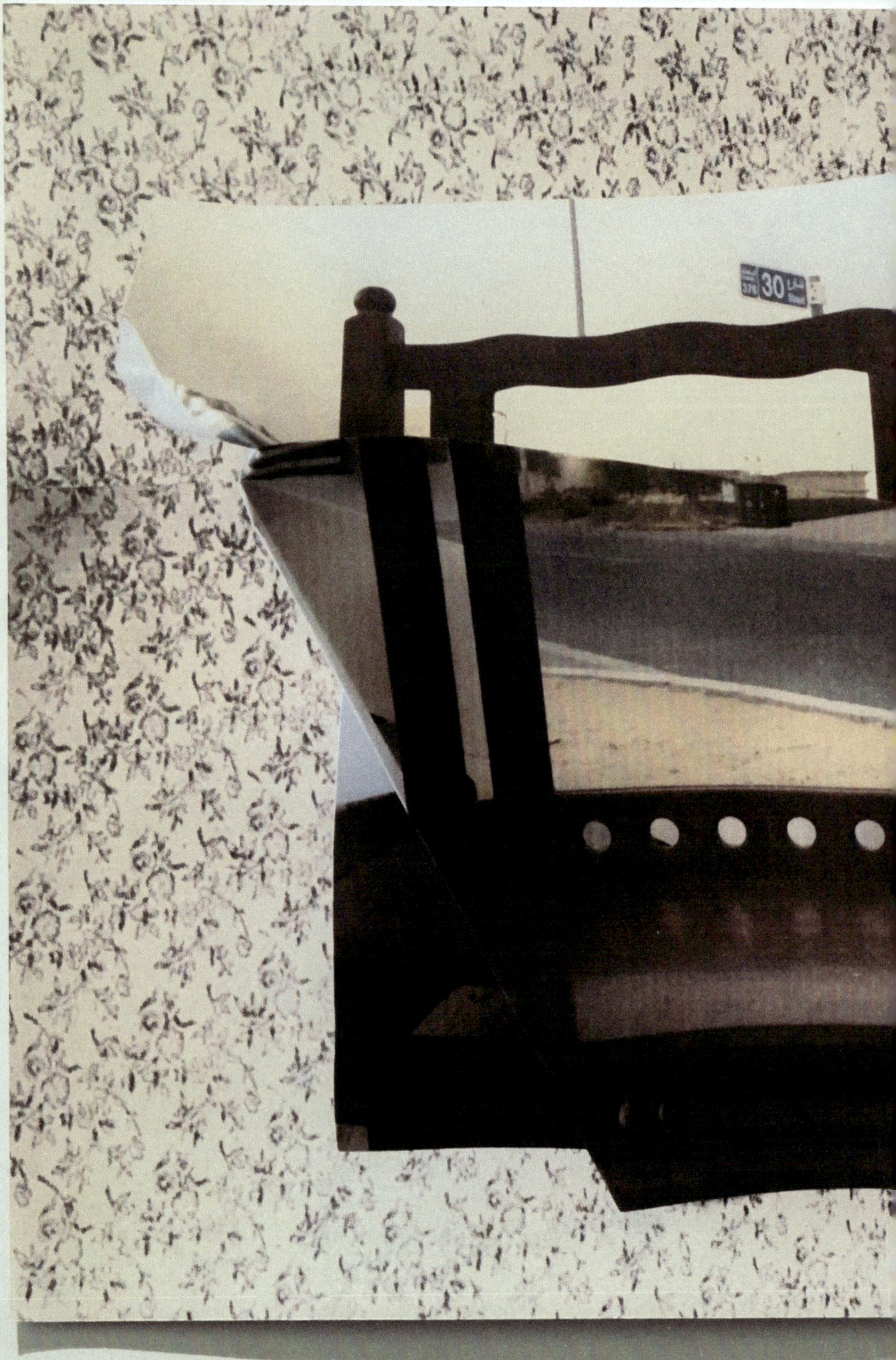
30

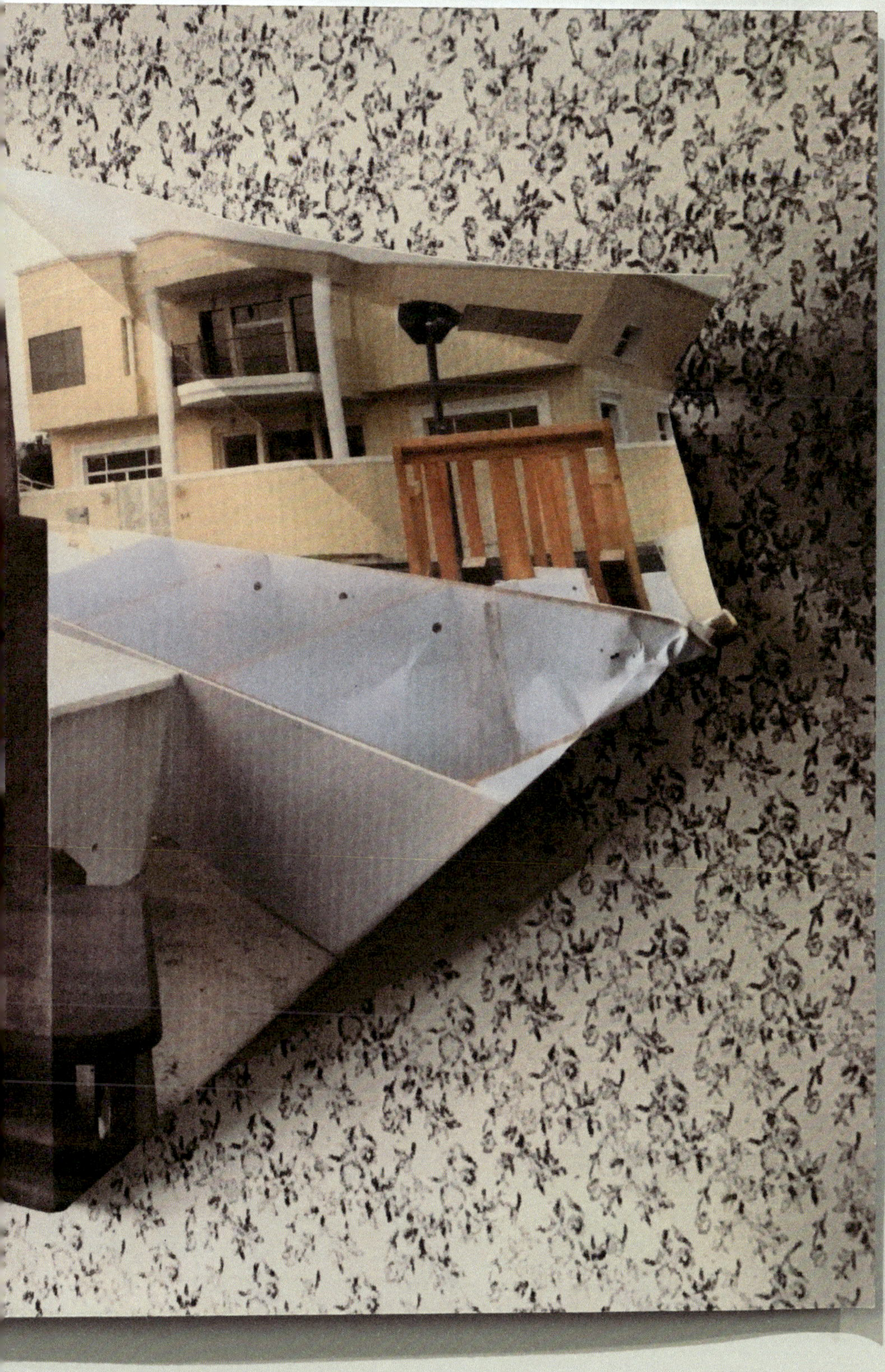

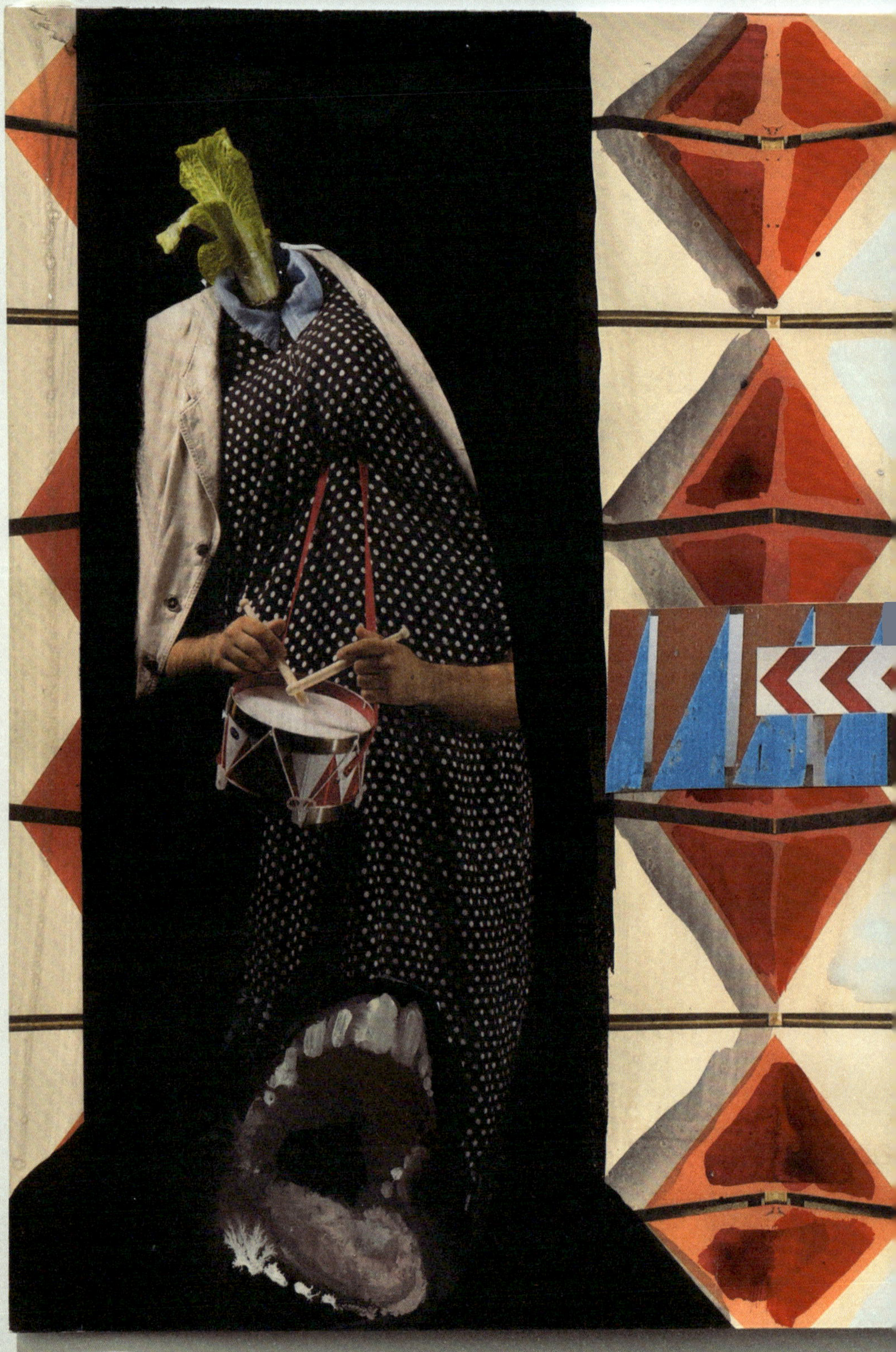

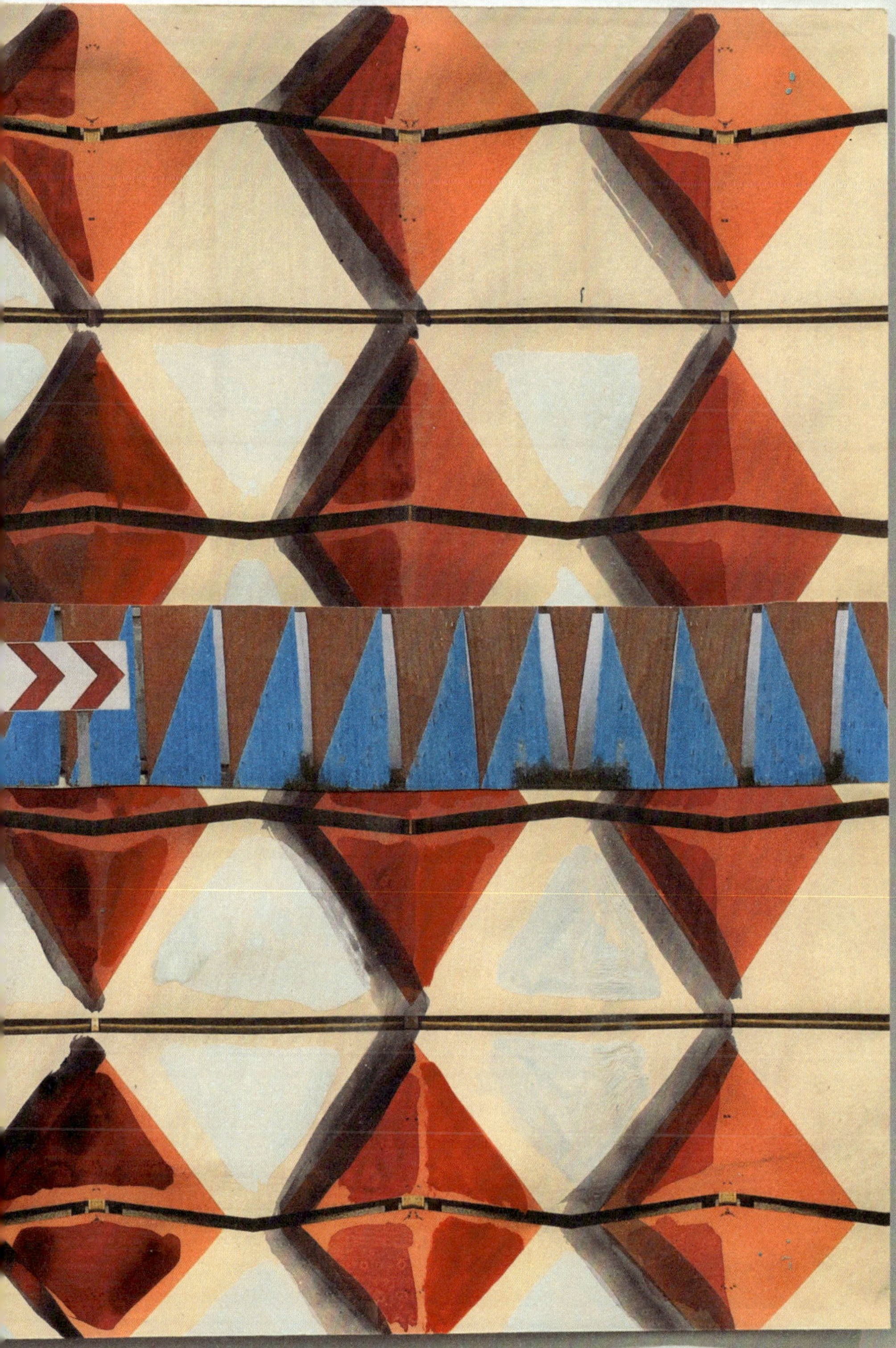

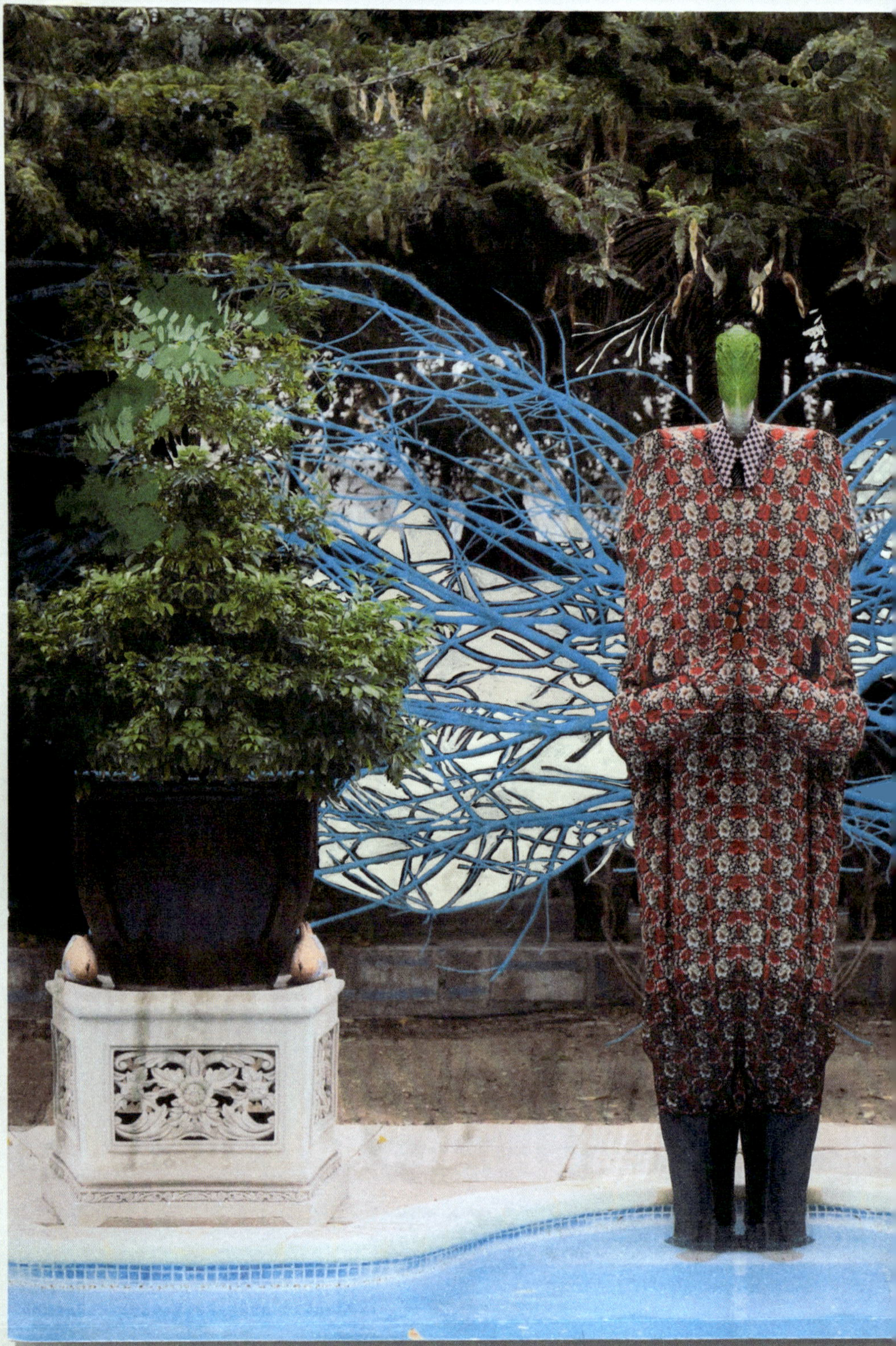

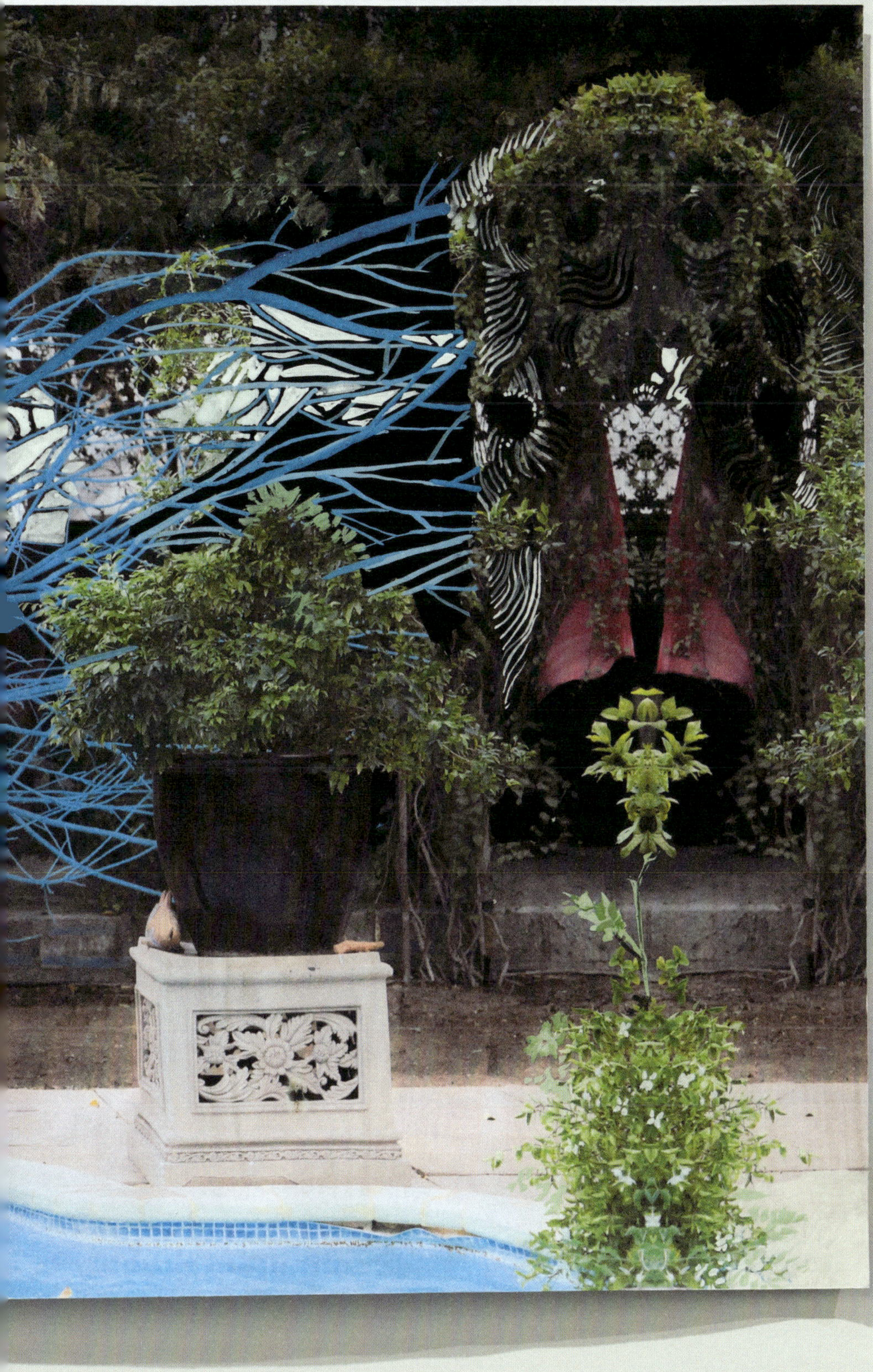

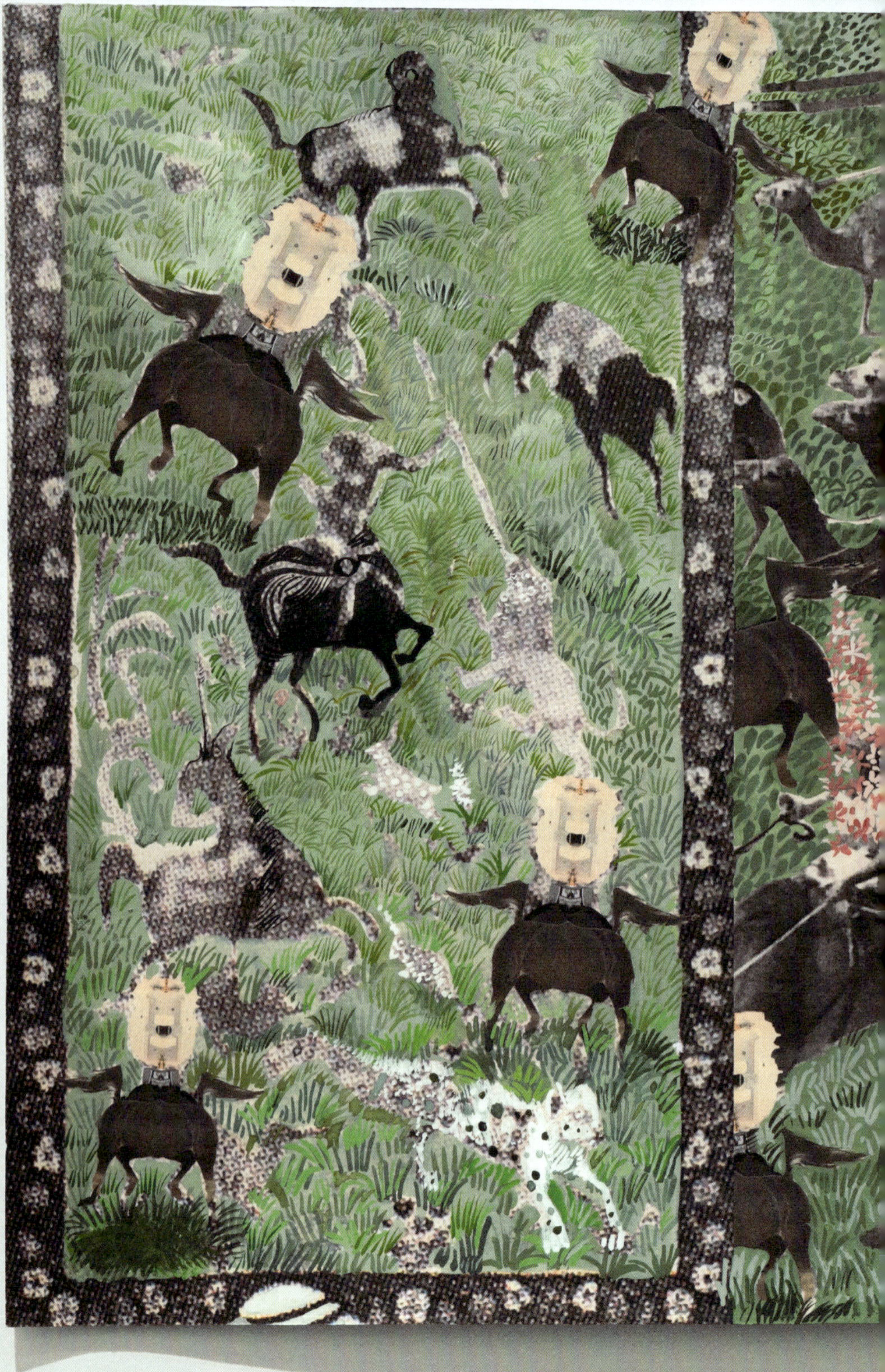

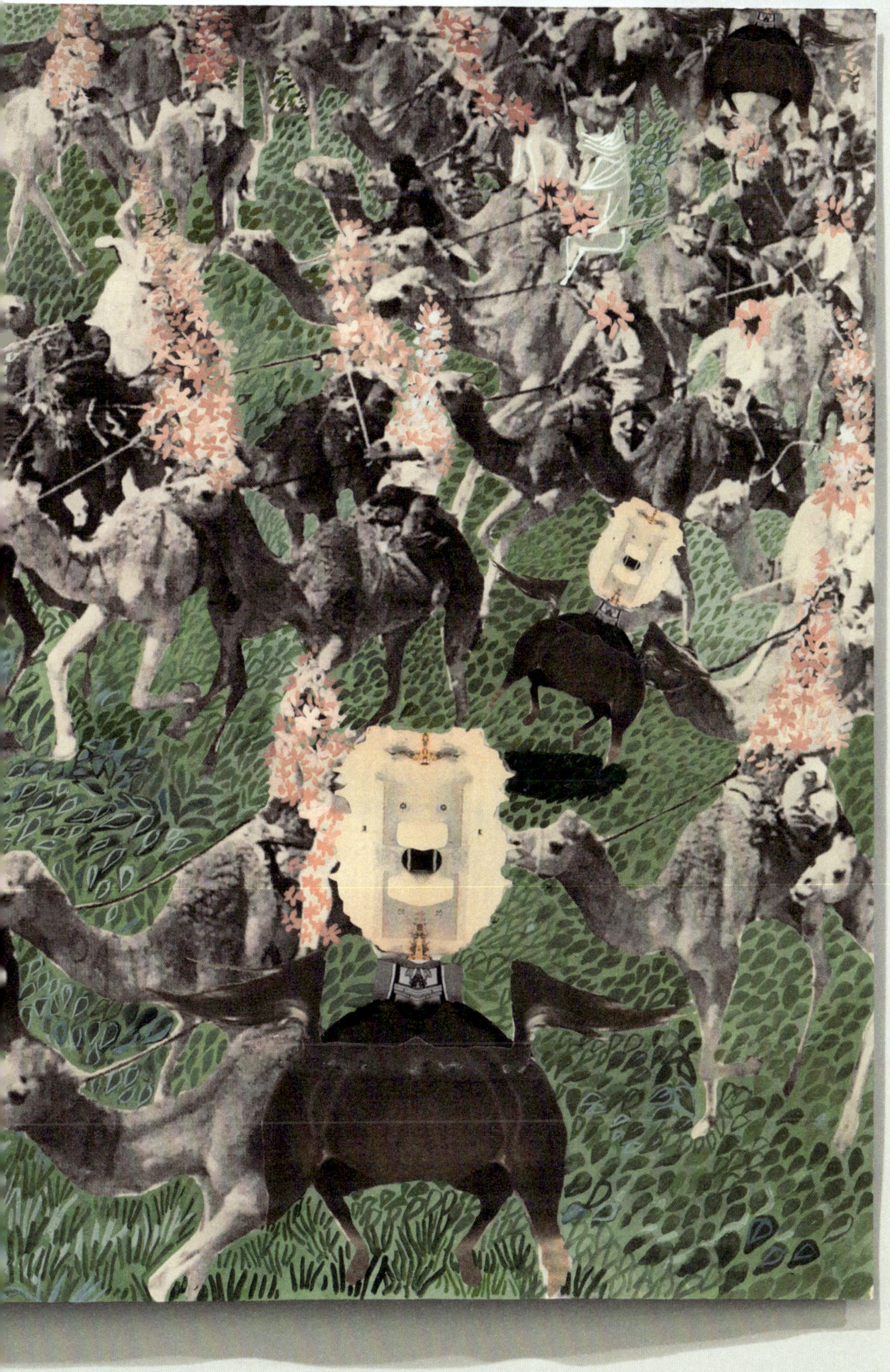

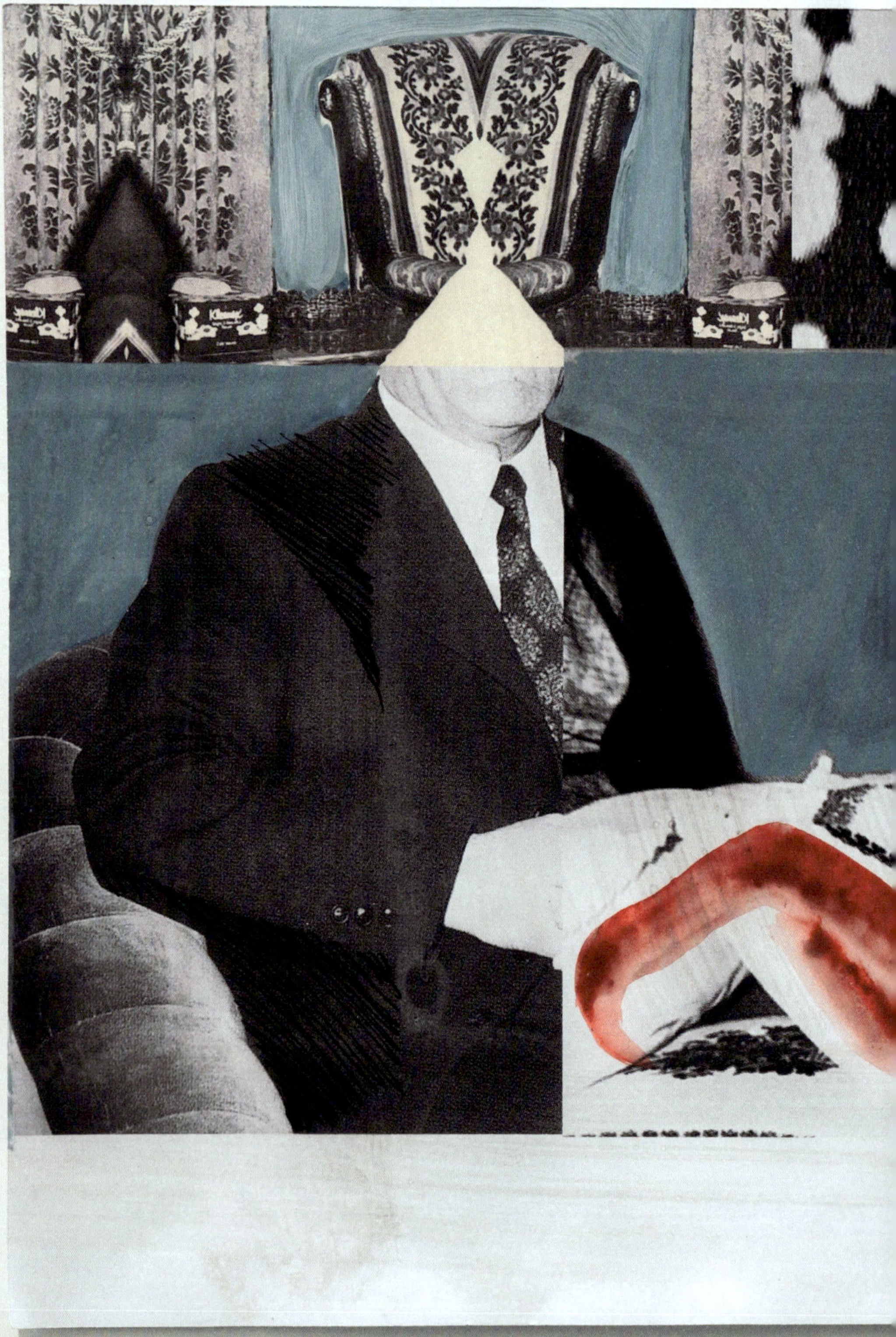

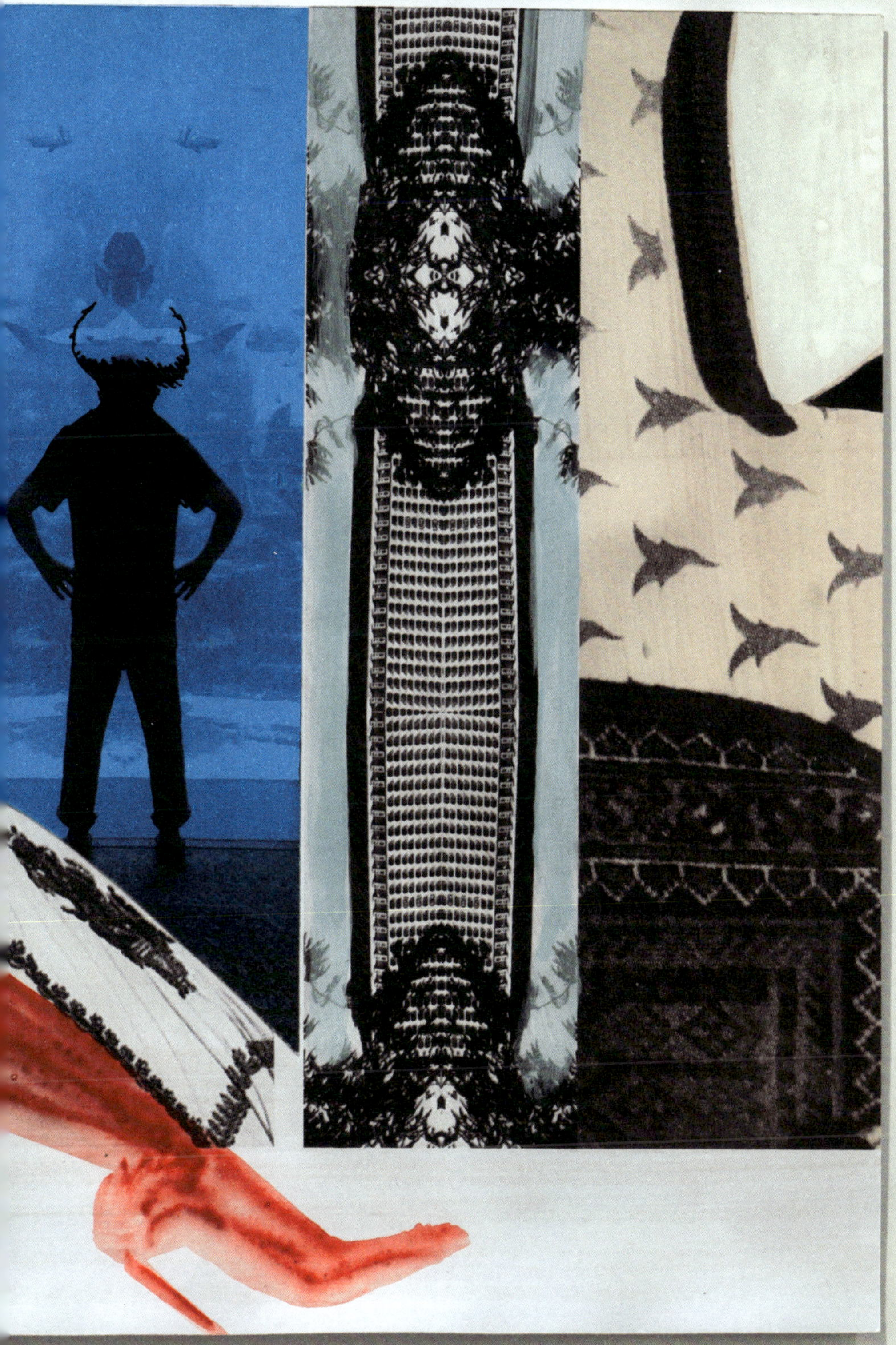

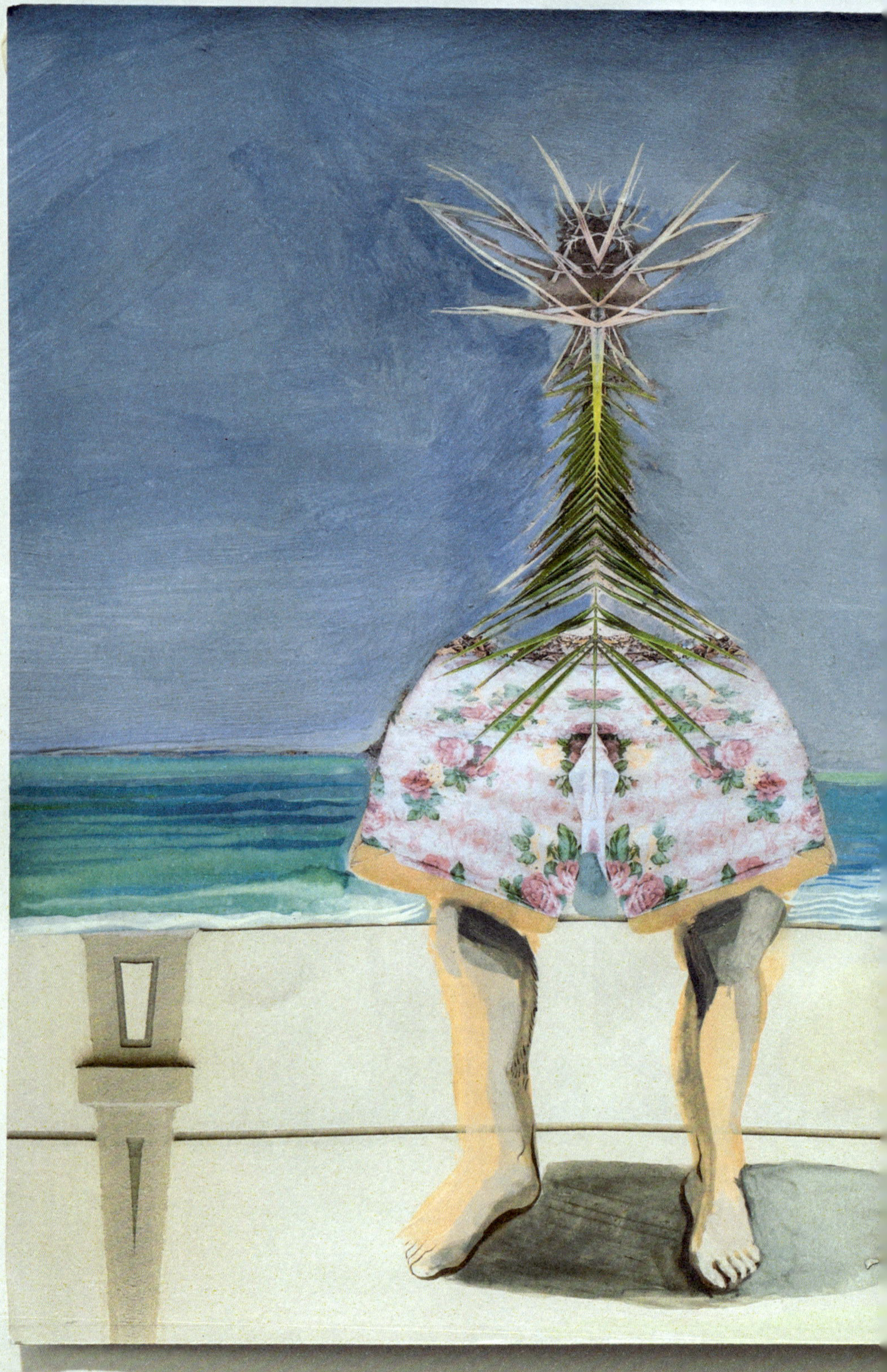

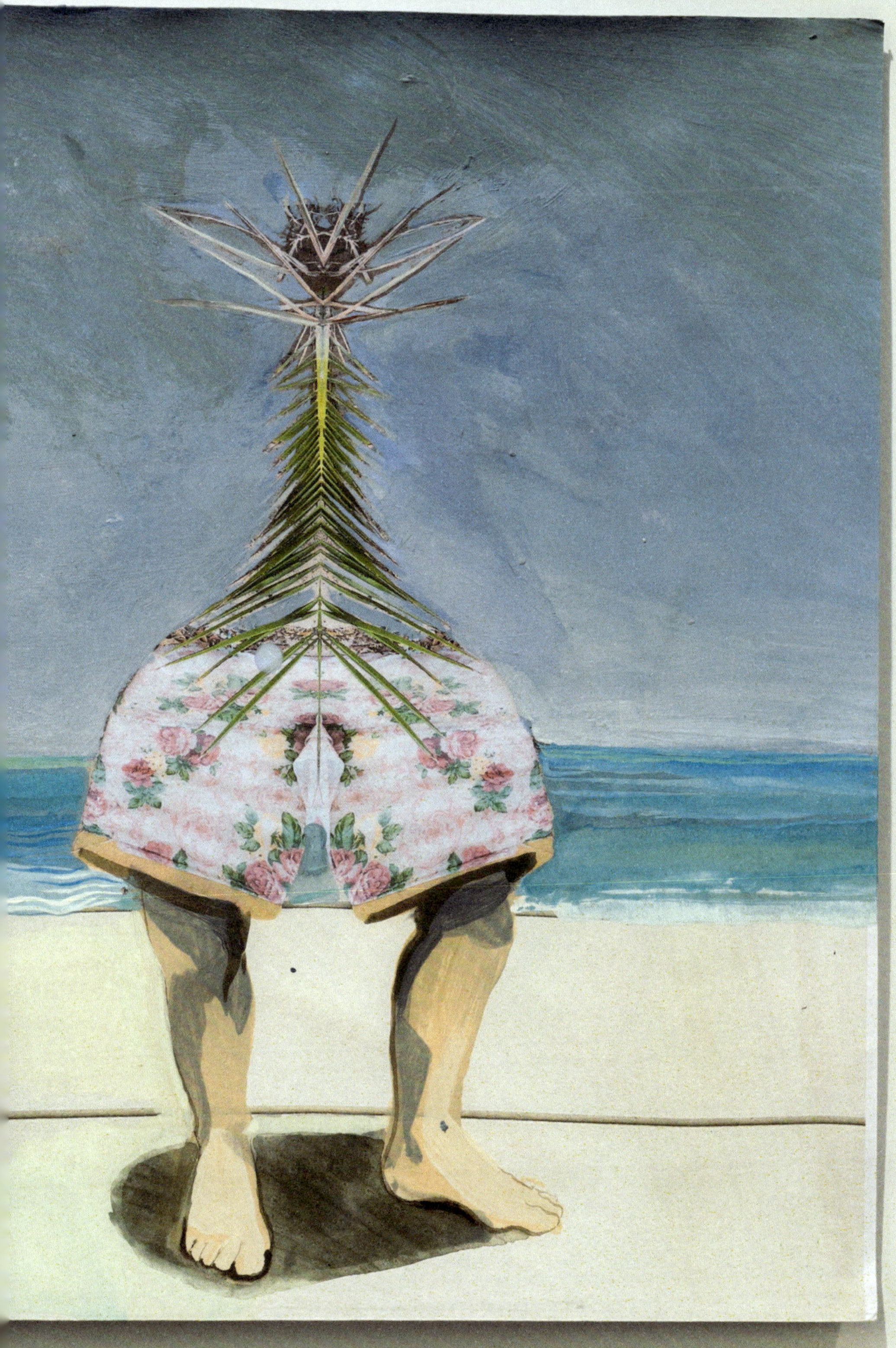

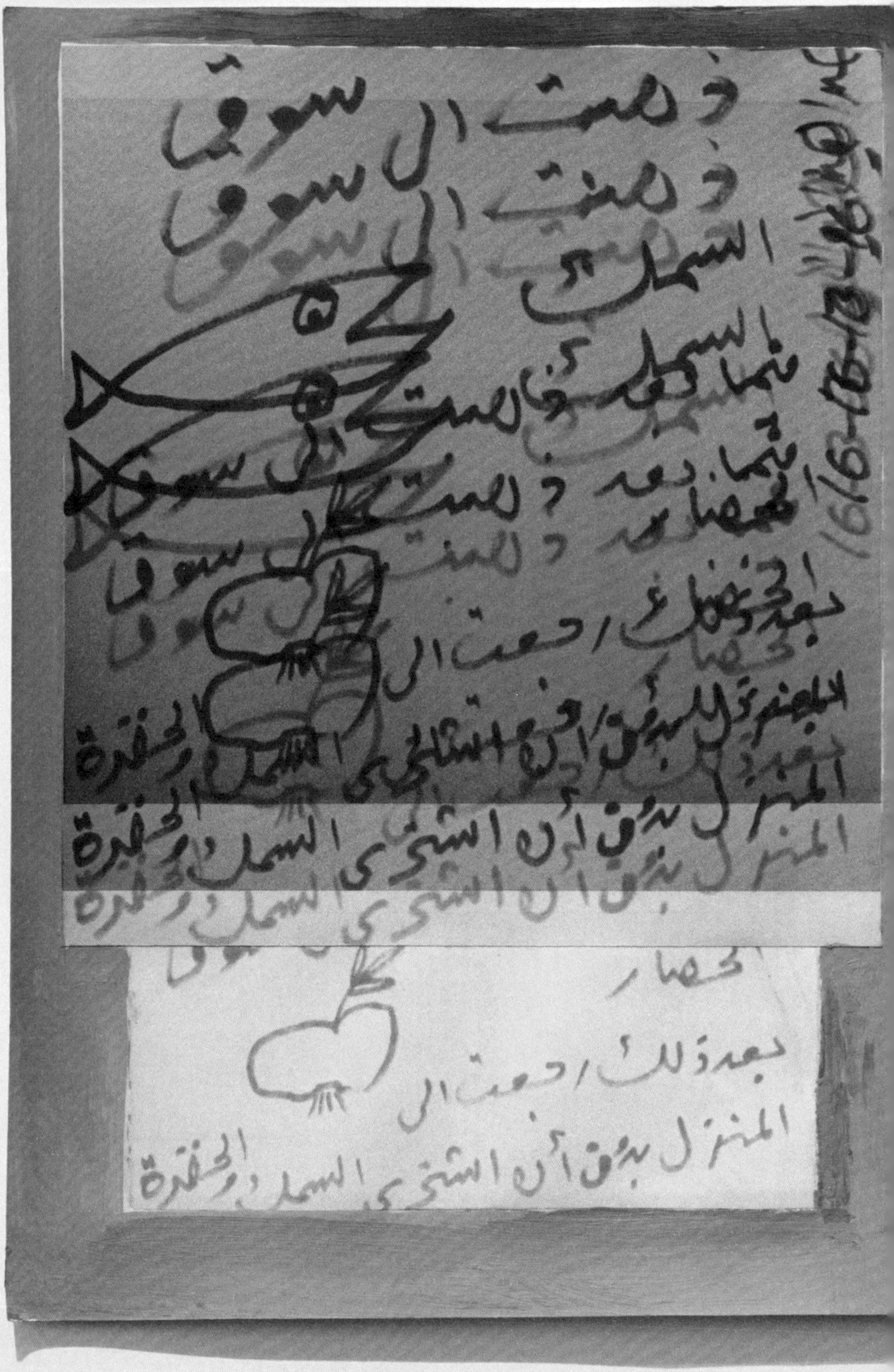

بعد ذلك رجعت الى
المنزل بدون أن اشتري السمك والخضرة

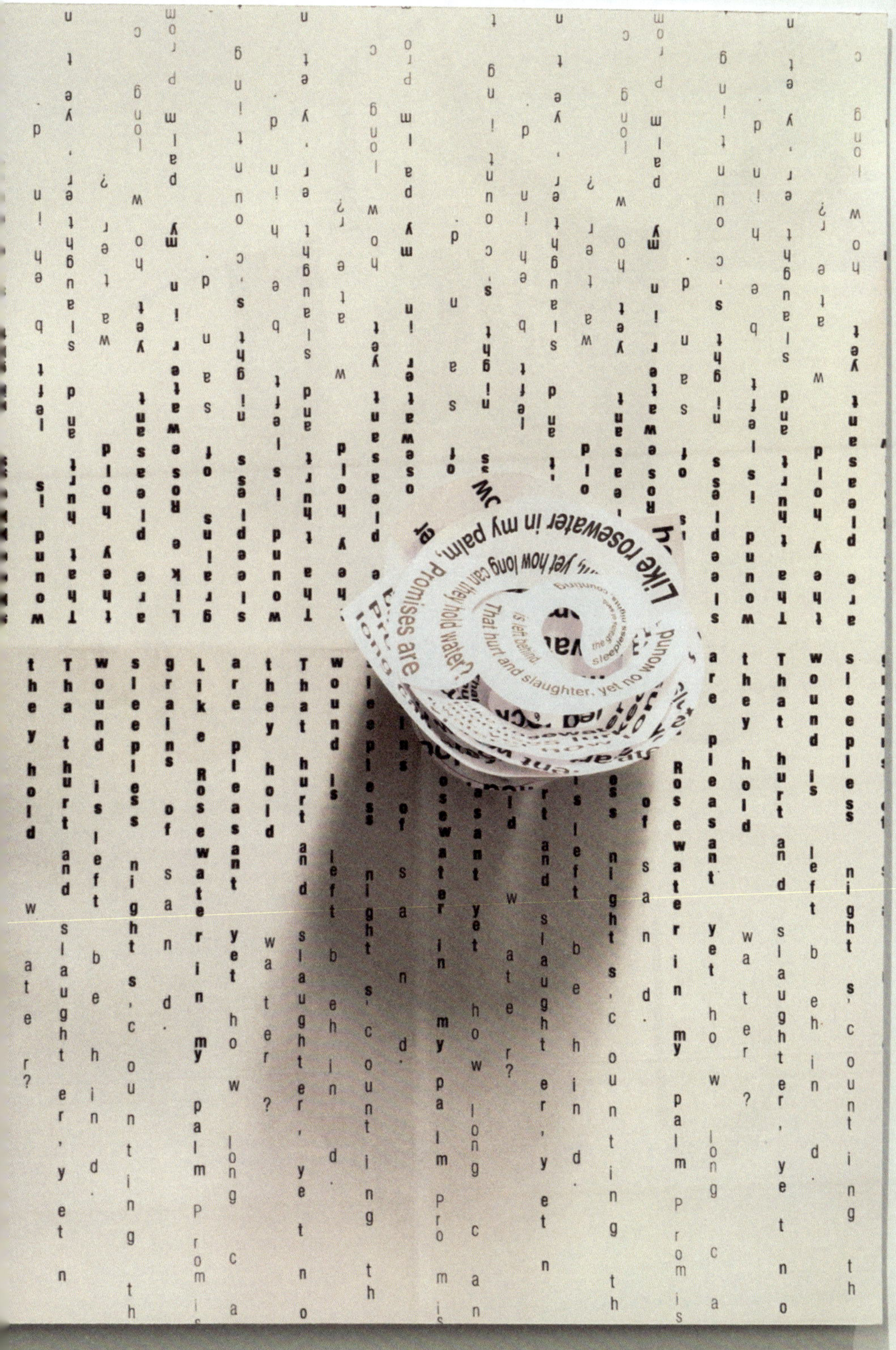

they hold water?
That hurt and slaughter, yet no
wound is left behind.
sleepless nights, counting th
grains of sand.
Like Rosewater in my palm Promis
are pleasant yet how long ca
Like rosewater in my palm,
yet how long can they hold water
Promises are
That hurt and slaughter, yet no wou
is left behind
the grains of
sleepless nights, counting

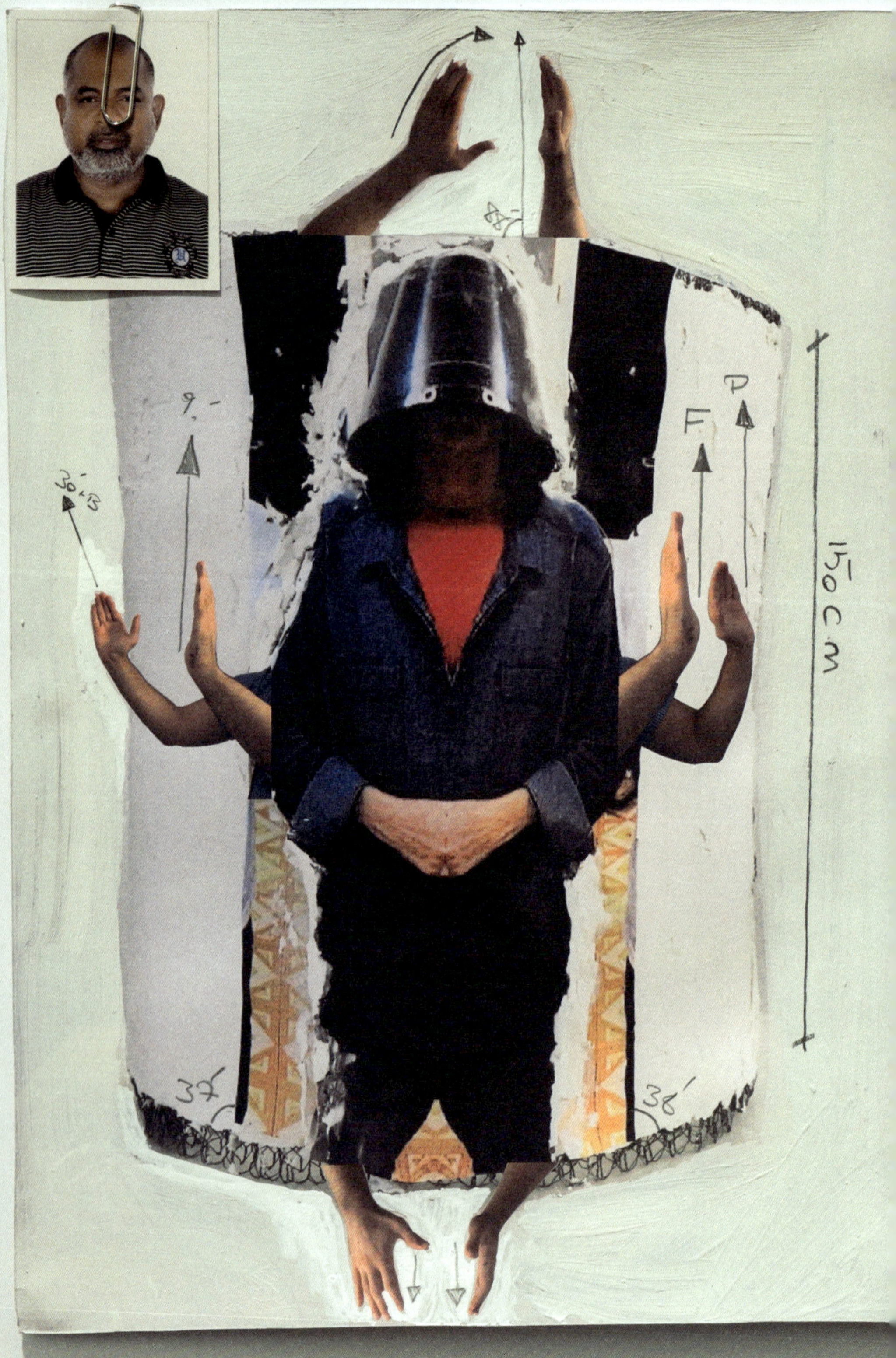
P
F
150 cm

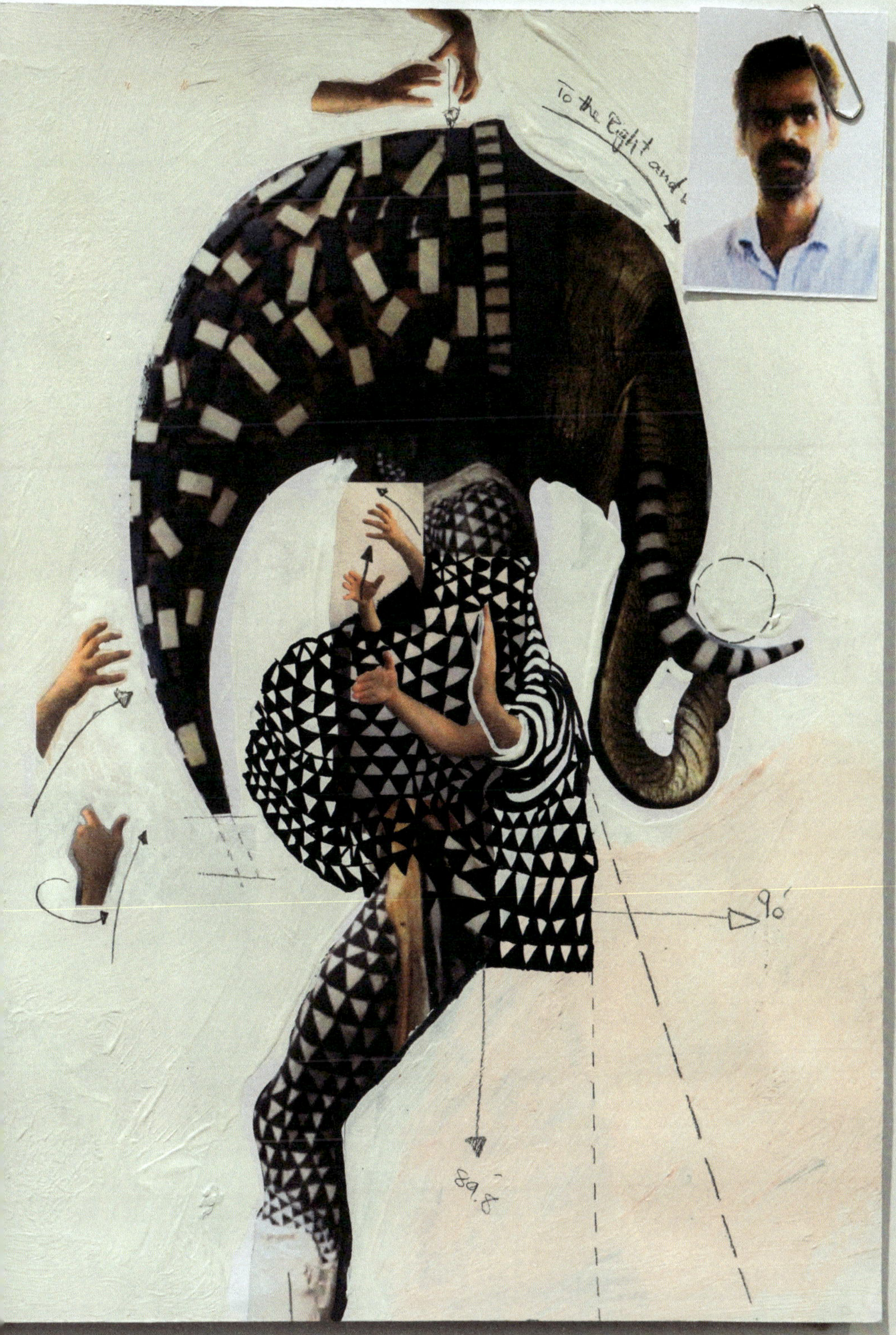
To the Right and
90
89.8

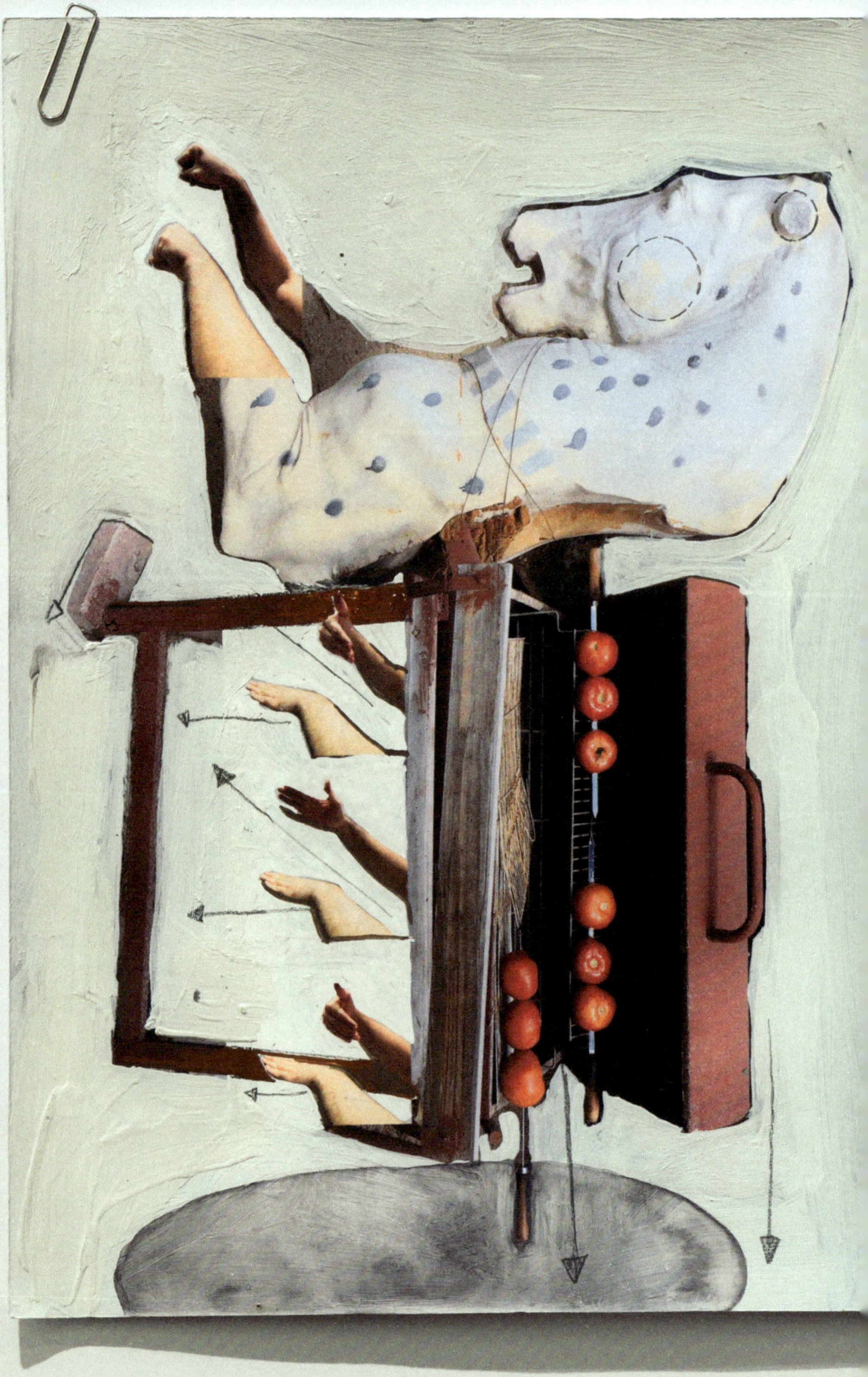

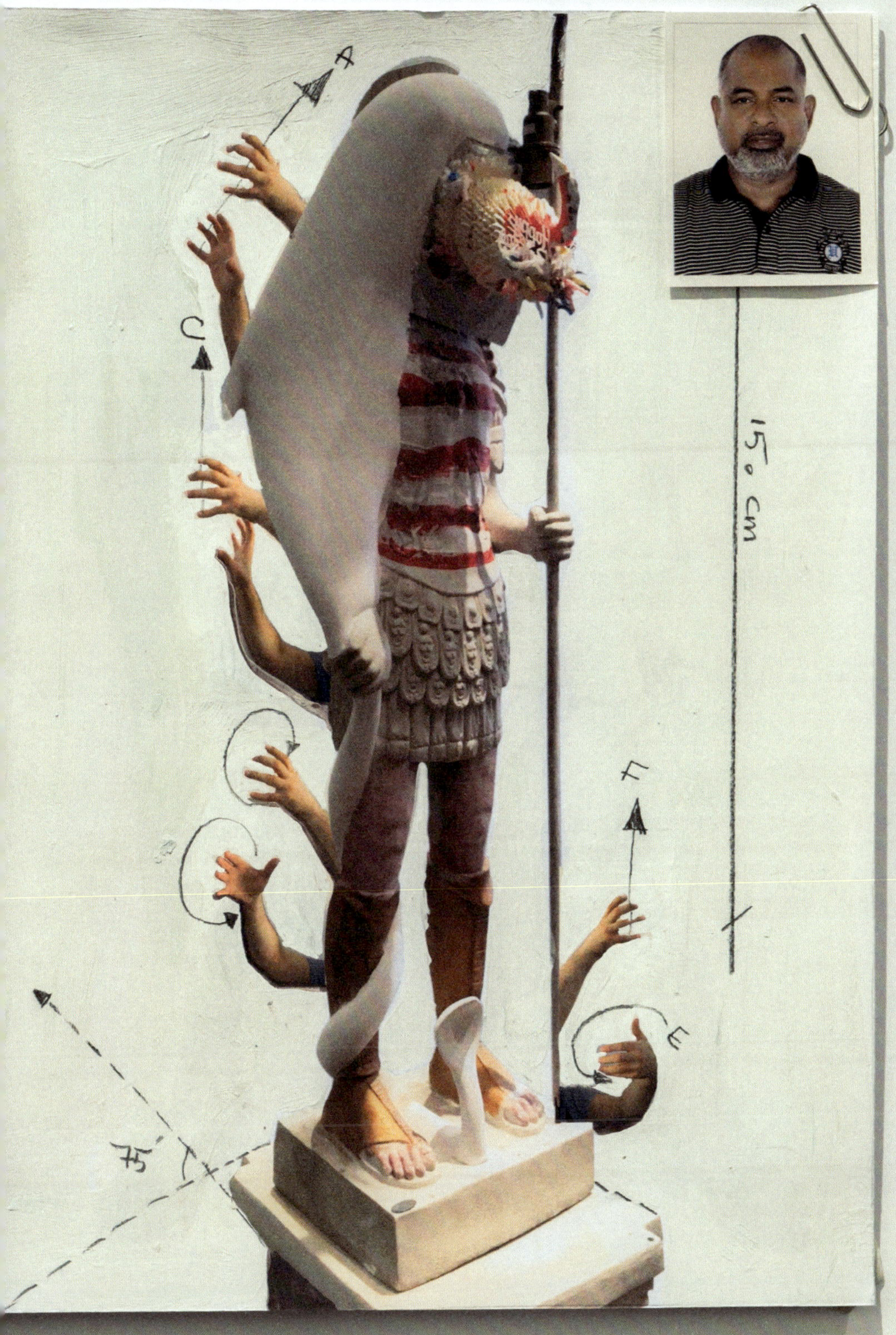
A
C
150 cm
F
E
75

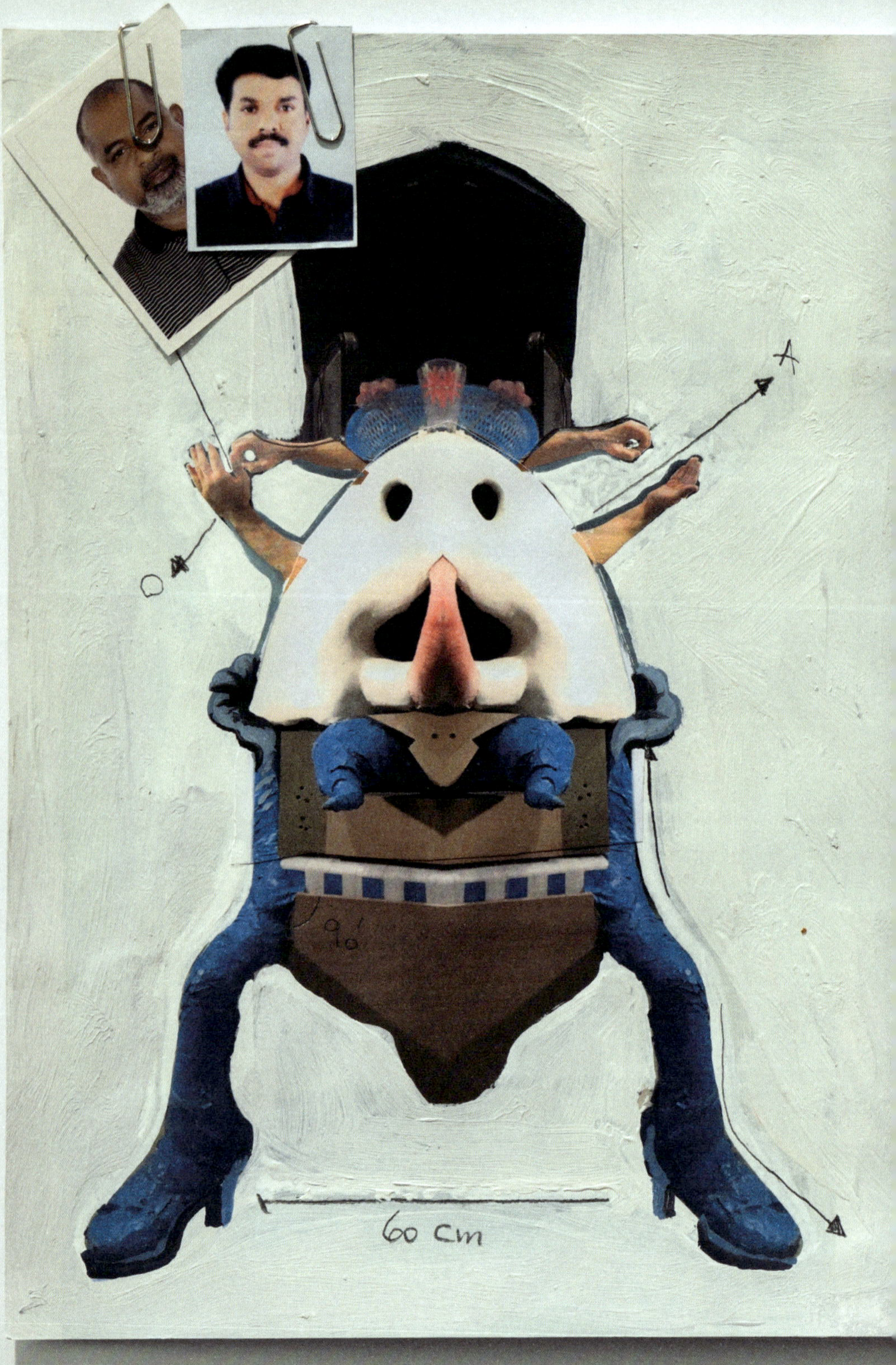
A
60 cm

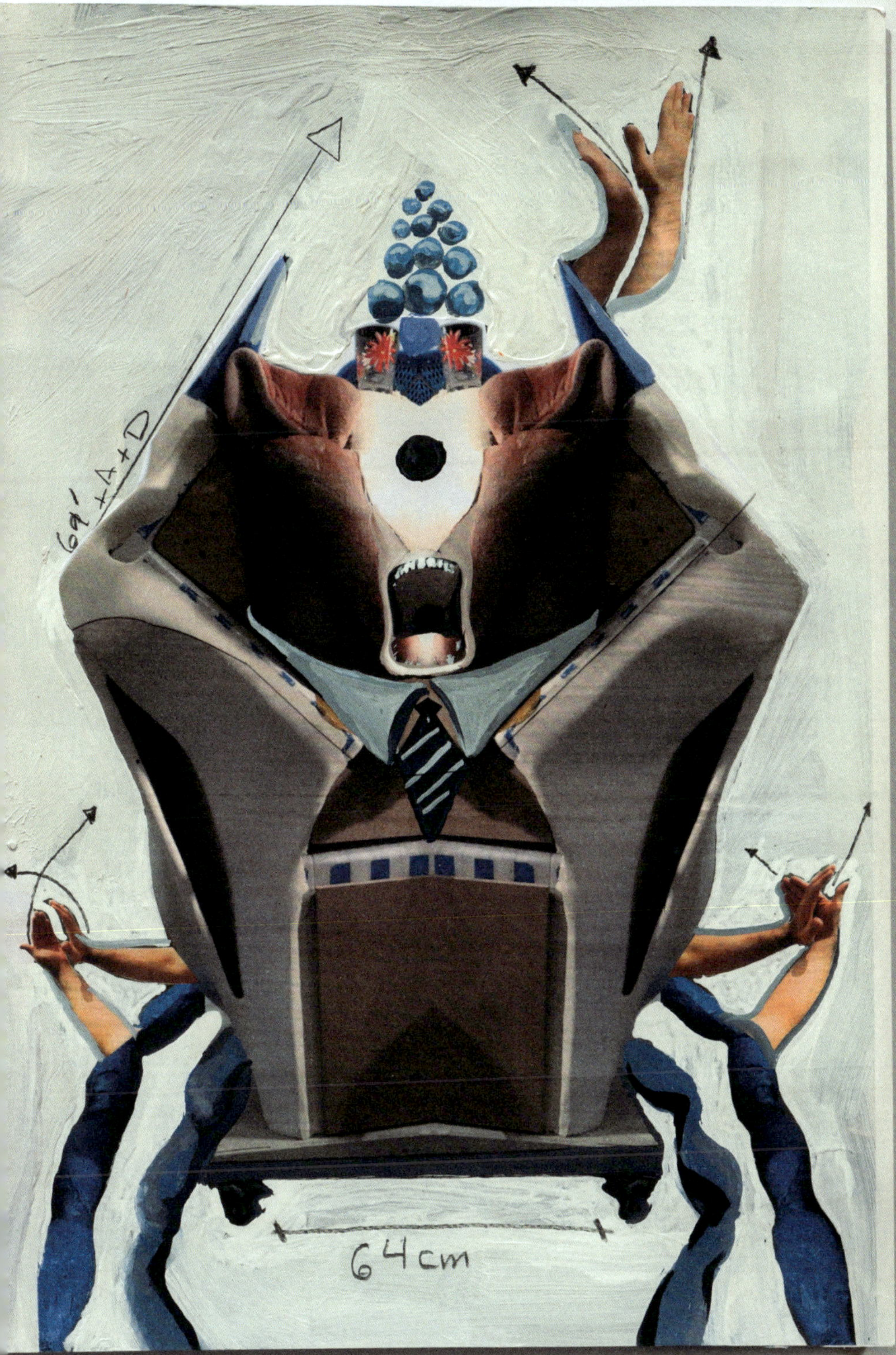
69' +A+D
64cm

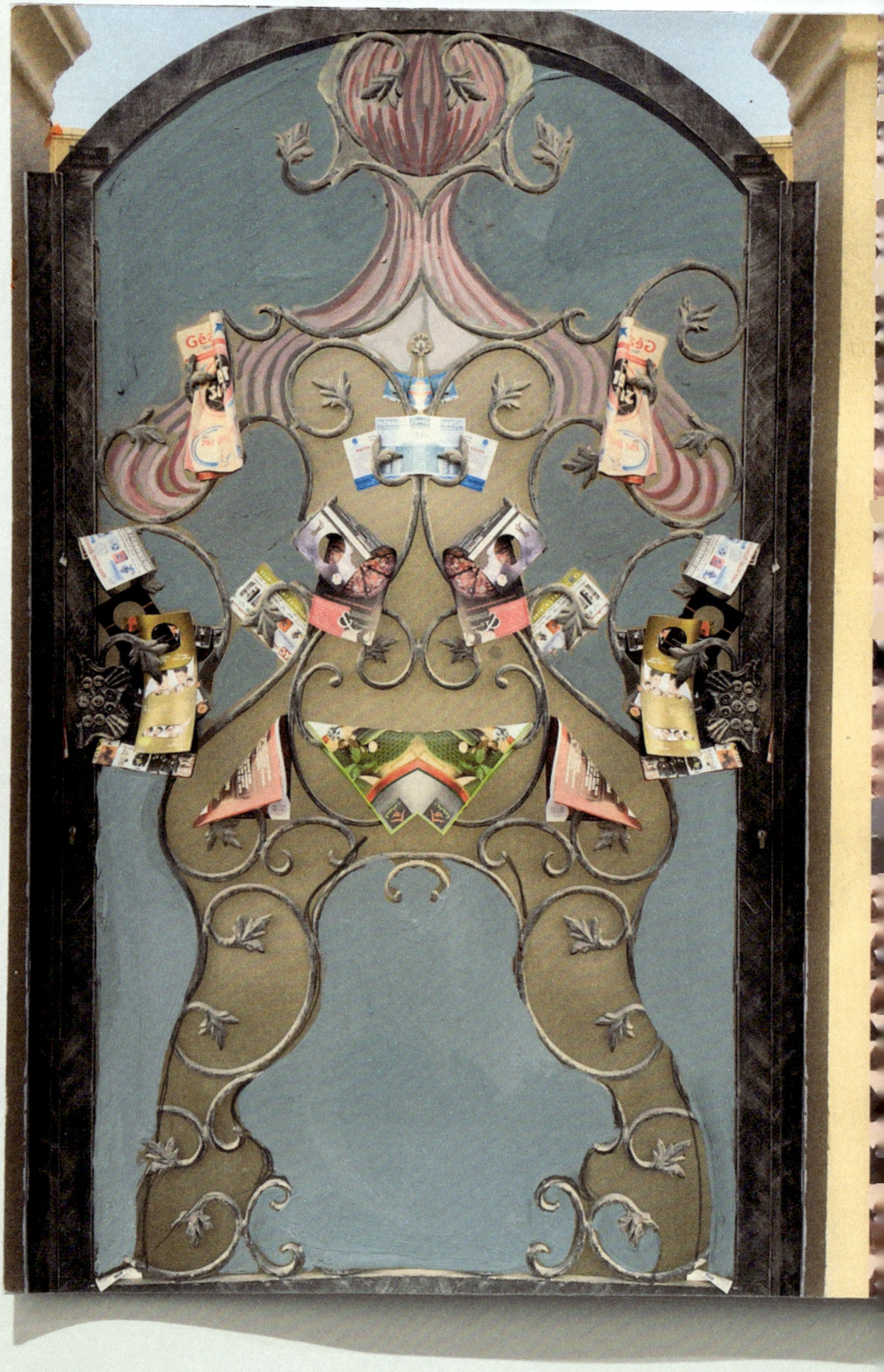

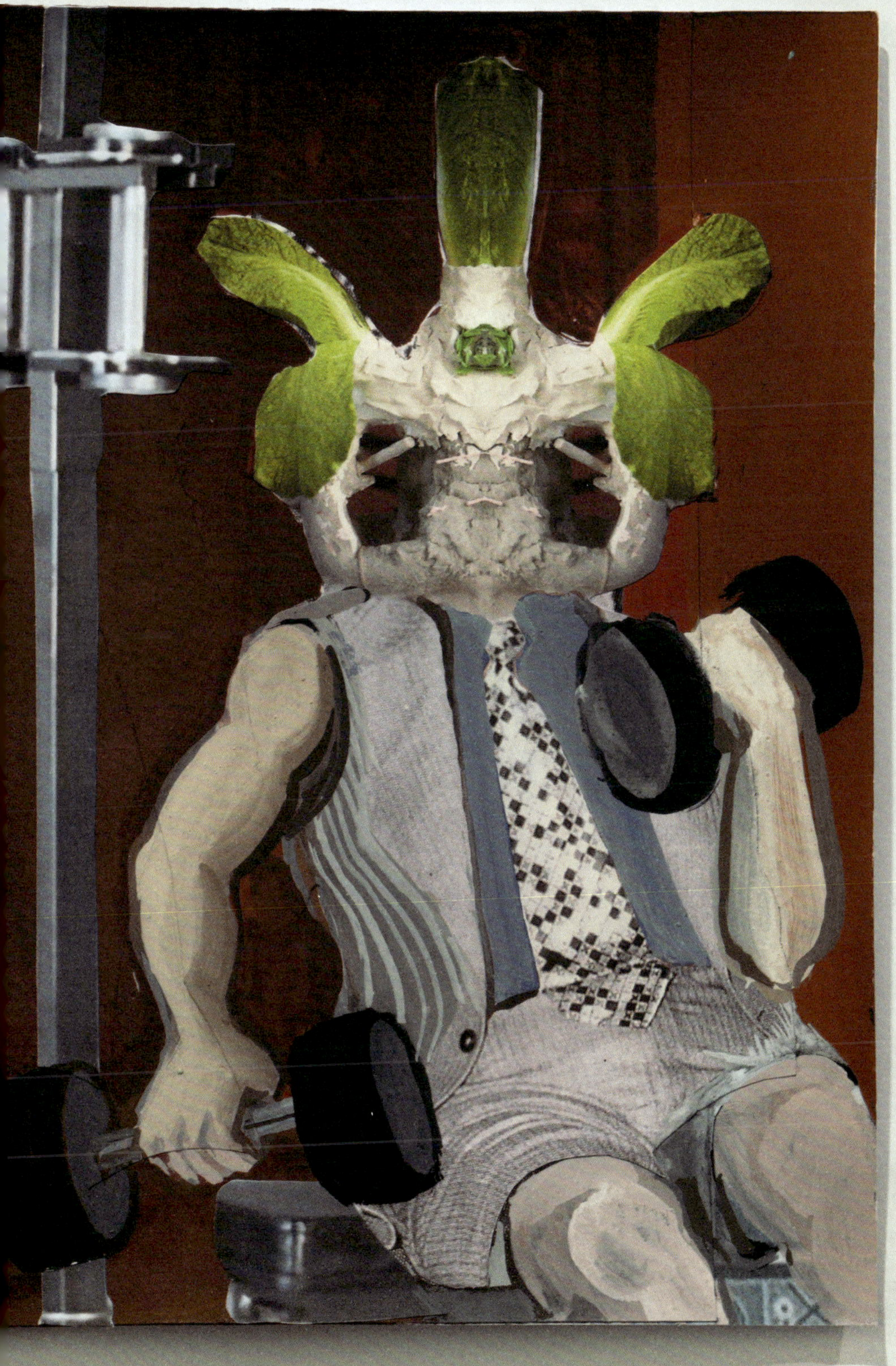

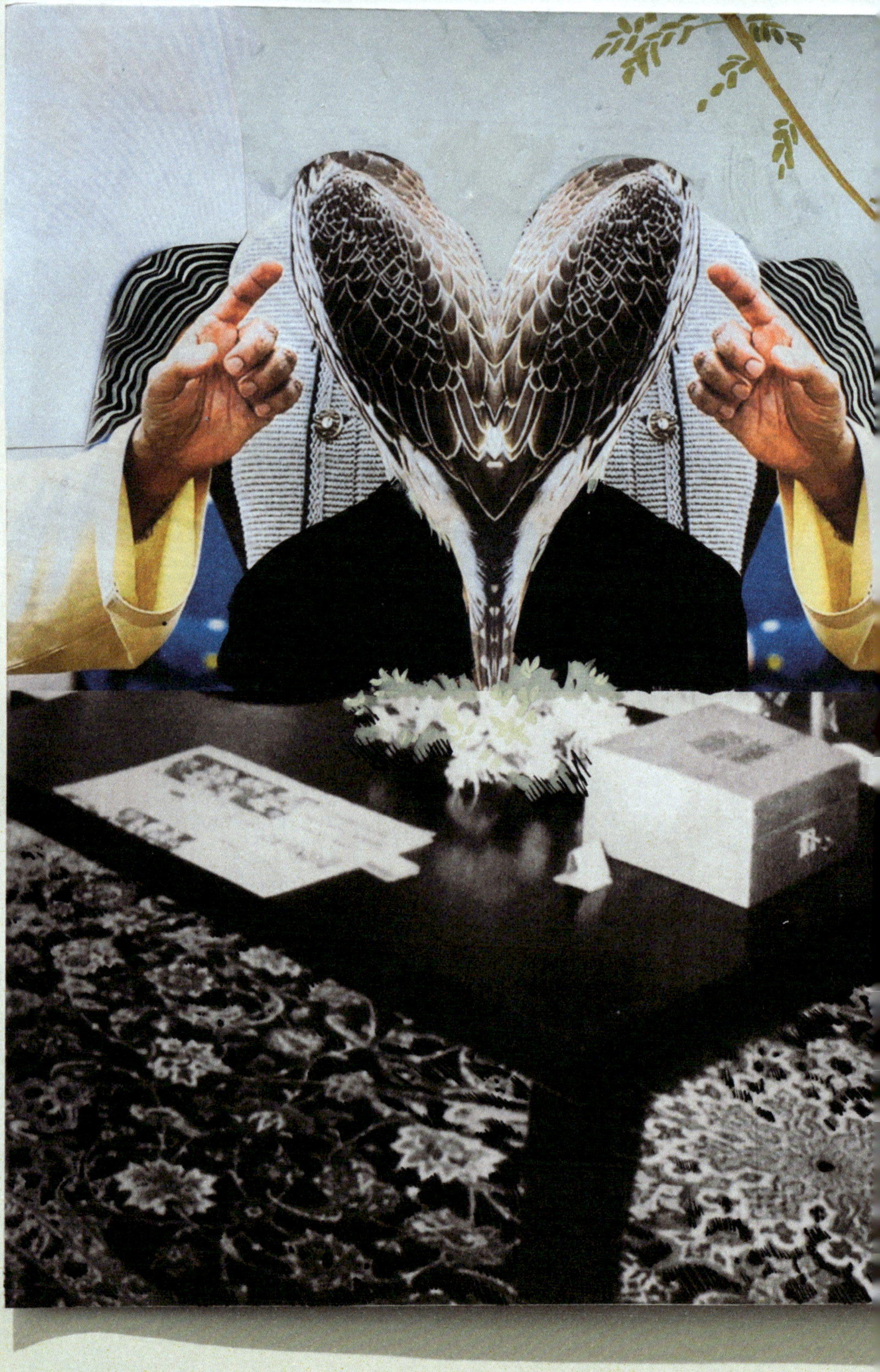

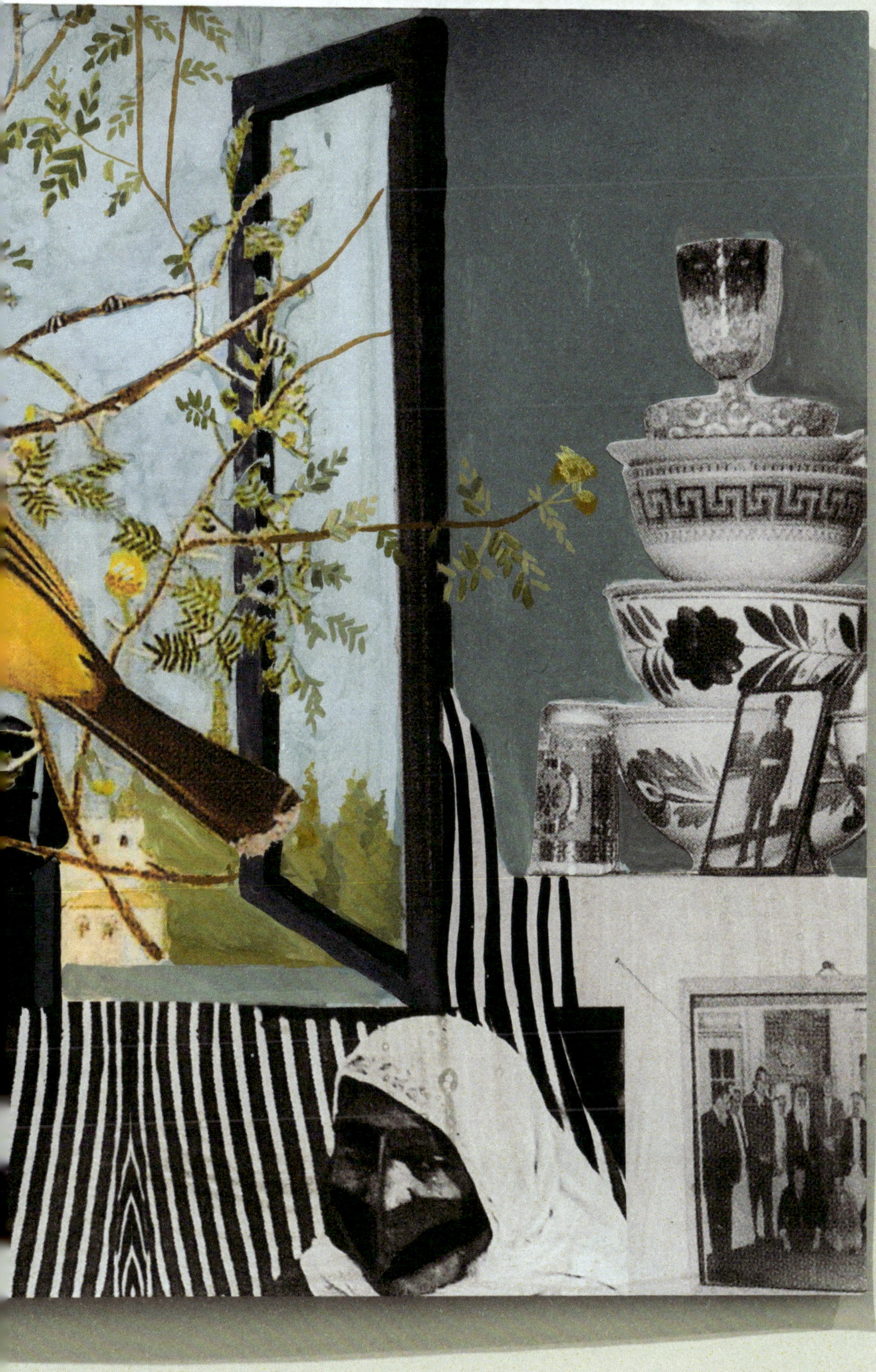

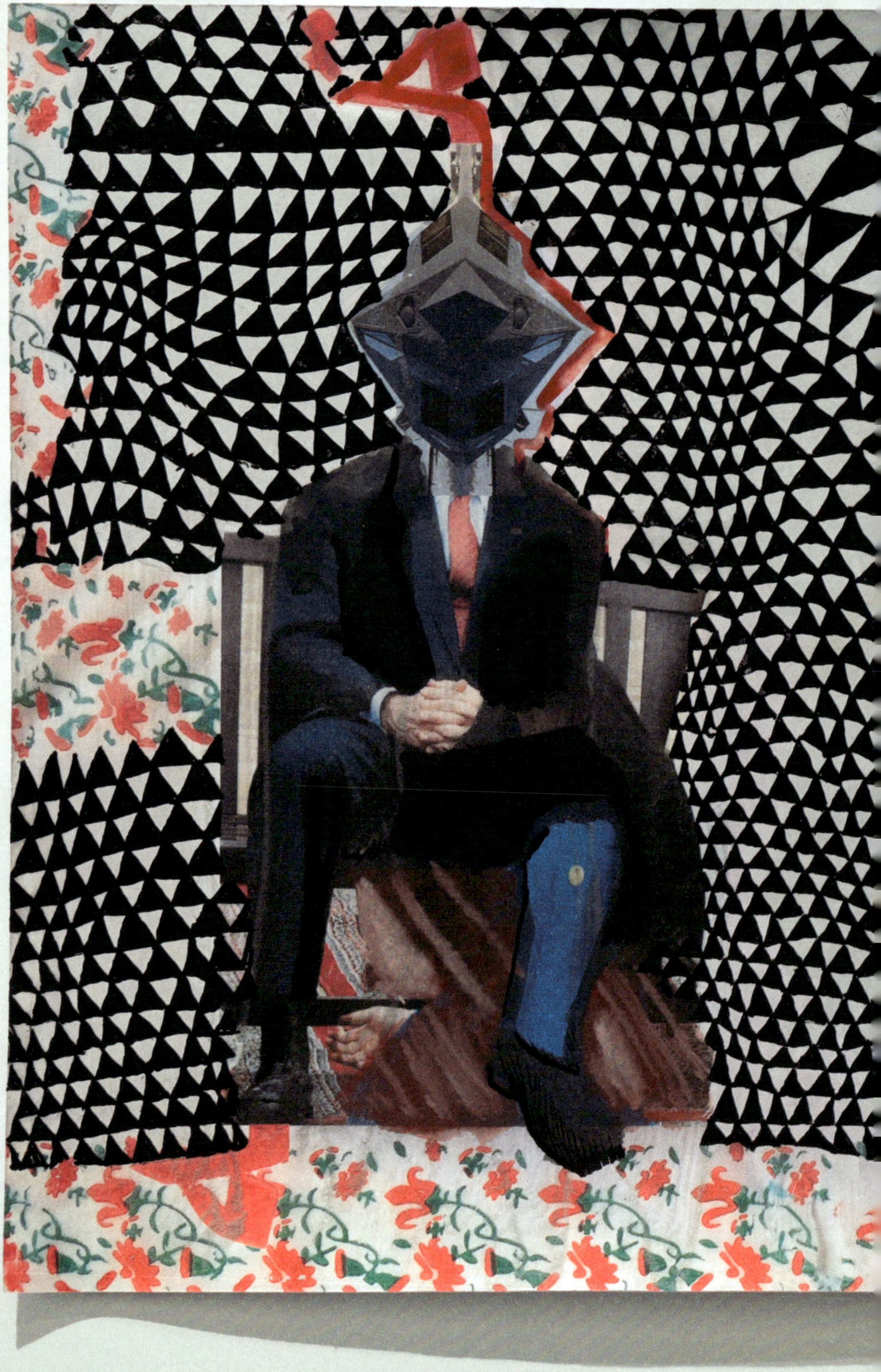

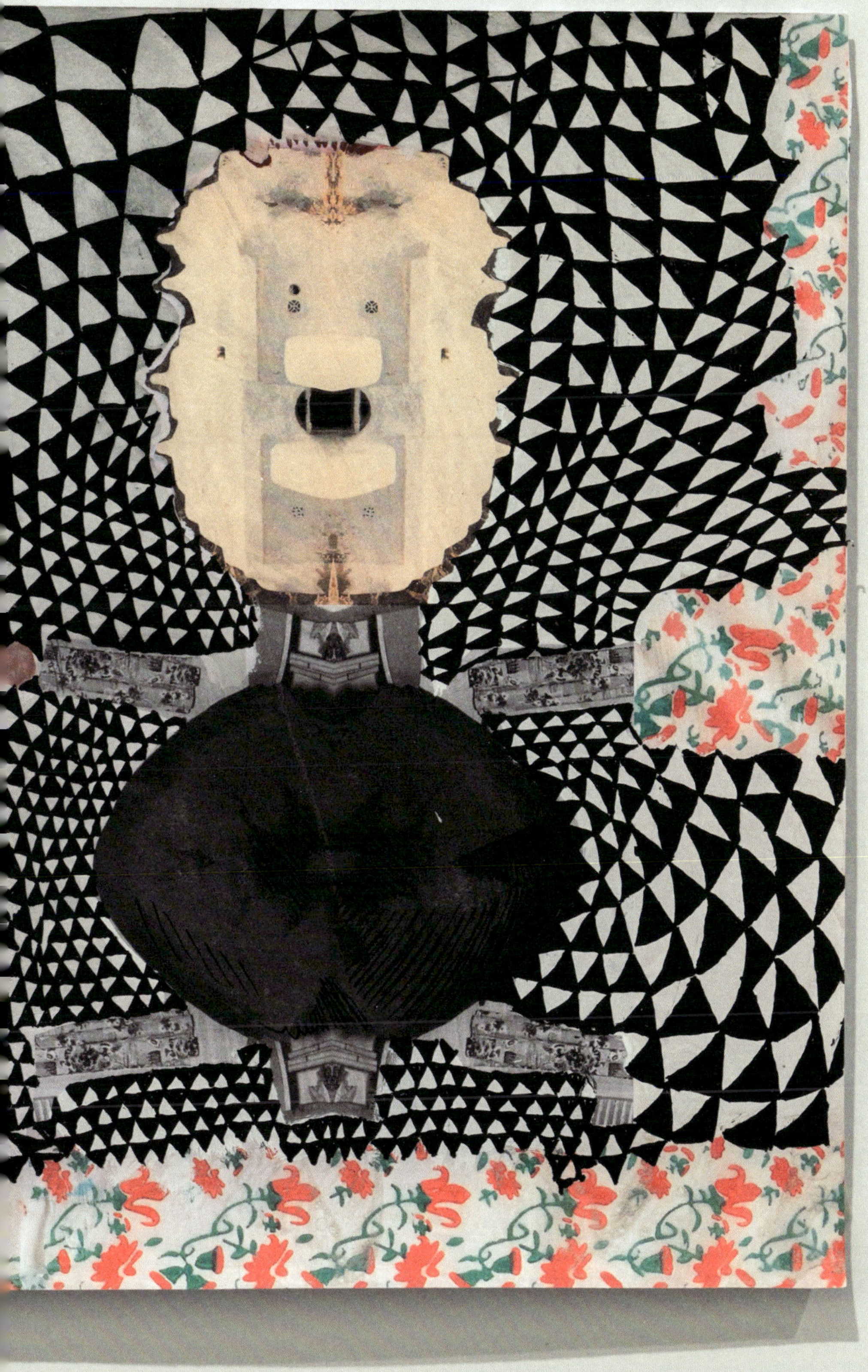

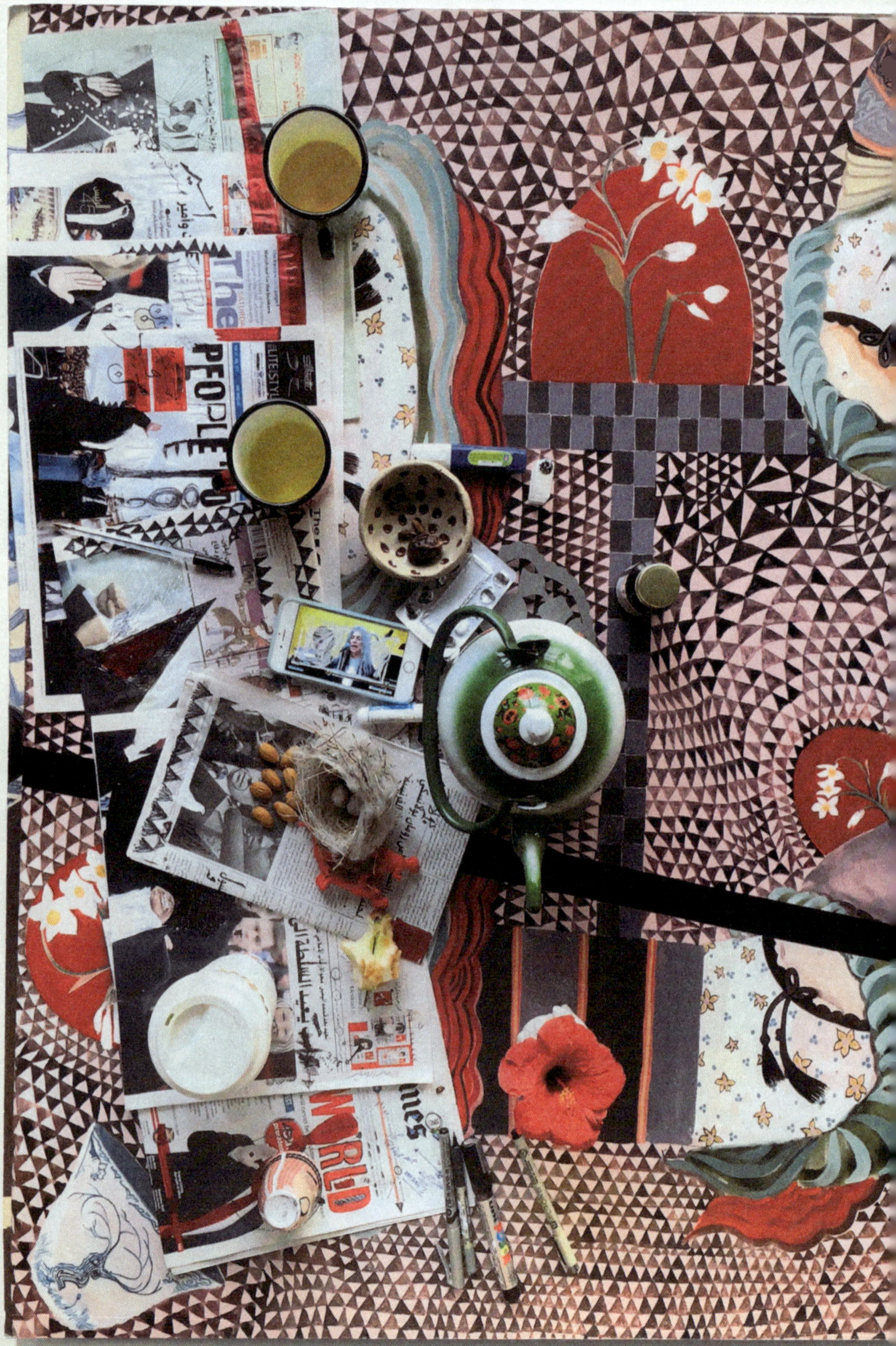

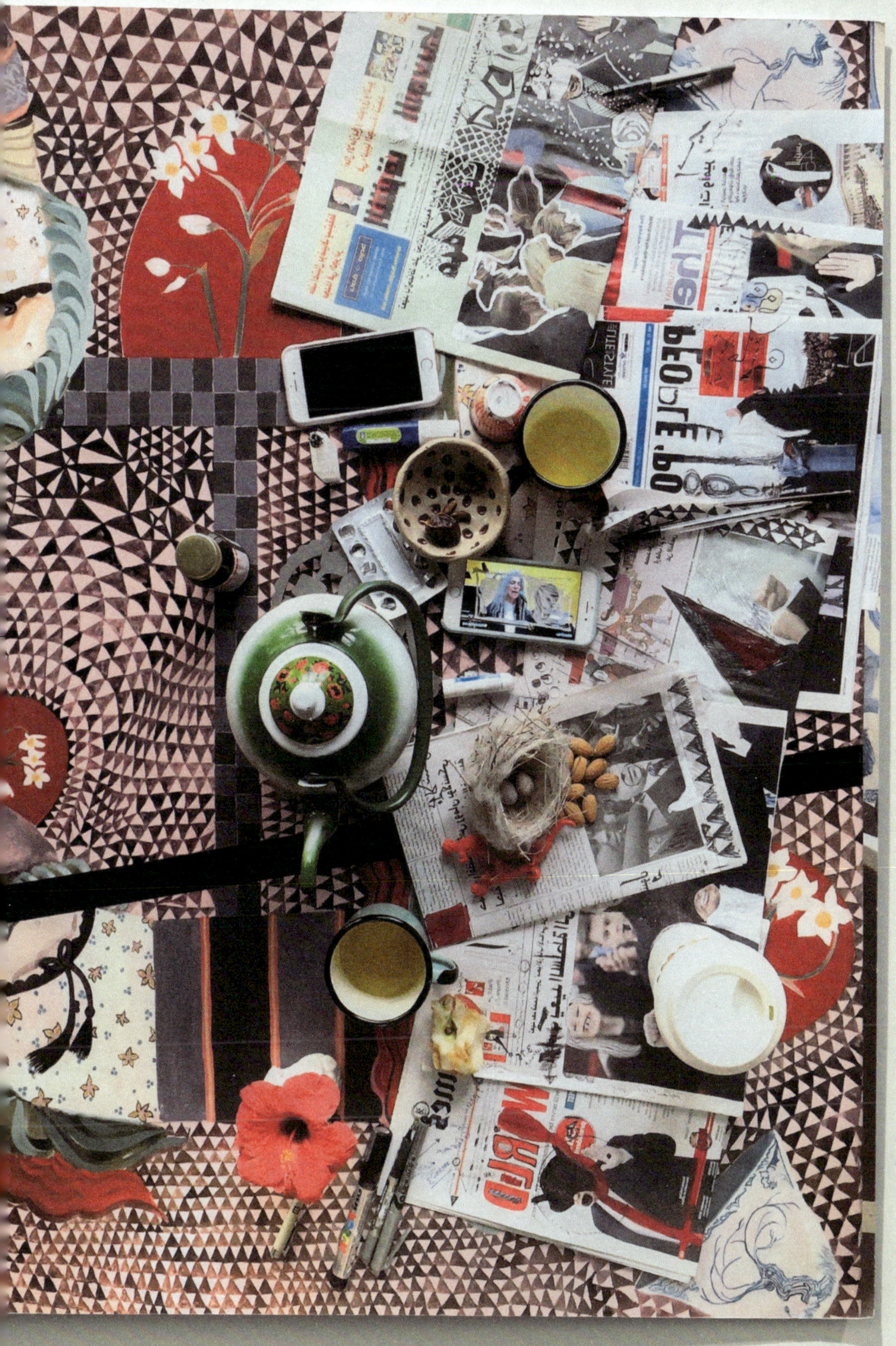

A Dialog between Rhythm and Form

Khalid Albudoor
and *Nujoom Alghanem*
in conversation with
Rand Abdul Jabbar,
Uns Kattan and
Hammad Nasar

UNS KATTAN I think a good place to start would be the 1970s. What was that period like for you? What was happening in your practice and in your life?

NUJOOM ALGHANEM In the late 1970s I was around 16 or 17 years old. Even though I was already working, I was still a little girl. Maybe the number of books I read when I was alone in my grandmother's house influenced me and formed the person I would become later on, but my view of the world at the time was shaped by the child in me. I wanted to write and do whatever I wanted to do because I was a free spirit.

KHALID ALBUDOOR My father encouraged my siblings and me to read. He was always reading. I started to collect books and I got interested in poetry and in around 1978 or 1979 I published my first poem. I was 19. I worked on improving my writing skills by reading and copying from different sources. At that same time a parallel movement was taking place. We were from a new country—there were a lot of talks about building the nation. Issues of identity and nationalistic ideologies were

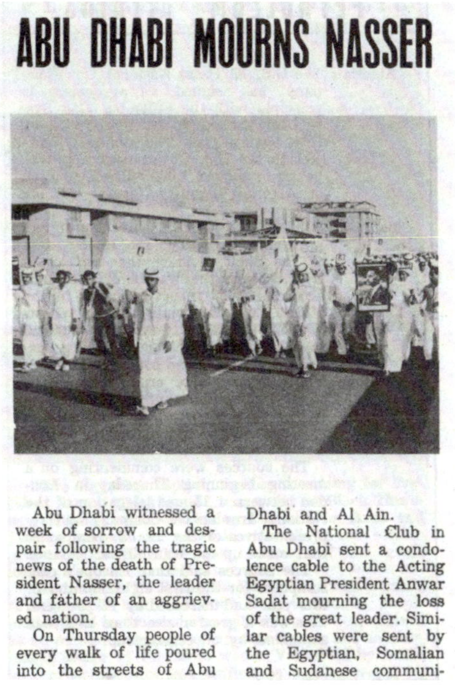

ABU DHABI MOURNS NASSER

Abu Dhabi witnessed a week of sorrow and despair following the tragic news of the death of President Nasser, the leader and father of an aggrieved nation.

On Thursday people of every walk of life poured into the streets of Abu Dhabi and Al Ain.

The National Club in Abu Dhabi sent a condolence cable to the Acting Egyptian President Anwar Sadat mourning the loss of the great leader. Similar cables were sent by the Egyptian, Somalian and Sudanese communi-

Abu Dhabi News, Thursday October 8, 1970
Courtesy of the National Archives, Abu Dhabi

swooping around the Arab world and we were affected by that. We used to read about Palestine and the revolution. We read about Che Guevara. I remember I used to draw his portrait. There were also some influences from my family. My uncles were publishing a magazine in Sharjah, *Al Azmina Al Arabiya*. They were very politically active, so I got some training as a writer at the magazine.

NA Gamal Abdel Nasser passed away around that time. That was a first for me, to see how a whole nation could become sad. We used to sing the Egyptian anthem at school here in the UAE. Egypt was a leading nation to us; it was like another home. When Nasser passed away, the whole country was mourning. They even organized a funeral ceremony for Nasser here and we all went.

KA Yes, I remember my father taking me. Everybody was crying.

NA That episode was very important in bringing concepts of nationalism to us. My father–I am sure your father too, Khalid–listened to Nasser's speeches on the radio, on *Sawt Al Arab*.[1] We felt like one big nation. Whatever happened in Egypt, Lebanon, or Iraq affected us as well. We were very much in touch with the rest of the Arab world. We were also the children of Sheikh Zayed. We repeated and believed his saying: "Arab oil is not more valuable than Arab blood!" We grew up with this great notion that we shouldn't love just our own land, but also the whole Arab world. It was all about being united.

KA We used to read works by Palestinian writers and poets like Mahmoud Darwish, Samih al-Qasim, and Ghassan Kanafani. We would read works by Egyptian writers and listen to music and patriotic songs.

UK I wonder why this view you held and shared often gets misread in your works by opposing parties. One would think that even "conservatives" held this same perspective of unity. Where did the clash between your practice and theirs come from?

1 *Sawt Al Arab (Voice of the Arabs)* was a Cairo-based transnational Arabic language radio service active from 1953 to 1967. Gamal Abdel Nasser is largely credited for its conception.

NA Most probably because we live in a paternalistic society where you have to get permission from the elders if you want to think differently! Okay, I will try to be honest. I think it came from those who were in control, particularly the heads of departments who could make decisions and devise plans for the cultural sections of newspapers. They were the ones with the power to write and to criticize, and they started attacking us. Unfortunately, most of those were Arab journalists. The only exception was *Al Khaleej* newspaper. They weren't as awful as the writers in other newspapers and that was because of Muhammed Al-Maghut and Dr. Yousif Aydabi who appreciated our talents and realized that we didn't have any intentions of destroying the Arabic language or the Arab historical archive!

KA It was also because the owners of *Al Khaleej*, Taryam Omran and Abdullah Omran, shared these ideas of Arab nationalism.

Playfulness in Form

HAMMAD NASAR Where did this impulse to break the meter and come up with new rhythms and play with established literary forms come from for you?

NA I think it's because of my poetry and literature background. I was just thinking about rhythm all the time. I wanted to write in free verse and create my own rhythm. When I started working with Hassan we had a conversation about rhythm, and I realized that he had similar concerns. When Hassan was in the process of making his work, he would repeat the rhythm they taught us during our first year of school. "Tafa tifi tafa tifi ta ta-ta ta-ta." I think there is an internal rhythm for every aspect of art. But to answer your question, I think the impulse to break the rhythm came from our readings and from our desire to imitate or to reflect on what was happening in Europe at the beginning of the 20th century. We were inspired by Dada, surrealism, and post-modernism. We wanted to form a group similar to those cultural movements in Europe and bring different art forms together–painting, music, performance, poetry, etc.

In the most bizarre modern art exhibition in the UAE:
Suspended Rocks, Scattered Papers, and Old Watches

Hassan Sharif: Art is a game… and organized "absurdity" is creativity!

By Mustafa Ghazal

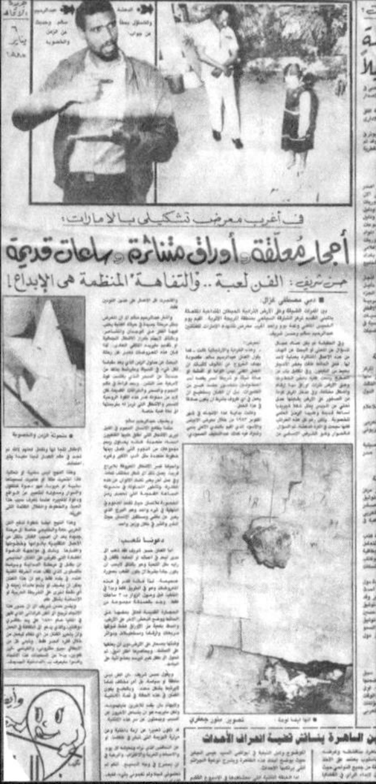
في أغرب معرض تشكيلي بالامارات:

أحجار معلقة.. أوراق متناثرة.. ساعات قديمة

حسن شريف: الفن لعبة.. والتفاهة المنظمة هي الإبداع!

Let's Play!

The artist Hassan Sharif has developed his works or playthings even further. Art, in his opinion, is like a game and therefore shouldn't be taken seriously with the condition that it is played properly. The artist conceived these installations on his way to the exhibition and three hours before visitors arrived. He happened to find a collection of old rocks and hung some of them on the wall and stacked others on the ground. He drew squares, rectangles, circles, and numbers on a bunch of papers. He pinned them to the ground and surrounded them with a nice frame, then he transformed himself into a big child, drawing spontaneously on the tiles.

Hassan Sharif says: "Art is not logic or politics, it is something altogether different unconnected to anything specific… Of course the artist in this state is entirely selfish and doesn't care to present to others something they can understand. What he wants is for people to ask questions and wonder about the secret behind this selfishness. Art might be an expression of inner conflict, the bitterness of failure that eats at our bones, or the contradictions that we see and live every day, the depression, estrangement, exile, and the desire to scream in everyone's face: you didn't teach me anything or give me anything of use, so how can I be of use to you? Children use play and you do what they do because you couldn't find in the world of adults anything that could hold your attention. And this attitude is not negativity or arrogance, for if you committed suicide, for instance, or left, we would have called that pessimism and escapism. It is more a call for optimism and dialogue and an attempt to express reality and ways to change it when we know the reason for this chaos and the lines and dark shadows these installations produced.

This approach is also a step toward pushing Arab art in general and Gulf art in particular into a new realm, for artists feel a sense of boredom about the colors, lines, and ideas of traditional works. Confronting the pressure on a Gulf artist to remain in the very preliminary stage of art-making, despite his ability to add to or continue what another colleague has begun at a different point in the Arab map and humanity in general."

Hassan Sharif points to the roots of this attitude going back to the Dadaist movement which called for absurdity in art and freeing oneself from any system in order to work through absolute free thought alone. The Italian artist Piero Manzoni and the French artist Yves Klein adopted this theory in the early 1960s and formed what they called Neo-Dada.

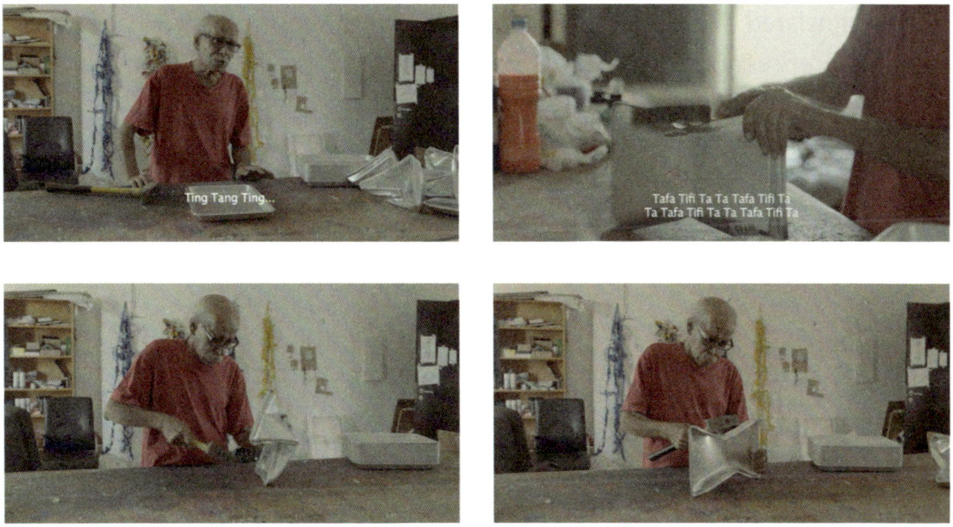

Stills from *Sharp Tools for Making Art*, ongoing documentary production on Hassan Sharif by Nujoom Alghanem, 2015–ongoing
Courtesy of Nujoom Alghanem

KA I would also add Arab names to the list. New poetry forms were written by al-Sayyab, Nazik al-Malaika, Nizar Qabbani, Mahmoud Darwish, and other free-verse writers who came later on, like Adunis. The work of Arthur Rimbaud and Charles Baudelaire also impressed me. Even though these movements were quite old, they were new to us, and they inspired us to dig further into it. We would also read Federico García Lorca, Pablo Neruda, and the Russian writers as well. We were reading translations–they were mostly translated in Beirut. At the first Sharjah International Book Fair in 1982, there were publishers and writers coming from all over the Arab world. We started building our personal library through the fair and these books were helping us build new ideas and forms.

NA Those translated books gave us insight into what was happening in Europe. Even though some of these things happened many years earlier, for us, it was as if they were happening in real time.

HN In some ways it sounds similar to what happened in China after Mao, where suddenly books that had been banned for 50 to 60 years were being translated all together, so people started jumping from what looked like post-impressionist thinking to conceptual art in one quick move.

NA That's a very good point because we felt that people here just wanted to gradually go to the next level, while we were ready to jump. They thought that in order for one to "grow" one would have to do this or that. We were past that, in a way, because we already had something going on.

HN You talked about creating a new movement and we are using this analogy of play, so who were you able to play with? Who could you recruit to this movement?

NA Friends like Hassan Sharif, Yousif Khalil, and Ahmed Rashid Thani.

HN Where were you meeting to share these ideas?

KA We were meeting in Sharjah, either in our apartment, at Hassan's place, or in cafés.

HN Take us to that moment of encounter, to your impulse to work with artists and to play with form. How did that conversation start for you?

NA I would say through literature. Literature brought us together. In order to understand art we had to read. We helped each other find the best books to educate ourselves. We were always talking about finding good resources to learn from.

KA When I visited the first exhibition of Hassan and

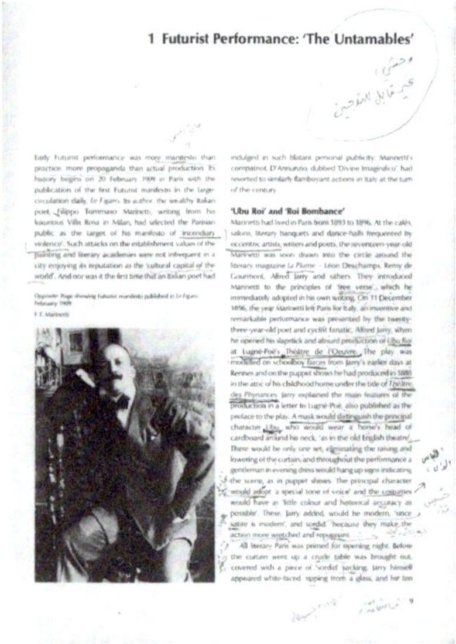

1 Futurist Performance: 'The Untamables'

Early Futurist performance was more manifesto than practice, more propaganda than actual production. Its history begins on 20 February 1909 in Paris with the publication of the first Futurist manifesto in the large-circulation daily, *Le Figaro*. Its author, the wealthy Italian poet, Filippo Tommaso Marinetti, writing from his luxurious Villa Rosa in Milan, had selected the Parisian public as the target of his manifesto of 'incendiary violence'. Such attacks on the establishment values of the painting and literary academies were not infrequent in a city enjoying its reputation as the 'cultural capital of the world'. And nor was it the first time that an Italian poet had indulged in such blatant personal publicity: Marinetti's compatriot, D'Annunzio, dubbed 'Divine Imaginifico', had resorted to similarly flamboyant actions in Italy at the turn of the century.

Opposite: Page showing Futurist manifesto published in *Le Figaro*, February 1909

F.T. Marinetti

'Ubu Roi' and 'Roi Bombance'

Marinetti had lived in Paris from 1893 to 1896. At the cafés, salons, literary banquets and dance-halls frequented by eccentric artists, writers and poets, the seventeen-year-old Marinetti was soon drawn into the circle around the literary magazine *La Plume* – Léon Deschamps, Remy de Gourmont, Alfred Jarry and others. They introduced Marinetti to the principles of 'free verse', which he immediately adopted in his own writing. On 11 December 1896, the year Marinetti left Paris for Italy, an inventive and remarkable performance was presented by the twenty-three-year-old poet and cyclist fanatic, Alfred Jarry, when he opened his slapstick and absurd production of *Ubu Roi* at Lugné-Poë's Théâtre de l'Oeuvre. The play was modelled on schoolboy farces from Jarry's earlier days at Rennes and on the puppet shows he had produced in 1888 in the attic of his childhood home under the title of *Théâtre des Phynances*. Jarry explained the main features of the production in a letter to Lugné-Poë, also published as the preface to the play. A mask would distinguish the principal character, Ubu, who would wear a horse's head of cardboard around his neck, 'as in the old English theatre'. There would be only one set, eliminating the raising and lowering of the curtain, and throughout the performance a gentleman in evening dress would hang up signs indicating the scene, as in puppet shows. The principal character would adopt 'a special tone of voice' and the costumes would have as 'little colour and historical accuracy as possible'. These, Jarry added, would be modern, 'since satire is modern', and sordid 'because they make the action more wretched and repugnant'.

All literary Paris was primed for opening night. Before the curtain went up a crude table was brought out, covered with a piece of 'sordid' sacking. Jarry himself appeared white-faced, sipping from a glass, and for ten

9

Hassan Sharif's notes in 'Futuristic performance: 'The Untamables' [in] *Performance: Live Art 1909 to the Present*. Courtesy of Khalid Albudoor and Nujoom Alghanem

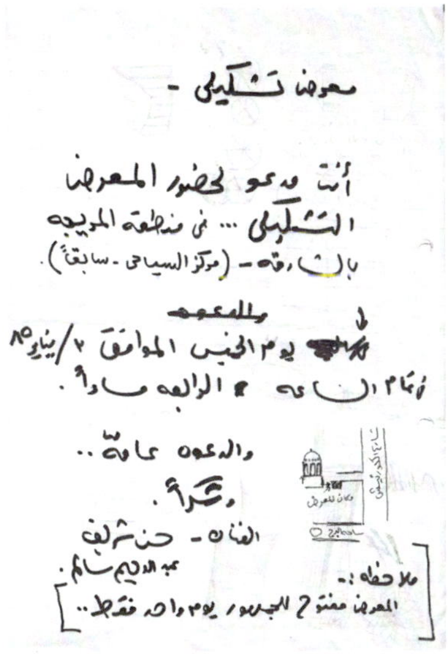
معرض تشكيلي -

أنت مدعو لحضور المعرض
التشكيلي ... في منطقة المريجة
بالشارقة - (مركز السياحي - سابقاً).

~~والمعرض~~
يوم الخميس الموافق ٢/يناير ٨٥
تماماً الساعة الرابعة مساءً.

والدعوة عامة..
وشكراً.
الفنان - حسن شريف
عبد الرحيم سالم.
ملاحظة :-
[المعرض مفتوح للجمهور يوم واحد فقط..]

Handwritten invitation by Hassan Sharif to the One Day Exhibition, 1985. Courtesy of Khalid Albudoor and Nujoom Alghanem

Abdulraheem Salim in Al Mareija[2] I found that Hassan's work was mirroring what was inside me. There was a sense of rebellion against political and literary conventions that I could relate to. I wanted to meet Hassan and Abdulraheem and try and understand why they put their artwork on the sand and on the floor. So we met and we got to talk. A few weeks after meeting Hassan, we were already in Al Mareija.

NA We found our stage.

HN Stage. That's a good word because it also brings in this idea of performance.

KA I would say I discovered the idea of play through Hassan. I would ask myself, could we play with art? Could we play with form and throw words on papers and simply declare that a poem? So I started writing poems in lines and in circles.

NA I saved a lot of these poems with drawings and dots but unfortunately I don't know where they are now.

RAND ABDUL JABBAR Why did Abdulraheem only participate in that exhibition and why didn't he continue his collaboration with Hassan?

NA I think Hassan realized that Abdulraheem had different ideas. Many people did not want to clash with the media or other cultural organizations. Maybe Abdulraheem wanted to be on the safe side,

2 An Art Atelier ran by Hassan Sharif in Sharjah in 1984.

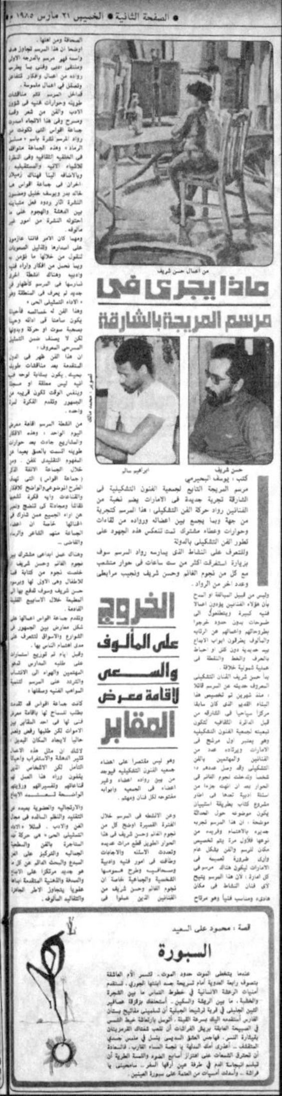

• الصفحة الثانية • الخميس ٢١ مارس ١٩٨٥م

من اعمال حسن شريف

ماذا يجري في مرسم المريجة بالشارقة

حسن شريف

ابراهيم سالم

كتب : يوسف البحيرمي

مرسم المريجة التابع لجمعية الفنون التشكيلية في الشارقة تجربة جديدة في الامارات يضم نخبة من الفنانين رواد حركة الفن التشكيلي : هذا المرسم كتجربة من جهة وبما يجمع بين اعضائه ورواده من لقاءات وحوارات وعطاء مشترك تمت تنعكس هذه الجهود على تطور الفن التشكيلي بالدولة

وللتعرف على النشاط الذي يمارسه رواد المرسم سوف بزيارة استغرقت اكثر من ست ساعات في حوار متشعب مع كل من نجوم القائم وحسن شريف ونجيب مرابطي وعدد اخر من الرواد .

الخروج على المألوف والسعي لإقامة معرض المقابر

وليس من قبيل المبالغة او المدح بأن هؤلاء الفنانين يؤدون اعمالا فنيه كبيرة ويتطلعون الى طموحات بدون حدود خرجوا بطروحاتهم واعمالهم عن الرتابه والمألوف يطرقون ابواب الابداع

قصة : محمود علي السعيد

السبورة

What's Going on in the Al Mareija Art Atelier in Sharjah?

By Yousif Al Buhairmy

Moving further away from the ordinary and seeking to create an exhibition amongst graves

Some studio activities include making one-day exhibitions. These ideas and projects came after long, deep conversations that don't revolve around the typical understanding of art. Through these conversations, the Aqwas collective aims for a clear and objective approach toward understanding ideas and convictions, while allowing for challenging ideas to mature and that take place in streets and markets in an attempt to gauge the level of people's interest in them. A few days ago, forms were distributed to students in schools calling for those interested in coming to and joining the studio to develop and nurture their artistic talents.

Aqwas applied for a permit to hold an exhibition in one of the cemeteries amongst the dead; they were denied permission and are now workin on finding an alternative just like Yousif Khalil, who withdrew from the Aqwas group right after publishing the first edition of *Silsilat Al Ramad*. Hassan had already decided that he didn't want to be a painter and Abdulraheem simply returned to his own practice. The way we heard it, Abdulraheem and Mohamed Yousif lobbied to keep us out of the Emirates Fine Arts Society (EFAS). They were concerned that we were going to plant the seed of destruction since we had supposedly "caused problems" in the Emirates Writers Union. So Hassan was in a dilemma.

Emirates Writers Union / Discussing Form

HN In the 1980s you were already members of the Emirates Writers Union.

NA We were founders–not only members.

HN With whom did you found it?

KA There was a group of around twenty writers, I think.

NA We were writing poetry and short novels. The problem started during one of the board meetings, when members of Union decided to include journalists, and we objected to it. We reminded them that there were principles in the establishment of the Emirates Writers Union. All candidates had to go through an application process and provide written work and publications to be reviewed by a committee in order to be granted membership. But the board members wanted to put this to vote and they brought about 15 journalists and writers who were essentially friends!

KA The board members were trying to publish the work of these friends and brought "written pieces" as evidence. Our argument was that just because you wrote a few pages, that doesn't automatically make you a writer. This fight went on for a long time but eventually they succeeded. A few of us fought back. We wanted to have creative writers only and not journalists.

HN So that was before the inauguration of the Emirates Writers Union?

KA Yes, that was two or three years before. The fight for quality-controlling the writers joining the Union came soon after that.

HN So you founded something, which was playing with form, and you were getting frustrated, as it became something else.

KA This came later on. The rebellious idea of being totally against form came four or five years later, in 1984–85.

NA They compared us to the early 20th century movements in Russia. They said we were formalists who did not care about meaning and social causes but only about form.

Hassan

HN So in April 1985 there was what you described as a moment of recognition. Hassan was doing something that shared some of your interests.

NA We realized that he knew all these artists we were reading about that were associated with Dada, surrealism, Pop art, and postmodernism. Hassan's experiments with lines and playfulness came from Wassily Kandinsky and Paul Klee. He was a fan of Marcel Duchamp until he died.

HN So, just like you were recognizing something in Hassan, how was he recognizing your view?

NA Hassan knew of our work before we met. He was an avid reader.

KA He shared with us the desire to create new art forms but he was distant from the content of our poetry. We connected through thinking. Many times he would say, "What are you writing about? Are you educating people with your ideas? We don't have to do that in art. We only have to work and do things!" I remember having these conversations with Hassan. He would also give us books to read and translate.

HN Did your earlier ideas of nationalism find any purchase at all with Hassan? Because I thought he would have been very antithetical to this.

KA No, when we met Hassan, that sentiment was already fading.

NA Our practice focused more on form then.

HN How did Aqwas form?

NA We just found each other and from the onset it was like love at first sight. Like, yes! That's the person! That's it!

KA After seeing the exhibition in Al Mareija. I was interested to learn more about this man. That was the starting point. We got to know each other and then a few months later we formed the group.

NA I always wanted to be an artist, ever since I was in high school. I was thinking about going abroad to study art but my father refused to let me go so I had to go to UAE University where I felt so suffocated. So I decided to work as a journalist. I didn't want to go to that university; I just wanted to make art. I started making sculptures and drawings. I didn't want to make art like my aunt.[3] Similar to poetry and free verse writing, I felt the responsibility to do something new.

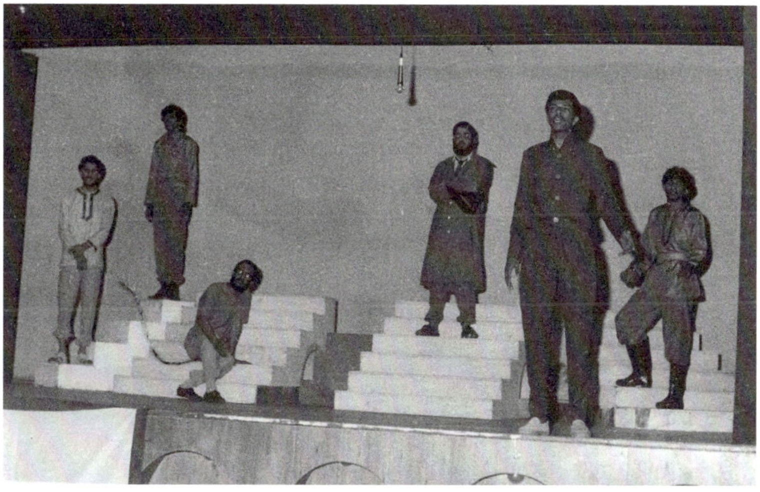

Ahmed Rashid Thani (seated) in Al Masrah Al Hur (the Free Theatre) in UAE University, circa 1981. Courtesy of Khalid Albudoor and Nujoom Alghanem

Silsilat Al Ramad Reappears:
Yousif Khalil withdraws from the publication.
"We will try to present something new in every edition"
"Our exhibition of nine rocks represents the pages of the journal"

By Muna Matar

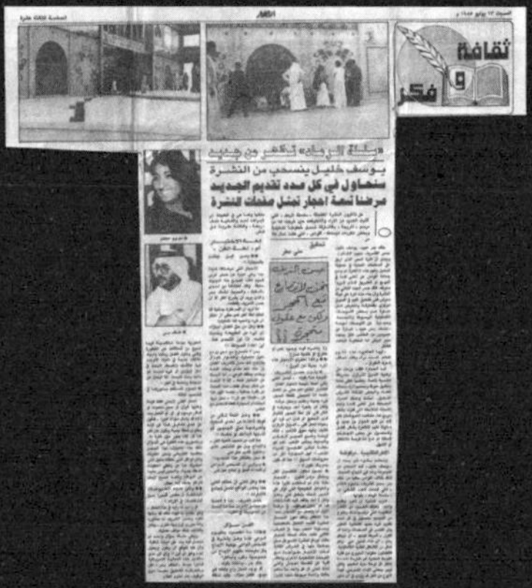
ثقافة و فكر

يوسف خليل ينسحب من النشرة

سنحاول في كل عدد تقديم الجديد

معرضنا تسعة احجار تمثل صفحات النشرة

Do you remember the surprising journal, *Silsilat Al Ramad*? It provoked many opinions and commentaries when it came out of the Al Mareija Atelier in Sharjah, showing abstract illustrations and contributions by members of the Aqwas collective, which includes Kahlid Albudoor, Yousif Khalil, Hassan Sharif, and Nujoom Alghanem.

It seems that the amount of ink spilled in local newspapers in an attempt to analyze and understand this phenomenon has not stopped Aqwas from continuing to move forward in this direction. A second edition of the journal has been published, and it came out in the form of an exhibition this time. Located in the Central Souq in Sharjah, the exhibition included a number of paintings and installations... and rocks. One of the installations by Khalid Albudoor was composed of two wooden poles with a rock suspended between them. The background was inscribed with these words: "Hey, spider on the frontiers of speech, the sky is a mirror. You stood still to tame your long hair."

The rocks were distributed on the floor of the souq in a specific geometric pattern. Some of them were covered entirely with colored scarves, some were half-covered, and some were simply laid on scarves. Seeing the group's determination to keep going and in the face of the questions rapidly increasing upon experiencing the artworks, it was necessary to reopen the conversation in order to understand the works better and to get some answers for questions we've had for a while.

Traditional Frameworks Are Rejected

To begin with, we know that Yousif Khalil withdrew from the group and decided to remain silent. The collective now includes Khalid Albudoor, Hassan Sharif, and Nujoom Alghanem, who introduced the second edition of *Silsilat Al Ramad* by saying, "We don't want the journal to appear in one form. There are many traditional frameworks that we reject, and as a way of innovating forms, we're going to try to present something new every time. The journal is evolving and it will not be constrained in pages but may be a video, or a live performance, which is one of the forms of fine art. The artists tried to go beyond the traditional idea of a painting bordered by a regular frame to one that takes place live, but not in the theatrical sense, because this type of art could be performed anywhere and isn't limited by a script, or needing a director or a stage."

Muna Matar: *Why did you choose rocks this time, instead of paper?*

Hassan Sharif responds: "The work of art is a product of the artist's choices. So the artist's choices are more important than the works themselves. I like the mundaneness of rocks. A rock is a simple and ordinary object that could be presented. But no one would have the audacity to present it in an artistic context, because rocks don't speak a language that everyone can understand as related to art. The Central Souq is clean and has gold stores, so we wanted to place the regular and mundane rock next to the gold. Yes, it was surprising for people going to buy gold!! Are rocks more valuable than the items showcased in the stores?!! We could answer that with either yes or no!!"

We are not competing with rigid rocks; we are battling with rigid minds.

Al Ittihad, Saturday July 13, 1985
Courtesy of Khalid Albudoor and Nujoom Alghanem

HN And Yousif Khalil coming in, how did that happen?

NA There was an event one night and he joined us, and we started talking about art and literature. Khalil had established the cinema club in Al Ahli Club–a sports club. He was also a writer and was involved in theater. We needed his input as well–he was showing many films and using these as conversation starters.

UK Ahmad Rashid Thani was heavily involved in the theater scene too. He would often write about it.

HN What's the origin of the name Aqwas?

KA It came out of one of Hassan's artworks — he had these arches in the atelier and he said, "these are *'aqwas,'*" and that was the name we decided on. That was all!

HN Earlier on you were talking about the scenes in Iraq or in Egypt. Was there anything else in the region you were also finding affinity to?

NA There was *Lotus* magazine in Beirut and the poetry scene in Bahrain. Qassim Haddad founded a magazine called *Kalimat* and we used to publish in there a lot. Haddad and Amin Saleh used to write manifestos and that inspired us to write more.

KA Qassim was an active political figure at that time. He used to come here and we would meet and talk. There was an intense epistolary exchange. But when we published *Silsilat Al Ramad*, he wasn't very happy. He thought we were messing with literature. He told us we were making enemies and that we had enough already at that point. He used to bring up the example of surrealist Arab writers like Abdul Kader El-Janabi in Paris and complain that they were not writing "literature" anymore.

NA But we owe Qassim a lot. He was an intellectual. He had a mission.

3 Artist Dr. Najat Meky.

HN Let's talk about your publication *Silsilat Al Ramad*. I was particularly struck by the word "*Silsilat*" and the fact that it was created with the intention of being a series from the very start. You also talked about the first issue as a manifesto. How did that came about? What were you hoping to achieve?

KA We wanted to tell the world that we were a group and that we had things to say. We were done with conventional ideas of art and poetry and the only way to tell people was to make a publication and to "shock."

NA I don't think we were trying to "shock" per se. I think we just wanted an outlet for our ideas and to be recognized as a legitimate group of artists.

HN Who said that you couldn't publish your own material?

NA The board members of the Emirates Writers Union.

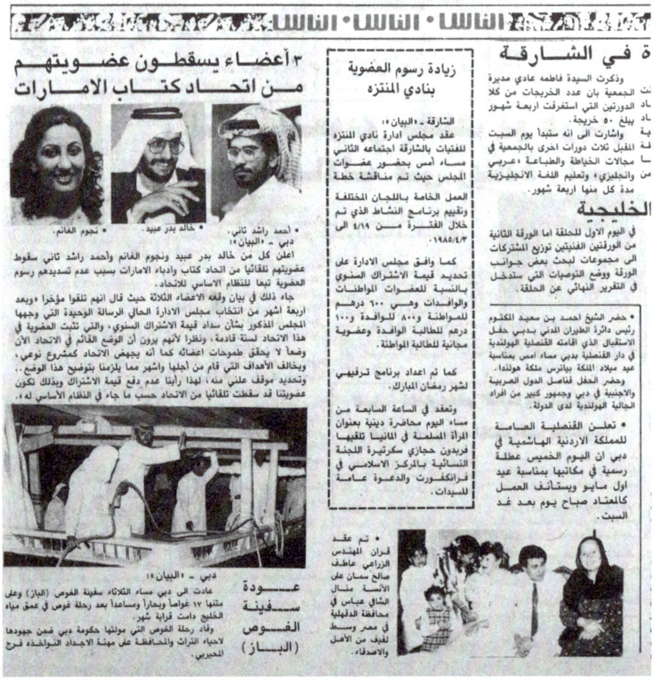

الناس • الناس • الناس

٣ أعضاء يسقطون عضويتهم من اتحاد كتاب الامارات

• أحمد راشد ثاني. • خالد بدر عبيد. • نجوم الغانم.

دبي ـ «البيان»:

اعلن كل من خالد بدر عبيد ونجوم الغانم وأحمد راشد ثاني سقوط عضويتهم تلقائيا من اتحاد كتاب وادباء الامارات بسبب عدم تسديدهم رسوم العضوية تبعا للنظام الاساسي للاتحاد.

جاء ذلك في بيان وقعه الاعضاء الثلاثة حيث قال انهم تلقوا مؤخرا «وبعد اربعة اشهر من انتخاب مجلس الادارة الحالي الرسالة الوحيدة التي وجهها المجلس المذكور بشأن سداد قيمة الاشتراك السنوي، والتي تثبت العضوية في هذا الاتحاد لسنة قادمة، ونظرا لأنهم يرون أن الوضع القائم في الاتحاد الآن وضعاً لا يحقق طموحات اعضائه كما أنه يجهض الاتحاد كمشروع نوعي، ويخالف الأهداف التي قام من أجلها واشهر مما يلزمنا بتوضيح هذا الوضع.. وتحديد موقف علني منه، لهذا رأينا عدم دفع قيمة الاشتراك وبذلك تكون عضويتنا قد سقطت تلقائيا من الاتحاد حسب ما جاء في النظام الأساسي له».

عودة سفينة الغوص (الباز)

دبي ـ «البيان»:

عادت الى دبي مساء الثلاثاء سفينة الغوص (الباز) وعلى متنها ١٧ غواصاً وبحاراً ومساعداً بعد رحلة غوص في عمق مياه الخليج دامت قرابة شهر.

وقاد رحلة الغوص التي مولتها حكومة دبي ضمن جهودها لاحياء التراث والمحافظة على مهنة الاجداد النواخذه فرج المحيربي.

زيادة رسوم العضوية بنادي المنتزه

الشارقة ـ «البيان»:

عقد مجلس ادارة نادي المنتزه للفتيات بالشارقة اجتماعه الثاني مساء أمس بحضور عضوات المجلس حيث تم مناقشة خطة العمل الخاصة باللجان المختلفة وتقييم برنامج النشاط الذي تم خلال الفترة من ٤/١٩ الى ١٩٨٥/٤/٣.

كما وافق مجلس الادارة على تحديد قيمة الاشتراك السنوي بالنسبة للعضوات المواطنات والوافدات وهي ٦٠٠ درهم للمواطنة و٨٠٠ للوافدة و١٠٠ درهم للطالبة الوافدة وعضوية مجانية للطالبة المواطنة.

كما تم اعداد برنامج ترفيهي لشهر رمضان المبارك.

وتعقد في الساعة السابعة من مساء اليوم محاضرة دينية بعنوان المرأة المسلمة في المانيا تلقيها فريدون حجازي سكرتيرة اللجنة النسائية بالمركز الاسلامي في فرانكفورت والدعوة عامة للسيدات.

ة في الشارقة

وذكرت السيدة فاطمه عادي مديرة الجمعية بان عدد الخريجات من كلا الدورتين التي استغرقت اربعة شهور يبلغ ٥٠ خريجة.

واشارت الى انه ستبدأ يوم السبت المقبل ثلاث دورات اخرى بالجمعية في مجالات الخياطة والطباعة «عربي وانجليزي» وتعليم اللغة الانجليزية مدة كل منها اربعة شهور.

الخليجية

في اليوم الاول للحلقة اما الورقة الثانية من الورقتين الفنيتين توزيع المشتركات الى مجموعات لبحث بعض جوانب الورقة ووضع التوصيات التي ستدخل في التقرير النهائي عن الحلقة.

• حضر الشيخ احمد بن سعيد المكتوم رئيس دائرة الطيران المدني بدبي حفل الاستقبال الذي اقامته القنصلية الهولندية في دار القنصلية بدبي مساء امس بمناسبة عيد ميلاد الملكة بياترس ملكة هولندا.

وحضر الحفل قناصل الدول العربية والاجنبية في دبي وجمهور كبير من افراد الجالية الهولندية لدى الدولة.

• تعلن القنصلية العامة للمملكة الاردنية الهاشمية في دبي ان اليوم الخميس عطلة رسمية في مكاتبها بمناسبة عيد اول مايو ويستأنف العمل كالمعتاد صباح يوم بعد غد السبت.

• تم عقد قران المهندس الزراعي عاطف صالح سمان على الآنسة منال الشاقي عباس في محافظة الدقهلية في مصر وسط لفيف من الأهل والاصدقاء.

"Three members drop membership from the Emirates Writers Union," *Al Bayan*, May 1, 1986. Courtesy of The Emirates Library, the National Archives, Abu Dhabi

KA They were the same people that ran the official newspapers and their cultural sections.

NA They sent out a press release asking all the newspapers not to publish our work. That was ridiculous! They also demanded that we seek their permission if we wanted to participate in any poetry festival or any cultural festival in the Arab world or abroad! They were a bit authoritarian in their distaste for our expressions.

HN So, faced with the quandary of wanting to create your own magazine but not being able to publish it, you decided to do photocopies. How did this unique method of distribution come about?

KA It was the only way. We made twenty copies of the first issue and we distributed them to newspapers and to other writers in our circle.

NA Hassan did the design and we conceived the content of the magazine.

HN Who brought in the idea of including sticks of chewing gum in it?

NA We wanted to insert a gift for our readers. It was a playful thing.

KA To add some sweetness to their reading experience. "Here, have a chewing gum and then read so that you are happy." The funny thing is that some journalist commented that it was an American chewing gum—so we were "Americanized."

NA Khalid drove to every newspaper and gave them the publication. We were determined for them to take it. But the authorities soon called Hassan and they told him that we needed permissions. We met again and thought to ourselves, what can we do? And Hassan said okay, if they don't allow us to publish, let's say the next issue is an exhibition. So we put together an exhibition in the Islamic Souq in Sharjah. It was a busy place. Just outside the Gold Souq.

KA We thought, let's hit the streets! Let's make an exhibition.

If He Were Resurrected to Life

By Abdullah Rasheed

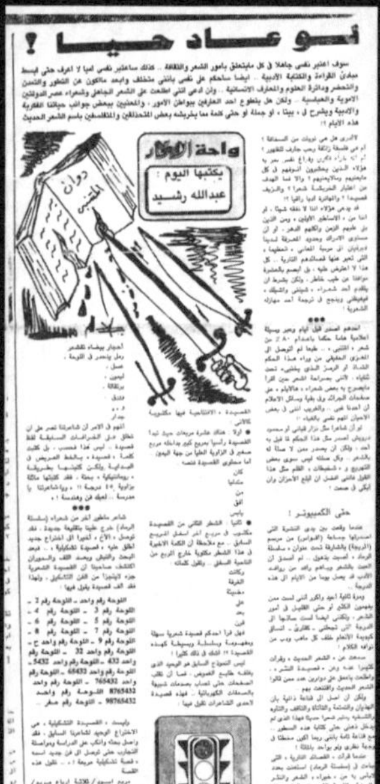
لو عاد حيا !

واحة الأفكار

يكتبها اليوم : عبدالله رشيد

جدول انسحاب أم جدول ضرب؟!

Even the Computer!

When I got hold of the journal titled *Silsilat Al Ramad* produced by the Aqwas collective from the Al Mareija Atelier in Sharjah, I was stunned. I couldn't believe that messing with poetry and one of the most important genres of literature could ever get to this point.

I am not an expert on poetry, but I am also not so naive a reader as to drift behind whatever is written in meaningless words!

I have heard about modern poetry and read a lot about it and about the art of prose, and I've delved deeply into several modern poetry volumes and found authenticity in them. But to arrive to an inner conviction that hallucinating, stuttering, and insulting is considered modern poetry is something that didn't happen even as I write these words, and I could be wrong in my perspective!

When I read the "fiery poems" published in the journal, I consulted with a good number of "experts" who understand poetry, prose, short story, criticism, and all genres of literature, culture, logic, and science. I couldn't find a single person who could guide me through or decipher the illustrated puzzles—I wonder if everyone I spoke to was stupid?! Maybe!!

One of them suggested that I buy a Japanese computer and feed it with everything published in the journal, all its "valuable" information and modern literature and poetry theory, to see if it can help me see the light. I liked the idea, but I changed my mind when I discovered that computers are designed to commit suicide should they be stricken with depression!

The strange thing is that the cover of the journal has a piece of gum stuck on it! Maybe it's because those who produced the pamphlet have a total personal conviction that whoever is unlucky enough to read it will chew the gum after throwing the rest of it away in the garbage. It wouldn't be far-fetched that if Al Mutanabbi came back to life, he would burn his own poetry diwans before committing suicide from bitterness and resentment...

Al Ittihad, January 20, 1985
Courtesy of Khalid Albudoor and Nujoom Alghanem

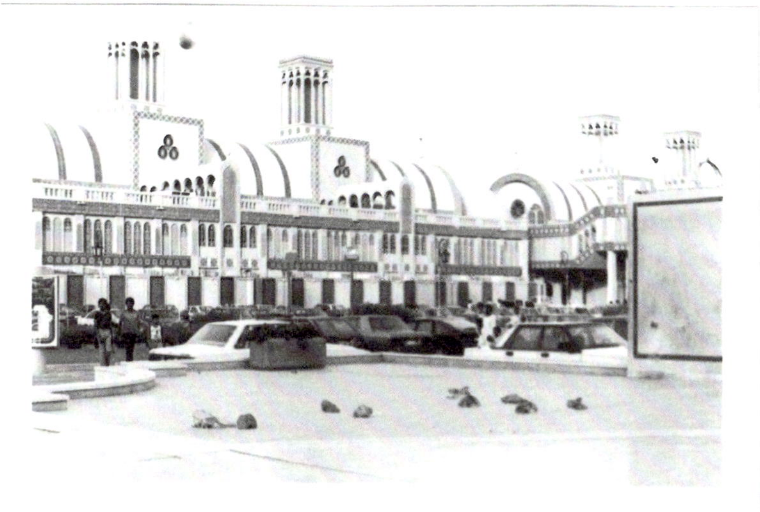

Silsilat Al Ramad, second edition,
Islamic Souq / Gold Souq, Sharjah, 1985
Courtesy of Khalid Albudoor and Nujoom Alghanem

NA We thought they wouldn't stop us but indeed they did. I made some drawings of my hands, Khalid made drips with paint, and Hassan had three groups of rocks, each composed of three rocks tied with a cotton rope that had a specific color representing each one of us. They were red, orange, and blue. I also made an animal spine sculpture painted in oil. People came over and ridiculed us. "Is this art? You think you are making art?" Some would kick the rocks around. Kids would play with them, too.

HN You placed rocks outside the Gold Souq–quite interesting ideas of value. There was then a second issue of the journal, and what happened to the third one?

NA It remained as a cover only. By then, we had to stop. The Department of Information and Culture in Sharjah informed Hassan first, because his studio was in the same building. Hassan was an employee in the Ministry of Youth and Sports. The Head of Authority told him that he could have a studio on the condition that he would give art classes in the afternoon. That's when he started teaching young people like Mohammed Kazem, Khalil Abdulwahed, Abdullah Al Saadi, etc. Hassan was very opinionated as a board member of EFAS. Those around him were constantly on their toes but they couldn't do much without him because he was so industrious. Abdulraheem Salim and others were playing on two fronts.

They were very smart. They knew when to deal with Hassan and when not to. He kept publishing *Al Tashkeel*[4] on his own and took care of everything from A to Z. They were lucky to have someone that would take care of it.

Anyway, with the closure of *Silsilat Al Ramad*, we had to endure a lot of public attacks in the press, and that was very heavy to take. People wrote that we were "kicked out" of the Emirates Writers Union. We felt like outsiders and aliens. We continued going to the atelier and doing translations. We would spend hours and hours writing. My English was not that great at the time, but I used to help Hassan with the Arabic translation of the books.

KA After all these fights I felt like I needed solitude. I wanted to be with my writing, with my books, to get out of the horrible situations we were in. Hassan got in trouble as well. So I spent most of my time reading and not even thinking about publishing anything. That period marked the separation between us and the whole scene, and that's when Nujoom and I started to work separately on our first poetry collection.

Lessons Learned

HN What did each of you take away from the experience of Aqwas and *Silsilat Al Ramad*?

NA We were determined not to give up our art, our creativity, but we also needed to educate ourselves and be stronger to face these difficult situations. So we got study leave and enrolled at Ohio University in 1994 but I had to pay for my own education during the first year. I got a scholarship afterwards.

KA Nujoom did her BA and I did my MA and then she went to Australia in 1997–1998 and then moved back to the UAE in 1999 where she joined Abu Dhabi TV.

4 A magazine issued by the Emirates Fine Arts Society.

NA I had studied film so the CEO made me Head of the Training Department for the whole organization. Soon after I began advising on strategies on the executive committee and as Director of New Media.

HN What do you think Hassan gained from your connection?

NA I think his work in publishing and education. We established that together and he kept doing that. He wrote for newspapers, even though he wasn't a writer. So, in a way, we helped each other in that early stage. When I went to university, I took a lot of art courses to improve my skills and allow myself to continue that cultural and artistic dialogue with him. Although we left the country, we stayed in touch. We would see each other when we would visit during the end of year or in summer.

RA I am curious, Nujoom, about your role as "female rebel," being the only woman in the collective.

NA It's true I was the only female within the group but not within the scene. There was Thabiya Khamis, who was a very brave woman, and Hamda Khamis. However, we never thought about it this way. It never occurred to us that I was the female, although the way people chose to see that was different. My poetry was criticized and misinterpreted for having presumed sexual connotations. But I didn't feel like a lone female amongst males. My views were respected and they respected me. We were all the same.

رسالة إلى المدعو «أحمد راشد ثاني»

لو رايت منظرا جميلا
لو انفعلت ذات يوم ...
لو جاشت نفسك بافكار واحلام وهواجس لا تعرفها ..
لو اشعلتك دمعه ...
لو عذبتك نظره ..
لو ضج بك طفل ..
لو ارهقتك انثى ....
لو احترقت في وطن ...
لو انكرك شارع ..
لو شئت ان تقول ...
فيا ترى كيف تقول ؟
بالطبع ... ستبحث عن اية ورقة...
على علبة سجاير
على غلاف كتاب
على ورقة مهملة ..
على اي شيء قابل للكتابة عليه ..

ستكتب الكلمة الاولى ... وفي الثانية ستجد نفسك في مدينة تشاهدها لاول مرة .. مدينة كاملة باحيائها وطقسها ورائحتها ولونها وسكانها .. وستخرج منك ومنها واليك امرأة ... امرأة لا تعرفها .. لها لونها وشكلها .. ستفاجئك بما تلبسه .. وبما تفكر فيه .. وبما تمارسه ...

وما عليك انت .. الا ان تأخذها وتحتضنها ... وتحترق ... اعرف انك ستحترق كثيرا ..

ولكن بعد ذلك ستحس بالراحة .. بشيء من الشعور بالسعادة والنصر ... بارهاق شديد وحالة غير عادية تماما ..
ستقرأ ما كتبته ...
ستستغرب ...
ستقول بلسان لا شعوري :-
هل انا فعلا كتبت هذا الكلام ..؟
ستقترب من المرأة ...
ستسأل نفسك واصدقاءك والكتابة ...
ستفكر بالعين التي اشترتك بزواياها

بعد ذلك .. ستتعود على هذه الحالة كما يتعود الانسان على كل الاشياء التي تعجبه ..

ومرة اخرى ستمارس الكتابة ..
بعد خبر تنازل جديد في جريدة تحبها ...
بعد مقال كتبه اديب جيل ...
بعد عيون امرأة ...
بعد الدخول الى قلب انسان نظيف لم تكن تعرفه ..
بعد حوار مع انسان لا يفهمك
بعد شيء جميل ينعشك
بعد فهم ...
بعد وعي ...
بعد حالة
بعد اصالة وبحر ..
بعد شعور بالحزن ستكتب ...
وتكتب..
قد يساورك الشك فيما تكتب
قد يطل عليك العقم وانت ما زلت في مخاضك
ولكن عليك في اللحظة التي تقررها .. ان تخرج

ليس مهما ان تجد وسيلة اعلامية ما تمنعك من الخروج ... وليس مهما ان تجد اديبا كبيرا من ادباء المهرجانات والبلاطات والمقابلات يقمعك ...

وليس مهما ان تجد زملاءك يضحكون من هذا المجنون الذي في داخلك ...

وليس مهما ... ان تكتشف في يوم ما ، ان العالم يكرهك لانك تضج بالدموع والامواج والحزن ... والاطفال والنساء ...

ولا يهمك السجن ... اذا دخلته وانت تبكي على وطن
ولا تهمك المشنقة ... اذا عانقتك وانت تصرخ في وجه طاغيه
ولا يهمك مجتمع يرفضك لانك احببته ...
اكتب ما تريد لا ما يريده غيرك ..
واكتب ما تريده اللحظة لا ما تريده انت
تصور انك كتبت
« هذه امتكم امة ضائمة
وانا شاعركم فلتلعنوني
هذه ابنتكم ابنة عاشقة
وانا عاشقها فلترجموني
وانا الخارج عنكم ..
فاسألوني عن خروجي
فاذا كان خروجي نحوكم ...
هيا اشنقوني
فانا يا سادتي جرمي عيوني
وانا يا سادتي ...
جرمي لساني
وانا يا سادتي ...
جرمي قصائدي
ولهذا ... الجرم واضح
لا يريد الآن ...
شاهد كان يعمل في جهاز الامن سرًا
اول دليل اخر من عين امي ..
ا، تعهد والدي في دفتر البحر كصياد فقير .
قد لا تجد جريدة تنشر لك هذا ..
قد يصادقها من لا تتوقع منه ذلك ...
قد يصادقك الشاهد الذي كان يعمل في جهاز الامن سرا ..

والآن جهرا ..
ويفاجئك بدليل من عين امك ..
وآخر من عين حبيبتك ...
سيفاجئك بتعهد والدك في دفتر البحر كصياد فقير
وبقصيدتك التي كتبتها ذات يوم على غلاف كتابك المدرسي .
المهم ان تتحمل ..
تحمل ان الاشياء مقبلة .
وذات يوم ستعرض قصيدتك على الناس ..
سيختلفون ..
(يختلف الناس ...
وتصبح انت الشيء المختلف عليه في اروعك
تكتشف سخفاء العالم ..
ان لم تكتشف نفسك
وهذا شيء لم يفعله احد قبلك)
المهم ان تتحمل ...
فلا عليك من ضجيج زائف يخلقه الكثيرون حولك ..

ولا عليك من جماجم عرفت الفاظا جاهزة وتعابير جاهزة تتكررها في كل مكان ...

ثم لا تؤمن بانسان ..

بمعنى لا تغتر بانسان ما .. فمن ترفعه سقوطه صعب عليك ...

انت يا من حاولت ان تكتب ...
ومن حاول الكتابة عشقا
ومن عشق اتخذ قرارا سياسيا ..
ومن اتخذ قرارا سياسيا طورد ...
ومن طورد تصعلك ...
والصعاليك احاسيس .
واقرأ كثيرا ...
وارفع صوتك بما تريد
وحدد صورتك كما تريد
فانت الموقف والصورة والانسان
كن كما انت ..
(ايها السادة ...
هذه اصابعي ..
خمس كما ترون
في كل اصبع فم
وفي كل فم سرير
وفي كل سرير جمجمة
وفي كل جمجمة قلب
وفي كل قلب بلده) .
وانت اولا واخيرا للناس ...
اكتب من الناس وعنهم ولهم ..
فكم انت جميل من تجاعيد شحي
وفي اصرار فتيات من اجل قضية
وفي عين ليلى ..
وفي وطنية كاسين
كن كما كنت واكثر ...
كن البحر ...
كن خورفكان ...
كن العالم كله
كن المواطن والصعلوك والانسان ...
انا اعرف ان كل هذا عذاب ...
وان كتابة القصيدة احتراق ...
انا اشعر بك وانت تتالم من وجوه ساذجة
تقابلك بعيون لا تفهمها ..
تتالم لانهم لا يعرفون ... كيف كتبت هذا ؟..
وكيف احترقت ؟
واعرف انك تلجأ الى مخدعك كل ليلة ... تفكر ...
تبحث عن امرأة في داخلك
عن وجه لا تعرفه في مرآتك
في عالم لا يفهمك
وتقرر ان تصمت احيانا ..
وان تتكلم احيانا كثيرة ...
كن هكذا كما انت ولا تتغير ...
رغم انني اعرف ان الاشياء تتغير عليك كل دقيقة ..
ثم لا عليك من كل هذه المهاترات التي تحدث حول الفن ...
لا تلتفت الى شيء تعرف انه ضدك وضد البحر وليلى
وكاسين وامك وحبيبتك ...
وفي النهاية لن يسود الا الذي كنت تحلم به دائما ...

الانسان الذي تمتزج فيه همومك وهمومه والارض والعشق والبحر ...

ثم انظر الى هؤلاء الذين امامك ...
المسرعون الى طبق ياكلهم
الغارقون في حديث يضحك عليهم
الملتهون بكرة تلعب بهم
كل لديه جرحه ...
والكل يبحث عن كتفه
حاول ان تقرأ لهم قلوبهم
انت ومن تحبه
ومن تحبهم وانت ...
وجود هؤلاء وجودكم ..
واندثارهم في دوائر خارجة عليكم ... اندثاركم
ثم كابد اختيار من تعشقها
وكابد اختيار من تتحدث معه ..
وكابد الكتابة في الذي تكتبه
وكابد النظر في الذي تحدق فيه ..
ثم ان رأيت وجهك السابق اصمت ..
اقرأ وادع الى القراءة .
فهذه الجماجم لو تثقفت خلقت ...
ولو خلقت كانت ...
ولو كانت لما كان هذا الوضع ...
الكل مثلك
له حجرته ...
وقلمه
وقلبه
وكتابه

ولكن انت من استطعت بطريقة وبمستوى ما ، ان تعرف حاجتك ...

حاول ان تعرفها اكثر ...
وتهدي اصدقاءك الى ما هم بحاجة اليه ...
واياك وتحديد نفسك ...
فالكتابة ليست هي الشعر
والعالم ليس هو لحظة ما ...
كن فنانا اينما كنت .
وكيف تكون ؟
فالفنان هو الذي يحمل فنه في كل جزء فيه ...
في كل لحظة يعيشها ..
انها ليست حرفة ..
ولا مفخرة
بقدر ما هي نوع من انواع الانسانية
فليس من السهل ان تطلق على شخص ما فنانا ..
جرب ذلك ..
ثم فكر بوعي وتركيز ..
وستعرف انك مخطىء كثيرا وكثيرا جدا ..
وما يأتي بسهولة يتلاشى بسهولة
فلا تطلق احكامك بسهولة
ولا تطلق الفاظك بسهولة
ولا تكتب بسهولة ...
وكن بسيطا ولا تكن سهلا ..
والفن هو كل شيء ..
فكن فنانا في كل شيء ..
قد لا تستطيع ان تمارس طريقة فنية معينة ..

ولكن متى ما استطعت ان تمارسها بشكل تظنه مرضيا ... مارسها بقرار تتخذه انت ولا تفرضه ...

ثم اخرج وتحدده ...

لا عليك من الرجم فالحجارة التي سوف يرجمونك بها ... ستخرج بينها بعد ذلك المشاب كثيرة ... وسنابل .

اخرج لتقرأ ما كتبت
وتقول ما فكرت
واشرح للعالم ما في جمجمتك
... قد يتطاول عليك لسان
قد تصفق لك يد
وفي النهاية ...
لا اريد ان يعنيك من الامر
سوى الكتابة ..
ورضاك عن نفسك
وضحكة تخلقها في وجه عاشق
ودمعة تذرفها في عين عاق

وموجة تظل دائما تذكر الناس بالبحار والشطآن والقوارب والصيادين ..

ثم لا يهمك مجافاة الناس لك ...
عدم بحثهم عنك ..
ابحث عنهم بصدق ...
ومتى اكتشفوا ذلك ...
سيبحثون عنك بلهفة لا تتصورها
وبحب لا تتصوره ..
ثم احرص على نبضك الصادق ...
واوراقك التي اردت ان تكون هكذا ،
وعين حبيبتك ..
ووطن لا يعرفك
وام لا تقبلك ...
وشعب لا يفهمك
وامرأة تبحث عنها
وصديق تفتقده
وشارع يشعلك
ووجه يفرحك ...
ودمعة تحزنك
وسرير يؤيك ...
وتجربة تشكلك
وقرار ينفعك
وفكرة خطرت ببالك
وقصيدة احرقتك
وكتاب صادقك
وعشب احياك ..
وقد اماتك ..
احرص على هواجسك المعنونة
وعفويتك الطاهرة
وبساطتك البريئة
احرص على استاذيتك التي لا تفهمها
وثرثرتك التي لا تقصدها
والصمت الذي يفاجئك
كن كما انت ..
كن كما انت ...
هذه نصيحتي لك ولمن مثلك في هذا العالم ..

التوقيع احمد راشد ثاني

Al Khaleej, December 14, 1981
Courtesy of the National Archives, Abu Dhabi

A Letter to Ahmed Rashid Thani
By Ahmed Rashid Thani

Al Khaleej
December 14, 1981

Should you witness a beautiful view
Should emotions overwhelm you some day ...
Should your soul overflow with emotions and dreams and obsessions unknown to you ...
Should a tear ignite you ...
Should a glance torment you ...
Should a child stir a din ...
Should a woman exhaust you ...
Should your love for a nation burn you ...
Should streets deny you ...
Should you want to speak ...
I wonder how would you speak?
You certainly will look for any piece of paper ...
On a cigarette pack
On a book cover
On a discarded sheet ...
On anything you can write on ...
You will write the first word ... and with the second, you will find yourself in a city you see for the first time.. A city so complete with its neighborhoods, climate, scents, colors, and people .. And a woman will emerge from this city, and within you and for you ... a woman you don't know ... with her own colors and features ... She will surprise you with what she wears... and in what she thinks ... and in what she does.
And all you have to do is take her and embrace her ... and burn ...
I know that you will burn a lot.
But soon after, you will feel a sense of relief ... some feelings of happiness and victory ... You will feel exhausted, and find yourself in an unusual state.
You will read what you have written ...
You will be surprised ...
You will unconsciously ask
"Did I really write this?"
You will come closer towards a mirror ...
You will ask yourself and your friends and your words ...
You will think of that gaze that captured you with its sharpness ...
And after that, you will return to a disenchanted state ...
as humans often do with all matters they like ...
And you will write once more ...
After a piece of news is released in a newspaper you love ...
After an article composed by a renowned author ...
After glancing in a woman's eyes ...
After getting to know a strange heart that is so pure ...
After a conversation with someone who does not understand you ...
After a beautiful something that refreshes you ...
After understanding ...
After realizing ...
After a state
After originality and depth ...
After sadness, you will write ...
And write ...
You might feel suspicious about what you write
And you might feel barren in the process
But it is then that you have to decide ... to exit
It is not important that you will find a medium stopping you, or a prominent author of festivals and foolishness and interviews suppressing you ...
It is not important that you will find your colleagues laughing at the mad man inside of you ...
And it is not important that you will discover, some day, that the world hates you for your preoccupation with tears, and emotions and sadness ...
and children and women
Don't be concerned with prison ... should you enter it crying for your nation

And don't be concerned about a noose that will embrace your neck as you scream against tyranny
And don't be concerned for a society that rejects you because you love it …
Write what you want and not what others desire …
And write what this moment dictates and not what you want
Imagine that you wrote this:
"This nation of yours is lost
And I am your poet so curse me
Here is your daughter, a lover
And I am her lover so stone me
And I am the outsider …
And if I launch towards you then go ahead and hang me
Come on hang me
For I, gentlemen, have eyes that criminalize me
And I, gentlemen, have a tongue that condemns me
And I, gentlemen, my crime is my poetry
And so it is clear, my crime does not desire
a witness who worked in the secret service
or another witness of my mothers eyes …
or my father's declaration in his book of sea as a poor fisherman.
You might not find a newspaper that would publish this for you …
It might be torn by the those you least expect …
You might encounter that witness from the secret service …
And he would publicly show you evidence from your mother's own eyes …
And another from your lover …
He will surprise you with your father's declaration in his book of sea as a poor fisherman
And with your poem that you wrote one day on your school's notebook
It is important that you persevere …
And that you know that things are coming …
And that one day you will show your poem to people …
They will react differently …
(People will disagree and you will discover that you, in your brilliance, are the point of their contention
You will discover those silliest in the world …
that is, if you do not discover your own essence, something that no one has done before you)
It is important that you persevere …
So don't worry about the fake noise people create around you …
And don't be concerned with skulls that repeat scripted sentiments and words everywhere …
And then, don't believe in any human being…
As in don't be fooled by anyone … for it will be hard to witness the fall of those you lift so high …
You who have tried to write …
And have tried loving writing
And those who love have to take a political stance …
And those who assume a stance are persecuted …
And those persecuted are wretched …
And the wretched have feelings.

Do read plenty …
And raise your voice with what you want to say
And draw your image as you like
For you are the situation, the image, and the person
Be you, however you are …
(Oh gentlemen …
These are my fingers
Five as you can see
In every finger there is a mouth
And in every mouth there lies a bed
And in every bed is a skull
And in every skull is a heart
And in every heart is a home).
You are after all for the people …
Write about and for them …
For you are so beautiful with wrinkles
And through the persistence of girls for a cause
And in the eyes of Layla …
And in the patriotism of two drinks
Be you, however you are and more …
Be the sea …
Be Khor Fakkan …
Be the entire world
Be the citizen, the wretched and the human …
I know all of this is torture …
And that writing a poem will burn …

I feel your pain from observing naive faces
That confront you with eyes you don't fathom ...
It hurts because they don't know ... How you wrote this?
And how you burnt?
And I know that you go to bed every night thinking ...
Looking for the woman inside of you
For the face that you do not recognize in your mirror
In a world that does not understand you
And at times you decide to remain silent ...
And say a lot to others ...
Remain as you are and do not change ...
Although I know that things change every minute ...
And don't be concerned with the art of polemics ...
And don't turn to something you know is against you, and against the sea and against Layla
And your drinks and your mother and your lover ...
At the end only your dreams will prevail ...
The person that holds to your concerns, and concerns of the earth and of love and the sea ...
Then look at those who are in front of you ...
The ones that rush towards a dish that eats them
The ones drowning in conversations condescending to them ...
The ones that play a ball playing them
We each have our own wounds ...
And we each look for a shoulder
Try to read their hearts out to them
You and whomever you love
And whomever you love and yourself ...
For their existence is yours ...
And their extinction in circles afar ... is your own extinction
Struggle to choose the one you love
And struggle to find someone to speak to ...
Struggle to write what you are writing
And struggle to look at what you are staring at ...
And then if you see your old face, then remain quiet ...
Read and encourage reading.
For if those skulls are educated, they will be recreated ...
And if they are created, they shall become ...
And if they become then things wouldn't have been as they are ...
Everyone is like you
With their own room ...
And their pen
And their heart
And their book
But it is you who recognized your own needs
So try and know that some more ...
And guide your friends towards their own needs ...
And don't you dare and limit yourself ...
For writing is not poetry
And the world is not just a mere moment ...
Be an artist wherever you are
And how shall you be?
For an artist is the one who carries his art in every part of his being ...
In every living moment ...
It is not a craft ...
Nor something to take pride in
It is a form of humanity
For it is not easy to call someone an artist ...
Try that ...
Then think closely and clearly ...
And you will know that you are mistaken, very mistaken
And what comes easy, vanishes easier
So don't judge prematurely
And don't utter your words prematurely
And don't write so easily ...
Be simple, but don't be easy ...
For art is everything ...
So be an artist in everything ...
You might not know how to practice a specific form of art ...
But when you can, then do so with a decision that you yourself take, not one that is imposed ...
Then go ahead and identify ...
Don't be concerned with the stoning you will receive ...
You will walk away with gray hair
Go on and read what you wrote

And speak what you think …
And explain to the world what lies inside your skull …
You might encounter obscenity
Or receive an ovation …
And in the end …
I want you to be only concerned with writing …
And with your own self contentment
And with a laugh you plant on a lover's face
And a tear you shed in an impious' eyes …
And a constant wave that reminds people of seas and beaches, and boats and fishermen.

Ignore people's indifference towards you
And how they won't look out for you …
For you have to look for them genuinely …
And when they discover that …
They will look for you with an eagerness you cannot imagine …
And a love you won't expect …

Then take care of your honest rhythm …
And of your papers as you wanted them to be
And of your lover's eyes …
And of a nation that does not know you
And a mother that does not accept you …
And of a society that doesn't understand you
And of a woman you look for
And of a friend you miss dearly
And of a street that inflames you
And of a face that you rejoice in
And of a tear that saddens you
And of a bed that engulfs you
And of an experience that shapes you
And of a decision that benefits you
And of an idea that crosses your mind
And of a poem that burnt you
And of a book that befriended you
And of grass that resuscitated you
And then killed you …

Take care of your self-made obsessions
And of your pure spontaneity
And of your innocent simplicity
Take care of mentors that you do not fathom
And of chatter that you do not mean
And of silence that surprises you
Be yourself, as you are
Be yourself, as you are
This is my advice for you and for those who are like you in this world.

7 1 1985

سلسلة الرماد 1.

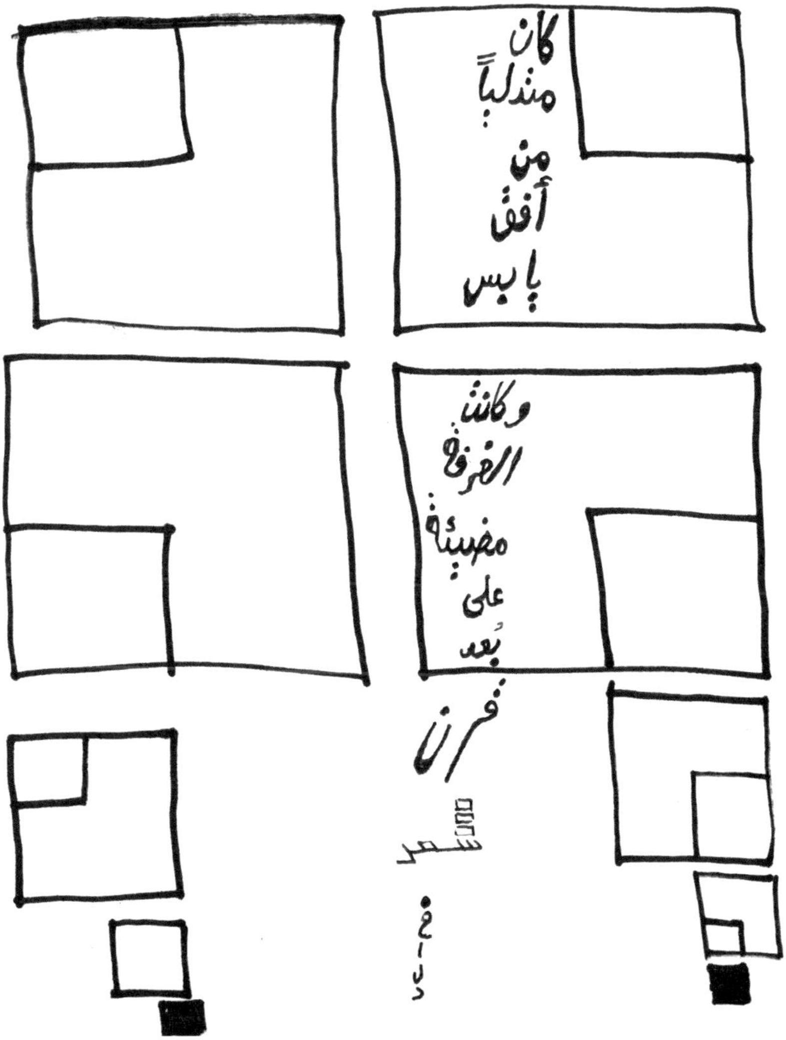

شعر

ح-د-اد

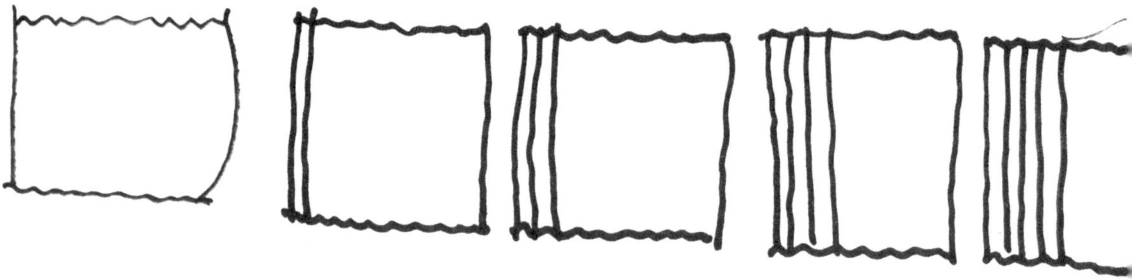

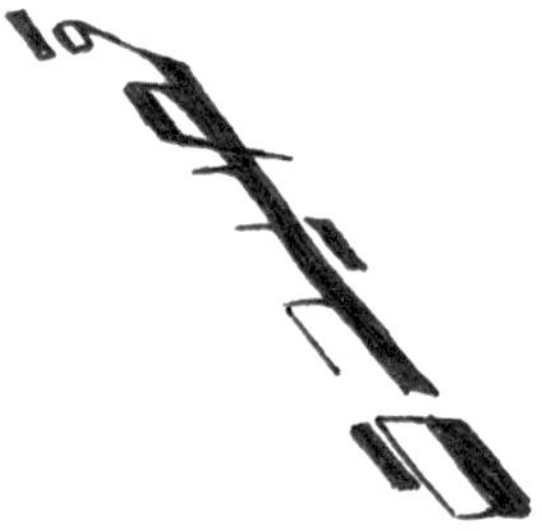

أحجار بيضاء تقشعر ..

رمل ينحدر في اللوحة ،

عسل ،

ليمون ،

برتقالة ،

وورد ..

و

جدار .

نجوم

١٩٨٥/١/٧

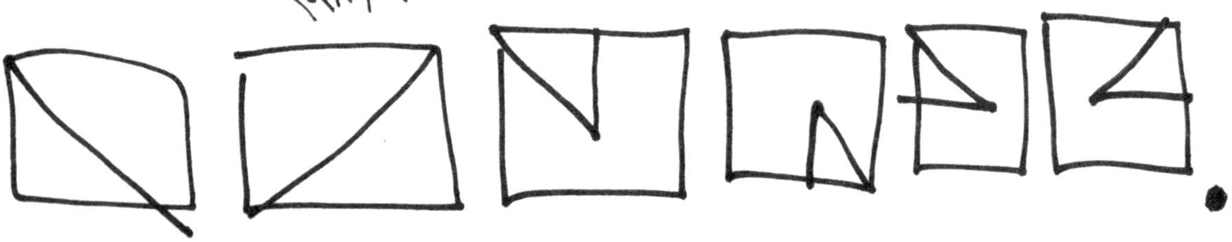

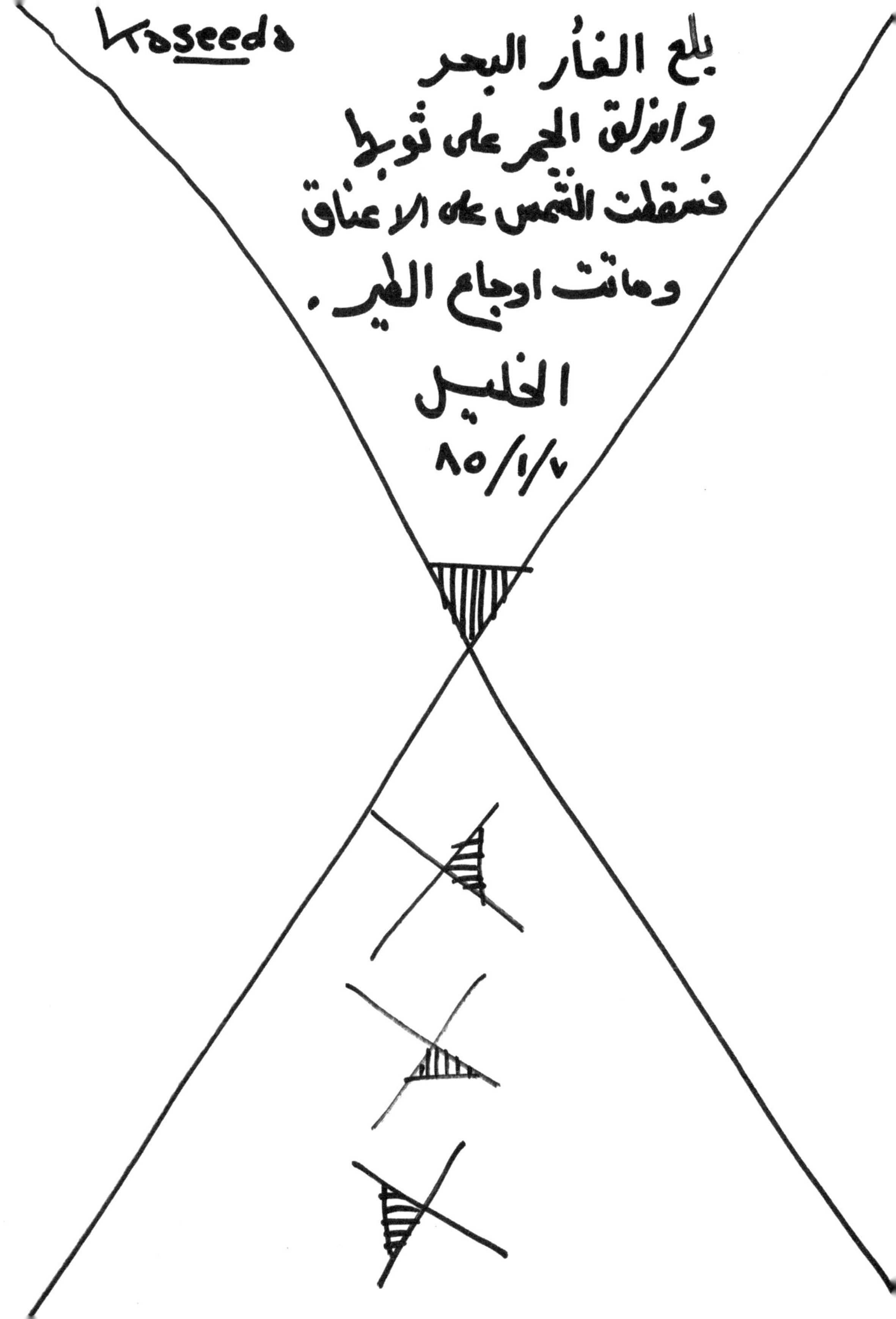
Kaseeda
بلع الفأر البحر
وانزلق الحجر على ثوبها
فسقطت الشمس على الاعناق
وماتت اوجاع الطير.
الخليل
٧/١/٨٥

اللوحة رقم واحد - اللوحة رقم 2 - اللوحة رقم 3

اللوحة رقم 4 - اللوحة رقم 5 - اللوحة رقم 6

اللوحة رقم 7 - اللوحة رقم 8 - اللوحة رقم 9

اللوحة رقم واحد 2 اللوحة رقم واحد 32 اللوحة

رقم واحد 432 اللوحة رقم واحد 5432 اللوحة

رقم واحد 65432 اللوحة رقم واحد 432

765 اللوحة رقم واحد 8765432 اللوحة

رقم واحد 98765432

"اللوحة رقم صفر"

توصيات تشكيلية

123456789
112345678
111234567
111123456
111112345
111111234
111111123
111111112
111111111

12
1213141516171819
1122113311441155
2211331144115511
6677889955443322
9988776655664433
9876543212345678
2324543256789999
3456789

حسن ألف

7-1-1985

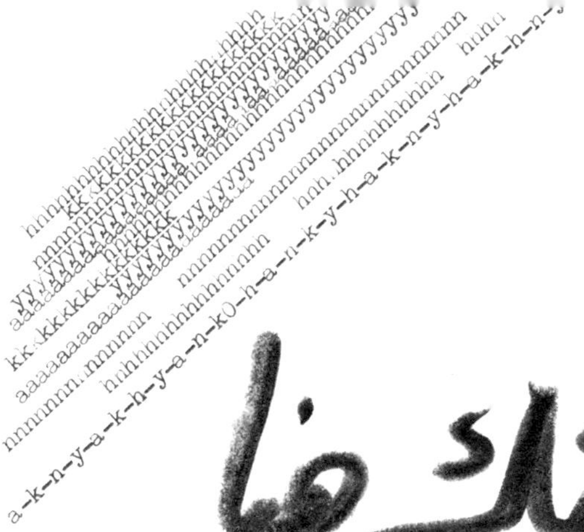

قصيدة

لو تدري انك هنا
الآن
لقلعت راسك برفق
ووضعته
على الطاولة

JAN 85

خصوصية

"زمن الرماد"

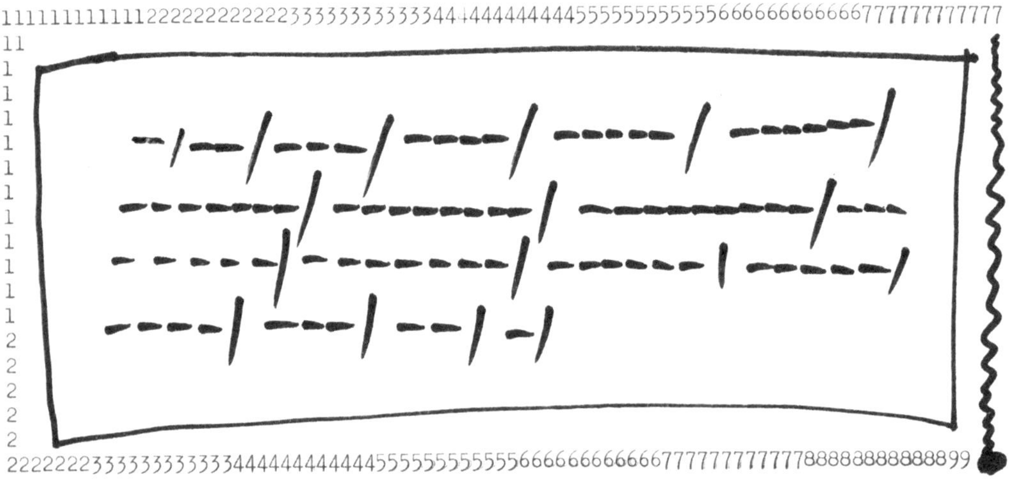

خيلا وقاسيا، كان. حال مولده
فقدته امه. عاد، يلبس الجمر
وينثر بالافاعي. خلفه هرولنا.. لكننا
لم نجده وتهنا وجدنا ظله

الخليل
٧/١/٨٥

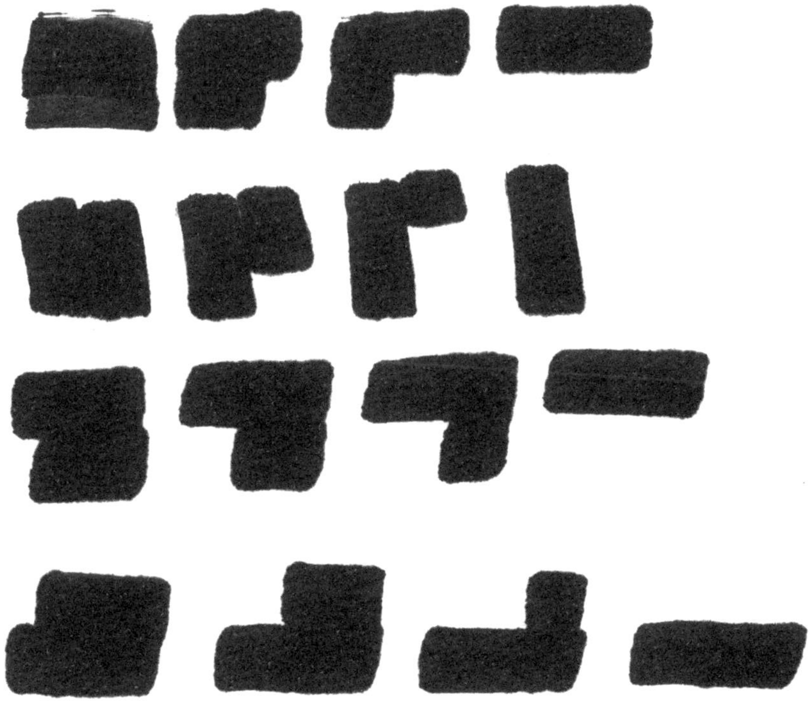

مربع أسود / ثلاثة أرباع مربع / نصف ثلاثة
أرباع مربع / ضلع مربع .

مربع أسود / ثلاثة أثلاث مربع / نصف ثلاثة أثلاث مربع
واحد .

مربع غير مستوى / مربع إلى غير مستوى / مربع شكل ٦
خط .

مربع قاعد / مربع نصف قاعد / مربع مستتر في مستطيل

• نقطة .

حسن/ألفو
٦-١- 1985

أعـــــلان
توقعوا في العـــــدد القــــادم
مفاجـــأة كبـــرى

نشـرة داخلية تصدرها جماعة (اقواس)
من مرسم (المريجة) الشارقة
١ ـ نجوم الغانم
٢ ـ حسن شريف
٣ ـ خالد بدر
٤ ـ يوسف خليل

Pages 173–180

Silsilat Al Ramad, Issue no. 1, 1985 (reproduced 2017)

Photocopied zine with poetry, writing, and drawings by Khalid Albudoor, Nujoom Alghanem, Yousif Khalil, and Hassan Sharif

English translation pages 182–183

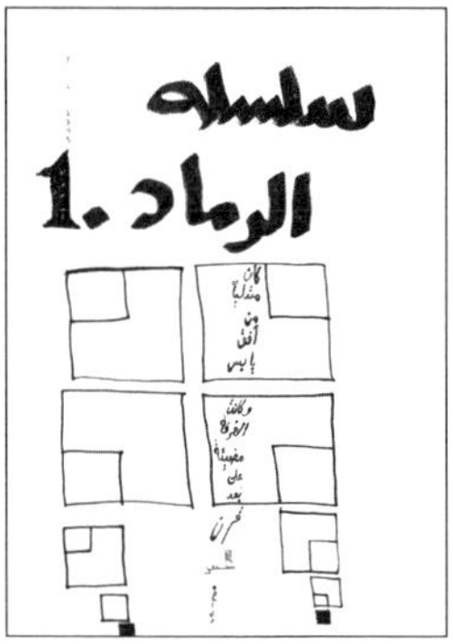

Silsilat Al Ramad .1

He was dangling from a parched horizon
And the room was lit, as far as a century

Poem
Khalid

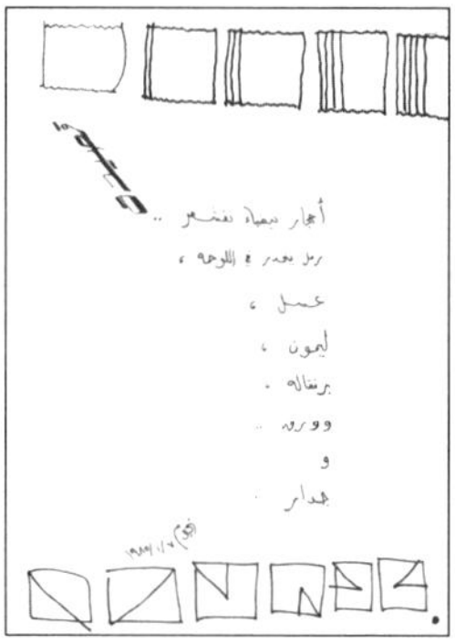

Poem

White chilling stones..
Sand descends into the painting,
Honey,
Lemon,
Orange,
And paper..
And
A wall.

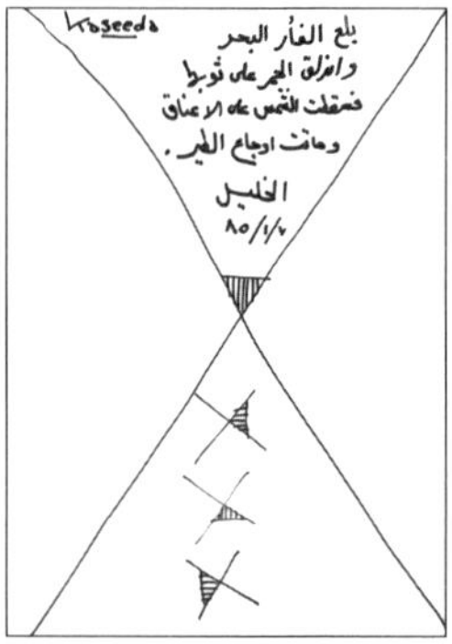

Nujoom, January 7, 1985
Poem

The mouse swallowed the sea
And embers slid on her dress
The sun fell on our necks
And the agony of the birds died.

Alkhalil
January 7, 1985

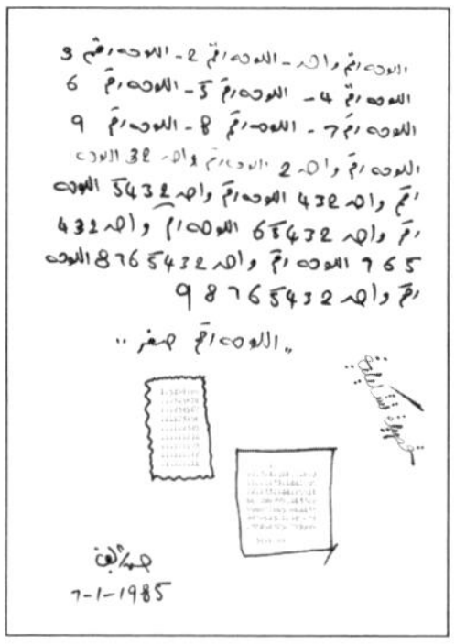

Visual Poem

Painting number one – painting number 2 – painting number 3
painting number 4 – painting number 5 – painting number 6
painting number 7 –painting number 8 – painting number 9
painting number one 2 painting number one 23 painting
number one 234 painting number one 2345 painting number
one 23456 painting number one 234567 painting number one
2345678 painting number one 23456789

"painting number zero"

Hassan Sharif, January 7, 1985

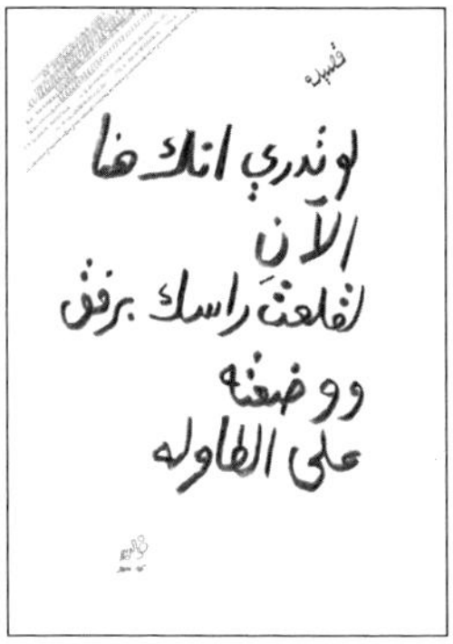

لو تدري انك هنا
الآن
لقلعت راسك برفق
ووضعته
على الطاوله

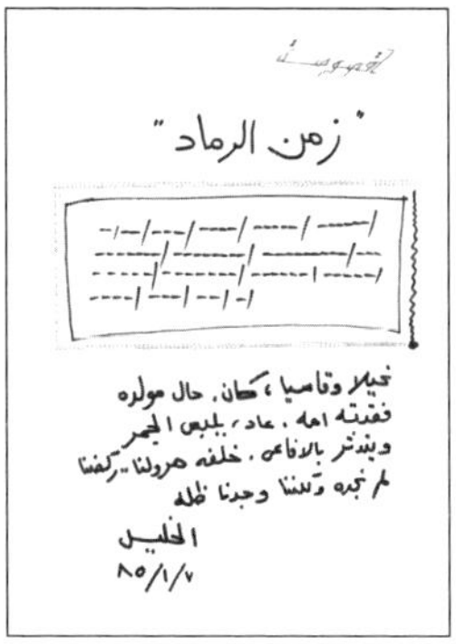

"زمن الرماد"

نحيلا وقاسيا كان. حال مولده
فقدته امه. عاد، يلبس الجمر
ويتدثر بالافاعي. خلفه هرولنا.. ركضنا
لم نجده ولكننا وجدنا ظله
الخليل
٨٥/١/٧

Poem

Should you know you are here
Now
You would have gently ripped your head off
and placed it
on the table

Khalid Albudoor
January 1985

Short story
"The Age of the Ashes"

He was lean and tough. The minute he was born his mother lost him. He returned once more, wearing embers and wrapped in serpents. Behind him we paced.. we ran. We couldn't find him but instead found his shadow

Alkhalil
January 7, 1985

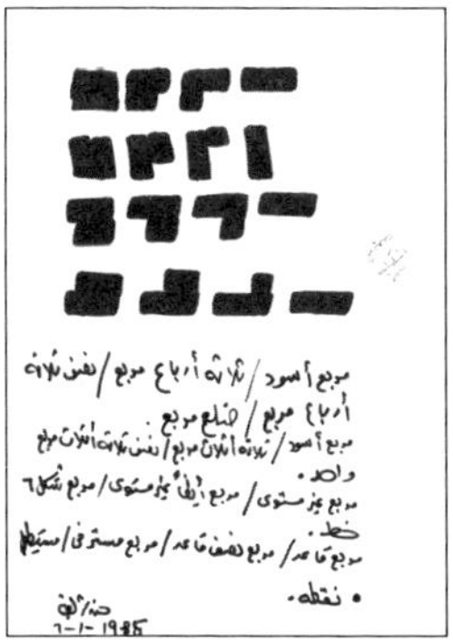

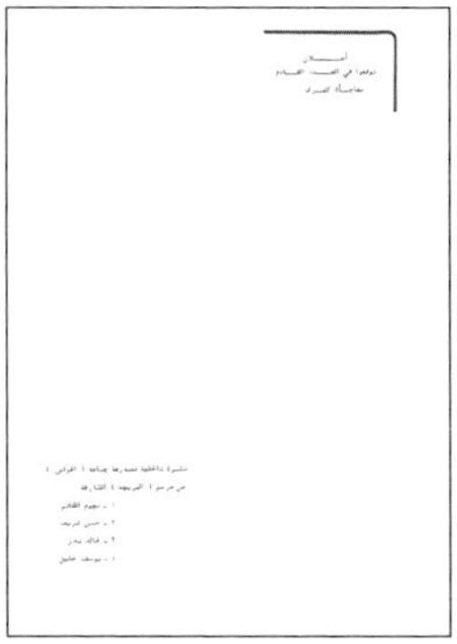

Visual Squared Short

Black square / Three-quarters of a square /
Half three-quarters of a square / Side of a square.
Black square / Three-thirds of a square /
Half three-thirds of a square.
Uneven square / Another uneven square /
A square in the shape of line.
A seated square / A half seated square /
A square flat on its back / A rectangle /
. Full stop.

Hassan Sharif
January 7, 1985

Announcement
Expect a big surprise in the upcoming edition

A journal published by the (Aqwas) collective from (Al Mareija) Atelier in Sharjah
1. *Nujoom Alghanem*
2. *Hassan Sharif*
3. *Khalid Albudoor*
4. *Yousif Khalil*

Nujoom Alghanem
Sara Al Haddad
Vikram Divecha
Lantian Xie
Dr. Mohamed Yousif

Texts by *Hammad Nasar*

Nujoom Alghanem

Nujoom Alghanem has worn many hats during her wide-ranging career as a filmmaker, poet, journalist, and artist. While Alghanem is best known as a prizewinning filmmaker in the UAE's contemporary artistic scene, her contributions to the UAE's Pavilion at the 57th Venice Biennale focus on her role in the lively exchange between the visual arts and poetry in the 1980s—a rich area for further exploration in the nation's cultural history.

Alghanem was a cofounder of the short-lived Aqwas collective (1985–86) with the poet Khalid Albudoor, the writer Yousif Khalil, and the artist Hassan Sharif. During this brief period while the group met and worked at the Al Mareija Atelier in Sharjah, Alghanem fully devoted herself to making art. She and Albudoor, along with the poet, writer, and cultural critic Ahmed Rashid Thani, were already founding members of the influential literary collective, the Emirates Writers Union. Straddling both groups, hers is a distinctive voice within the formative and collective conversation carried out in a language of rhythms and forms between artists and poets in the UAE (see pp. 148–167) for an interview with Alghanem and Albudoor).

A key example of the fruits of this interdisciplinary collaboration is the self-published art journal *Silsilat Al Ramad* (1985, pp.173–183). It was a collective endeavor by the members of Aqwas, and coincided with a period in which Albudoor, Alghanem, and Thani faced an unofficial "ban" on the publication of their work by the Emirates Writers Union. *Silsilat Al Ramad* was not simply an alternative mode of publishing, but a declarative platform against convention. Experimental in form and content, it included drawings, free verse, sketches, and even a numerical poem by Sharif. The first issue of *Silsilat Al Ramad* was produced in a photocopied edition of twenty, and distributed by hand to key editors and cultural commentators in the UAE. A stick of chewing gum was attached to the cover as a playful gesture. This humorous offering, however, was unable to sweeten the many scathing responses by a critical establishment that frowned at what they saw as the group's assault on poetic form.

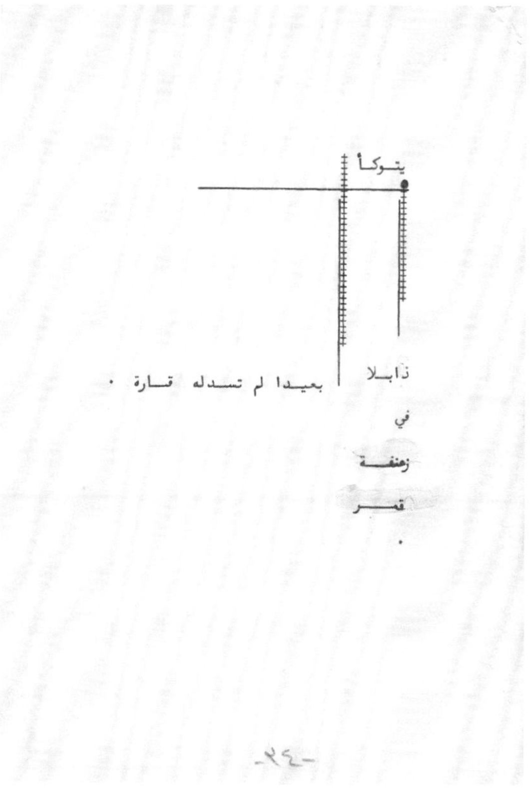
يتوكأ
ذابلا
بعيدا لم تسدله قارة .
في
زعنفة
قمر
.
-٢٤-

Leaning, 1984
Typed manuscript

Silsilat Al Ramad, issue no. 1, has been reproduced as part of Alghanem's contribution to the presentation at the Venice Biennale.

Alghanem sought new playful rhythms in free verse even as her poetic experimentation took liberties with the meter of classical Arabic poetry. Her efforts benefited from a period of dynamism in Beirut's literary and publishing scene: poetry and writings on art and culture from diverse sources were being translated, and a vital new stream of Arabic writing was emerging from the region, inspired in part by Gamal Abdel Nasser's visions of pan-Arabism. From this heady mixture, ranging from regional poetry magazines to Dada and Surrealist wordplay to the haikus of Basho and Issa, Alghanem sampled widely.

Her ambitions extended beyond the sphere of literary forms. She was investigating simple ways of injecting visual strategies into the construction of her own form of concrete poetry. *Leaning* (1984, above) and *Space* (1984, p. 190) are hand-typed exemplars of this experimental period, which juxtapose geometric forms and spatial arrangements of her free verse. Neither of these poems was realized in print form in the manner she envisaged—publishing constraints meant that publishers were unable to match her sense of adventure.

Space has been reproduced for the pavilion in a new, stand-alone form.

After the disbanding of Aqwas, Alghanem gravitated toward journalism, a more economically viable career option than testing the interstices of poetry and visual art in 1980s UAE. As the structure of her unpublished early poem, *An Unusual Day* (c. 1983, pp. 196–197), portends, she eventually ended up working with film, utilizing a professional scholarship to study first in the United States (1993–96), and then in Australia (1997–99). During her student days, she again found the opportunity to experiment, staging an elaborate outdoor performance set to a text, *Between Heaven & Earth, the Body I Borrowed* (1994). For her presentation at the Venice Biennale, Alghanem has rerecorded the text as part of a sound installation accompanied by a selection of the documentary photographs of the original performance.

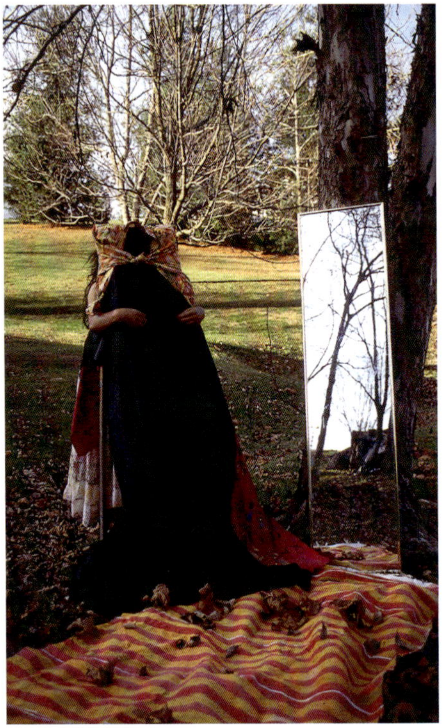

Between Heaven & Earth, the Body I Borrowed, 1994
Text, documentary photographs of performance, sound (rerecorded 2017)

Her films have covered a diverse array of subjects, and frequently foreground bold female characters such as Fatima Bint Ali Alhameli, the UAE's pioneering camel owner who enters her beasts in camel beauty pageants. But Alghanem's investment in the visual arts is also evident in her documentaries, most obviously in her film on the pioneering painter and sculptor Dr. Najat Meky (*Red, Blue, Yellow*, 2013), and an ongoing project on Hassan Sharif (*Sharp Tools for Making Art*, 2016–ongoing).

In her video/performance project, *Dancing with Shadows* (2012–ongoing, pp. 198–199), a man dances in a bare, crypt-like room. The camera follows him as he shifts from recognizably Sufi whirling to ritualistic trance to dance and back again. His mantra, expressed in the form of breathing, and the sound of his movements furnish the only soundtrack. Alghanem has shown this work as a single-screen projection, but also has ambitions to realize a multi-room installation choreographing movement, sound, and light, doing with the moving image what she did with the written word in the 1980s.

Central to all of her multiple interests—poetry, documentary filmmaking, and performance projects—is an undiminished commitment to experimentation with rhythm and form.

Nujoom Alghanem is an Emirati poet, artist, scriptwriter, and award-winning director based in Dubai. She has directed and produced several short fictional films and feature documentaries, and is a film, media, and cultural consultant to educational and professional institutions in the UAE. Her recent films include *Honey, Rain & Dust* (2016), which premiered at the Dubai International Film Festival (DIFF); *Nearby Sky* (2014), winner of Best Non-Fiction Prize in the Muhr Feature Competition at DIFF; *Sound of the Sea* (2014), which was awarded a Special Jury Prize at the Alexandria Mediterranean Countries Film Festival; and *Amal* (2011), winner of the Special Jury Prize at the Beirut International Film Festival. Her work has been shown in "Mind the Gap" at Tashkeel, Dubai (2017) and "Homage Without an Homage" at Art Dubai (2017). She earned a master's degree in film production from Griffith University School of Film in Australia, and a bachelor's degree in television production from Ohio University.

Space

One step

Two steps

Stop

Don't read

Paint an image

And disappear within it.

Space, 1984
Typed manuscript

.. فضاء ..

خطوه .

خطوتان ..

قف .

لاتقرأ .

أرسم لوحه 

وافل فيها .

Between Heaven & Earth, the Body I Borrowed
By Nujoom Alghanem

Not far from this nook the sky is gathering itself to meet the ground. The dragonflies migrate while the leaves of the fall pile up making homes for the arriving creatures. My voice is passing through the wind avoiding getting lost between heaven and earth. What's lighter than my body now but the flake of snow that fell earlier onto my back yard, adding more whiteness to the wilted grass with the milky color of morning? I have a curved spine and slightly unbalanced shoulders, just like my thoughts. On my face, two holes called the eyes given to me at birth. I cannot remember now the shade they had when I learned how to gaze at the horizon, trying to count the distant traveling ships. My lips had moved for three decades or so. My tongue learned to speak when it had to say something, yet never recognized why it had to speak all those lines. But, I can recall all the sounds that were left there in that little box called memory. Was it my memory though or the neglected safe of that body I borrowed when I came to earth?

The snow filled my plant pots with its sweet brightness but brought darkness to my room for several days. I lit candles to relieve the spirits of the night and to read my old poems so that the air would feel less quiet. In that darkness I became friends with my hands and feet. I could be at peace with the senses I had distrusted. Nevertheless, those nights threw all of my hidden fears back to me, the memories and their tendency to contaminate my days with their dullness.

If I have to tell you something my friend then let it be this:
let me tell you about the bruises I inherited from my mother.

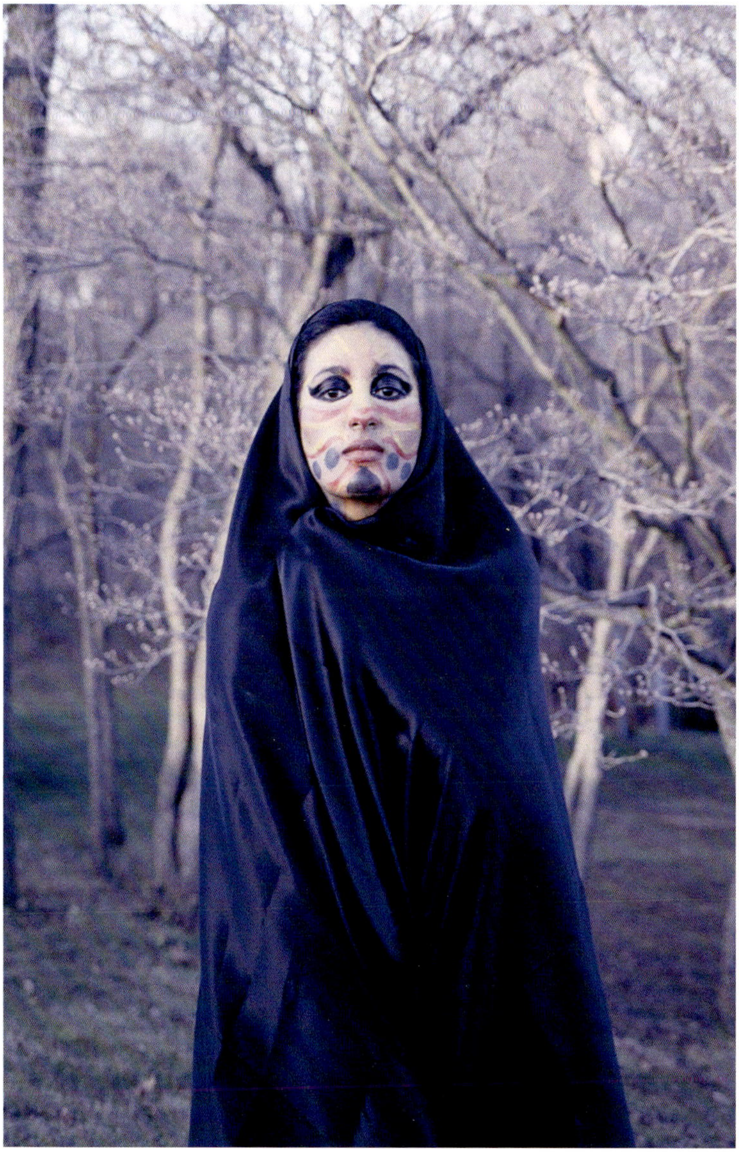

Between Heaven & Earth, the Body I Borrowed, 1994
Text, documentary photographs of performance,
sound (rerecorded 2017)

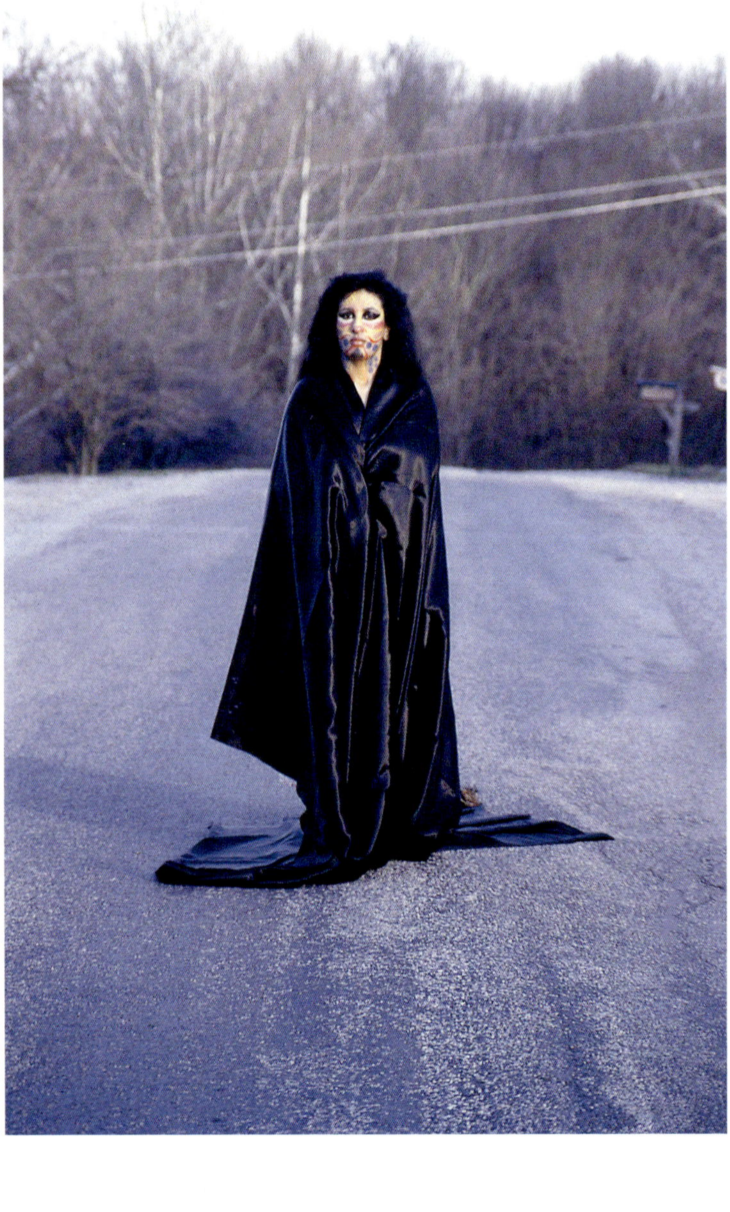

She gave me her sadness to care for like a small plant that never stops wanting to be watered with tears. She hid her night cries in my heart and never tried to take them back. She touched my hair with her wrinkled fingers but didn't realize that they might also touch my thoughts. I took after her in so many other ways, the gray hair, the trembling voice, the early symptoms of old age and the hunched back. I took after her in talking with myself, cursing life and blaming the angels for not backing me with my hopes for my children. And now I could see that I even inherited her red moles, her anger and cracking joints.

But I don't want to be like my mother.

I'll find myself a planet to call home, new wishes to trace or become sisters with life; I told myself when I saw her break as if she were just a frond.

Nothing remains the same, and this piece I wear above my bones will soon be dust to be blown in another sphere or back to dirt where I fear.

I'll celebrate the lakes before they dry, the woods before they become ashes, the beaches before they withdraw from our lands, and the desert before it swallows me.

Why cannot I believe you? Why is it every time I say we are companions you turn and walk away, leaving me with no replies or consolation. The mirror I received for my last birthday doesn't say a thing. The reflection coming through stares at me, no words to be heard.

I guess the remaining sky seen through the only window is getting narrower. The body that used to be tied tight to its ground is floating away. Was that the body I knew, or the soul that was just freed with the fall of the new snow that was carried by the light air, lost between my heaven and earth?

Between Heaven & Earth, the Body I Borrowed, 1994
Text, documentary photographs of performance,
sound (rerecorded 2017)

An Unusual Day

1.
Three women
and eight children
Half of them playing
and the other half walk clumsily.

2.
Two
A woman and a man
They disappear
quietly

3.
A veiled woman walks with a man
The woman is talking
The man is disgusted.

4.
A child passes by for the twentieth time
On a bicycle

5.
Three veiled women
and a "SriLankan" female carries a child

6.
An Ice-cream man
is stopped by a woman
She buys two kinds of ice-cream
She hums and eats...
The ice-cream man returns
She forgot her pen on his cart
I wonder what was she writing

7.
Four men
Why are they fighting?!!

8.
A veiled woman
Another woman leads two children
What brings them together?

9.
A lonely girl
Passing quietly near a check point
In front of the sea
What is she thinking?!
Here she is now
Rushing back...

10.
Blood on the pavement

11.
I will commit suicide,
a woman said.
Then she came back to kiss a man sitting on the pavement

12.
A terrible pain
Invades half of my body
and the other half is in oblivion.

An Unusual Day, c. 1983
Handwritten manuscript

13.
A local man walks alone on the corniche
He is sad
Maybe he had a fight with his wife
Maybe he hasn't spoken to his lover
And maybe…
Strange
A local chap alone.

14.
Three men cross the road
But
Without affection.

15.
I love you to yearning

16.
Again, a veiled woman…
Why is she frowning while looking at me?!

17.
You are far from me now
I love you
I wait for you to call
The lines of that unusual day had ended
Yet, I am in yearning for another day
An un-ordinary one as well

18.
…

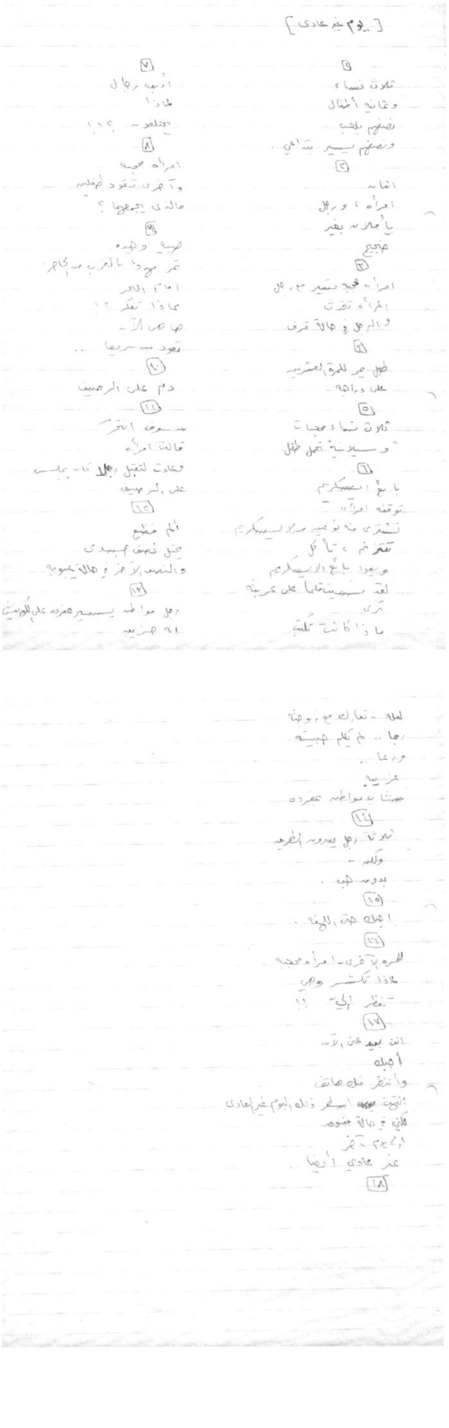

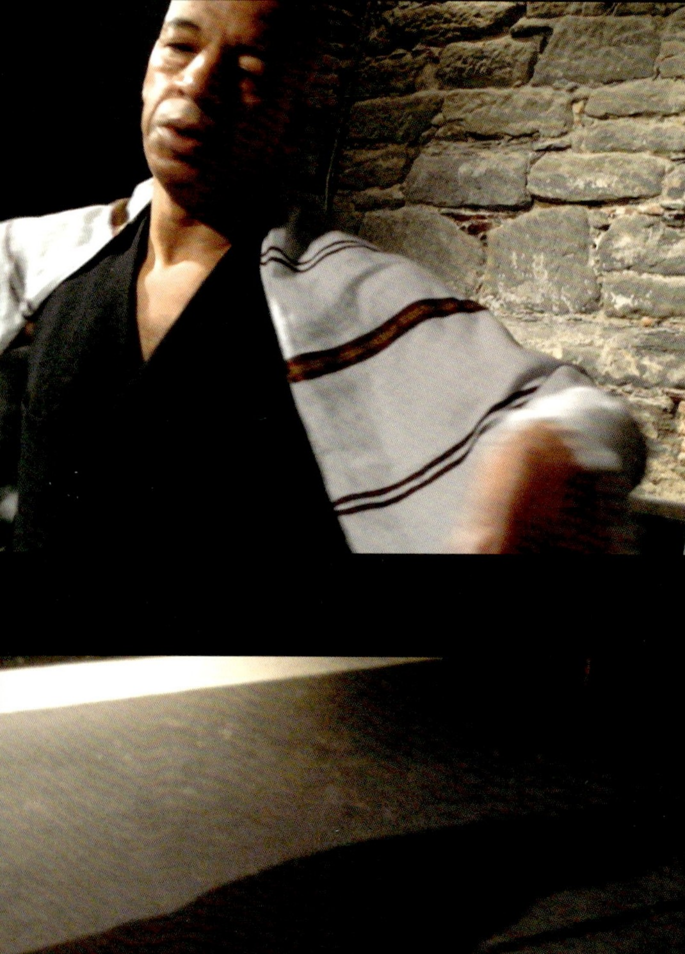

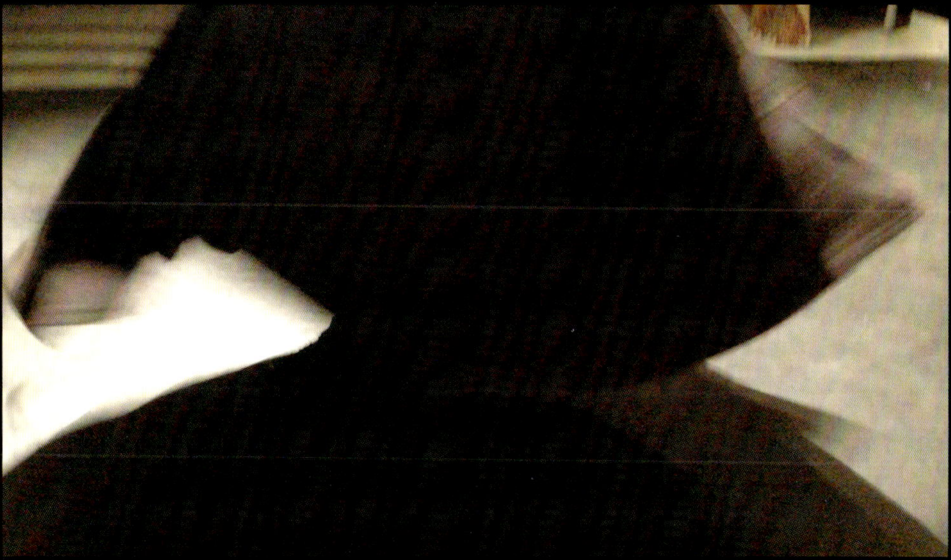

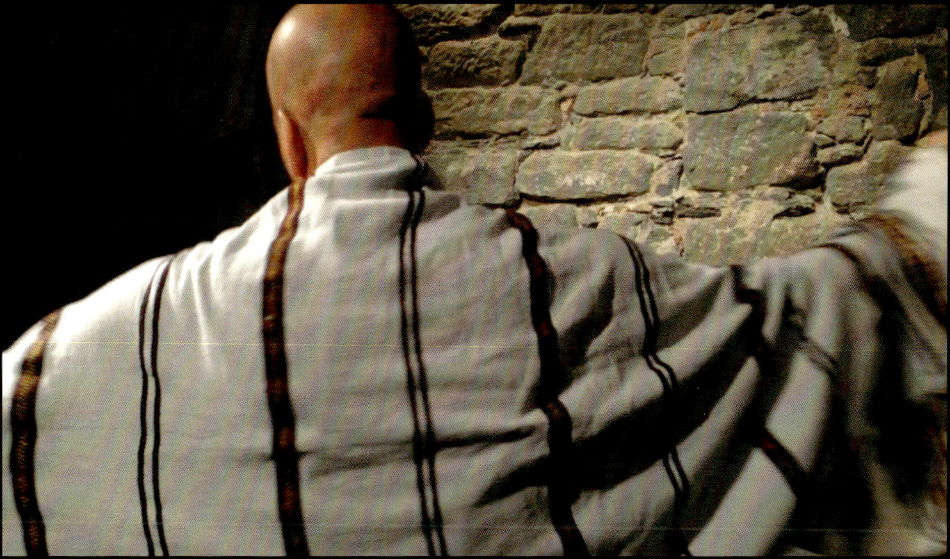

Sara Al Haddad

Sara Al Haddad works with yarn and fiber, crocheting, knitting, and stitching to create objects that can be hung, wrapped, piled, arranged, and stretched to occupy space. In doing so, Al Haddad also occupies time. Hers is a slow art, where the labor of making—always hers—is paramount.

This privileging of time and her hand is not in service of a vague idea of formal perfection, but embodies the conception of her work as a daily practice. It recalls the South Asian musical tradition of *riyaaz*—a regime of ritual-like diurnal exercises. But given that Al Haddad has often spoken about her art as embodying "internal struggles"—the doubts, fears, loneliness, insecurities, and challenges that comprise the messy business of life—it is perhaps therapy, meditation, and the physical workout that serve as more apposite analogies. Not in the singular, but as a chronic condition.

Al Haddad's series, *filling holes* (2012-ongoing, see opposite and p. 209), is an extended self-portrait. Initially shown as a set of thirty panels, each work features a word or phrase stitched in different colored embroidery thread on polyester film paper. The words reveal emotional states: desires (*i want more*), foibles (*i get jealous sometimes*), and compromises (*oh well*). At a superficial level, they recall Tracey Emin's neons and proto-Instagram confessional works (*I've Got it All*, 2000), but with the narcissism strained out. There is something transparent and diaristic in Al Haddad's efforts. In her choice of words, one can see flashes of what Louise Bourgeois, in her own diaries, called "our volcanic unconscious"—a state that can only be accessed through relationships and encounters with other people.

The transient nature of relationships is the subject of *"passing clouds," he said* (2016, p. 211), an arrangement of six crocheted sculptures arrayed on the floor, seemingly unable to contain the small stones that spill out of them. The sculptures' bright colors (pink, purple, yellow, green...) are insufficient to camouflage a patina of mild melancholia that pervades this work. Even the exhibition label—with each sculpture being mapped onto a single initial and a range of dates—is structured like a set of tombstones: memento mori to friendships.

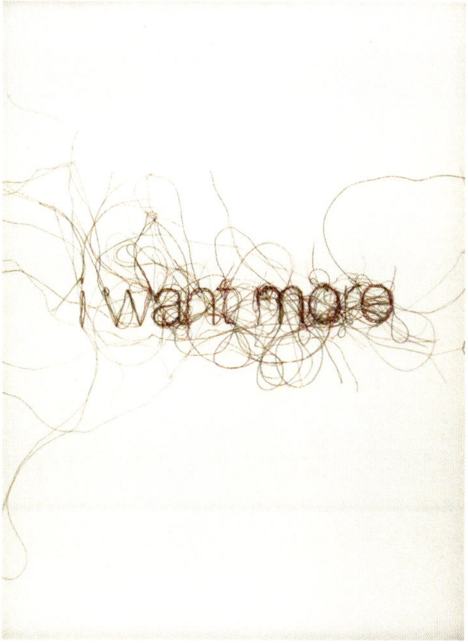

filling holes, 2012–ongoing
Embroidery on polyester film paper, 44 x 32 cm

This urge to document is clearly visible in *recordings: passing clouds* (2016, pp. 210). These drawings marry a rough outline shape for the passing clouds sculptures with the numbers of stitches in each row logged at the end of every day's work. They look like coordinates, a coded message, or a cipher. In a reversal of the usual relationship between sketches and sculpture, here the drawings record the sculptures as she shapes them. These drawings thus become functional objects, akin to musical notation for her improvisations.

For her presentation at the 57th Venice Biennale, Al Haddad presents a variation on an existing work and creates two new commissions responding to the pavilion space.

as you try to forget me (2015, pp. 204, 205) recalls earlier projects in which Al Haddad wrestles large-scale yarn sculptural installations into inhabiting a space, in the vein of *without* (2013) and *therefore; thereafter* (2014). But unlike the site-specific nature of her previous installations, *as you try to forget me* evolves through display. It was first exhibited suspended from the ceiling. Half-twisting in space, half-resting on the floor, it suggested a seated figure, "legs" crumpled and trailing, as if struck down by the unrequited love contained in the work's title. In its second showing the sculpture was draped, towel-like, on a railing suspended from a high ceiling, one end snaking on the floor to suggest a tidal flow—marking time through presence. At the Venice Biennale Al Haddad experiments with a new arrangement: another stage, perhaps, in the creative process of forgetting.

In *can't you see how i feel* (p. 206), a new commission, Al Haddad sheaths one of the black steel pillars supporting the pavilion in different sized layers of pink yarn. In an earlier work, *distractions* (2011, p. 208), Al Haddad fashioned a headdress from crocheted and knitted yarn. The work's photo documentation shows the artist wearing her creation, partially hiding her face but making her performative intent clearly visible. In *can't you see how i feel* Al Haddad substitutes the pillar for her own body while playfully adorning the pavilion's most masculine architectural feature in an avowedly "girlie" pink. The pillar ceases to be a pillar; it simultaneously goes into hiding and invites the viewers' touch.

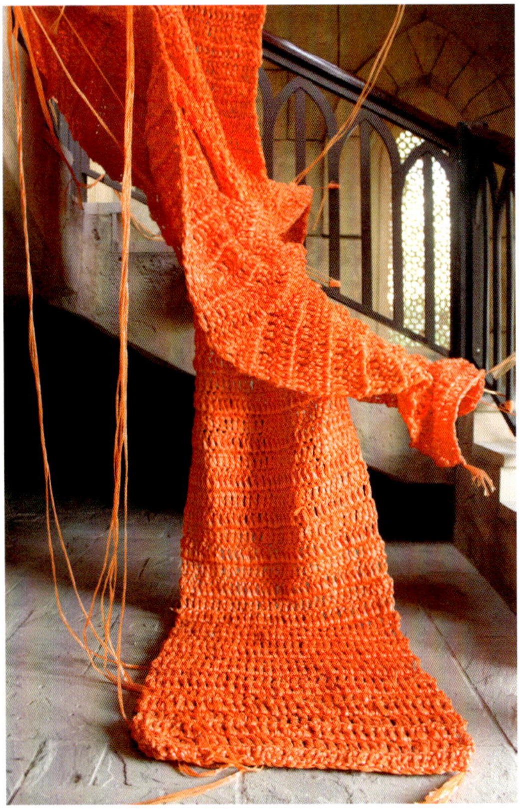

therefore, thereafter, 2014
Plastic yarn; dimensions variable

Al Haddad's second commission, *don't you ever leave me alone* (p. 207), also colonizes the pavilion's architecture by knitting a screen between the two pillars at its southern entrance. Materially, the fine embroidery thread recalls a spiderweb, echoing art history (Faith Wilding's *Crocheted Environment* (1972) or Louise Bourgeois's multiple sculptures of spiders); and contemporary politics ("separation barriers" from North America to South Asia). It also recalls a popular story of the *Hijrah* (the historic migration from Mecca to Medina) during which the Prophet Muhammad (peace be upon him) and a companion took shelter in a cave while being pursued by assassins. They were saved from discovery by a spiderweb spun overnight to cover the mouth of the cave.

For Al Haddad, "things that separate," such as a screen, offer the opportunity of perspective. *don't you ever leave me alone* does this by introducing an additional character—shadows cast on the floor—to the stage of the pavilion, but also by creating a border, marking territory. And in an unintended irony, lent import by current geopolitics, the neighboring pavilion Al Haddad partly screens from the UAE is none other than Mexico's.

Al Haddad's art—from the choice of materials and forms (sheathing a phallic steel column in pink yarn, for instance) to her working methods embedded in daily practice—is anchored in trajectories of recognizably feminist practice. But it spills beyond feminism's lightly patrolled borders to become an art of gentle occupation and surreptitious performance. Through presence, relationships, and the passage of time, she is *settling*—making a space home.

Sara Al Haddad is an artist based in Dubai. She was a Fulbright Scholar at the Maryland Institute College of Art in Baltimore (MFA, Sculpture, 2016), and earlier graduated from the American University of Dubai (2011). Al Haddad has had two solo exhibitions, "i know, i knew" at the Gallery of Light in 2013 after completing a two-month residency at the Dubai Community Theatre & Arts Centre (DUCTAC), and "Bursting at the Seams" at Pavilion Downtown Dubai in 2012. Her recent group exhibitions include "Bayn: The In-Between," Warehouse 421, Abu Dhabi (2017); "ACADEMY 2016," Connersmith, Washington, DC (2016); "Ramadanization," Gallery of Light, Dubai (2016); "not really here," Platform Gallery, Baltimore, USA (2016); and "Beyond," Abu Dhabi Art (2015).

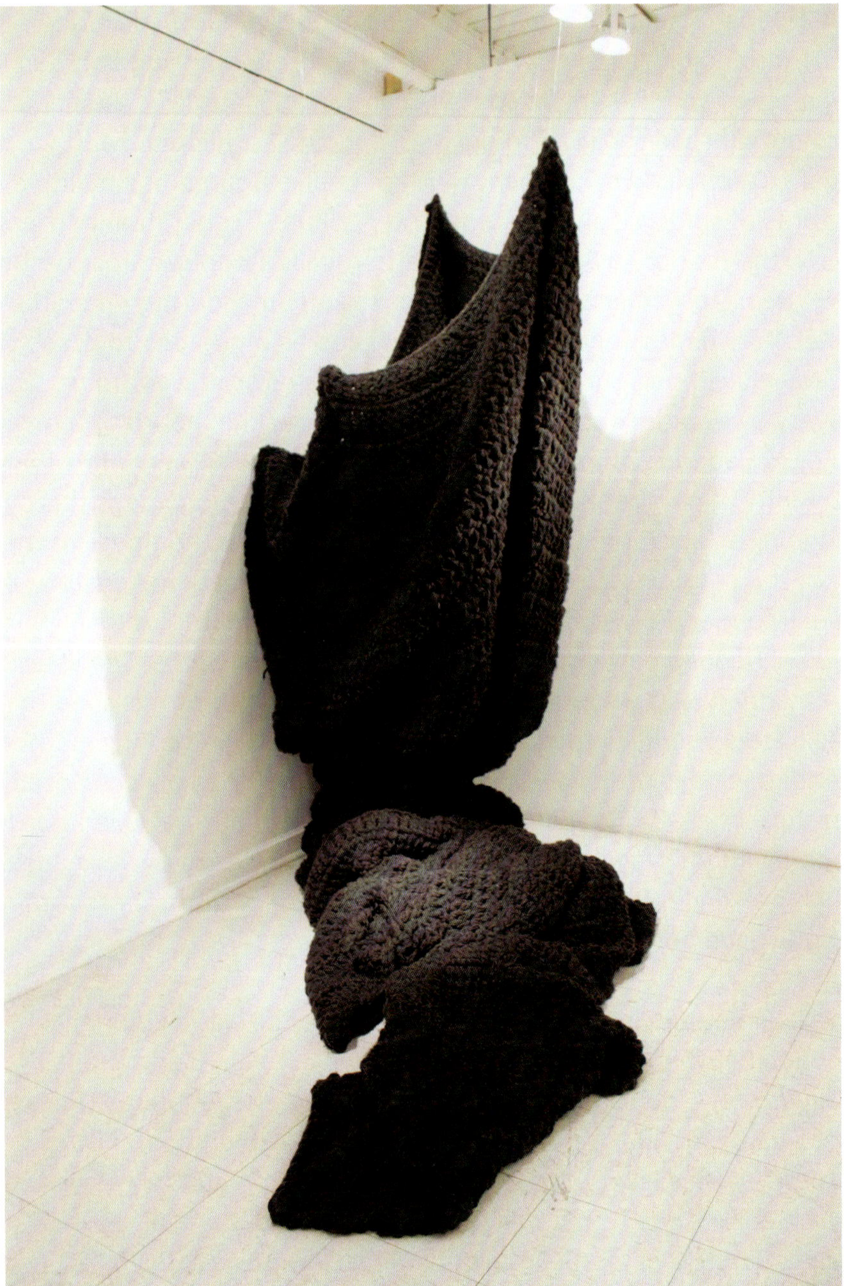

as you try to forget me, 2015
Yarn, metal rings, and cardboard; dimensions variable

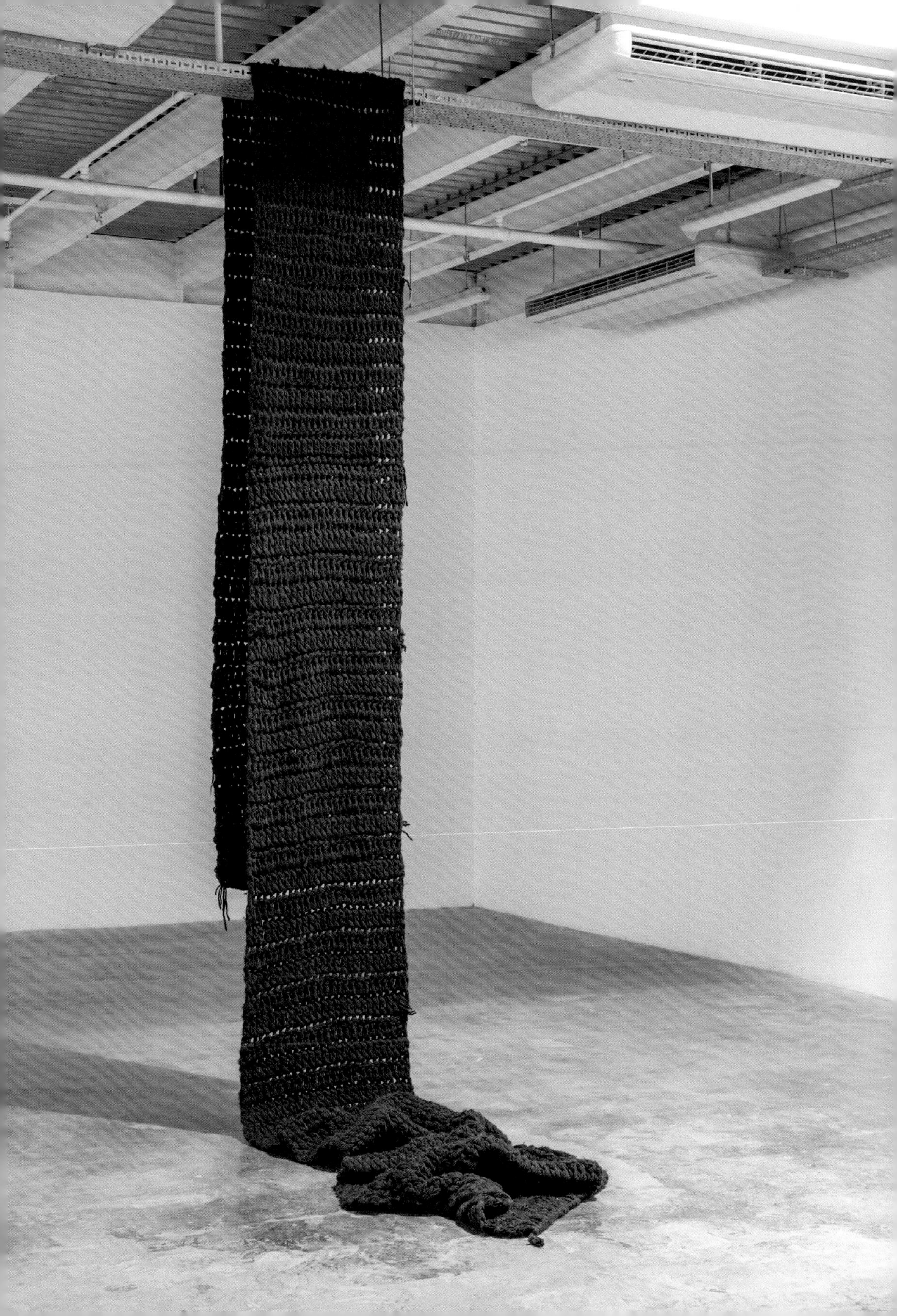

Sketch for *can't you see how i feel*, 2017
Crocheted yarn; dimensions variable

Commissioned by the National Pavilion of the United Arab Emirates
for the 57th International Art Exhibition – la Biennale di Venezia

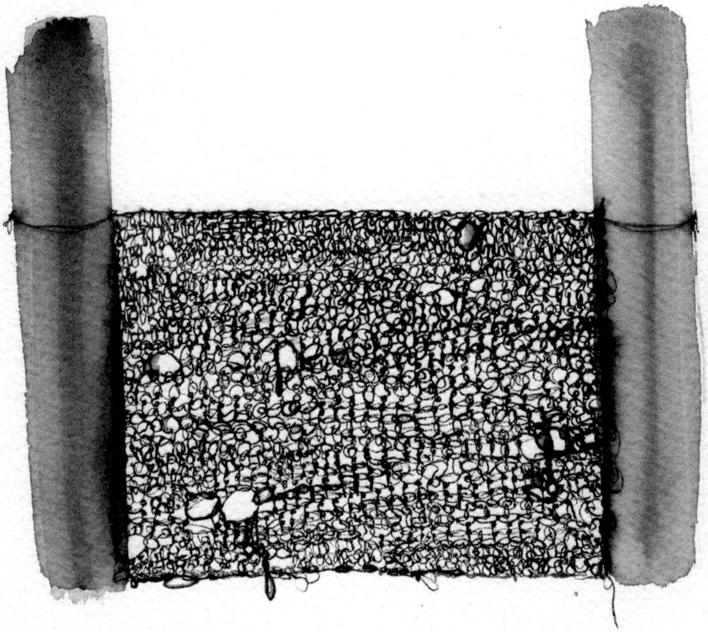

Sketch for *don't you ever leave me alone,* 2017
Crocheted embroidery thread; dimensions variable

Commissioned by the National Pavilion of the United Arab Emirates
for the 57th International Art Exhibition – la Biennale di Venezia

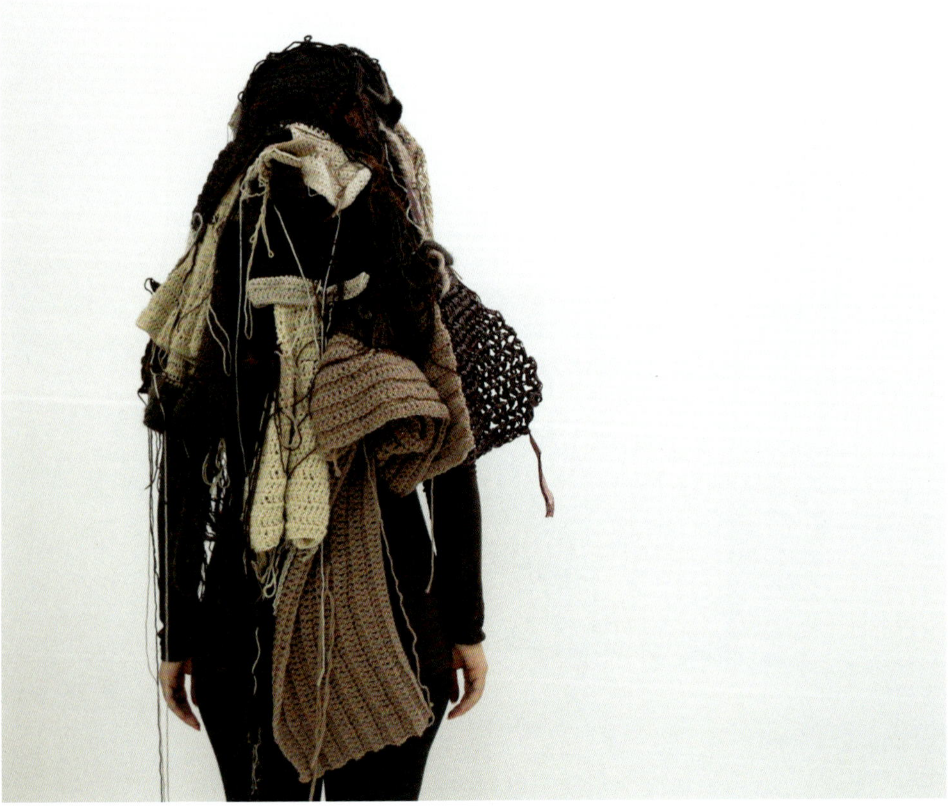

distractions, 2011
crocheted and knitted yarn and plarn; dimensions variable

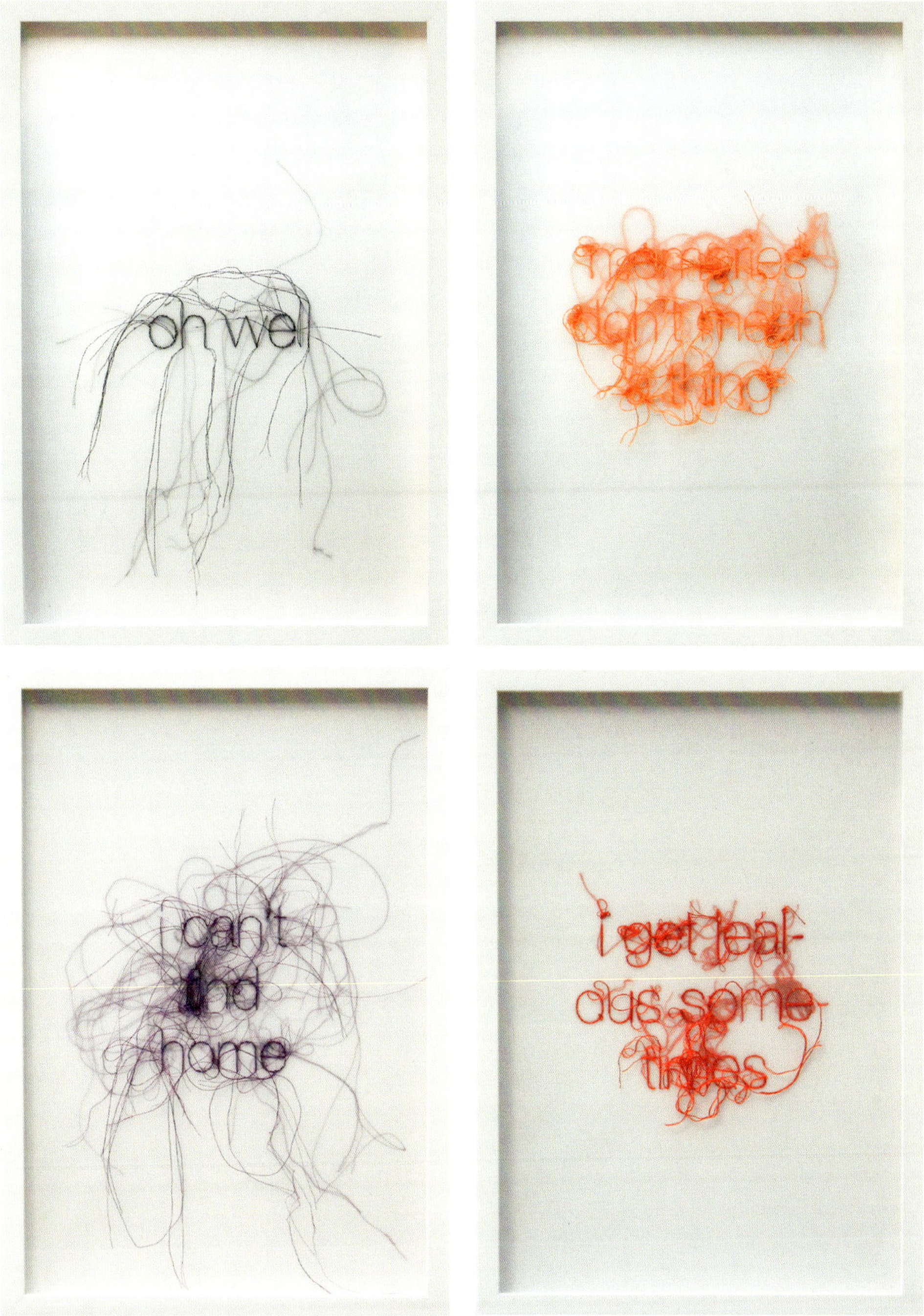

filling holes, 2012–ongoing
Embroidery on polyester film paper, 44 × 32 cm

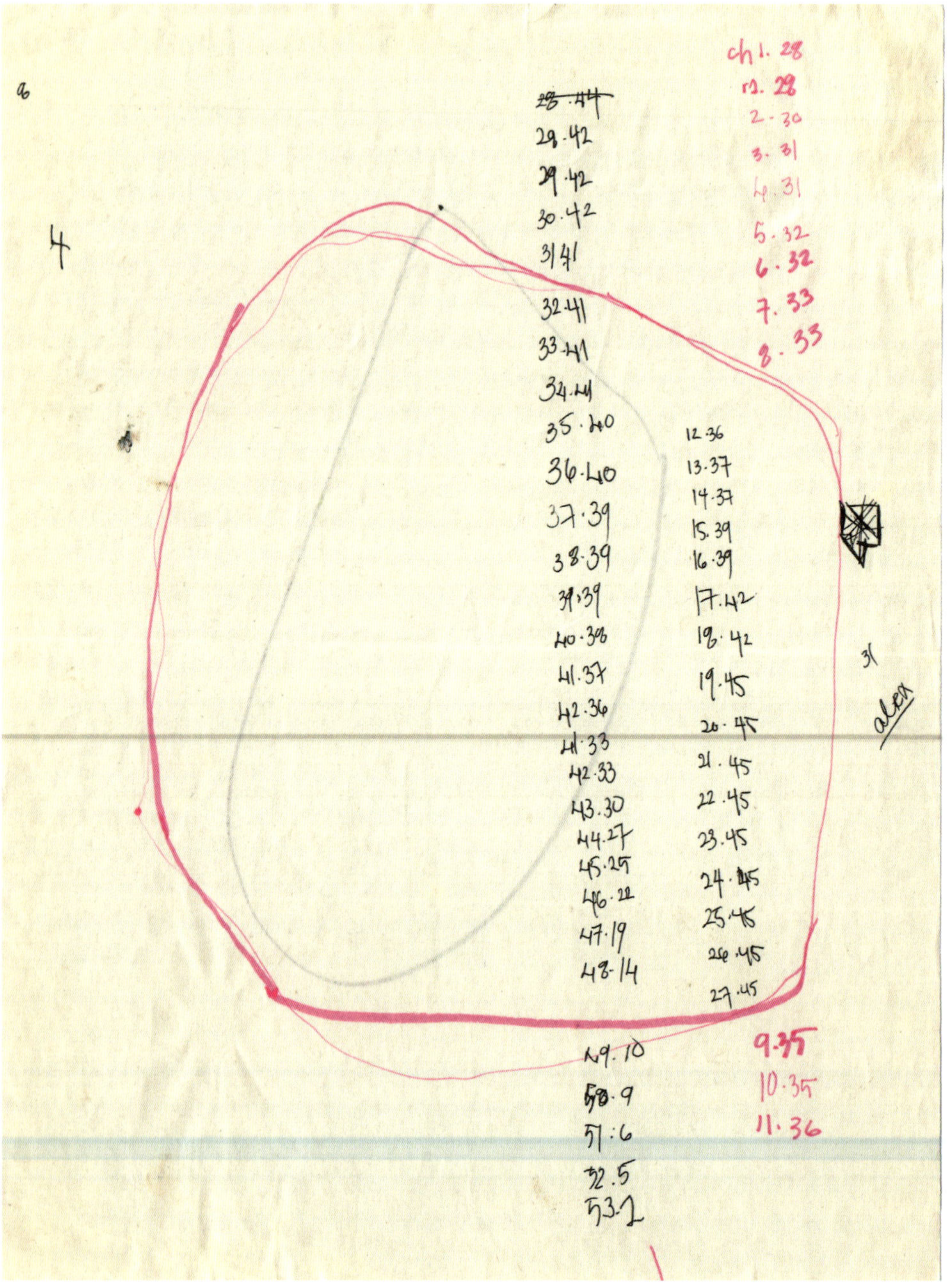

recordings: passing clouds, 2016
Pen on paper

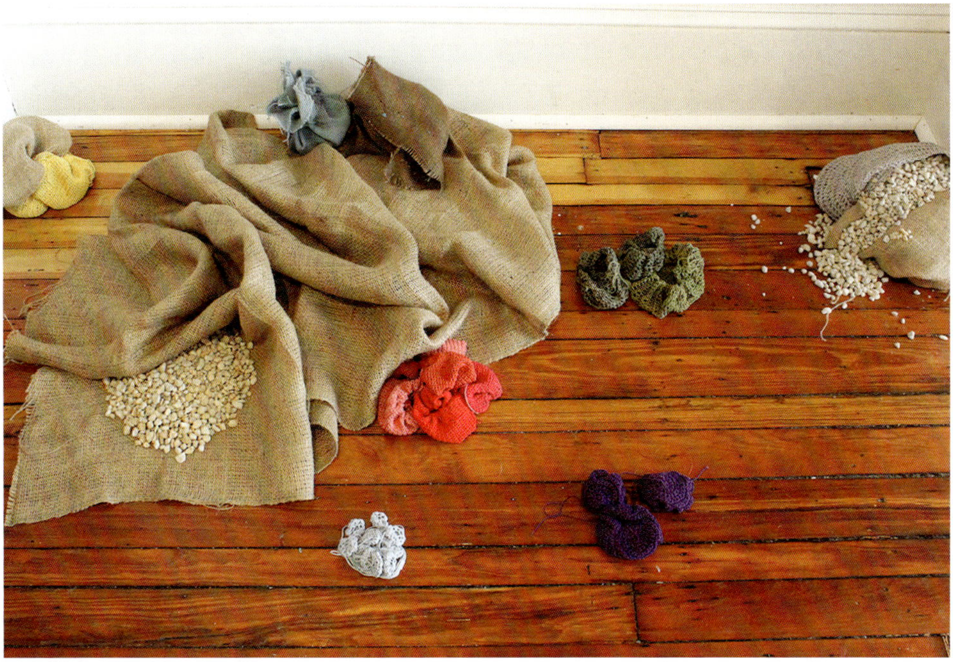

"passing clouds," he said, 2016
Chain stitch 3
rw 1 – 3
inc 2
rw 2 – 5
1, 2, 3, 4, 5, 6, 7

M. 2007 – 2015
N. 2011 – 2015
T. 2011 – 2015
L. 2014 – 2015
G. 2011 – 2015
N. 2003 – 2015
M. 2011 – 2015

Cotton thread, burlap and stones; dimensions variable

Vikram Divecha

Vikram Divecha's work often takes form as site-aware sculptural installations that produce affect through an elaborate orchestration of "found processes" such as waste collection, hedge trimming, road repair, and other banal workings of a city or community. He brings curiosity and wonder to the unlikely junction where everyday economics meets formalist aesthetics.

This working mode is made possible by the privileged access granted to him as a South Asian professional man in the UAE, with the social fluidity to traverse the UAE's complex demographics and multiple constituencies—in particular, art world patrons, municipal and city authorities, manual laborers. His works neither celebrate nor obscure these enabling conditions, often bringing questions of agency, ethics, and value into conversation with the manifold histories and discordant aesthetics, vernacular and modernist, of a fast-changing Dubai.

The Warehouse Project (2016, see pp. 222, 223, 224–225) is exemplary of these multivalent ambitions integral to his practice. Divecha arranged for a warehouse in Dubai's principal art district to function in the service of a regional distributor of toys, while simultaneously displaying its fluctuating stock as a dynamic sculptural installation. This complex situation opened up kaleidoscopic vistas into multiple strands of practice in art history—Carl Andre's formalist arrangements, Andy Warhol's popular appropriations, Rasheed Araeen's participatory installations, and Joseph Beuys's social sculpture all come to mind. It also engaged the UAE's long history as an entrepôt, home to a mercantile form of Indian Ocean cosmopolitanism. By composing this choreography of simultaneous labor and consumption—laborers moved boxes to fulfill orders, while art audiences toured the warehouse—he made visible the trade between real estate and art. The warehouse thus became a point of exchange of both form and value—where capitalism briefly rested as art, before becoming commodity again, echoing, in its slippage between different circulatory networks, his earlier work, *Boulder Plot* (2014, see p. 228–229).

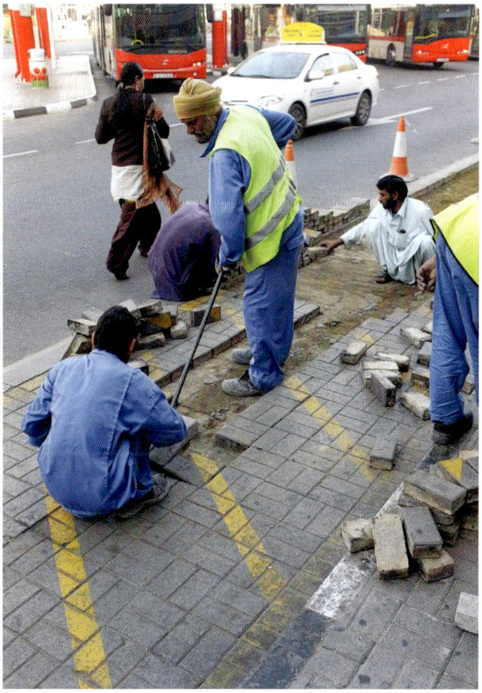

Degenerative Disarrangement, 2013

For his presentation at the Venice Biennale, Divecha has been invited to extend his project, *Degenerative Disarrangement* (2013). In its first iteration, he had arranged for the bricks comprising a section of pavement at a Dubai bus stop—which was painted over with diagonal yellow lines—to be "uprooted" and rearranged to form the courtyard of a historic house, with the yellow paint on the bricks dispersed. The work was completed within a fixed time frame determined in relation to the masons' daily wages. These four tons of bricks have now been "relocated" to Venice, where a different set of workers has arranged them in an order of their own making.

The work operates in a visual register that recalls geometric abstraction—a visualization of the interrupted rhythms of jazz. But similar to *The Warehouse Project*, it makes literal the transformation of value when objects from one system (municipal) enter another (the art world). It also mirrors the large-scale movement of labor from South Asia to the UAE in search of economic opportunity: "let's go to Dubai"—the translation not quite capturing the urgency and opportunity of the Urdu phrase that reverberated through 1990s Pakistan, *Dubai chalo*.

The "relocation" of this bricks-turned-art to Venice creates a parallel enhancement of value, one that may only be realized when these bricks find their way back home to the UAE—an enrichment alluded to in yet another common phrase heard in South Asia: *Gulf Return*, associated with the return home (to South Asia) of laborers whose stint in the Gulf has enhanced their store of economic and social capital.

Divecha's second work in the pavilion is a new commission, the video *Bathing Boulders* (2017, see pp. 220–221). The work began as documentation of the making of *Boulder Plot*—washing a series of boulders before arranging them to form a short-lived sculptural garden. But it has been transformed through the editing process to create a sort of moving meditation set to the rhythm of its gestures, the flow of water, and movement of shadows. It triggers associations that are simultaneously spiritual (*wuzu*—ritual ablutions before Muslim prayers, bathing deities in Hindu temples), pastoral (bathing elephants in Sri Lanka's famed elephant orphanages), and sensual.

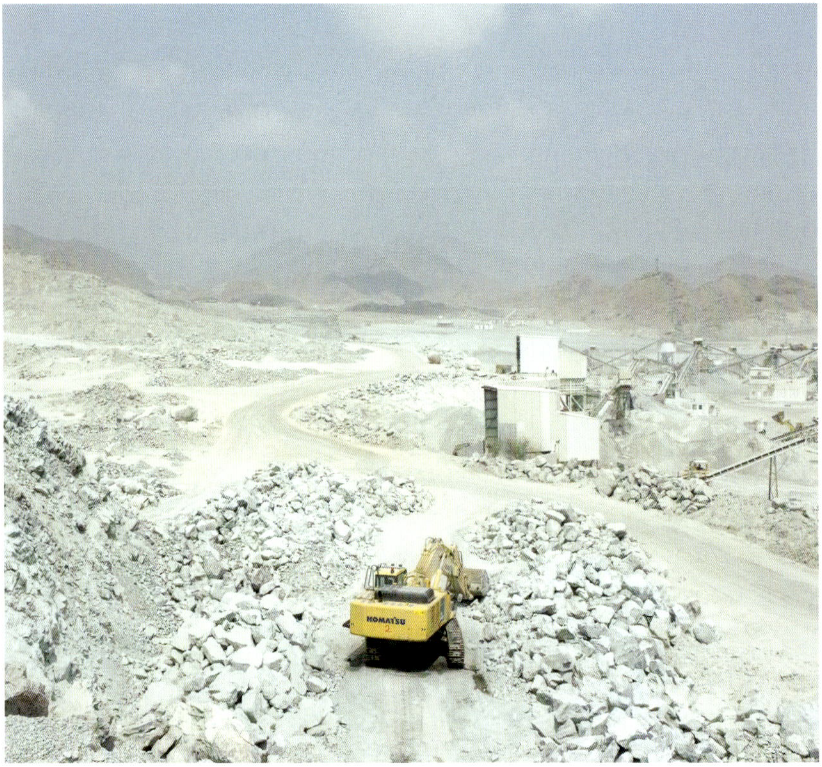

Boulder Plot, 2014

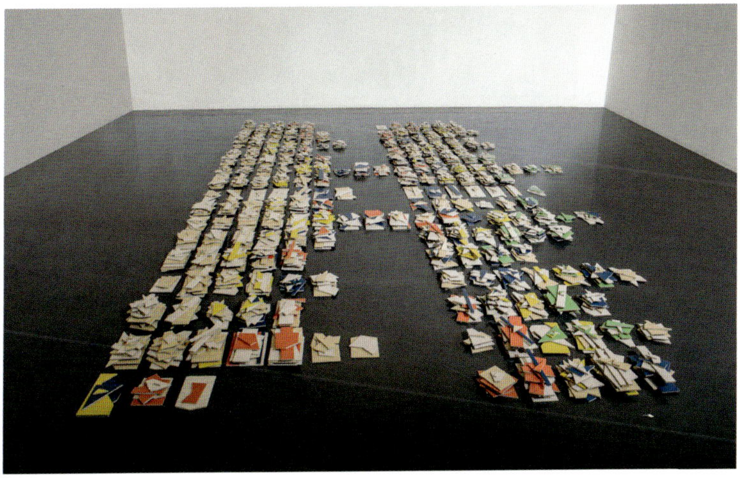

Negative Heaps, 2015
Porcelain tiles; dimensions variable
Commissioned by Unlimited Arab Exploration, Dubai

Divecha's practice can be seen as a social form of sculpture: shaped through negotiation, persuasion, and a spirit of mercantile entrepreneurialism; and realized by means of memos, contracts, and workshops. He realigns social and economic relations across diverse networks to produce "glitches"—ripple-like effects that are often transient but a source of aesthetic charge and of beauty, like pebbles in a pond.

Mumbai-bred Vikram Divecha (born 1977, Beirut) is an artist based in Dubai. Exhibitions include Sharjah Biennial 13, "Tamawuj" (2017); "Binary States India—UAE," Kochi (2016); "Portrait Sessions," Tashkeel, Dubai (2016); "White Cube... Literally," Gallery Isabelle van den Eynde, Dubai (2016); "Warehouse Project," Alserkal Commission (2016); "DUST," Centre for Contemporary Art, Ujazdowski Castle, Warsaw (2015); "Accented," Maraya Art Centre, Sharjah (2015), among others. Recipient of the 2014 Middle East Emergent Artist Prize, he has also created projects for The Arab Fund For Arts and Culture's public art commission "InVisible" in 2014.

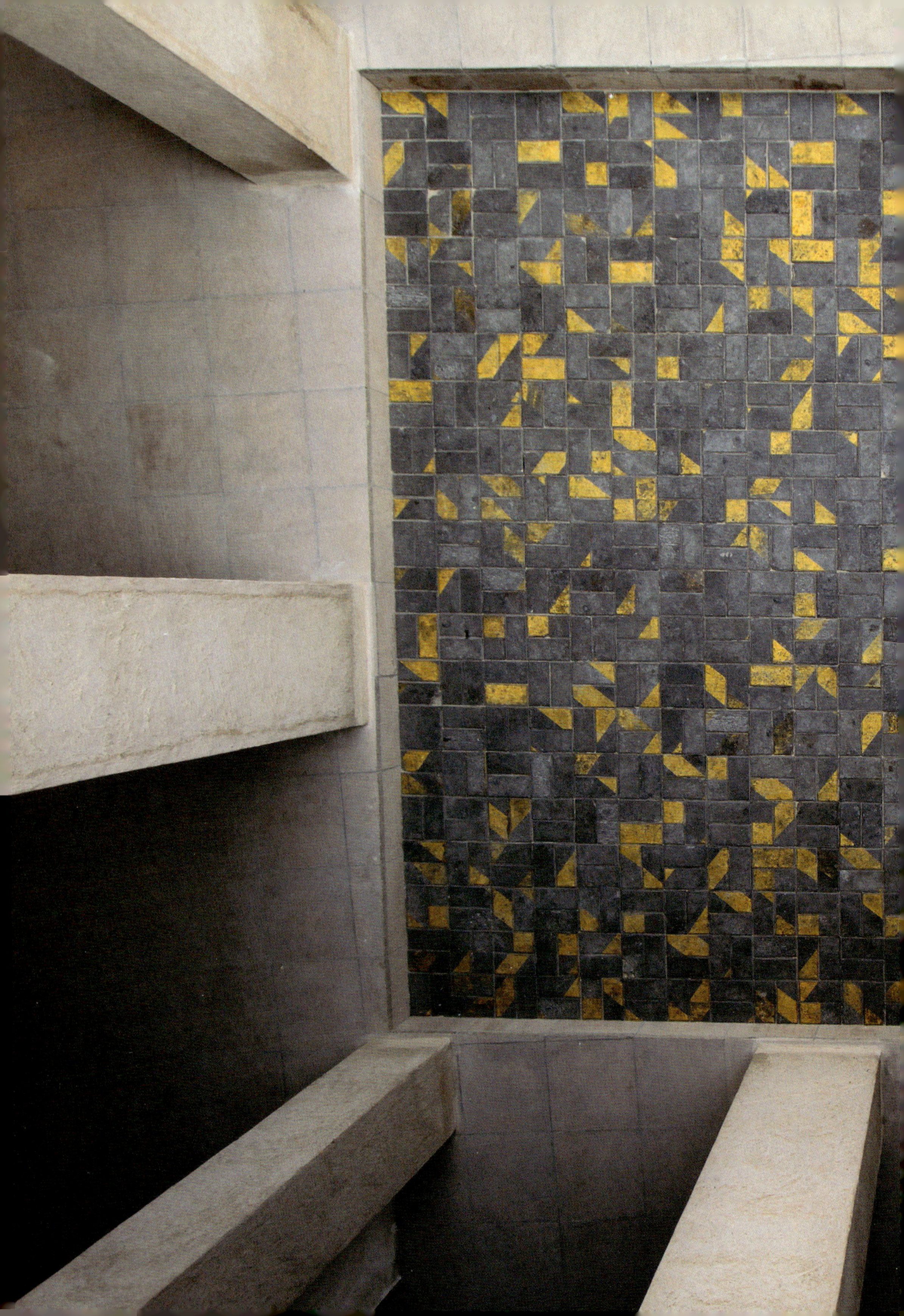

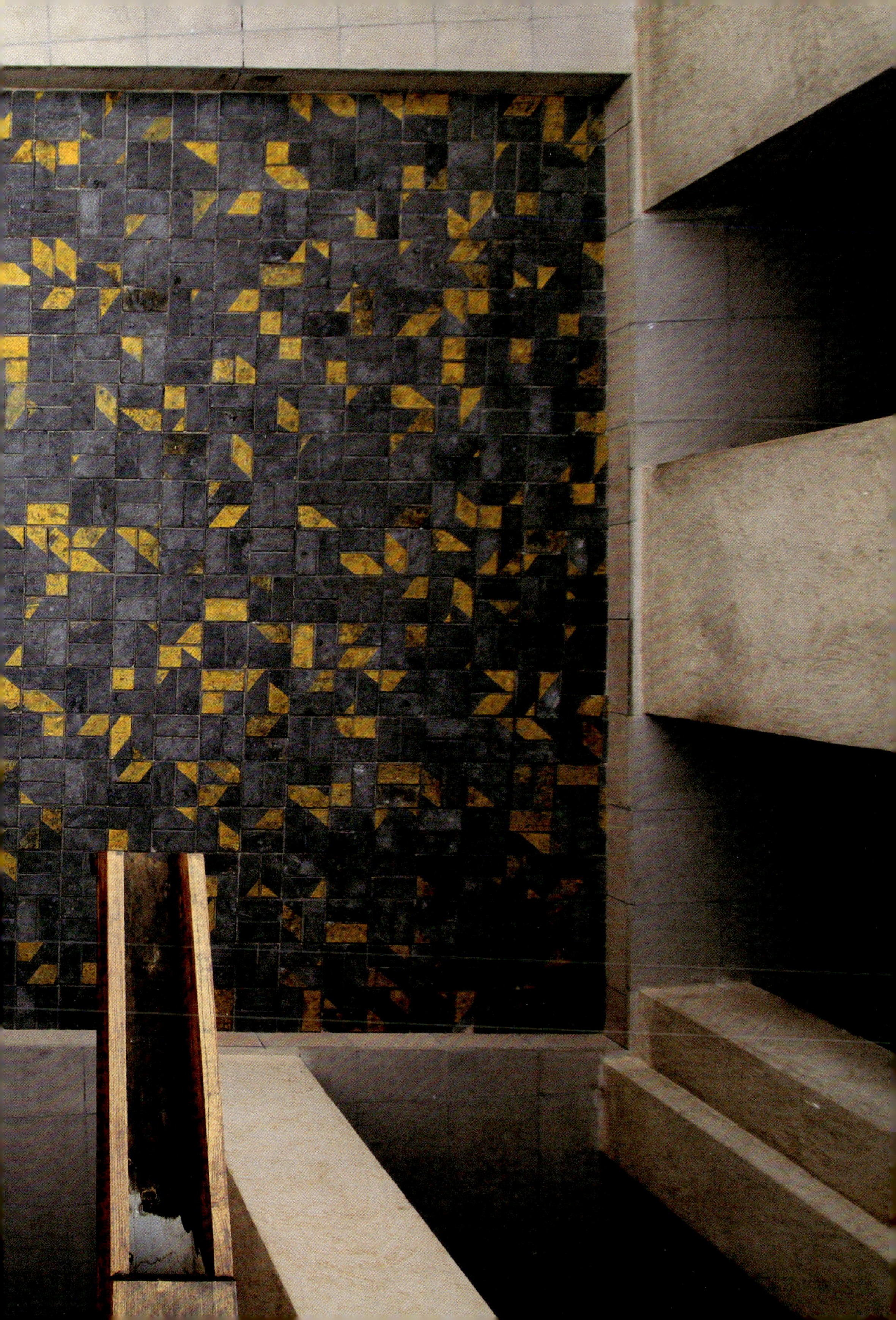

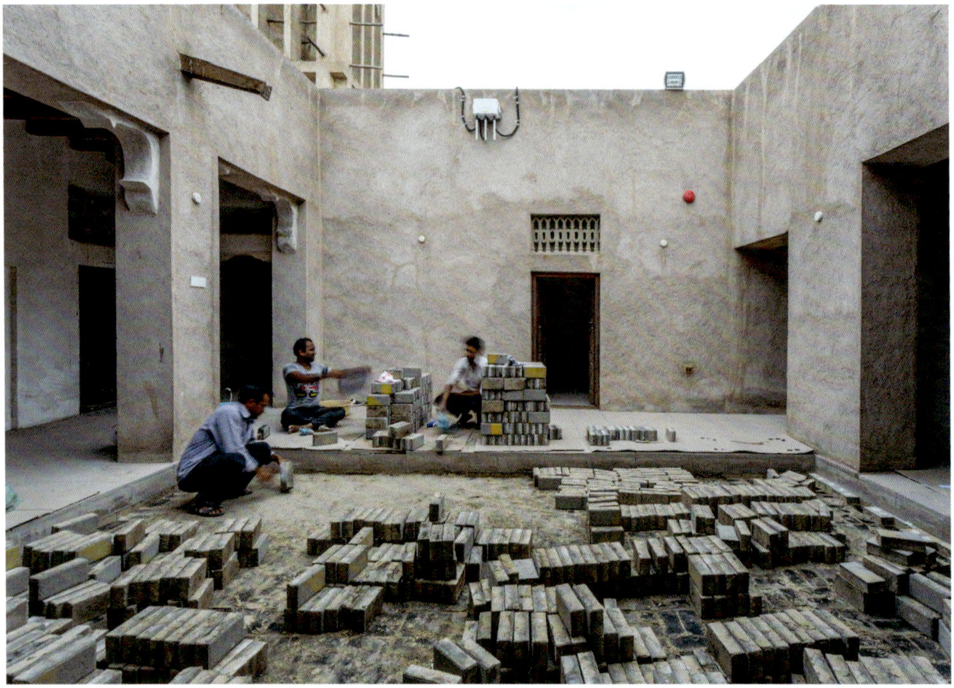

Degenerative Disarrangement, 2013
Interlocking pavement bricks; dimensions variable
Relocated from Al Fahidi Historical Neighborhood, Dubai, 2017
Uprooted from Al Ghubaiba bus stand, Dubai, 2013
SIKKA 2013, Commissioned by Dubai Culture & Arts Authority

Inspired by the scrambled patterns often created when pavements are repaired in the UAE, Divecha negotiated for bricks from a Dubai bus stand to be moved and rearranged to form the central courtyard of a house. The painted bricks that comprised the yellow lines directing parking on the street were arranged into a random geometric pattern determined by masons working under their contractual time constraints.

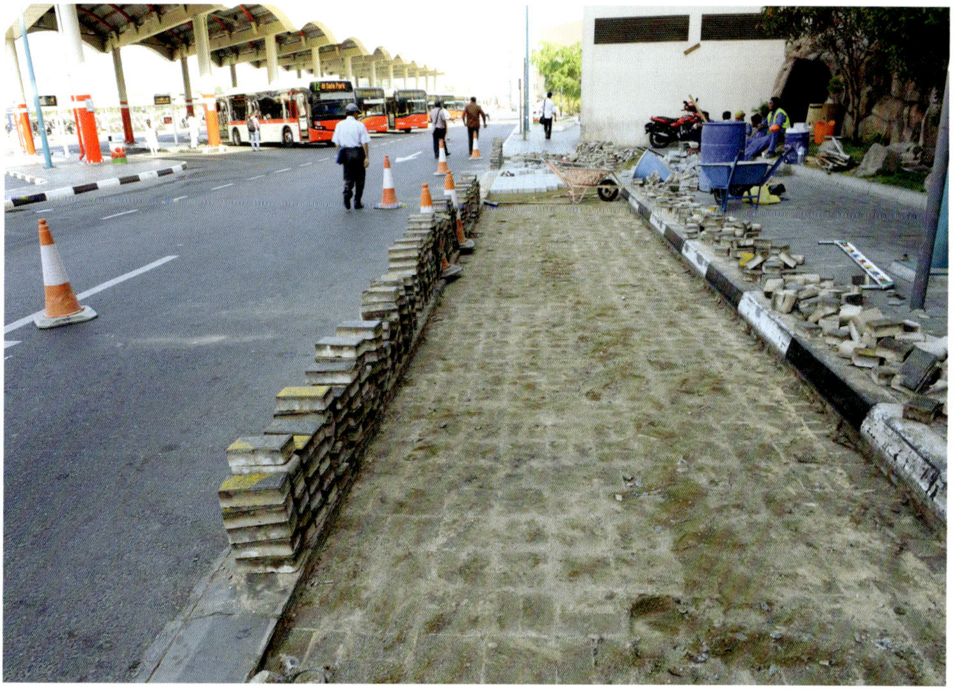

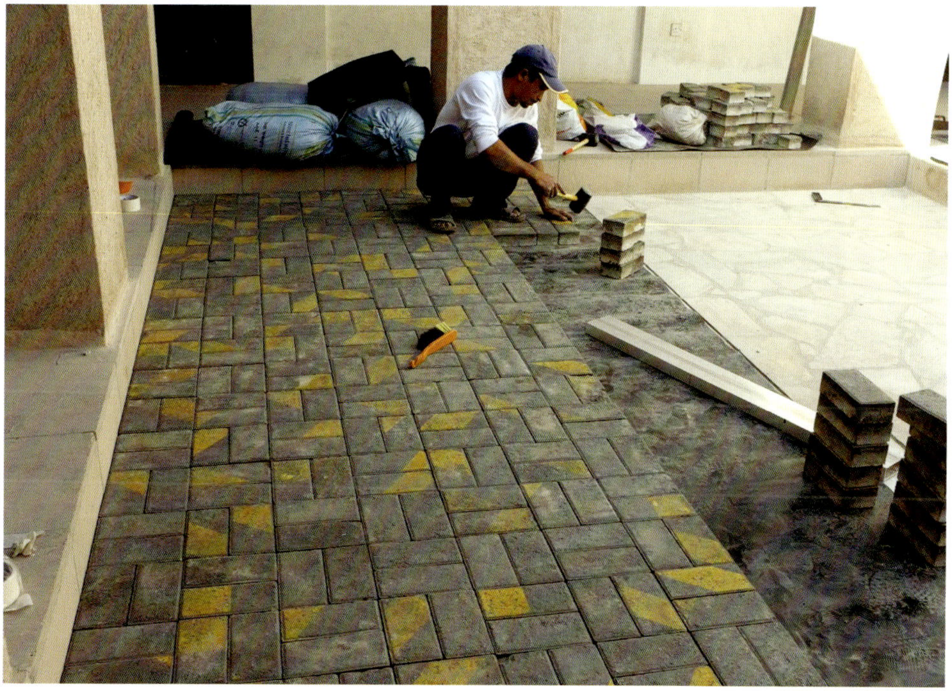

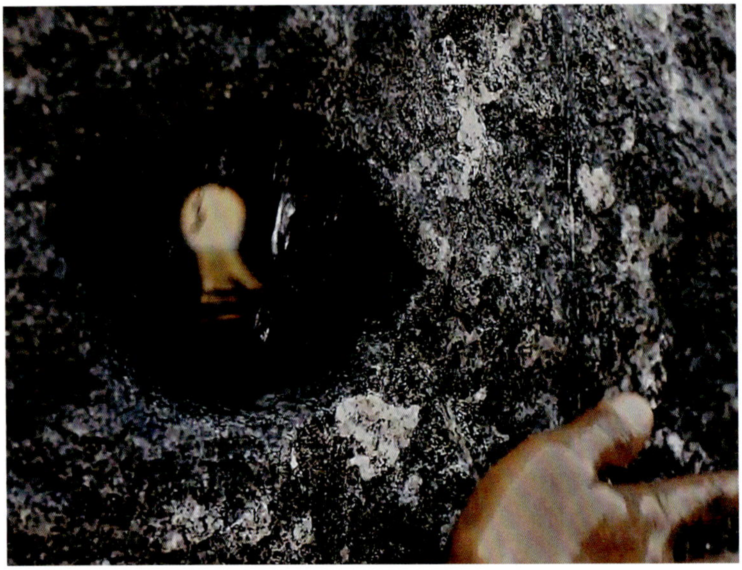

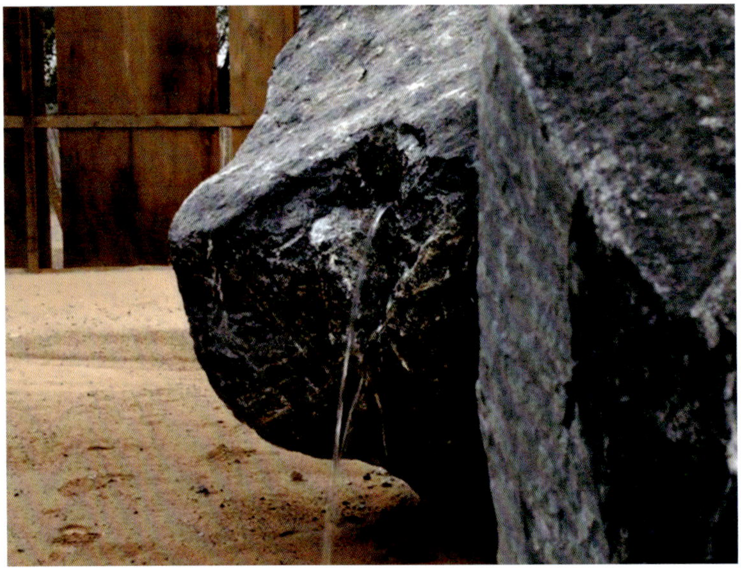

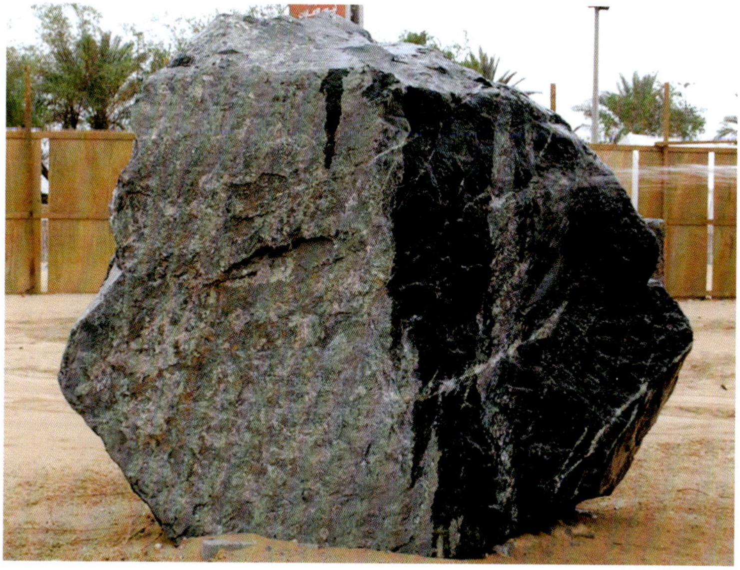

Bathing Boulders, 2017
Video stills from HD video, silent, color, single channel, 04:24 min

Washing Assistant: Helal Thakur Titon Thakur; Videography: Vikram Divecha, Swapna Kurup; Editing (Blacktop Films): Dominique Petrot; Post Production (White Light Studio): Nuttacha Khajornkaitsakul (Colorist), Sorawich Khunpinij (Digital Conform), Nathamon Thatthanakan (VFX Artist), Max Tersch (Post Supervisor), Siripun Sangjun (Post Producer)

Commissioned by the National Pavilion of the United Arab Emirates for the 57th International Art Exhibition – la Biennale di Venezia

As part of the process of preparing the gouged boulders in *Boulder Plot* (2014, see p. 229) for display, Divecha's assistant hosed them down with water. Struck by the aesthetic charge of this ritual-like action, and the associations it prompted, Divecha decided to record the process. The raw footage has been edited to produce a new video work, *Bathing Boulders*, as a commission for the UAE's presentation at the Venice Biennale.

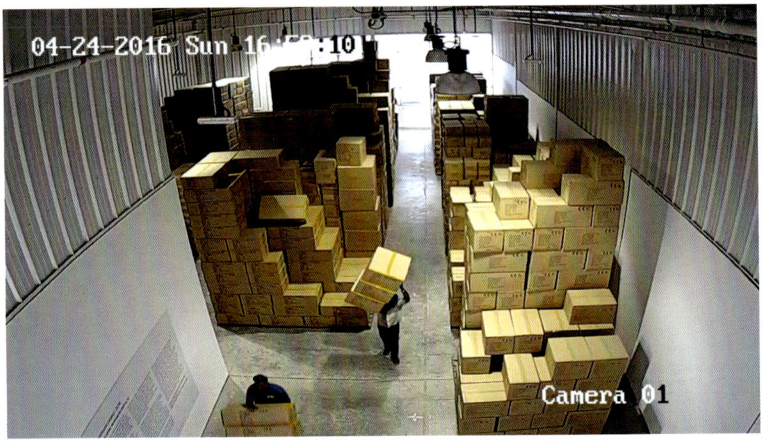

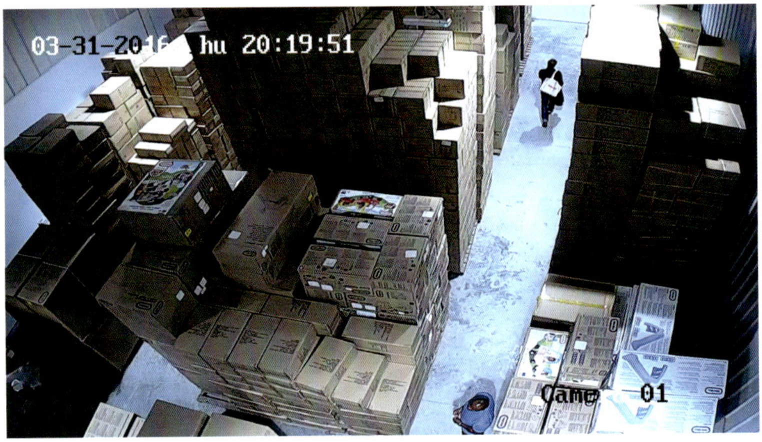

Pages 222–225
Warehouse Project, 2016
Wholesale goods, warehouse 82
Commissioned by Alserkal Avenue, Dubai

During his four-month residency at Dubai's Alserkal Avenue arts district, Divecha was allowed the use of a warehouse identical to those repurposed by neighboring international galleries. The artist then entered a barter arrangement with a general trading company, importing toys from China (Zippy, Hello Kitty, etc.) for regional distribution—allowing them free use of the warehouse in exchange for permitting him to display their fluctuating stock of boxed goods as art.

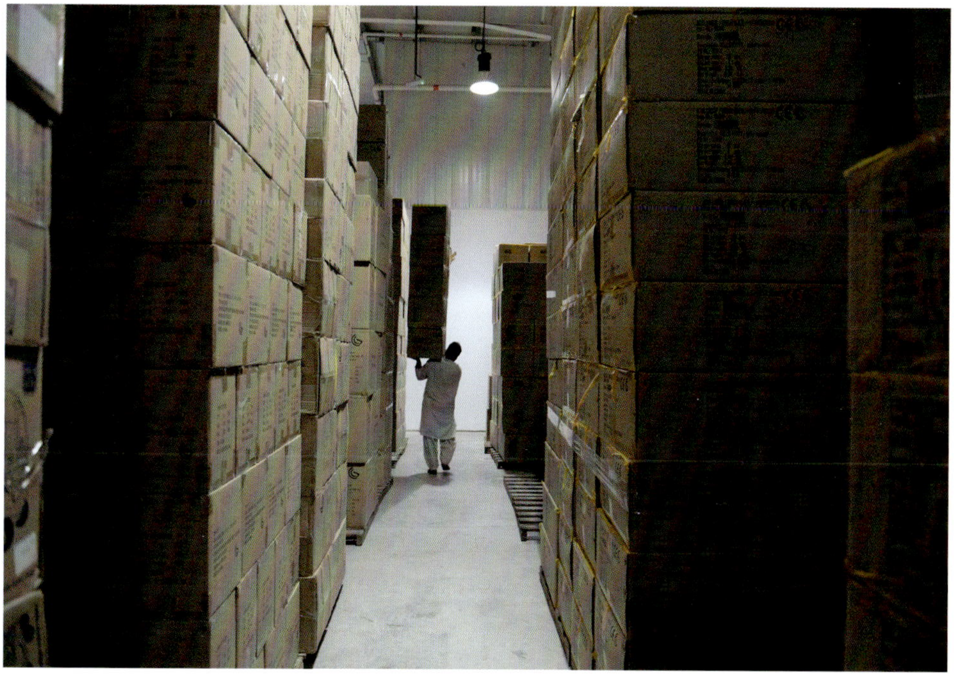

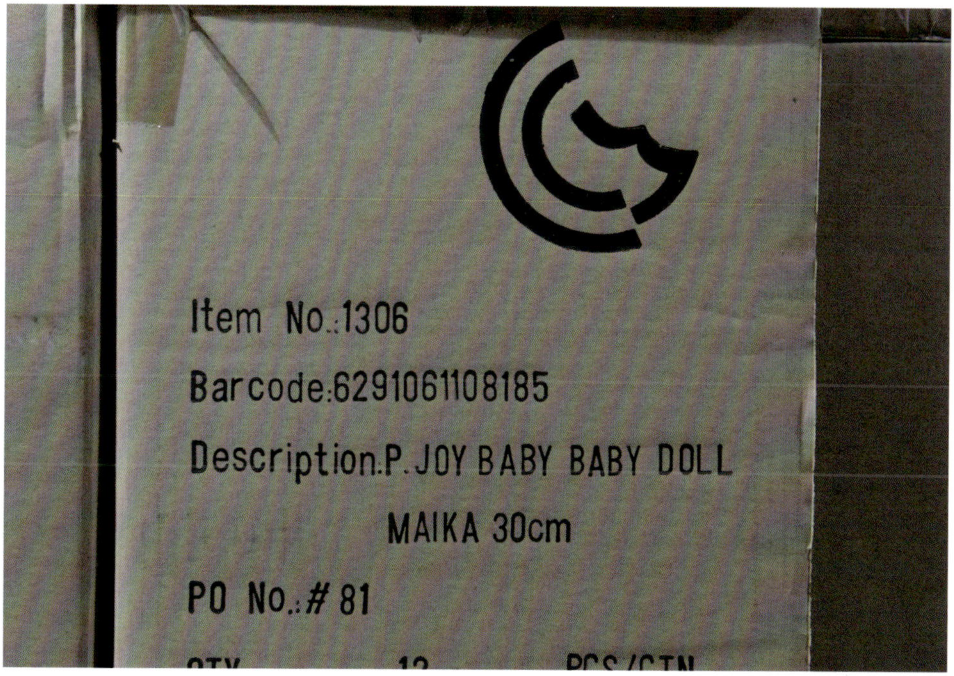
Item No.:1306
Barcode:6291061108185
Description:P.JOY BABY BABY DOLL
MAIKA 30cm
PO No.:# 81

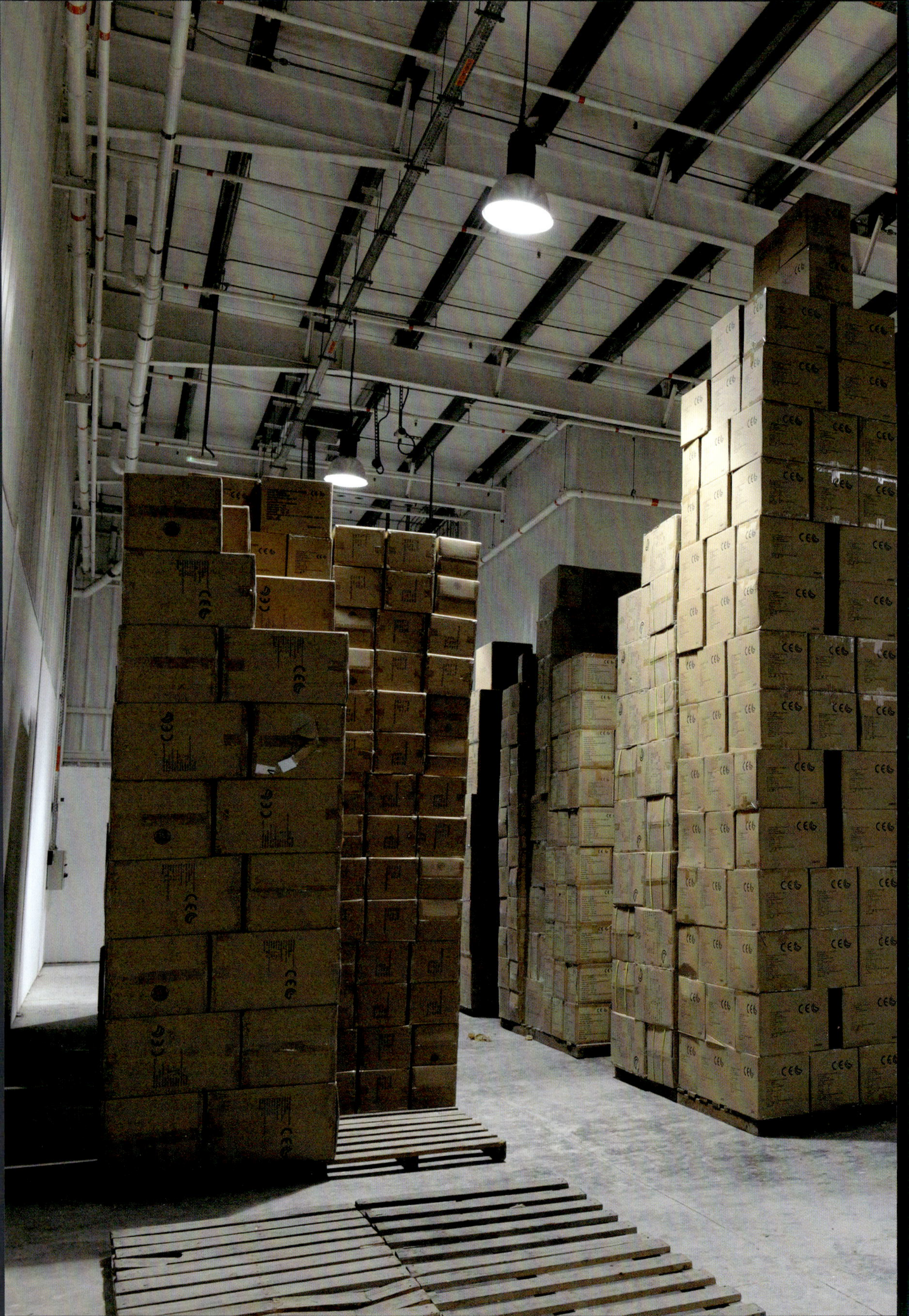

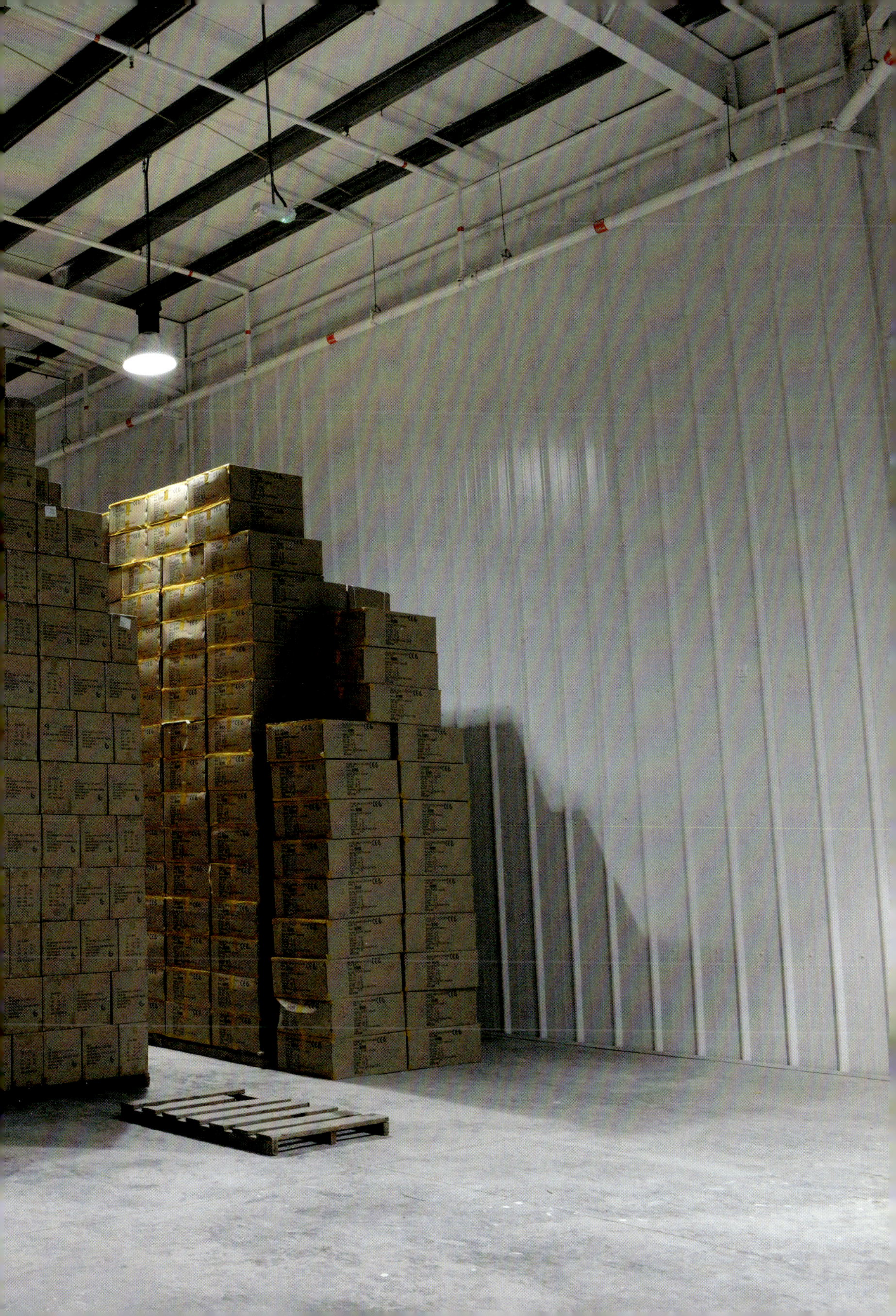

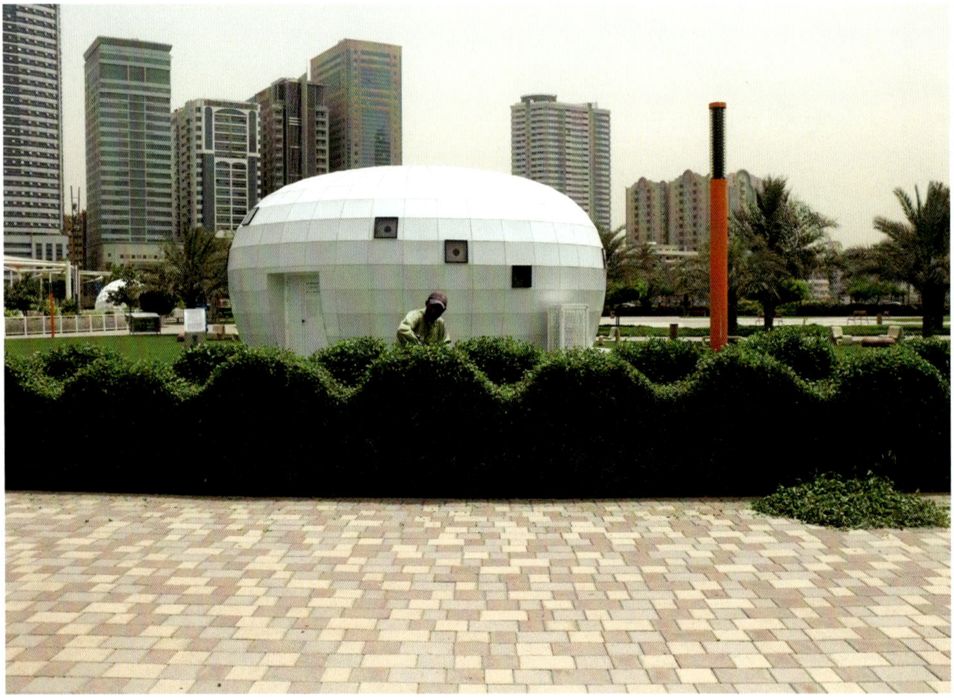

Shaping Resistance, 2015
100m hedge, 5 patterns
Site-specific intervention, Al Majaz Park, Sharjah
Commissioned by Maraya Art Centre, Sharjah

Artists: Tariq Mahmood, Muhammad Riaz Ahmed,
Sajad Hussain Bughio, Muhammad Shabbir Ahmad Din,
Vikram Divecha, Shahid Ahmad Bashir Mahmood,
Mohammed Mostafa Mohammed Junu Mia

Divecha's public project in a Sharjah park injected, in Murtaza Vali's words, a "playful irregularity into its precisely manicured shrubbery." The realization of the project required Divecha to obtain permission from the Sharjah Municipality to work with the Pakistani and Bangladeshi gardeners responsible for the park's upkeep. Through a series of drawing workshops, the gardeners were encouraged to select a set of shapes that appealed to them aesthetically, and then trim the park's hedges to realize these shapes and maintain them for the duration of the exhibition. This is now a permanent work.

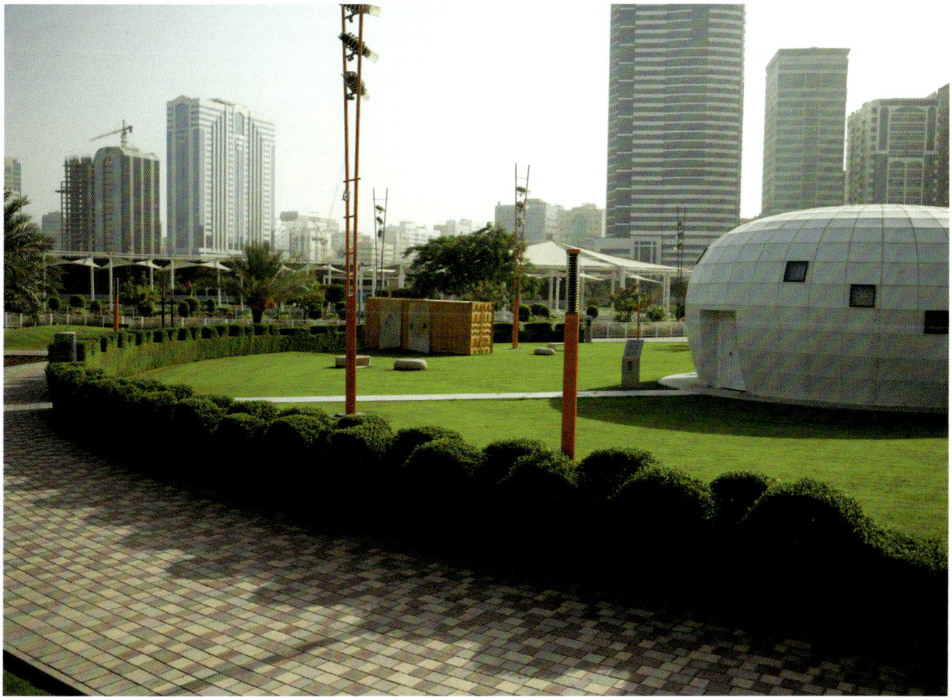

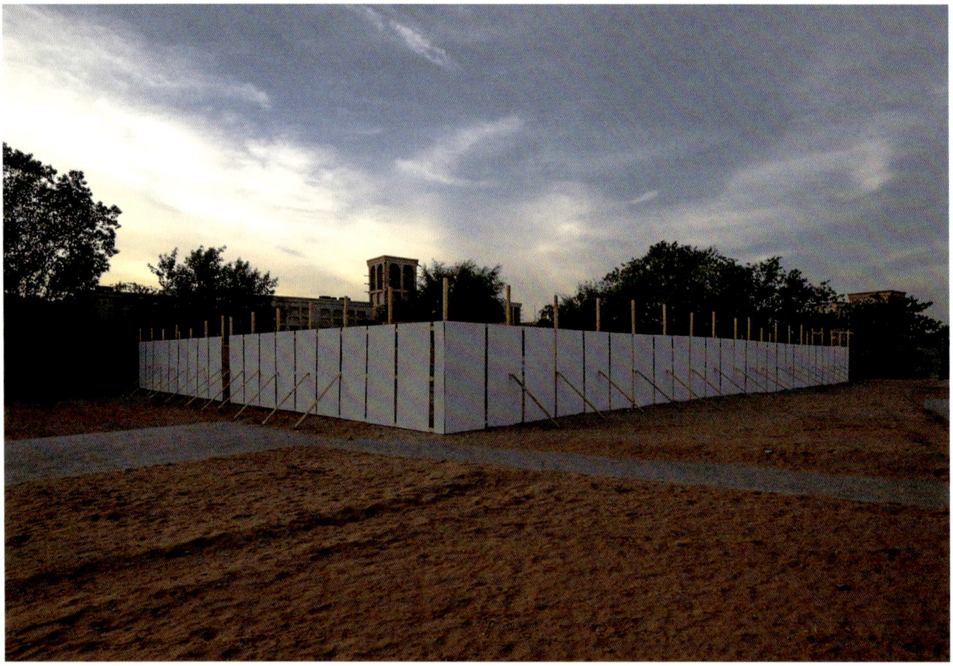

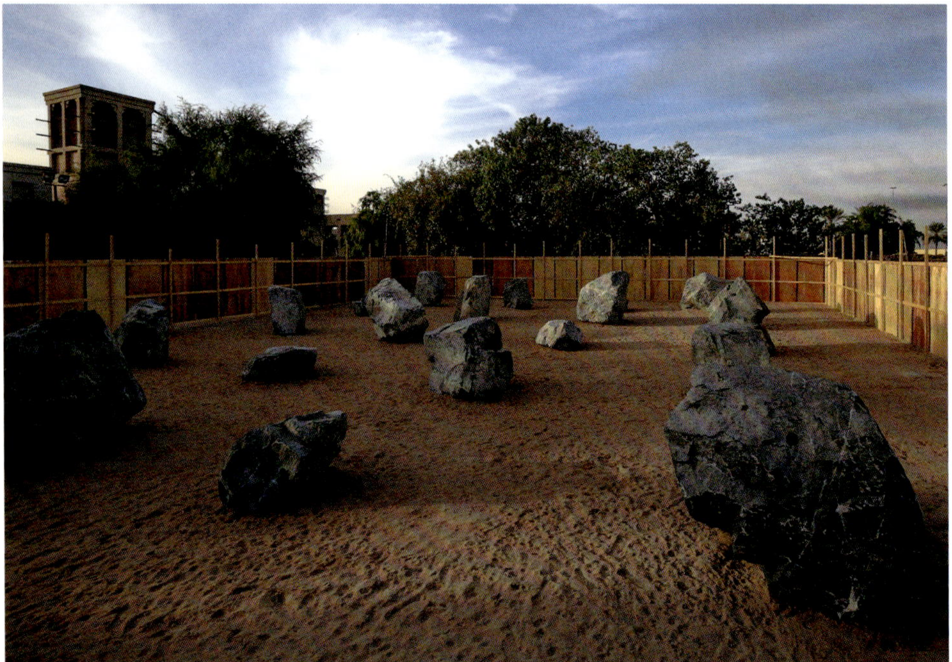

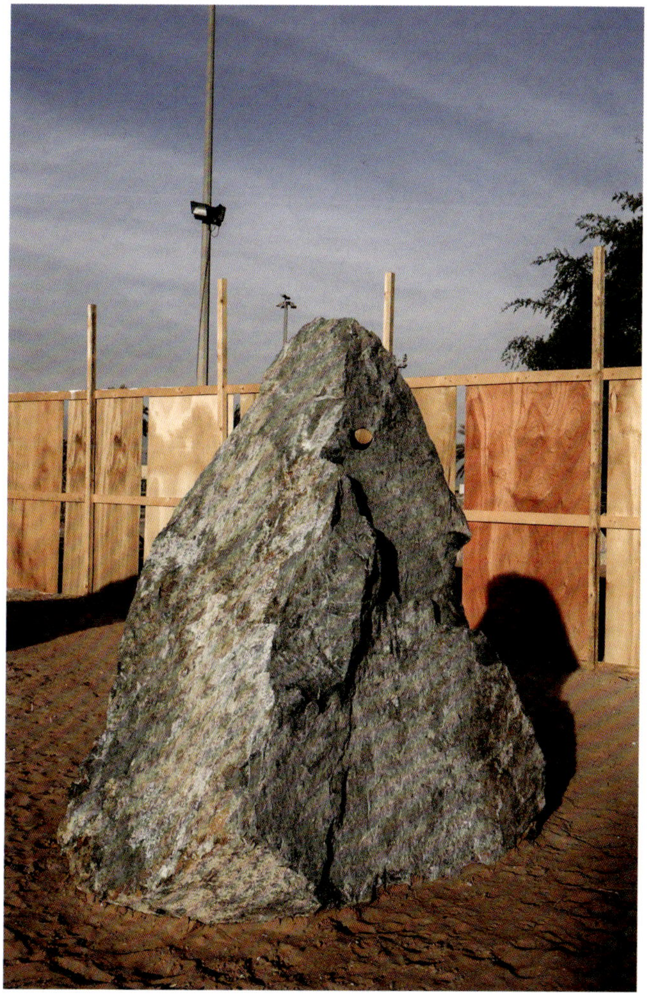

Boulder Plot, 2014,
24 gabbro rock boulders (4–7 tons), construction fencing
Installation dimensions: 35 m × 25 m. Boulder dimensions variable
Shindaga Heritage Village, Dubai
Commissioned by the Arab Fund for Arts and Culture (AFAC), Beirut

Boulder Plot comprised 'gouged boulders' from a quarry in Fujairah arranged on a plot in Dubai surrounded by hoardings routinely used to hide urban construction sites. The exhibited boulders all bore the cylindrical holes drilled into the mountain face to house the explosive charges used for rock blasting. In most instances these holes do not survive the blast. This unlikely sculpture garden comprises those rare instances where they did, and this ephemeral, almost surreptitious, display functioned as an aesthetic pause for the boulders, before they were trucked back and crushed to feed the construction industry.

Lantian Xie

Lantian Xie makes work about sites, itinerancy, and the communal occupation of time. He creates moments of encounter that poke gently, as if with a feather, at fixed ideas of belonging. His method is to introduce barely perceptible disturbances into how we feel, see, or understand our lived experiences—to nudge us into sensing the syncopation in the rhythms of life.

His sites of choice—hotels, cafés, and restaurants—are private spaces that behave as if they are public. In a series of works—*Metropolitan Hotel, Chicago Beach Hotel, Advertisements for Chicago Beach Hotel* (opposite and pp. 246-251)—Xie explores the international modernism of hotels. His interest lies in their often-formulaic material embodiment of collective aspirations and in the web of aesthetic, social, and economic regimes that govern their unspoken and unstable publicness.

Xie is invested in the itinerancy of people, practices, and meanings. His sustained engagement with music, for example, is at least partly driven by its capacity to harbor stowaways—histories, imaginaries, and political affinities—in its circulation.

His work at the Shanghai Biennale, *The Sidewinder* (2016, see pp. 244), is exemplary of this trajectory. A Volkswagen Santana—a ubiquitous taxi and police car, and the first joint-venture car built in China—is parked outside the exhibition space, engine running and lights blinking. The muffled jazz playing inside is a medley of Lee Morgan's classic "The Sidewinder" (a rattlesnake and an American missile are namesakes) and Salah Ragab's "Egypt Strut." Ragab, the "father of Egyptian Jazz," was the head of the army's marching band in Gamal Abdel Nasser's Egypt. "Egypt Strut" was included on the album *Egyptian Jazz* (2006) and produced with the assistance of the legendary American jazz bandleader, poet, philosopher, and father of Afrofuturism Sun Ra.

Ragab's album was a sonic translation of Nasser's Pan-Arab aspirations, which were a source of inspiration for the region, and in particular for the founders and rulers of the UAE. The open issue of *Life* magazine, that

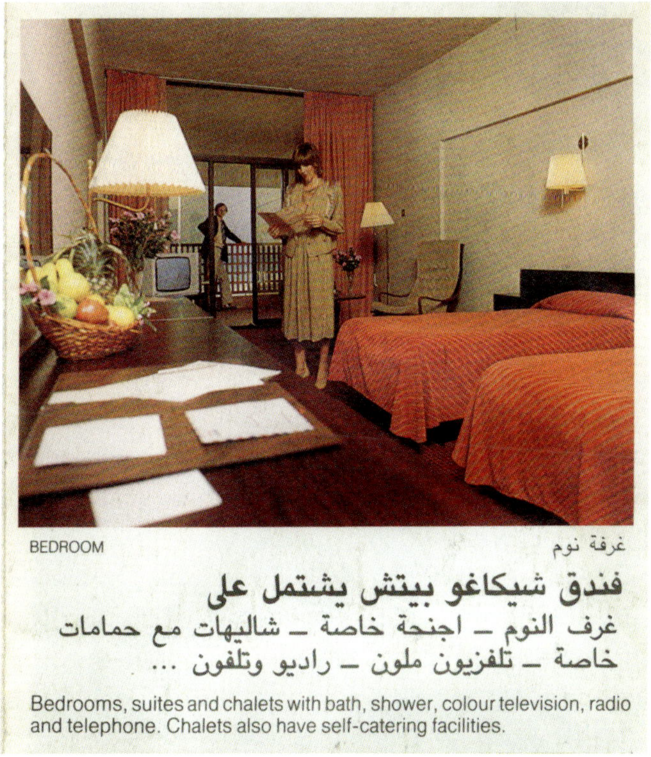

Advertisements for Chicago Beach Hotel, 2015

quintessential carrier of American conceptions of Cold War modernity, on the front seat adds an additional layer of meaning. The car resonates with the vibrations of the engine and the music, but also with different narrative strands of power—modernization, postcolonial nationalisms, solidarity movements, Cold War cultural diplomacy, and capitalist trade—that it brings into momentary union.

Gestures like smoking, talking, and eating are exemplary of Xie's interest in the communal passage of time. In *Woodland Fern No. 4* (2014, p. 233), he reproduces the green "accent wall" of his local branch of the popular Eat & Drink Restaurant chain as an exemplar of a vernacular form of cosmopolitanism: at ease with the multiple cuisines and peoples of the coastal Arabian Sea, and fluid in its ability to straddle differences in class, ethnicity, language, and taste. The color green nods to the "green screen" or "Chroma key" postproduction technique that allows a separately filmed background to be inserted in a scene. Eat & Drink Restaurant's accent wall, like its menu and clientele, becomes a machine of possibilities.

Indian Ocean cosmopolitanism is also explored in *Half Cup Saffron* (2016, p. 242). A cup of chai sits on a hot plate, waiting in anticipation of something that is yet to happen or the continuation of what has been interrupted. Chai was originally brought to the Gulf from South Asia, and has since seeped across class and ethnic distinctions to become one of the most popular hot drinks in the region. *Half Cup Saffron* is one of three existing works, alongside a major new commission, that forms Xie's presentation at the Venice Biennale.

A second work, *Hassan's Ashtray* (2014, p. 243), comprises a nondescript ashtray—purportedly stolen from an artist's studio—complete with cigarette butts and ashes, adjacent to a disposable lighter. The ashes are physical residue, but also evidence of the casual intimacy inherent in smoking and talking in company, as one's inhaled smoke is expelled and breathed in by fellow smokers.

Taxidermy Peacock (2014, p. 240-241) is the third of Xie's existing works in the pavilion. Peacocks are engineered for display. The Peacock Throne was the extravagant literal, and symbolic, seat of power of the Mughal Empire captured by a Persian king and since lost. The Peacock Alley—connecting the two buildings of New York's legendary Waldorf Astoria hotel—was where one could observe a "daily promenade of notables." The peacocks of Dubai are royal pets. In *Taxidermy Peacock*, what does the limp body of a flamboyant, regal peacock, hidden from our line of sight, signify? Is this escape, theft, or subterfuge?

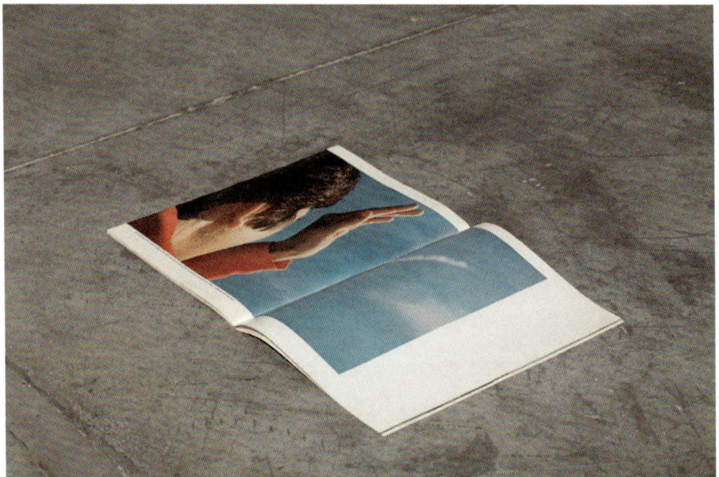

The Sidewinder, 2016

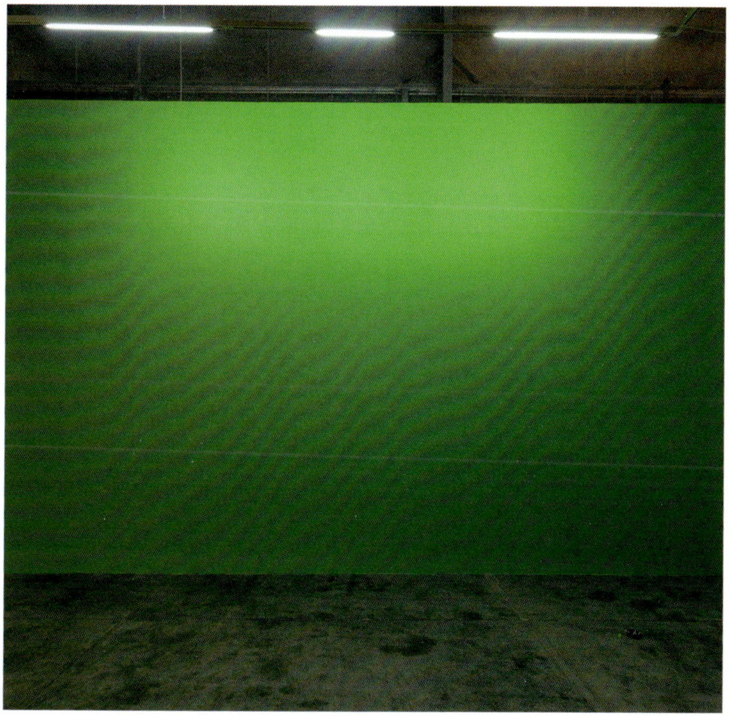

Woodland Fern No. 4, 2014
Paint, wood, fluorescent lights

In *A rumble interrupted our chat* (2017, pp. 235–239), a major new commission for the Venice Biennale, Xie introduces objects, stories, and situations through a short script-like text. Xie's "regular" cast is immediately recognizable: an itinerant band responds to an eclectic set in a Venetian hotel; friends in a café drink coffee and smoke cigarettes while ruminating on home. New "characters" include a seagull carrying french fries. Their roles are sketched but left dangling between fact, fiction, and possibility.

Completing this filmic or theatrical staging is a series of "props" in the exhibition space: Xie's existing three works, a can of insect repellent, and a painting. The painting is a reproduction of a painting within a painting by the Palestinian artist Suleiman Mansour. The "original" *Memory of Places* (2009) features an elderly man wearing the Arab keffiyeh standing in front of a painting of olive trees: iconic tropes for referencing place, home, and memory. The copy is a method Xie has often deployed, notably in *HHSM* (2012, pp. 245), in which a number of identical paintings of His Highness Sheikh Mohammed bin Rashid Al Maktoum, monarch of Dubai were commissioned by art workers in Dafen, China. But this particular copy is just of the painting of the olive trees in Mansour's original. The old man is missing. Perhaps he has wandered off to a hotel lobby to smoke and listen to jazz, enveloping not just the pavilion but the entire city in an expanded mise-en-scène.

Through this orchestration of multiple narratives, fluid time, and expanded possibilities, Xie invites viewers to participate in the work by building their own structures of meaning and feeling as the story unfolds over time and in multiple sites, including their imaginations. Channeling the parable of "an elephant in the dark"—the Indian fable popularized in Rumi's poem—viewers are challenged to imagine or feel a "whole" they are only able to see or touch in fragments.

This fragmentary, temporally dispersed yet loosely shared set of possible encounters can be read as metaphor for that slippery act of belonging. Xie's work asks whether belonging can be enacted, not as a flag-waving polemic, but as a daily practice of presence and imagination.

Lantian Xie (born 1988) is an artist from Dubai who makes images, objects, stories, and situations. Xie holds an MFA from the School of the Art Institute of Chicago and is Editor at Large of the Dubai-based publishing practice *THE STATE*. His recent exhibitions include the 11th Shanghai Biennale (2016), curated by Raqs Media Collective, and the 3rd Kochi-Muziris Biennale (2016), curated by Sudarshan Shetty.

Pages 235–239: *A rumble interrupted our chat*, 2017
Things that happen; live band, group of friends, party, painting, object
Researcher: Michelle Wong

Commissioned by the National Pavilion of the United Arab Emirates
for the 57th International Art Exhibition – la Biennale di Venezia

A short screenplay-like text introduces a series of durational performances that happen in different locations over the course of the Biennale, a set of objects in the pavilion, and fictional narratives that could happen. The pavilion itself, including prior works by Xie, becomes part of an expanded mise-en-scène for a deconstructed stage.

OPENING WEEKEND of the Biennale—a band from Hong Kong plays live music every night in the lobby of Hotel Danieli.

Month of JUNE – every morning a group of friends meet at Cafe Ala Bragora on the corner of Calle De La Morte. They talk, and smoke, and talk and talk.

ONE DAY a seagull appears with french fries in its mouth.

ONE DAY a water taxi waits at Ca' Di Dio Dock. Suitcases on board with red luggage tags.

AUGUST & SEPTEMBER – every day two friends wear matching Vans Old Skools as they go about their days.

One of them OCCASIONALLY asks to borrow a lighter from a passerby.

NOVEMBER 25th – a party happens in a house in Castello.

A painting of a place with olive trees leans against a wall in the UAE pavilion.

NEARBY a can of cockroach repellent sits beside the welcome desk.

SOMEWHERE a dog barks.

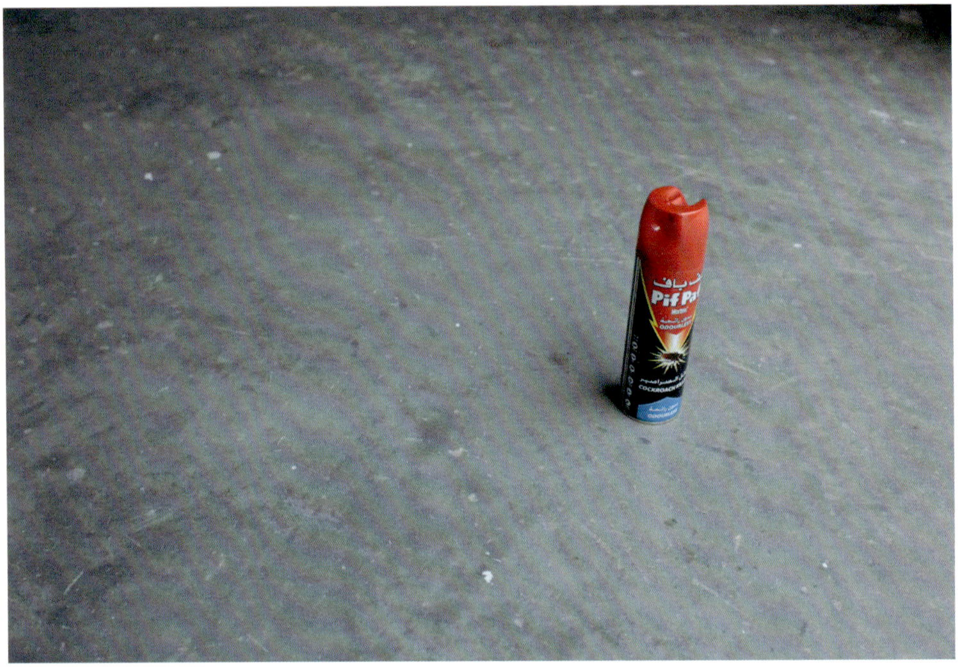

Excerpts from *A rumble interrupted our chat,* 2017

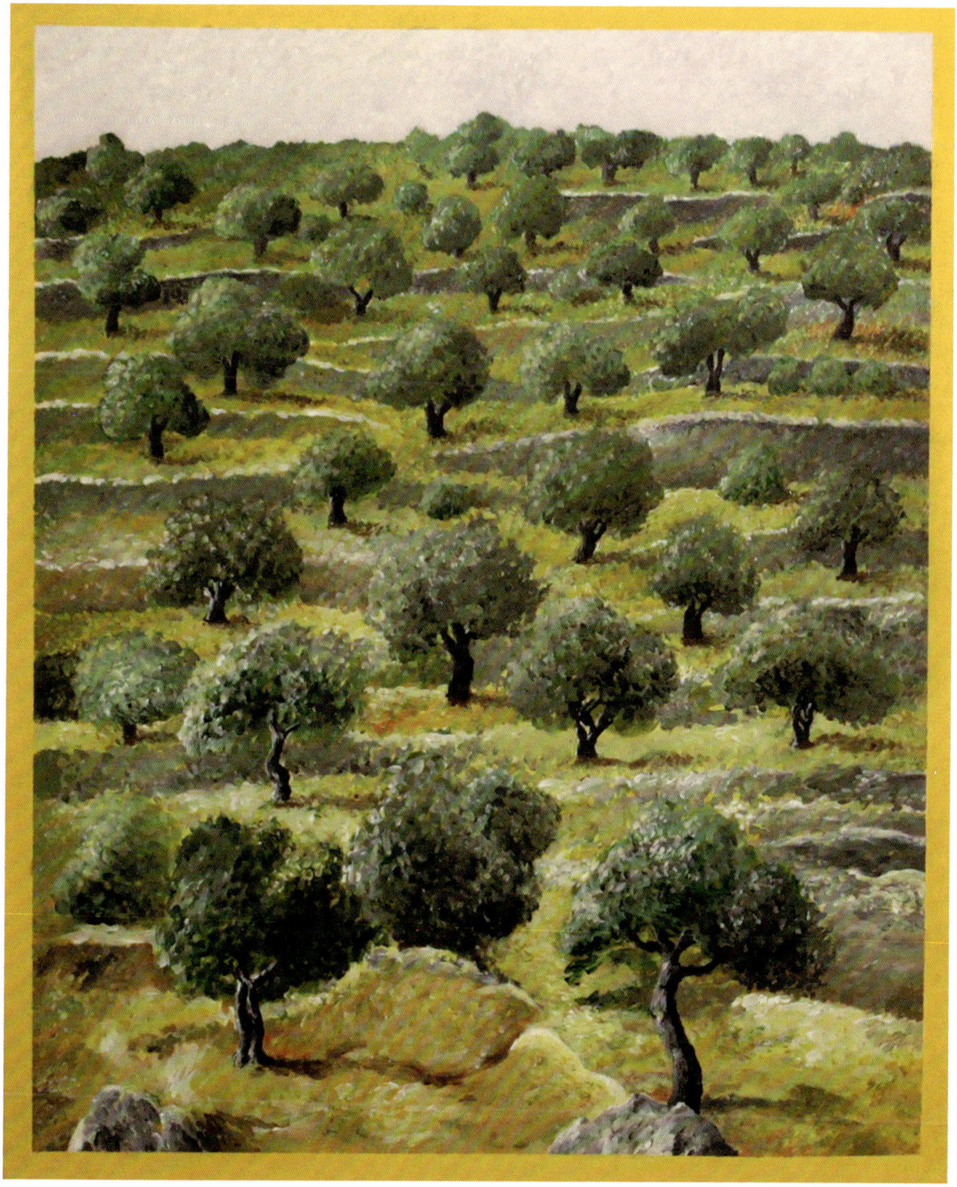

A SPECULATIVE SET LIST, TITLED 'RUMBLE'

- There's A Small Hotel (Dorothy Ashby)
- Corcovado (Oscar Peterson at Palmyra Hotel, Lebanon)
- Choucoune (Issa El Saieh)
- Misirlou (Xavier Cugat, Waldorf Astoria Hotel, New York City)
- Maria Elena (Xavier Cugat)
- Miami Beach Rhumba (Xavier Cugat)
- Egypt Strut / Sidewinder / Watermelon Man (medley; Salah Ragab, Sun Ra, Lee Morgan)
- Ramadan in Space (Salah Ragab)
- The Sheik of Araby (Sidney Bechet)
- Ticke Me Not (Chic Chocolate, Taj Mahal Hotel, Bombay)
- Bombay Meri Jaan (Mohammed Rafi Geeta Dutt)

Notes for *A rumble interrupted our chat*, 2017

CUT TO:

EXT - CAFÉ - MORNING

On a narrow-ish cobblestone street lined with shops, enclosed by buildings on all sides. Lots of shadows. Amber light from inside café. Shiny metal tabletops and chairs on the street outside, next to café window display full of pastries.

A group of friends is sitting at one of these tables. Saucers, ashtray, bowl of chips on tabletop. They are all wearing sandalwood perfume, smoking cigarettes, drinking coffee, lost in heated conversation.

They listen to each other intently, sometimes laughing, sometimes interrupting, sometimes arguing. Their dialogue is said in rapid pace.

It is impossible to tell where they are from.

THEN . . .

Pages 240–241
Taxidermy Peacock, 2014
Courtesy of the artist and Grey Noise, Dubai

Peacocks—pets in Dubai's royal household—are regularly sighted in the morning and at dusk when they leave the Palace for a frolic amid the traffic of Dubai's financial district or a wander through the backyards of neighboring houses. Here a taxidermy peacock is stashed out of the line of sight: its limp body and hidden location, suggestive of something sinister.

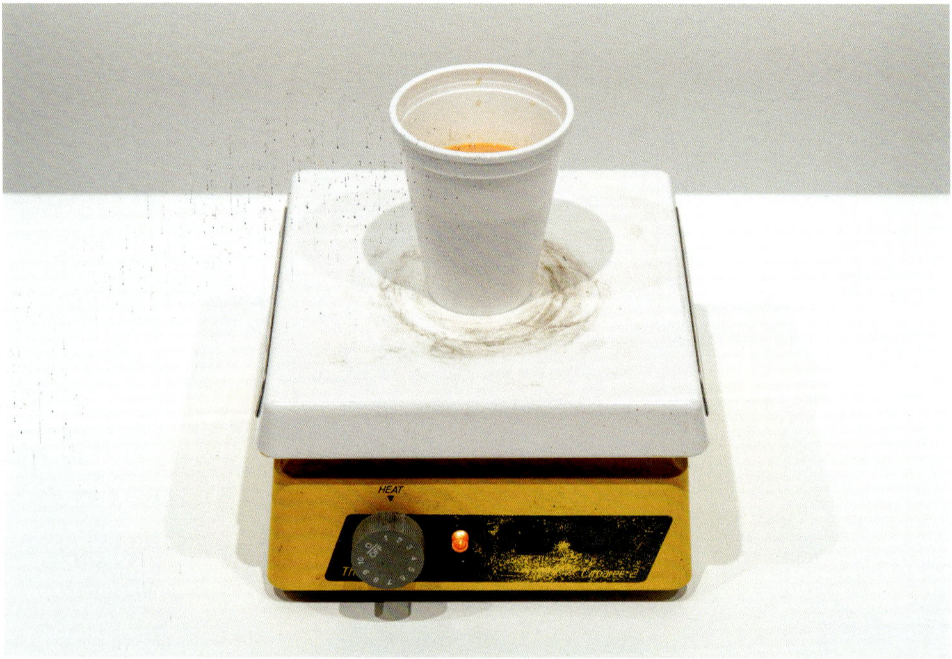

Half Cup Saffron, 2016
Saffron, Rainbow condensed milk, Lipton tea, styrofoam cup, hot plate
Collection of Art Jameel

Chai (black tea boiled with milk, sugar, and cardamom) is among the most popular hot drinks in the UAE. A cup of chai, made with condensed milk and a few threads of saffron to intensify the flavor, is being kept warm.

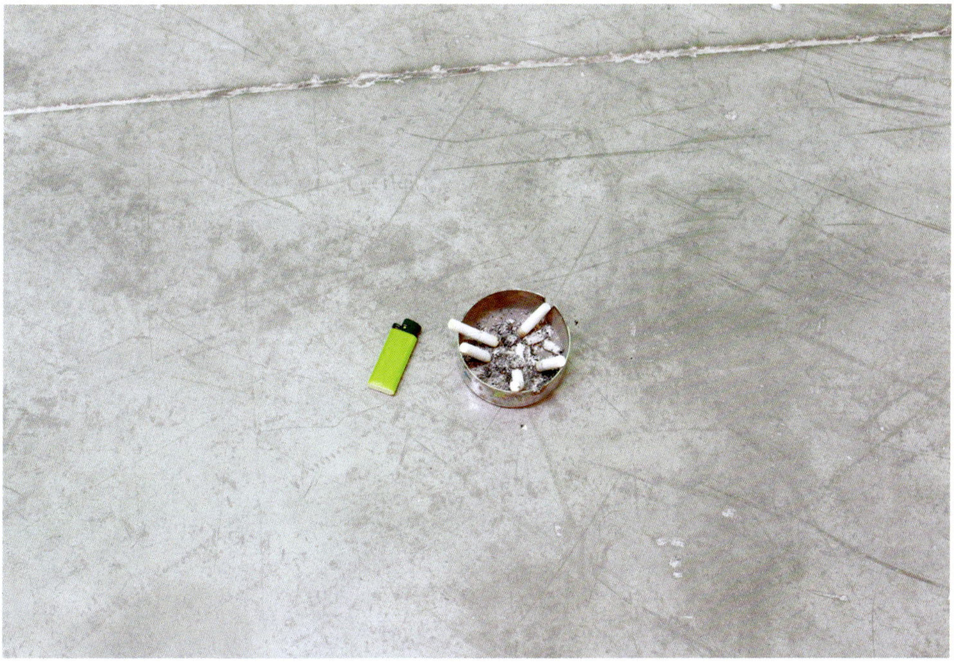

Hassan's Ashtray, 2014
Ashtray, ashes, cigarette butts, lighter
Courtesy of the artist and Grey Noise, Dubai.

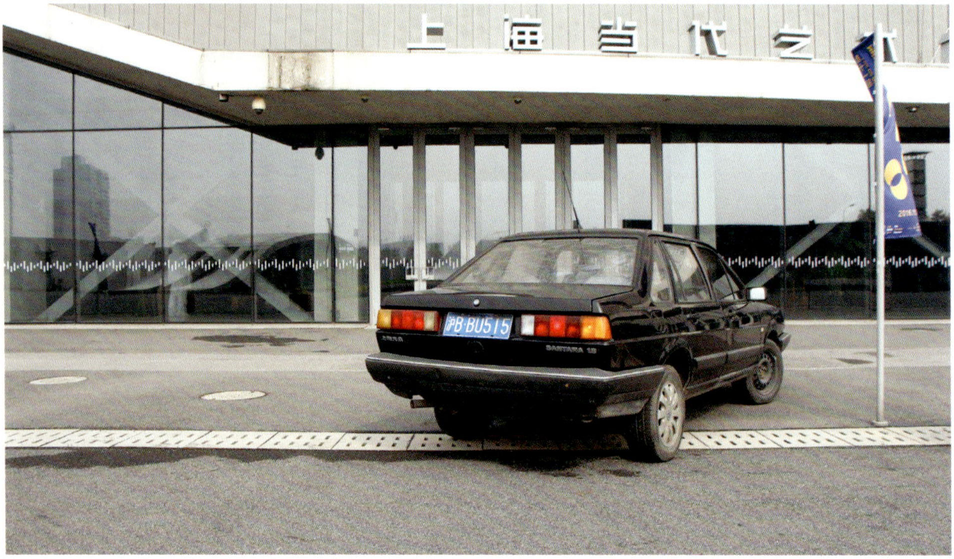

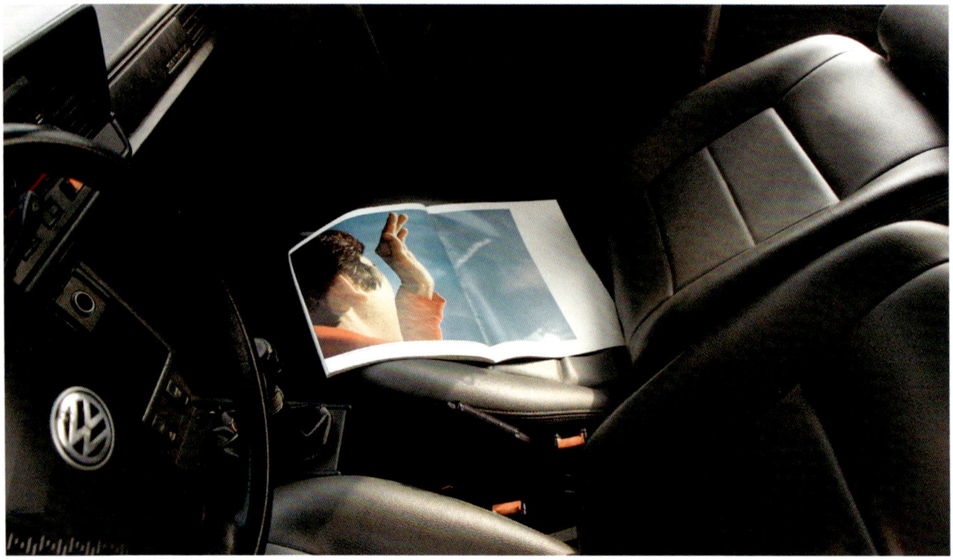

The Sidewinder, 2016
Volkswagen Santana, audio excerpts from Salah Ragab's "Egypt Strut" and Lee Morgan's "Sidewinder," *Life* magazine

A car is parked outside the exhibition space, its engine humming and emergency lights flashing. Muffled jazz—oscillating between American and Egyptian jazz—plays on its stereo. A magazine sits on the front passenger seat, open to an image of someone witnessing a line of flight.

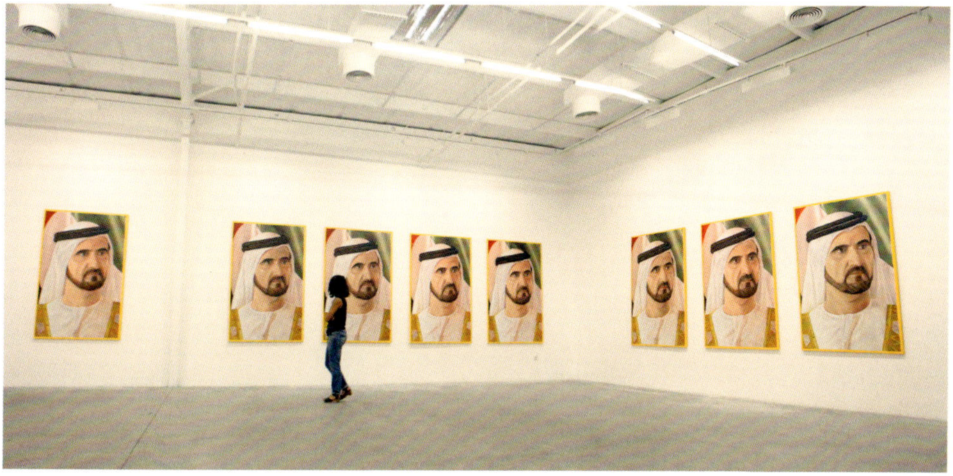

HHSM, 2012
Oil on canvas, State mandate
Courtesy of the artist and Grey Noise, Dubai

Art workers in China produced twelve paintings copied from a widely distributed state portrait of His Highness Sheikh Mohammed bin Rashid Al Maktoum, the ruler of Dubai. On exhibition, the Dubai Media Office issued a mandate barring the paintings from sale.

The work now comprises the series of paintings and the mandate.

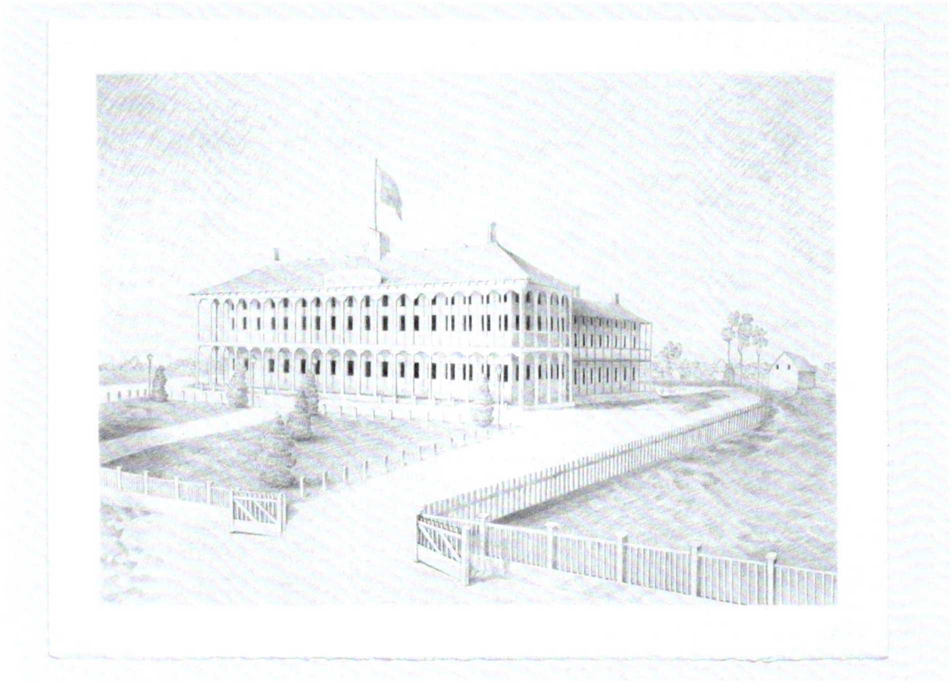

Metropolitan Hotel no.115, 2016
Fifteen colored pencil drawings on paper

Suite of drawings depicting various hotels throughout
history and geography, all named Metropolitan.

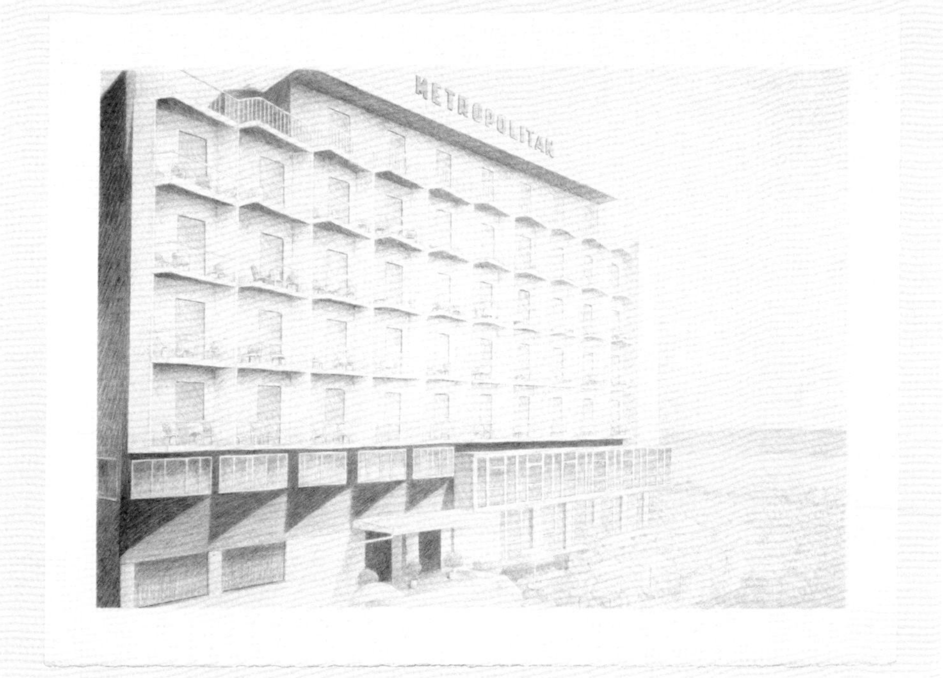
METROPOLITAN

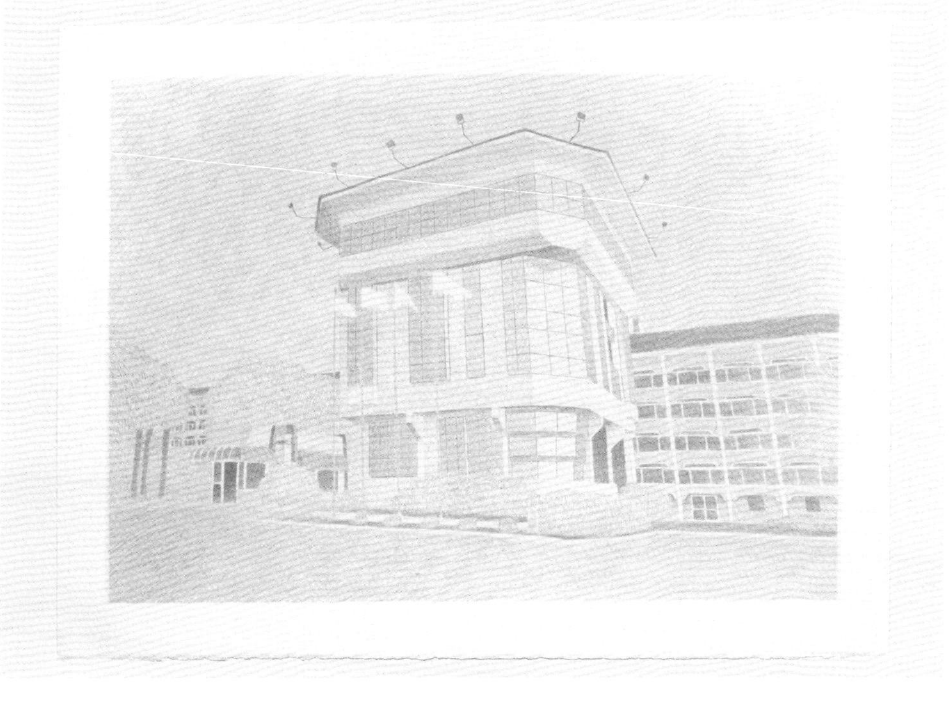

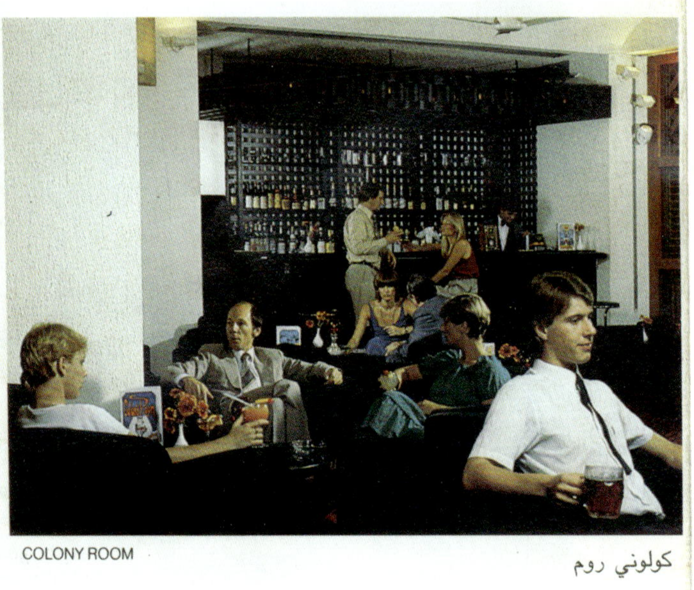

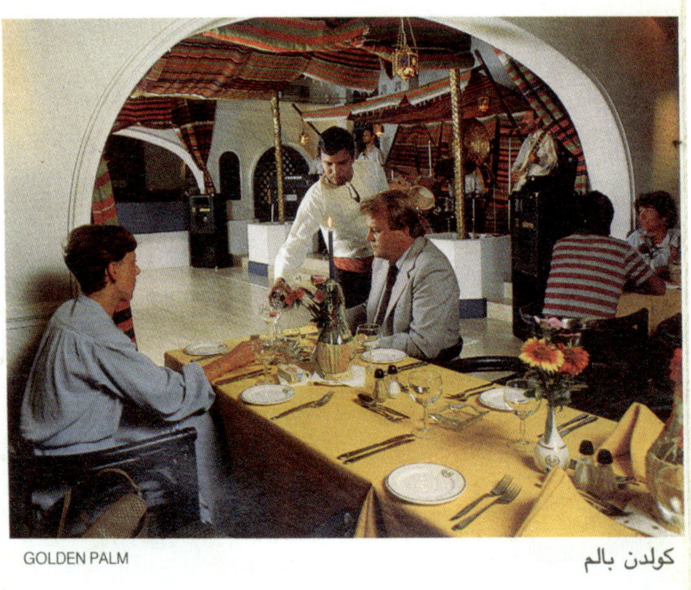

Advertisements for Chicago Beach Hotel, 2016
Images compiled from marketing collateral—printed matter,
brochures—from Dubai's Chicago Beach Hotel

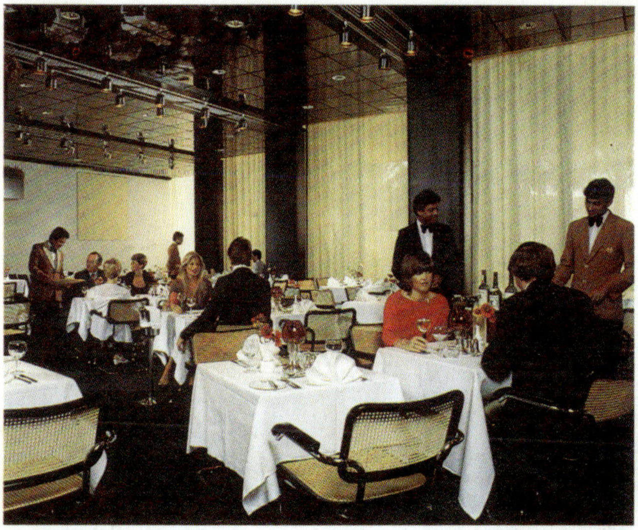

LES IMAGES ليز يماج

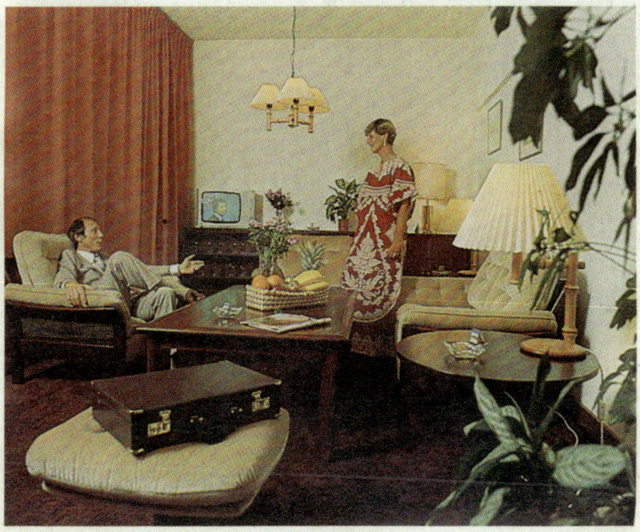

SUITE جناح

15 -New Chicago Beach Hotel Chicago, Ill.

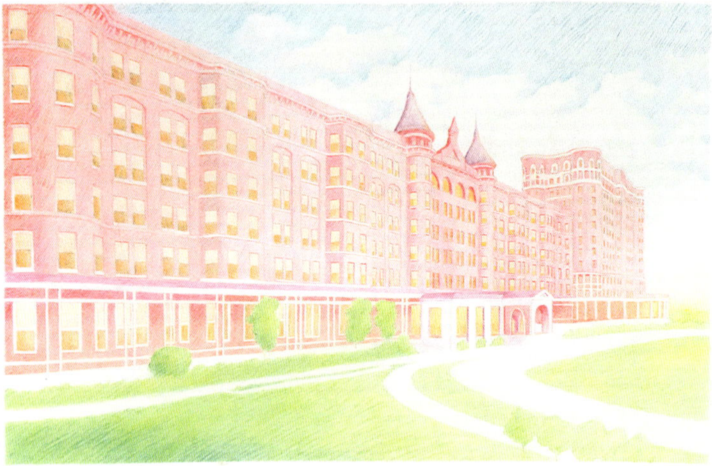

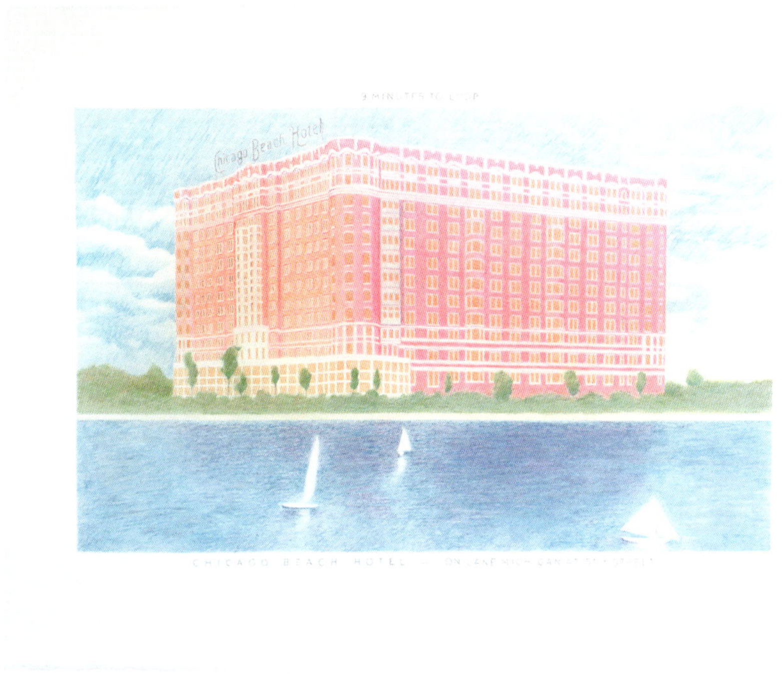

Chicago Beach Hotel, 2014
Color pencil on paper
Courtesy of the artist and Grey Noise, Dubai

Chicago Beach Hotel was Dubai's first resort hotel. Built on "Chicago Beach"— named after the Chicago Bridge & Iron Company, which constructed Dubai's offshore undersea oil storage tankers in the 1960s—the hotel remained a landmark until it was demolished in 1997. Chicago Beach Hotel was also one of Chicago's grand hotels, built to accommodate visitors to the World's Fair of 1893, and demolished in the early 1970s. The two pencil drawings are of the Chicago hotel, and its extension.

Dr. Mohamed Yousif

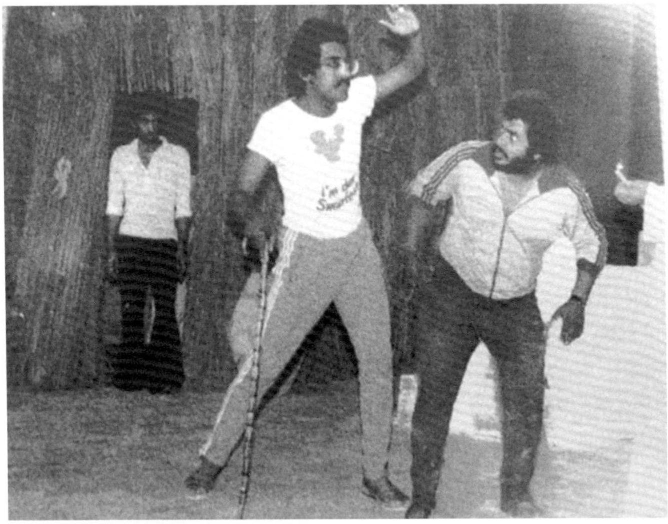

Dr. Mohamed Yousif (center), rehearsal of *Lail Ya Lail*, a play by Abdulrahman Al-Mannai, performed in Africa Hall, Sharjah, 1982

Dr. Mohamed Yousif straddles both the visual and performing arts—he has chaired the boards of the Sharjah National Theater and the Emirates Fine Art Society (which he cofounded in 1980) and was Head of Art in the UAE's Education Department. But for an ostensible "pillar" of the UAE's cultural establishment, his artistic trajectory seems surprisingly precarious.

Drawn to sculpture during his undergraduate training in Cairo (1973–77), he returned home to face a backlash from a conservative social milieu intolerant of figurative sculpture. This was not unusual. But while many of his peers, such as Abdul Raheem Salem and Dr. Najat Meky, were able to divert their energies into their painting practices, Yousif's commitment to sculpture meant that he had to leave it for nearly nine years; much of his early work is lost or destroyed.

Yousif returned to sculpture during the course of his postgraduate studies in the United States (1998–2000), where he developed the initial strands of his lifelong project, "nature to nature," which was also the title of his PhD thesis at Ranchi University, Jharkhand, India (2005). In his thesis, Yousif maps out his fields of engagement: the movement of camels in the desert and sailboats on the sea; the flow of water and sand; the biological rhythms of life, from the water cycle to bees, pollination, and the production of honey. Taking inspiration from aspects of Buddhist art, the ecologically oriented practices of David Nash and Andy Goldsworthy, and the landscape and visual footprints of everyday culture (from henna patterns to the bows of sailing boats) in his native Sharjah, Yousif has carved out a practice that aligns with his interest in nature as material and subject and that has allowed him to sensitively navigate the shifting possibilities for sculpture in the UAE over the last four decades. The body is absent but almost always a palpable presence in his work.

Yousif privileges natural materials such as chopped wood, twigs, sand, leaves, and twine from natural fibers, often working with materials collected from the trees in his own backyard. Over the last two decades he has frequently produced series (or "families") of sculptural forms that are suggestive of the human figure rather than direct representations. He arranges them with theatrical flair, like characters in a play.

Gypsy Dancers, *Na'ashat*, *Hide & Seek*, and *Incense Burner* (all 2008, pp. below, 260–261) exemplify this aspect of his practice. They communicate a corporeal sense of movement without direct representation. *Naashat* uses a simple alignment of wood, twigs, and palm leaves to convey the choreography of the folk dance of the same name—women in

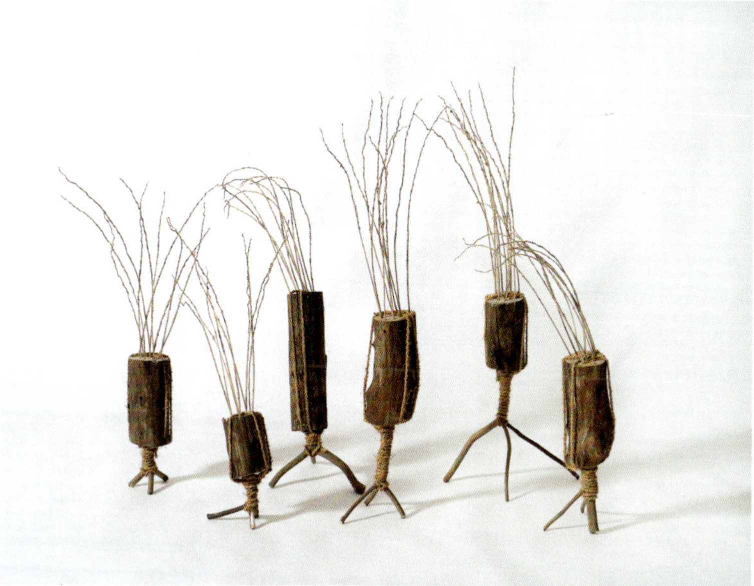

Incense Burner, 2008
Tree branches, palm tree parts, wood; dimensions variable

groups sway and toss their heads from side to side, their long hair carving out figure eights in the air—with an easy economy of means. The work simultaneously echoes Nash's sustained experiments with shaping what could be termed an organic modernity.

The Sea and the Desert (1994–2005, pp. 262–263) epitomizes Yousif's engagement with landscape. The installation covers the gallery floor to create two surfaces in an unequal balance: a "sea" of tree branches painted different shades of blue, with the "foam" of the waves rendered in white; and a "desert" of sand, with chopped slices of wood suggesting camel tracks. Traces of movement, of the wind, can also be read into the undulations of the "sea" and "desert." They mirror each other, under a shared sky. There is a discernable intent of transporting the viewer elsewhere, unfixing earthly orientations, and creating new ones in the realm of imagination.

For his presentation at the Venice Biennale, Yousif has reconstructed two previously lost works.

Al Shawahid (1981–2017, p. 259) is an assemblage of handmade aluminum spoons mounted on a wooden board painted white that recalls the size and shape of a gravestone. Contained within a coarsely fashioned plaster arch, the anthropomorphic spoons are arranged roughly by size, as if posing for an intergenerational family photo. Below their "feet" is a burial mound with a small mirror affixed in its center. The work is hung with the mirror at eye level. The different "generations" of spoons are witnesses to this cycle of life, which is embodied by the family. Viewers are invited to reflect on their own mortality staring back at them from the mirror. *Shawahid* stages an affective field of tender yet hopeful solemnity.

In *Al insiyabiyya bil majadeef taht al maa* (the flow of underwater paddles) (1995–2017, pp. 256–257), Yousif has suspended a series of ten wooden oars that fan up to the double-height ceiling of the Pavilion. In a nod to traditional craft practices, the arms and blades are bound together with rope. The oars carve out a volume in space, reminding us that most of a ship is always hidden from sight beneath the surface of the water—a perspective familiar to the artist from his childhood spent at Sharjah Creek observing boats being hauled onto land for cleaning and repair. But these oars are not immobile. The oars are arranged at varying angles and orientation, embodying movement, not just in the sense of propulsion but also of rhythm. Seen from the side, they are musical notation made concrete.

Music and rhythm are integral to the labor of every fisherman or rower. In rowing, the coxswain keeps time; coordinates the direction, power, and rhythm of the rowers; and maintains morale. For the fishing boats, song plays the same role. The oars sway gently in the air with the movement of audiences walking by, but also with the rhythm of all the songs and journeys they have absorbed. And if in *The Sea and the Desert* Yousif had given us a Google Earth view of the meeting of water and sand, in *Al insiyabiyya bil majadeef taht al maa* he takes us to the ocean floor and encourages us to look up in childlike wonder at the gentle movement of these oars and the crossings they suggest.

Like drawing, music and movement too are skills that come naturally to every child and that, paraphrasing Picasso, every artist spends a lifetime relearning. And it is this inner song of the everyday, orchestrated through the movement of the cycles of life—dancing bodies, undulating seas, shifting sands, and falling leaves—that Mohamed Yousif seeks to frame in his works. His sculptures are characters on a stage, resonating with life's rhythms.

Dr. Mohamed Yousif (born 1953, Sharjah) has exhibited in art events around the world. He has participated in all exhibitions organized by the Emirates Fine Arts Society since its inception in 1979 and previously showcased one of his works at "1980–Today: Exhibitions in the United Arab Emirates," the National Pavilion of the United Arab Emirates at the 56th Venice Biennale. He received a PhD in Fine Arts from Manav Rachna International (Ranchi) University, India; an MFA from Webster University, Missouri, USA, in 2000; and a Bachelor's degree in Fine Art from the Cairo College of Fine Arts in 1978.

Following page:
Al insiyabiyya bil majadeef taht al maa, 1995 (re-fabricated in 2017)
Wood, rope

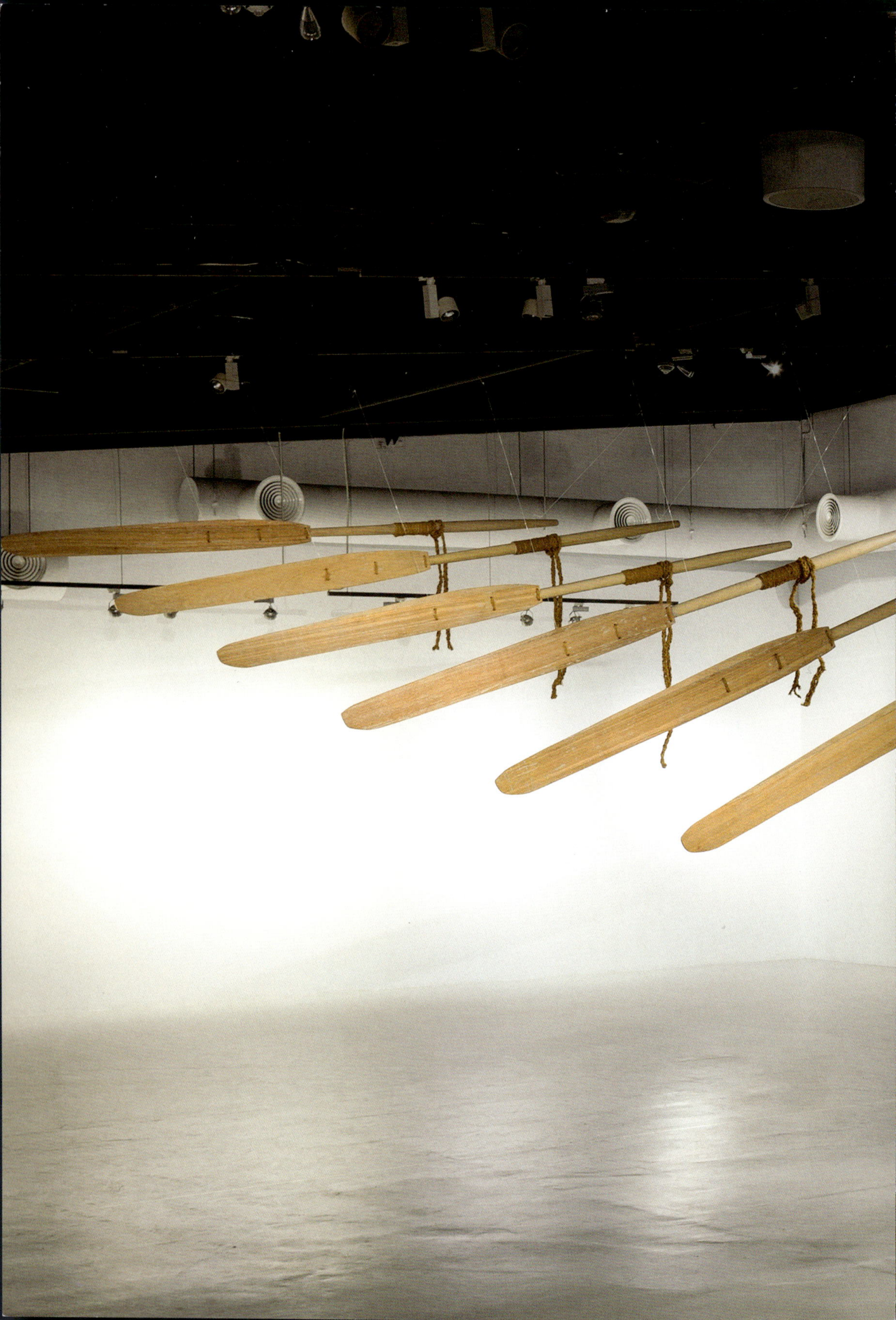

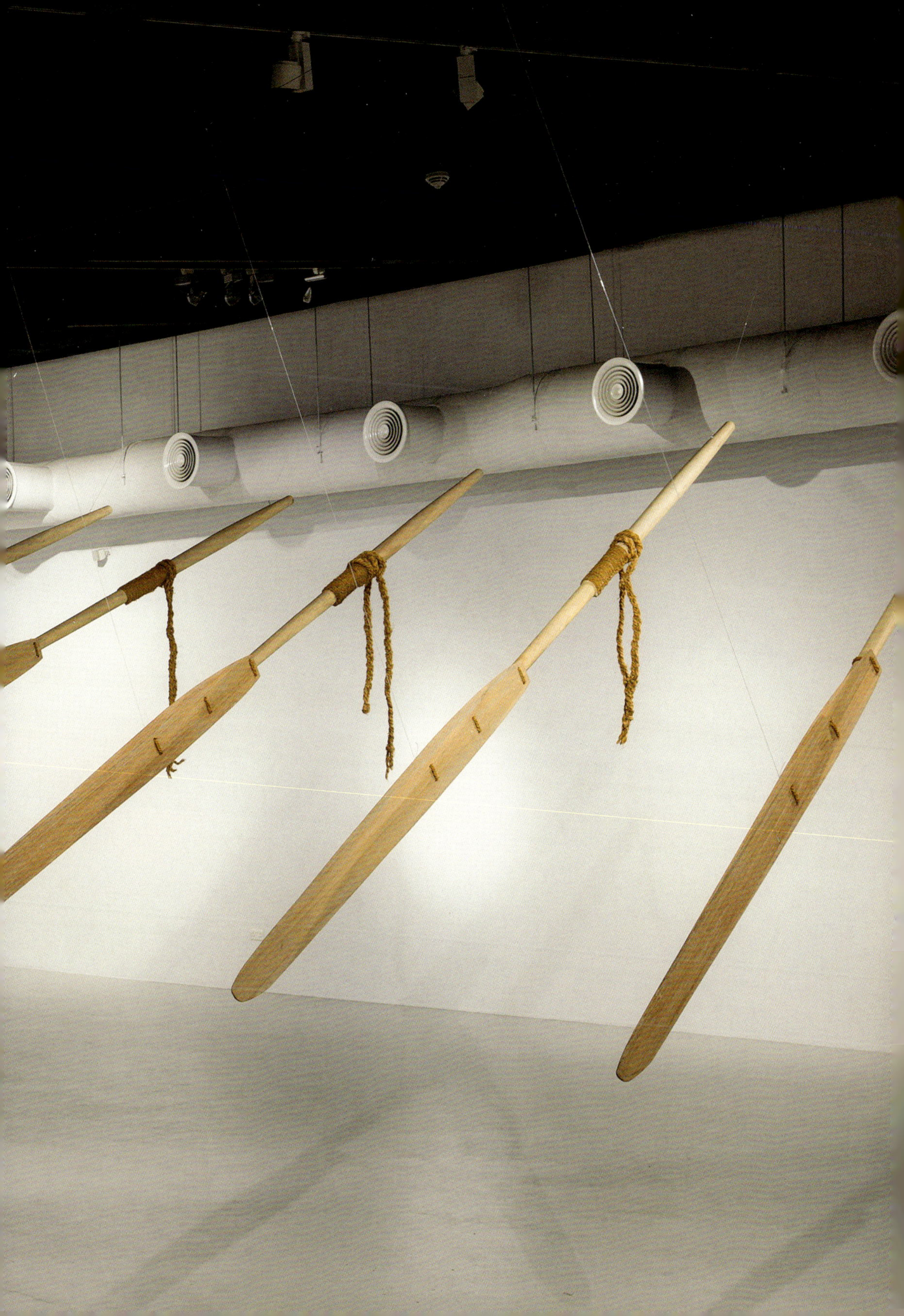

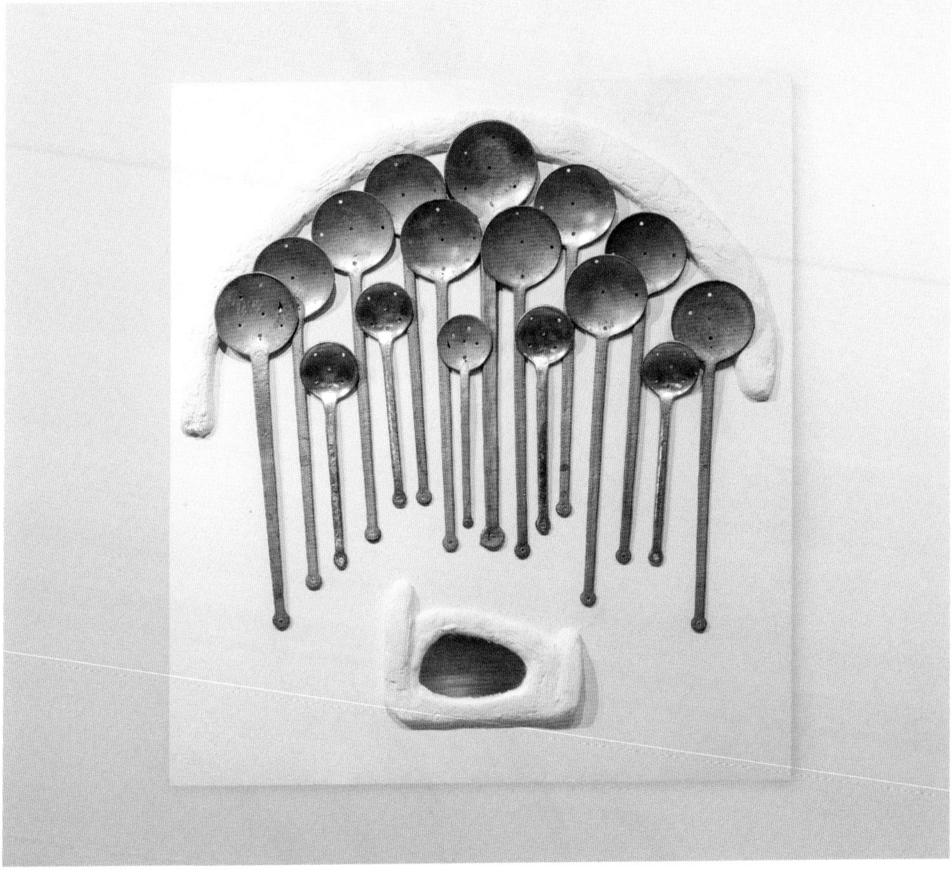

Al Shawahid, 1981 (re-fabricated in 2017)
Handmade aluminum spoons, wood, mirror, plaster, emulsion paint;
dimensions variable

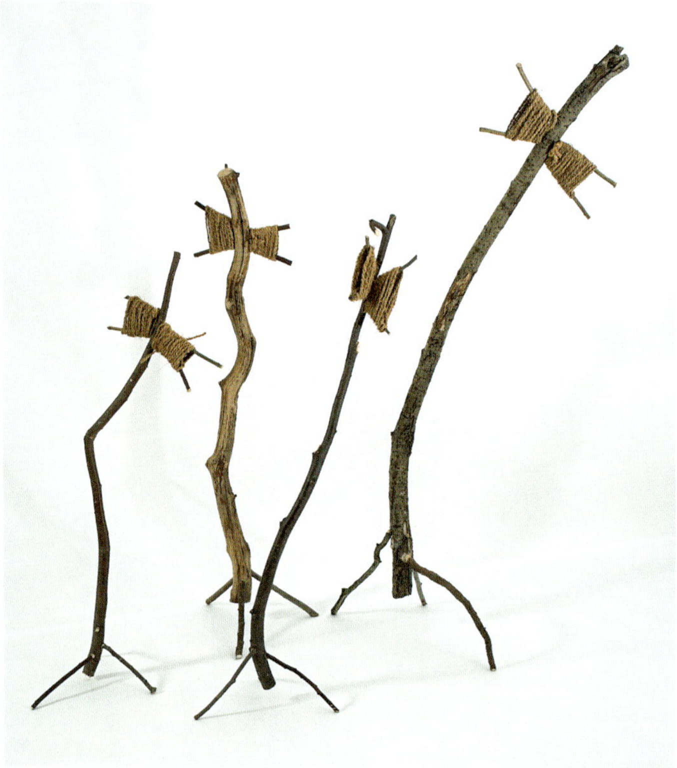

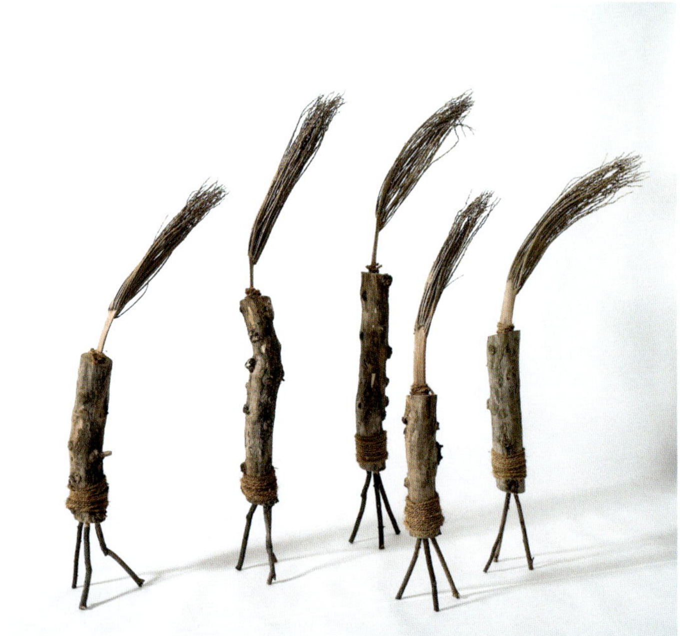

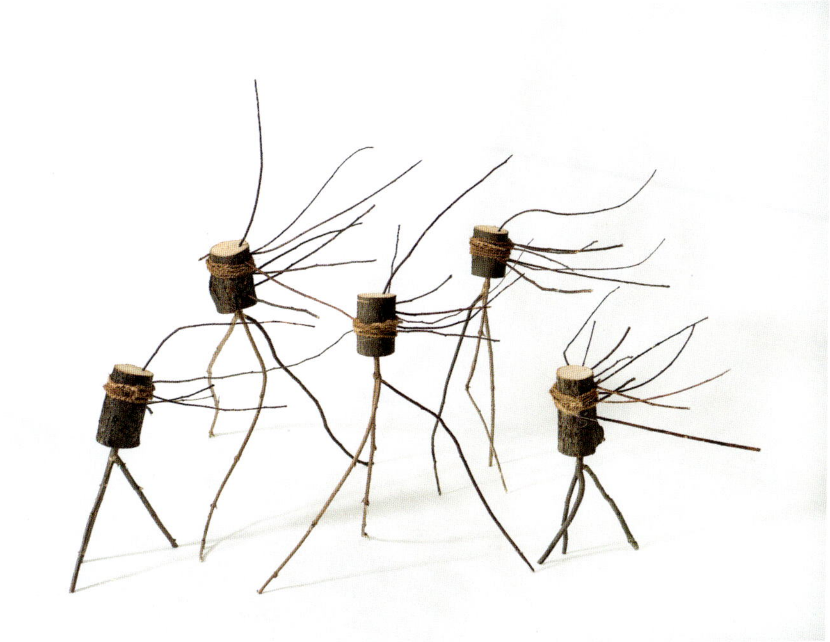

Gypsy Dancers, 2008
Na'ashat, 2008
Hide & Seek, 2008
Tree branches, palm tree parts, wood

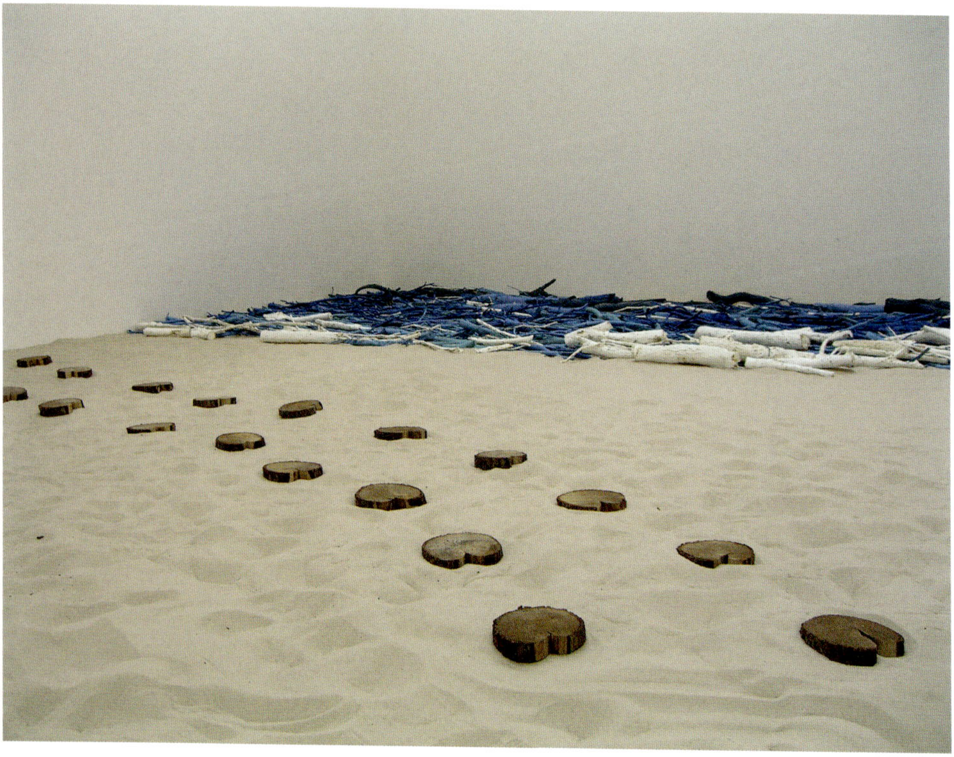

The Sea and the Desert, 1994–2005
Sand, chopped wood, tree branches, emulsion paint;
dimensions variable

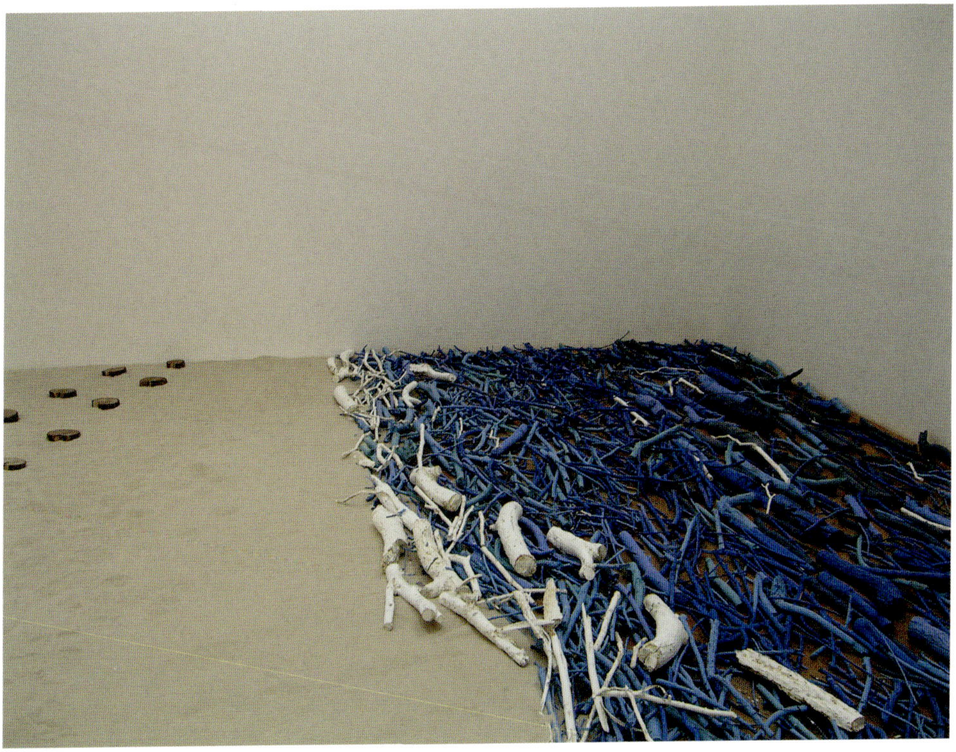

Contributors

HAMMAD NASAR is a London-based curator, writer, and researcher. He was Head of Research and Programmes at Asia Art Archive, Hong Kong (2012–16), and earlier co-founded Green Cardamom, a non-profit arts organization, in London. He has curated or co-curated numerous international exhibitions, including: "Lines of Control: Partition as a Productive Space" (2012–13); "Beyond the Page: The Miniature as Attitude in Contemporary Art from Pakistan" (2006–10); and, "Where Three Dreams Cross: 150 Years of Photography from India, Pakistan and Bangladesh` (2010). Nasar frequently publishes on art and its institutions in journals, magazines, catalogs and edited volumes; and is a regular speaker at symposia and conferences on international art.

KHALID ALBUDOOR is an award-winning poet, writer, lecturer, documentary film maker and cultural advisor. A founding member of the Emirates Writers Union and a former member of the Dubai Cultural Council, he was the recipient of the Al-Khal Poetry Award for his first collection of poetry, *Lail* (1992). His documentaries and television programs about Emirati cultural heritage have received awards and recognition, both locally and internationally.

MAISA AL QASSIMI is the Programmes Manager for Guggenheim Abu Dhabi. Amongst the exhibitions she curated are "The Creative Act: Performance, Process, Presence" (2016); "Seeing Through Light" (2014); and, together with Reem Fadda, two editions of "Emirati Expressions" (2013 and 2015). She has been a member of the board of directors of the Dubai International Art Center and a Professor of Photography at the Sharjah University College of Fine Arts.

DR. AISHA BILKHAIR is a Research Advisor at the UAE National Archives and a PhD in ethnomusicology. She is a member of several international associations and committees, among them the UNESCO Intangible Cultural Heritage Preservation Committee, the American Oral History Association, the GCC Society for History and Archaeology, and the Arab History Society. Dr. Bilkhair is the first Arab woman to represent Asia in the International Oral History Association.

REEM FADDA is a curator. Until 2016 she was Associate Curator for Middle Eastern Art for the Guggenheim Abu Dhabi. Between 2005-07, she was Director of the Palestinian Association for Contemporary Art (PACA) and worked as Academic Director to the International Academy of Art. In 2013 and 2015, alongside Maisa Al-Qassimi, she curated two editions of "Emirati Expressions" in Abu Dhabi. Fadda was also the curator of the United Arab Emirates at the Venice Biennale (2012), and the 6th Marrakech Biennale (2016).

RAMIN HAERIZADEH (b. 1975, Tehran, Iran), **ROKNI HAERIZADEH** (b. 1978, Tehran, Iran) and **HESAM RAHMANIAN** (b. 1980, Knoxville, USA) are artists based in Dubai. Their communal living and collaborative practice represents a radical redefinition of the collective, incorporating from time to time friends, writers, artists, and musicians.

UZMA Z. RIZVI is Associate Professor of Anthropology and Urban Studies at the Pratt Institute of Art and Design, Brooklyn, NY, and is currently a Visiting Researcher in the Department of International Studies at the American University of Sharjah, UAE. Rizvi has been a lead tutor, together with Murtaza Vali, of Art Dubai's seminar program Campus Art Dubai (CAD) since 2014 and directed with Amal Khalaf Art Dubai's 2016 Global Art Forum (GAF), "The Future Was." She is a regular contributor *The New Inquiry* and *LEAP*.

MICHELE ROBECCHI is a writer and curator based in London, where he is a Commissioning Editor for contemporary art at Phaidon Press and a Visiting Lecturer at Christie's Education. He is the author of a monograph on the work of Sarah Lucas (Electa, 2006), and, together with Francesca Bonazzoli, of *Mona Lisa to Marge: How the World's Greatest Artworks Entered Popular Culture* (Prestel, 2014).

OSMAN SAMIUDDIN is a sport journalist based in Abu Dhabi. He is Senior Editor at ESPNcricinfo, an editor for *The Cricket Monthly*, and the author of *The Unquiet Ones: A History of Pakistan Cricket* (Harper Collins, 2014).

DEEPAK UNNIKRISHNAN is a writer from Abu Dhabi. He has studied and taught at the Art Institute of Chicago and presently teaches at New York University in Abu Dhabi. His book *Temporary People* (Restless Books, 2016) was the inaugural winner of the Restless Books Prize for New immigrant Writing.

MURTAZA VALI is a writer, art historian, and curator. An independent critic since 2005, he has contributed regularly to *Art Review, Art India, Bidoun Magazine*, and *Art Asia Pacific*. He has been a visiting critic at Yale's School of Art and Cornell's College of Architecture, and was the recipient of the Winter 2010 Lori Ledis Curatorial Fellowship. He has written monographs on the work of Emily Jacir, Reena Saini Kallat, and Laleh Khorramian, and edited *Manual for Treason*, a multilingual publication commissioned by the Sharjah Biennial (2011).

WTD MAGAZINE is an independent publication that uses narratives, conversations and visual essays to reflect on the built environment of the present-day Middle East. These temporary parameters represent an attempt to initiate a discourse that highlights architecture, urban thought processes and their relationship to the societies in which they are created.

NATIONAL PAVILION
UNITED ARAB EMIRATES 2017

Commissioner
Salama bint Hamdan Al Nahyan Foundation

Curator
Hammad Nasar

National Pavilion United Arab Emirates
Laila Binbrek, Coordinating Director
Mouna Khorchid, Communications Manager
Rand Abdul Jabbar, Exhibitions Coordinator
Jay Yambao, Office Coordinator
Maria Bagnara, Internship Coordinator
Emanuela Semiani, Venice Coordinator

Exhibition design
Milk Train, Rome

Visual identity, typography and book design
Luke Gould and Joseph Pochodzaj, London
Design Assistant
Shamma Buhazza, UAE

Co-publisher and distribution
Mousse Publishing, Milan

Installation & lighting
Tosetto Allestimenti
AV installation
Murer Cantieri Audiovisivi
Photography
Seeing Things
Press and PR
Brunswick Arts

ACKNOWLEDGMENTS

Supported by
UAE Ministry of Culture and Knowledge Development

Lenders
Art Jameel
Artists
Gallery Isabelle van den Eynde, Dubai
Grey Noise, Dubai

Research
Uns Kattan
Research in Collaboration with Art Jameel

Organizations
Alserkal Avenue
Art Dubai
The Art Gallery at NYU Abu Dhabi
Asia Art Archive
Central Saint Martins, University of the Arts, London
Hotel Danieli
Maraya Art Centre
National Archives, Abu Dhabi
Sharjah Cricket Club
Sharjah Art Foundation
Sharjah National Theatre
Tashkeel
Warehouse421
Whitechapel Gallery

مؤسسة سلامة بنت حمدان آل نهيان
SALAMA BINT HAMDAN AL NAHYAN FOUNDATION

UNITED ARAB EMIRATES
MINISTRY OF CULTURE & KNOWLEDGE DEVELOPMENT

الإمارات العربية المتحدة
وزارة الثقافة
وتنمية المعرفة

Individuals

Musthafa Aboobacker
Awatif Adnan
Fiza Akram
Maya Allison
Feras Albastaki
Khulood Al Atiyat
Mubarak Al Dhaheri
Amal Ahmed Al Hadhrami
Meitha Al Mazrooei
Maryam Al Muqaddam
H.E. Sheikha Hoor Al Qassimi
Sultan Sooud Al Qassemi
Shamsa Rashid Al Qubaisi
Munira Al Sayegh
Abdelmonem Alserkal
Ritu Arya
Myrna Ayad
Joan Ayunan
Michelle Bambling
Obaid bin Sandal
Umer Butt
Miriam Butti
Roxana Calin
Antonia Carver
Iftikhar Dadi
Anita Dawood
Alaa Edris
Isabelle van den Eynde
Rami Farook
Paolomaria Giannotti
Kathleen Hoare
Jill Hoyle
Claire Hsu
Jean Jimenez
Kevin Jones
Vilma Jurkute
Bana Kattan
Mohammed Kazem
Munjid Kattan
Pete Kelly
Amal Khalaf
Mazhar Khan
Cristiana De Marchi
Laura Triggs Metzler
Angela Migally
Salwa Mikdadi
Giuseppe Moscatello
Maria Mumtaz
Haadi Elia Nasar
Jaami Shaakir Nasar
Hetal Pawani
Jack Persekian
Venetia Porter
Anne Preussel
Sunny Rahbar
Shafi Saidu
Reem Shadid
Abdulrahim Sharif
Mohamed Somji
Yassmin Tukan
Chris Wan
Jonathan Watkins
Tamsin Wildy
Michelle Wong

Photo credits

Dr. Aisha Bilkhair (pp. 91), George Braz (p. 214), Vikram Divecha (pp. 216–217, 218, 219, 220, 221, 222, 223, 224–225, 226, 227), Peter D'souza (228, 229), Lamya Gargash (pp. 98–9, 100–101, 102–103), Taher Ismail (p. 85), Irma Nazario (p. 88), Shafi Saidu (pp. 218, 219), Ekta Saran (pp. 213, 218, 219), George Edward Shahda (p. 215), Mohamed Somji (p. 39), *WTD Magazine* (pp. 18, 22, 76, 80, 81, 83, 112, 113, 114, 115, 116, 117).

And thanks most of all to the artists and contributors for their generous participation, enthusiasm and inspiration.

All images courtesy of the artists unless otherwise noted.

#positionsinplay
#nationalpavilionuae
#uaeinvenice

This book accompanies the exhibition, "Rock, Paper, Scissors: Positions in Play"
The National Pavilion of the United Arab Emirates at the 57th International Art Exhibition – la Biennale di Venezia
May 13–November 26, 2017

Curator
Hammad Nasar

Participating artists
Exhibition
Nujoom Alghanem
Sara Al Haddad
Vikram Divecha
Lantian Xie
Dr. Mohamed Yousif
Publication
Ramin Haerizadeh, Rokni Haerizadeh & Hesam Rahmanian
Deepak Unnikrishnan
WTD Magazine
Program
Hind Mezaina

la Biennale di Venezia
57. Esposizione Internazionale d'Arte

Editors
Hammad Nasar with Michele Robecchi
Artist commissions
Ramin Haerizadeh, Rokni Haerizadeh & Hesam Rahmanian
Deepak Unnikrishnan
WTD Magazine
Essays by
Dr. Aisha Bilkhair, Hammad Nasar, Uzma Z. Rizvi, Osman Samiuddin, Murtaza Vali
Contributors
Khalid Albudoor, Nujoom Alghanem, Maisa Al Qassimi, Reem Fadda
Translations
Ila Al Amam, Uns Kattan
Researcher
Uns Kattan
Copyediting and Proofreading
Priya Bhatnagar
Designers
Luke Gould and Joseph Pochodzaj
Publisher
National Pavilion United Arab Emirates
La Biennale di Venezia, Abu Dhabi
PO Box 62086, Abu Dhabi, UAE
www.nationalpavilionuae.org
Co-publisher and distribution
Mousse Publishing
Corso di Porta Romana 63
20122 Milan, Italy
www.moussepublishing.com
Printing
Pureprint, UK

ISBN 978-88-6749-275-6